Dining with the Rich and Royal

Dining with Destiny Series
as part of the Rowman & Littlefield Studies in Food and Gastronomy

General Editor: Ken Albala, Professor of History,
University of the Pacific (kalbala@pacific.edu)

Rowman & Littlefield Executive Editor:
Suzanne Staszak-Silva (sstaszak-silva@rowman.com)

The volumes in the Dining with Destiny series explore food biography, examining the private eating lives of icons from across the span of literature, art, music, politics, and revolution. If you've ever wondered what Lenin lunched on, whether George Orwell really swigged Victory Gin, or if there's such a thing as a Freudian supper, then the Dining with Destiny series is for you. Behind every great man and woman is a great meal. Their peccadilloes are explored anecdotally against the backdrops of history and culture, with accompanying recipes. Taste the disconsolate marriage of Marilyn Monroe to Arthur Miller, make red gravy and pasta Sinatra-style, or shake up the kind of chocolate malted that Woody Allen likes. How about a banana sandwich with Queen Elizabeth? Or a road trip picnic with Hemingway and F. Scott Fitzgerald?

Dining with Destiny is not just for all the "foodies" out there—the night-time cocoa will lie forgotten as you realize that Malcolm X entered the civil rights movement by rejecting anything piggy on his plate and as the Swinging Sixties are revealed through the hedonism and hashish cookies of Mick Jagger and Bob Dylan. The reader will dream of sitting at the table prepared by Hitchcock, Nelson Mandela, or Picasso. But beware: Dalí's lobster in chocolate sauce means that he has a desire to sleep with you rather than paint.

Each of these figures took part in landmark historical and cultural events that have shaped and defined our way of life—but they also had to eat. Now it is time to reveal the real man by looking in his fridge to discover what makes him a revolutionary, a hero, a rogue! Dining with Destiny lets you taste what's on Darwin's fork.

Dining with the Rich and Royal

Fiona Ross

ROWMAN & LITTLEFIELD
Lanham • Boulder • New York • London

Published by Rowman & Littlefield
A wholly owned subsidiary of The Rowman & Littlefield Publishing Group, Inc.
4501 Forbes Boulevard, Suite 200, Lanham, Maryland 20706
www.rowman.com

Unit A, Whitacre Mews, 26-34 Stannary Street, London SE11 4AB

British Library Cataloguing in Publication Information Available

Library of Congress Cataloging-in-Publication Data
Names: Ross, Fiona, 1966– author.
Title: Dining with the rich and royal / Fiona Ross.
Description: Lanham : Rowman & Littlefield, a wholly owned subsidiary of The
  Rowman & Littlefield Publishing Group, Inc., [2016] | Series: Dining with
  destiny series as part of the Rowman & Littlefield studies in food and
  gastronomy | Includes bibliographical references and index.
Identifiers: LCCN 2016013295 (print) | LCCN 2016017848 (ebook) |
  ISBN 9781442252271 (cloth : alk. paper) | ISBN 9781442252288 (electronic)
Subjects: LCSH: International cooking. | Rich people—Social life and
  customs. | Royal households—History. | Dinners and dining—History. |
  LCGFT: Cookbooks.
Classification: LCC TX725.A1 R6625 2016 (print) | LCC TX725.A1 (ebook) | DDC
  641.59—dc23
LC record available at https://lccn.loc.gov/2016013295

♾️™ The paper used in this publication meets the minimum requirements of American
National Standard for Information Sciences—Permanence of Paper for Printed Library
Materials, ANSI/NISO Z39.48-1992.

Printed in the United States of America

I would like to dedicate this book to these special people,
lost and found, and their food:

Alastair Ross's marvelous breakfasts
Moira Ross's skirlie forever; it was poetry, and so were you, my love
Roberta, Louise, Ginny, and Bob Catizone's incredible pasta sauce
(those Italians in Pennsylvania sure had some fun)
Ian and Dorothy McWalter's rhubarb pie and apple snow
MMM's lamb, Jane Levy's semidefrosted fish, and Lindsay Monroe's
spaghetti bolognaise
Amanda Duncan's last song; here's hoping heaven is kind to you
Jaja and Jojo's roast chicken with Sophia on Sundays (possibly with Jojo's
kipper stock)
Jimmy Turner's Waltzing Matilda
Elsie Gordon's Swiss milk toffee (hidden in Tupperware from my brother,
Alasdair Ross)
Olive Bucket's coconut buns in God's glory
Alex Ross's lamb chops and permanently bad-tempered dogs, all called Angus
Sarah Parry's caipirinha; Simon Saunders's risotto; and Gemma Keaney's
bean stew
Glenys and Glynn Sanger's kitchen of kindness

Here's tae us, wha's like us?
Damn few and they're a deid.

Contents

Acknowledgments

L ike all books, this one owes its life to many people. Apart from the rich and royal figures who crowd its pages, I want to thank my kindly and talented editor, Ken Albala, for his advice and support. The library staff in the hot and dusty Upper Reading Room of the Bodleian Library have been wonderful, carting endless volumes of peculiar books from deep down in the stacks. Thank you to my dear friend Gillian Harrison for introducing me to the Bodleian and for all her fine companionship there in the golden hours. Thank you to Harry Harrison for his many kind lunches. Thanks to my darlings Moira and Alastair Ross for teaching me (a.k.a. Chones) and Little Alasdair how to hold our knives and forks and for feeding us so well and for not letting the seven dwarves take Little Alasdair. I'd also like to thank the magnificent Margaret Conway and her husband, Ken Lovesey, for filming me while I curried a goat in their kitchen; Simon Saunders for his inspiring and beautiful ideas; Shelley Couper for helping me roast a suckling pig on a makeshift spit in her backyard; and the Allen and Harris property-renting agency for allowing me to marinate the aforementioned pig in the bathroom of the apartment they rented to me. To Mary Birtill and Irene Tominey I owe a debt for inspiring me with the Going Foot, and to all my Camino friends for walking the way with me. Jane and Dan Ganly have been a great help with IT advice and Jane's intimate knowledge of chocolate; also to Nathan Shelton of Bread and Butter Creative I owe eternal thanks for all his wonderful design work on my website and blog. To Yorick, Roberta, Octavia, Zoe, Woody Wilks, and Louise Guthrie

I would like to express gratitude for all those mad dining experiments in the Allam Street kitchen, while Pompey hid bananas in her dog basket and Miss Honey mated with my shoulder. Jean and Richard Haigh I must thank so much for advice on hope and the vast subject of vegetables. Thank you, dear Dr. Emily Gray, for letting me camp in your attic, and thank you to Marijke, Willem, Max, and Steve for so much laughter. Much of what I know about the royals I owe to conversations with Cabbage Murray and the Duke of Back: a big kiss to all Murrays (especially The Aunt) and Cuthberts! To Oscar Hughes I owe a debt for baby wonderfulness. I'd like to send a kiss to Roisin Ross for being my best, kindest girl forever; as Moira said to me, so I say to you: Even when I'm dust, that dust will love you. Even when I'm dust, I hope that dust still knows you're my daughter.

Finally, I'd like to express deep-hearted thankfulness to my dear husband and best friend, Gareth Sanger, for all the immense generosity, love, and belief he has shown in giving me a room of my own and £500.

Introduction

As with all the Dining with Destiny books, writing *Dining with the Rich and Royal* has felt like entering another world—this time one of ermine, oysters, spies, and champagne foot baths. While normal human beings occupy their time usefully, I have spent mine buried in the Oxford University Library, slinking about its spidery recesses, secretly eating sweets behind bookshelves, and picking up books from the stacks that make me blush as I whip them open in the reading room, elbow to elbow with professors of Anglo-Saxon; one book on Hugh Hefner had lots of nude bunnies rubbing bubble bath on their breasts. Everyone else is reading Einstein or Herodotus as I leaf through the confessions of Zsa Zsa Gabor, trying to keep the cover plastered against the table, hoping the Oxford angels assume I am a high-minded feminist scholar, studying Hefner and Zsa Zsa because I'm penning a brilliant indictment of the commodification of women. But what I'm really after is their supper . . . and what it tells us about them.

I begin to see food connections, parallels, and common eating "psychologies" shared by the rich and royal. Hugh Hefner and Conrad Hilton were single-minded, driven careerists whose hedonism focused, in the case of the former, on porn and, in the case of the latter, on hotel complexes. Both were mundane, clockwork eaters. A real food sensualist like Zsa Zsa Gabor was, then, disastrously mismatched with Conrad Hilton; their marriage was farcical. She dreamed of Hungarian food, paprika chicken, goulash, and cabbage rolls (interspersed with powder puffs, flowers, diamond rings, negligees, sapphires, and Cadillacs to match her hair color), while

1

Conrad mooned about his next hotel and the way the lobby might look. Ari Onassis and Maria Callas, in contrast, sprang from the same food DNA. Their relationship was Greek dynamite, and the fuse was set by their private blowouts on spanakopita, baklava, and moussaka. Greek food made them intimates to the exclusion of all those around them.

When Howard Hughes got together with Katharine Hepburn—with her "beet-root hair" and "rocking horse nostrils," as Cecil Beaton wickedly put it—they were never going to last. Her lavish, no-nonsense appetite perplexed Hughes, who was afraid of food all his life, handling it as carefully as nuclear waste. Food obsessions encompassed his entire workforce of Mormons; there was an embargo on garlic and onions. Employees and lovers would "sneak eat" in Hughes's coercive, totalitarian food kingdom, and the diet of his wife Jean Peters was ludicrously under surveillance.

More unexpected food links appear between Howard Hughes and King Ludwig II of Bavaria. The lives of both were changed by bad teeth: Ludwig ate too many sweets, and Hughes drank too much enamel-eroding orange juice. Dentists might have been off-putting in Ludwig's time—think poorly sharpened pocket knives and local blacksmiths—so Ludwig's oral hygiene is excusable (plus false teeth would be borrowed from the mouth of a living or dead human being, with their plaque still gluey in either case), but Howard Hughes's rotted teeth went untreated due to his utter, compulsive horror of dentistry. For a man who gave his Mormon assistants twenty closely typed rules on how to open a tin can without transferring any of their bacterial material to Hughes's mouth, you can imagine that a dentist and their reused instruments (even sterilized) would have been the stuff of a Hughesian nightmare. So both men became addicted to pain-relief drugs, dragging each into a personal hell of illusion—and to their deaths.

When you are rich and royal, you have great connections. This means that *Dining with the Rich and Royal* is also packed with lots of "extras," in themselves the movers and shakers of history. Have you heard of the American Miss Elsa Maxwell, a "fixer" of astoundingly influential parties? Elsa had the appearance of a large, well-risen scone and dressed in what seemed to be stitched-up floral tablecloths. Nevertheless, Elsa was fluent in persuading top restaurants to feed her and her guests at cost price as she drew celebrity, wealth, talent, and crowned heads to her like flies to the proverbial . . . Elsa could put you on the "map" if you were beautiful; you became part of her "living decorations." Cole Porter adored her; Marilyn Monroe stepped out with her; the Duchess of Windsor (temporarily but bitterly) loathed her. It was Elsa who fixed up Aly Khan, son of Aga Khan III, with Rita Hayworth (still bruised by her marriage to Orson Welles). Elsa appears at the piano, side by side with Maria Callas, having just fixed the party where Callas was to forgive Ari Onassis for marrying Jackie Kennedy—she had also introduced

Callas and Onassis. (Elsa may have been more than a little in love with Callas, so it was bad luck for her.) Characters like Elsa confirm Charles Bukowski's point in *Ham on Rye*: "I . . . noticed that both in the very poor and very rich extremes of society the mad were often allowed to mingle."

There are the Chinese eunuchs who pretended, with great, solicitous emptiness, to feed the starving Dragon Emperor; Rasputin, undone by his lust for rose-flavored cakes; Maurice de Rothschild, whose postdinner pastime was to spit orange pips down his nurse's cleavage; and Chillie Langhorne, Nancy Astor's rambunctious, plantation-owning Southern father, whose lips were brown with tobacco juice and who prided himself on making cocktails that winded the British.

The rich and royal are as prone as the rest of us to affirming their identities through food. When the ancient Aga Khan III managed to break free from his caregivers, he was distracted from his escape by a very delicious meal that had been set up for his staff, coincidentally of all the things he remembered loving to eat before his sorry existence on a pensioner's diet. He dived in and ate six plates of quail. He remembered Paris when he rolled the mulch of Poires Belle Hélène about his tongue; with each contraband mouthful, he was the man, the great imam, he had been. The shah of Iran's wife Farah, sharing his exile, wanted nothing more than a mouthful of dried mulberries, leavened with sand, to reopen the cicatrix of her memories of Iran. She's no different from us, is she?

F. Scott Fitzgerald understood the rich: "Let me tell you about the very rich. They are different from you and me. They possess and enjoy early, and it does something to them." This rings true, but I want to add: They are different from you and me; they hardly ever cook for themselves. Wallis Simpson may have started life with oven gloves on, but when glory came her way as wife, post-abdication, to Edward Windsor, she *approved* menus sent to her by her chefs. Nancy Astor was the same. Princess Diana, despite having taken a cookery course, spent hours puzzling over a microwave, trying to work it out; it may as well have landed at Roswell. If any of us were to become suddenly royal or formidably rich, we might have to learn to be like them, imitate the upper crust. But if this happens, don't lose heart; they find it very hard to be like us, too. Both Queen Victoria and her son Bertie tried to be ordinary commoners but betrayed themselves in being unable to queue in restaurants or by, respectively, booking tables under such obscure pseudonyms as "Lady Churchill" or "the Duke of Lancaster," which, presumably, they thought as unassuming as "Mr." and "Mrs."

As a society "dwarf," I feel a certain foolish, sneaking revolutionary satisfaction in knowing that millionaires can't slice onions. Those famous aristocrats, the Mitfords, are a clear exception and express their characters through their cooking. Diana Mitford, incarcerated for Fascism, still quaffed champagne and cooked sausages in white wine in prison—her account with Harrods remained active. Her

Communist sister Jessica (to be instrumental in the American civil rights movement) settled into the common, wild lands of the East End of London and had to throw away the Boulestin cookbook a posh friend had given her. She was determined to learn that electricity was something you paid for and how to eat fish and chips. The daughters of the last tsar finally learned to bake bread from the cook who was to die with them as they innocently awaited their brutish deaths in Yekaterinburg, while lots of guests of the millionairess art collector Peggy Guggenheim wished to God she wouldn't insist on cooking anything (Peggy thought cooking was wildly bohemian) but dreaded most of all her chocolate chicken.

While the rich tend to offer an entertaining and eclectic mix of eating foibles, *Dining with the Rich and Royal* also conjures up the forgotten great tables and banquets of the twentieth-century monarchies, the anecdotal meals that offer us the last glimpses of some of these monarchies. What was it like to drink kvass and pick at zakusky with Tsar Nicholas (he would always have given you a moment of his time, drawing up a chair next to you, and if you liked Sherlock Holmes, so much the better)? Or catch the first glimpse of a dynasty in its inception when Ibn Saud, the towering founder of Saudi Arabia, ate apple pie with Franklin Roosevelt. In the twentieth-century, Communism shook its blanket and out fell a score of monarchs. The fall of the Qing dynasty in China and the last Dragon Emperor can be followed through food. After some decent Communist reeducation, the erstwhile emperor, Comrade Pu Yi, ate in canteens and let other people jump on the bus before him. As Hitler plundered Europe, great, wealthy families like the Jewish Rothschilds abandoned their banks; a posse of monarchs took refuge in Britain, never to be restored to their thrones. Unity Mitford, the daughter of Lord Redesdale and Hitler's foolish companion at too many shameful lunches, put a gun to her temple and shot herself in the English Gardens in Munich. Instead of ending her existence, as she'd planned, she gave herself a lobotomy. Left permanently brain damaged, Unity spent the rest of her years catching the squeaky local bus into Oxford, lunching half-witted and happy on terrible stew in the soup kitchen there. Even Hirohito stopped being divine, but his partiality to Western, "democratic," and non-Japanese bacon and eggs helped rehabilitate him. With independence, India became a republic and sovereigns lost their rights. Gaddafi turfed out Idris of Libya. Feisal, the king of Iraq, was assassinated. Ismailism and the Aga Khan survived. Everything changed. Many Ozymandiases lay in the dust, croaking, "Look on my works, ye Mighty, and despair!" Every monarchical fall can be seen through the prism of food. Although a parsimonious eater himself, the shah of Iran's vast dinner at Persepolis spelled the end of his reign. An absence of any inkling of the ordinary, debilitating food poverty of his subjects' lives was unforgiveable—as was also the case when King Farouk of Egypt, a great, likeable glutton, was cast out of Egypt in the 1952 revolution and General Abdel Nasser's coup d'état. Farouk's portly form haunted the gaming tables of Monaco, and he died over his (very tasty) supper, supposedly poisoned.

The idea that excess leads to downfall comes close to the truth when you consider the vast, libertine consumptions of the emperors Nero and Varius. Woolly-bearded chump Nero ended up botching his own suicide (while whimpering, "What an artist dies in me"), and Varius's body was dumped in a sewer.

Remaking food from the past is one of the ways you can get back to the past. Whenever you peel potatoes, you may see your mother's and grandmother's hands in your own and hear the warm burr of their voices in the kitchen. *Dining with the Rich and Royal* is about the same thing. The re-creation of the past through food anecdotes and also some recipes—re-created by me in my small kitchen—capture the key, episodic eating moments in the lives of the rich and royal (many of whom didn't cook and, if they did, rarely wrote out their recipes). Often the formal meals they ate are the preserve of the famous chef's book, but these recipes so often belong to a grand, formal moment and offer no contextual narrative. I hunt for the food that reveals the characters of the rich and royal. There will be no chefs on hand to make these dishes for you, but you could try and find the odd servant to bark at.

1

Glitterati Grub

Menus for Movers, Shakers, and Millionaires

All the glamour of the jet set on a plate, from the silver spoon to the last Kleenex wipe. Follow the food adventures of the great transatlantic dynasties: the Vanderbilts, the Astors, and the Rothschilds. Ari Onassis had his hands full dating Maria Callas and Jackie Kennedy: How would you satisfy the appetites of these ladies? Discover the mad meals of eccentrics like Howard Hughes and "Dog Nose" Peggy Guggenheim. What was dinner like with Conrad Hilton—an American dream or a room full of farts? Refuel in the Playboy Mansion with the inside story of how Hugh Hefner amuses his bouche, or dine in shimmering, smoky Monaco with the likes of Maurice de Rothschild. When the world is at your feet, what is on your table?

IT'S ALL GREEK TO ME:
ARISTOTLE ONASSIS AND MARIA CALLAS

Aristotle Onassis was a shipping magnate, had a face like knotted olive wood, and was husband to America's darling, widowed Jackie Kennedy. Maria Callas was a gifted, sloe-eyed, world-famous diva. What drew them together? Magnetism? Sexual allure? Yes, certainly, but also—and very importantly—food. As biographer Nicholas Gage writes, "Only Maria, who had lived in pre-war Athens surrounded by neighborhoods of tenements overflowing with refugees from Anatolia, could understand the sadness evoked by the plaintive wailing *rebetika* songs and the joy conjured up in Aristo's breast by a recitation of elaborately spiced dishes rich with currants and pine nuts."

Ari Onassis fondly recalled growing up in the tangled, exciting Armenian quarter of Smyrna (now Izmir) on the crumpled west coast of Turkey. His grandmother, the splendidly named Gethsemane Onassis, was the matriarch who cooked for him. She dished up buttery pilav, gigantes, and milk-based sweetmeats, served with almonds and pistachio nuts. Gage also mentions the "aromatic meatballs in tomato sauce that Hadji-néné [Grandmother] would make especially for her grandson." On Sundays, after Ari had been trading cigarettes at the docks (his first successful venture into business), the women of the family made pastries steeped in rose-flavored syrup. Ari never forgot that taste. "You can smash the vase," he mused sentimentally, "but the scent of flowers never quite goes away."

Rose Water Syrup Konafa

Another version of konafa that is just as delicious uses ricotta cheese—in the case of this recipe, about half a pound—replacing the walnuts, pistachios, and raisins with the ricotta and adding the ricotta in a layer at the same point in the recipe. If you decide to try the ricotta-filled konafa, eat it when it is warm and straight from the cake tin.

INGREDIENTS
¾ cup granulated sugar
½ cup water
Juice of ½ a lemon
1 tsp. rose water
½ lb. konafa pastry dough
¼ lb. butter, melted

¼ cup whole almonds
½ cup walnuts, chopped
½ cup pistachios, chopped
¼ cup raisins
1 tbsp. granulated sugar
1 tsp. ground cinnamon

METHOD
Preheat the oven to 180°C. Butter an 8-inch cake tin.

In a saucepan, combine the water, sugar, and lemon juice. Bring to a boil, stirring, and then let it simmer until it becomes syrupy. Cool and then add the rose water.

Empty the konafa dough into a large bowl and loosen it up with your hands, encouraging its hairy strings to separate. Now add the melted butter and mix through.

Place the whole almonds on the base of the cake tin and then spread half the konafa dough on top. Now sprinkle on the walnuts, pistachios, and raisins. Dust with sugar and cinnamon. Cover with the remaining konafa dough and bake in the oven for 30–40 minutes. Remove from the oven and drizzle with the rose water syrup. Allow to cook. Turn out of the tin and serve.

A pogrom against Christian Greeks in Turkey followed by his own social and commercial hustling was to take Ari far from the dusty, honeyed comforts of Smyrna. It was all spaghetti in butter sauce in Buenos Aires or cold toast in the back rooms of a shipping office in London as Ari moved restlessly from tobacco trading into ship buying, an entrepreneurial visionary in foreign lands, too young, pomaded, and ambitious to be undone by homesickness. When in Argentina, he worked the midnight shift in a telephone company, trying to improve his foreign languages by listening into international calls. It was in piggybacking on one of these conversations that Ari got his first big break. While the Great Depression ruined many, to young Ari it was a golden opportunity to buy devalued ship stock.

Ari's culinary guardian angel was an early girlfriend, the older, sophisticated, and polylingual Norwegian divorcée Ingeborg Dedichen. She took Ari not just to her bed but also to Maxim's and gave him instruction on how to read a menu, how to order food and drink, the niceties of eating etiquette, and how and when to tip (even though he once farted in her face as a practical joke). By the time Ari made his move to New York to start shipping oil, he was ready for the stiff wine lists of the Plaza Hotel and to take on the zebra-striped glitz of El Morocco. His relationship with Ingeborg, however, frayed when forty-year-old Ari met seventeen-year-old Athena (Tina) Livanos. Ari's abandonment of Ingeborg was almost a dress rehearsal for the way he was to shake off Maria Callas when he met Jackie Kennedy. Tina presented an opportunity to marry into the staggeringly rich Livanos family of shipping magnates—in short, too lucrative an opportunity to let Ingeborg get in the way.

Ari's yacht, *Christina*, was a real honey trap. He might sit cradling a glass of ouzo at the glassed top of the semicircular bar. Beneath the glass was set a seascape, complete with miniature models of ships, each vessel representing another stage in the development of seacraft. One tiny basket floated among them, a flag lettered with "Moses—the first ship owner," conveniently linking Ari to the heroes of the Bible. The cleverest part of this device was a series of magnets allowing Ari, as if he were an Olympian god, to move the ships, lending a surreal and yet deliberate sense that he was moving mortal men and craft over miles of sea. To complete this fantasy of Poseidon, Ari's whaling boats had procured the paddle-like teeth from leviathan whales, which were set as footrests into the wood, and he slouched on a white-topped bar stool, its "leather" famously tailored from Minke whale foreskin (one of Ari's standing wisecracks was that you were sitting on the largest penis in the world). Other teeth, carved with tableaux telling the journey of fabulous Ulysses, acted as handholds, fixed to the bar. The swimming pool, decorated with a bullish Minotaur mosaic, was used as a holding bay for live blue speckled, barnacled lobsters for the evening meal but could also be drained and converted into a dance floor (Ari liked to surprise smoochers by flooding it while they were still dancing). But, as a reminder that all was not as it seemed in the close, internecine world of the Greek shipping magnate, the bathroom had a two-way mirror through which Ari could spy on any dealings in his office from a very different sort of throne. Once, almost predictably, this mirror was replaced wrongly and Ari was very surprised to find some members of his board staring in at him.

Fidelity was never one of Ari's strong points, and, while married to Tina, his eye was apparently caught by the inimitable Eva Perón. He let it be known that he'd appreciate meeting Eva in informal circumstances. They met at Eva's villa at Santa Margherita on the Italian Riviera; afterward, they ate an omelet together, prepared by Eva. To do justice to the omelet, Ari grandly announced he would give $10,000 to Eva's favorite charity. Bitching privately, however, Ari told a friend that he'd tasted better eggs than Eva's, grumbling that it was the "most expensive omelet I ever ate." A deep, perceptive cynicism underlay most of Ari's romancing. In Paris, at one mad cabaret show at the Crazy Horse Saloon, Ari, rather too encouraged by the nude shows there, offered a member of the paparazzi an exclusive photo of the real secret of his success. Ari staggered into the crowd, the journalist in his wake. Promptly, Ari whipped out his penis and let it rest on the tips saucer. "That says it all," he sniggered. "Sex and money—that is my secret." Methinks he'd had one too many. If he did wake up the next day with a hangover, Ari swore by a spartan hangover pick-me-up of Fernet-Branca and pickled pearl onions. Ouch!

Meanwhile, the small, stout child who was to metamorphose into one of the greatest divas of the twentieth century, Maria Callas, was growing up in Washington Heights, Manhattan, with her Greek immigrant parents and sister Jackie. Maria was willful, bright, and rather naughty (her mother used to smear pepper on her lips if she was caught lying). Two things delighted her: food and music (although what she really wanted to be was a dentist). Her thick glasses mirroring the black and white piano keys, Maria's music could already stop a street full of people. The comfortable smell of homemade bread often wafted through the family's apartment, and on special Thursday nights she liked nothing better than the family outings to eat slippery, flavorsome chop suey in a Chinese restaurant in Washington Heights. She surpassed her sister Jackie in her ability to demolish food, drinking quarts of milk and biting into chunks of macaronada. Her mother, Evangelia, recalled, "Macaronada . . . is like Italian macaroni but with my own special sauce. I would fry onions and a little garlic in sweet butter with chopped meat, add tomatoes, fresh or canned or tomato paste and cinnamon and sugar, and let the sauce stand for an hour before pouring it over the cooked macaroni. There was never any left when we had macaronada for supper." But of all the treats, what Maria loved most was her own post-supper invention—it was similar to saganaki. She would fry two eggs and slide on top of the sizzling eggs an exact square of soft Greek feta or kasseri cheese. She loved crunchy fried potatoes too, on the side. Always (or at least until she broke all contact with her mother), even after the largest of meals, she would pipe up, like a plaintive baby cuckoo, "Where are my eggs and cheese?"

Mrs. Callas soon realized she had a child protégé on her hands, and when Maria was thirteen and Jackie nineteen years old, Mrs. Callas (minus the rather useless Mr. Callas, who insisted girls would be better taught to cook and clean) left the United States for Greece in order to train Maria's voice. By now, teenage Maria was all pimples and podge, her black bangs covering a rash of spots. The stifling heat of Athens made her sweat, but there was little she could do to mask the chimp-like teenage body odor, as she was allergic to deodorants and perfumes. Moving into her grandmother's house in Athens did little to help with dumpiness. Grandmother Dimitriadou had a marvelous Greek cook, and they dined like kings every night. Then, moving into their own house at Patission 61, they were greeted by a large kitchen, gas stove at the ready, where during World War II the family's maids, Athena and Filio, baked oregano-scented kota riganati and glorious spanakopita from black-market goods and chickens and vegetables courtesy of the undercover markets in Athens or bought in the surrounding mountains.

Maria ate rich food at odd hours, picking over morsels whenever she had a break from her music practice—she had won a scholarship to a conservatory and was determined to push herself as far as she could go, refusing to leave her piano for meals. The family kept canaries, whose vocal range Maria envied. She practiced singing with the canary David, putting her fingers against his tiny, feathered throat to work out how he warbled his tune. One of the meeker canaries, Elmina, fainted

Kota Riganati

INGREDIENTS

3 lb. chicken, on the bone
4 cloves of garlic, crushed
1 tbsp. dried oregano
Juice of 2 lemons
3 tbsp. olive oil

2 tbsp. melted butter
Freshly ground black pepper
Sea salt
4 potatoes, peeled and sliced

METHOD

Place the joints of chicken in a large bowl. In a smaller bowl, mix together the garlic, oregano, lemon juice, olive oil, butter, pepper, and salt. Pour this over the chicken; massage it in with your hands. Cover, refrigerate, and marinate overnight.

Heat the oven to 230°C. Place the chicken in a roasting tray—skin side up— and blast it at 230°C for 5 minutes. Then reduce the heat to 170°C, add the potatoes, roll them around in the marinade, and cook for an hour.

Spanakopita

INGREDIENTS

3½ lb. spinach
1 tbsp. olive oil
1 clove of garlic, chopped
8 scallions, very finely chopped
1 handful of fresh parsley,
   very finely chopped
1 handful of fresh dill, very finely
   chopped
½ tbsp. fresh mint, very finely chopped

Black pepper
Sea salt
2 cups crumbly feta cheese
1¾ cups ricotta cheese
½ tsp. nutmeg
3 eggs, beaten
Filo pastry, about 13 sheets
4 tbsp. melted butter

METHOD

Preheat the oven to 180°C. Wash the spinach. In a large, roomy frying pan, heat the olive oil and add the garlic. Add the spinach and cover. Turn the pan down to low. Allow this to cook for about 5 minutes, until the spinach has wilted. Drain in a colander, pressing down with a spoon to remove any excess water. Set aside and allow to cool.

In a large mixing bowl, combine the scallions, parsley, dill, mint, black pepper, and sea salt. Now add the feta cheese and the ricotta. Grate half a teaspoon of nutmeg over this. Add the spinach and mix well. Pour in the 3 beaten eggs and again mix thoroughly.

Now get a square or rectangular baking dish and grease with olive oil. Have the thin, papery sheets of filo to hand. Keep a damp cloth over the rest of the pastry. Lifting a sheet of pastry at a time, brush each with the melted butter and place in the baking dish. Do this for 5 layers. Finally, do another 2 sheets, but lay them crossways, allowing the top and bottom of each to hang over the sides. Pour the spanakopita filling on top of the pastry layers and then fold in the last two sheets' overhang. Finish with another 5 sheets, each individually brushed with melted butter. Brush the top of the spanakopita with the last of the butter. Finally, bake in the oven for 30–40 minutes. Cut into squares and serve warm.

when Maria sang her arias and had to be revived with brandy. When she allowed herself a break, Maria would scoff tubs of ersatz ice cream and help herself to sacks of rations on the floor, her large bottom framed by the door. The canaries' room was used to hide two British officers from the occupying Axis powers; giggling, the girls dyed the blonde officer's hair black. The day after the British officers left, a fist pounded on the front door and a troop of sixty-one suspicious Italian soldiers poured into the house, their revolvers cocked at the ready. The Callas family had been betrayed. Maria, however, was seated at the piano, playing Tosca. The Italians slowly melted into a seated circle around the piano's legs, lost in Maria's music. The day after, they came back with votive offerings of ham and bread and macaroni to heap on the piano. And it was to be singing Tosca that Maria made her first professional public performance at the Royal Theatre in Athens before an audience of German and Italian soldiers. (In case you were wondering, the canaries survived starvation during the Greek Civil War but then met a sticky end when some nervous Communists, catching sight of shadows in the room, swept the room with machine gun fire. Only a charred feather or two remained, floating to the ground.)

Maria's fortunes changed for the better when, at age twenty-six, she met the puffy, fifty-six-year-old brick manufacturer Battista Meneghini, who became her manager and married her in 1949. With marriage to Battista came wealth, and this, with her increasing success as an opera singer, had an unpleasant effect on Maria's personality. She snubbed other cast members, became increasingly vain and self-centered, and shook off those who displeased her, including intimate relations—namely, her mother and sister. In desperation, Mrs. Callas wrote to her daughter, asking if Maria (by now a millionairess) could let her have $100 a month just to get by. A snarling reply came: "Mother, I have your letter . . . I can give you nothing. Money is not like flowers, growing in the gardens . . . I work for a living. You are a young woman . . . and you can work. If you can't earn enough to live on throw yourself out of the window." To her sister Jackie, who wrote asking to join Maria in Italy, Maria's riposte was "If, as you say, you still have no money, you had better jump in the river and drown yourself."

Maria and Battista owed their romance to a cutlet. They first met in the Pedavena restaurant in Bra Square, Verona, when Maria kindly insisted that local potentate Battista have her cutlet, as the waiter had regretfully informed them it was the last one available (though, uncharitably, one could note that by this point, Maria was always dieting sporadically, uneasy with the expectation that opera singers be overweight). Having snared her ancient Romeo, Maria became part of his family and watched wide-eyed while Battista's mother cooked. Mama Battista's cooking instructions were gold dust as Maria dutifully learned to make Meneghini family Veronese favorites such as lesso con la pearà, with its sublime sauce of buttery bone marrow breadcrumbs and anatra fredda con polénta calda—chilled duck with hot cornmeal pudding—as well as how to soak and cook the dried, salted codfish baccalà. No matter how delicious these were, Maria forbade herself more than one lingering mouthful of each. Stealing food was not beyond her, either; Maria was extremely pushy about what other diners ordered. Franco Zeffirelli recalled Maria sweeping up the menu and peremptorily ordering for everyone at the start of one meal; she then loved to lean over and sample a forkful of what was on another plate. Always half-hungry, she fantasized about meals to come, collecting recipes voraciously wherever she went, vicariously savoring the ingredients with each penned word: cold unsalted butter; heavy cream; béchamel sauce; pound cake; rich, puffed, warm chocolate beignets.

Lesso con la Pearà

INGREDIENTS

4 tbsp. olive oil
1 lb. veal or beef
1 chicken, quartered
1 calf's head
1 lb. pickled tongue
2 raw Italian sausages
3 carrots, peeled and quartered

4 onions, chopped
4 celery ribs, chopped
4 tomatoes, chopped
Sea salt
Black pepper
2½ pints water

FOR THE PEARÀ . . .

2 tbsp. butter
3 tbsp. beef marrow (I usually find
    that one marrow bone, split in half,
    renders more than enough fat)
1 clove of garlic, crushed
2⅓ cups fresh breadcrumbs

Freshly ground black pepper
Sea salt
The rich beef stock made above—you
    will add this by the cupful
½ cup freshly grated Parmesan
½ tsp. crumbled, dried chili

METHOD

In a very large, deep, heavy-bottomed pan, heat the olive oil. Slowly cook the chopped onions and celery until they are softened. Next add the tomatoes, salt, and black pepper, followed by the veal/beef, chicken, calf's head, tongue, sausages, and carrots. Add the water. Bring to a boil; remove the scum and then turn down to a low simmer. After 1 hour, drain and change the water. Return to a boil and keep removing any scum—this stock will be the base of the pearà. After another half hour is up, start on the pearà.

To make the pearà, melt the butter and beef marrow in a saucepan. When they are completely melted, add the garlic and breadcrumbs. Stir thoroughly to allow the breadcrumbs to fully absorb the butter and marrow, letting them toast in the fat. This will smell divine—keep stirring, though, as you don't want the breadcrumbs to stick or burn. Season with freshly ground black pepper and salt. Drain 2 cups of the stock from the meat. Stirring constantly, add these cups to the breadcrumbs and cook very gently. Keep adding more stock by the cupful over the course of an hour; the pearà should be like a medium porridge, with a smooth, creamy consistency.

Continue to cook the meat in the diminishing stock for another hour.

When you are ready to serve the pearà, stir through the crushed chili and the grated Parmesan. Finally, drain various meats you have cooked in the stock, arrange on a large serving dish, and serve the scrumptious pearà alongside.

Chocolate Beignets (this recipe will make about 20 beignets)

INGREDIENTS

3 eggs
½ cup milk
⅓ cup vanilla granulated sugar (this
   is made by keeping a vanilla pod
   or two embedded in pot of sugar)
2 tbsp. sunflower oil
2 cups all-purpose flour

1 cup unsweetened cocoa powder
2 tsp. baking powder
Pinch of sea salt
1 large bar of bittersweet chocolate,
   broken into ½ in. pieces
3–4 pints sunflower oil for deep frying

FOR THE CHOCOLATE DUST . . .

2 oz. powdered sugar
1 tbsp. unsweetened cocoa powder

2 tsp. powdered cinnamon

METHOD

In a large mixing bowl, whisk together the eggs, milk, sugar, and sunflower oil. Now place a sieve over the bowl and add the flour, cocoa powder, baking powder, and sea salt. Whisk the ingredients together; a thick, sticky, wickedly dark chocolate batter will form, which no longer adheres to the walls of the mixing bowl.

Now make the chocolate dust. In a bowl mix together the sugar, cocoa powder, and cinnamon.

Pour the 3–4 pints of sunflower oil into a large, roomy, and deep pan. Heat until the oil becomes silent—test it with a tiny blob of beignet batter; on falling into the oil, it should quickly rise, surrounded by bubbles.

Now scoop up about a 2-inch blob of beignet batter. Push a hole into it, pop in the chunk of bittersweet chocolate, and then seal the beignet. Drop 1 beignet into the oil at a time, making sure that you do not crowd the pan. Cook each for about 2 minutes, remove with a slotted spoon, and pop onto paper towels to absorb the oil. Do all the beignets this way.

Finally, roll each beignet in the cocoa dust and sink your teeth in! A cup of thick cream alongside is also good; lacking the stamina of Maria Callas, you may be able to eat no more than two—any more and start writing your will.

Battista recalled Maria ate "like a goat"—plates of vegetables without any dressing—attacked shaggy meat bones like a wild cat, and could never eat her fill of flesh, especially juicy steaks alla florentina, courtesy of some obliging Tuscan cattle. Yet, at the same time, Maria was tortured by her "elephant-like legs"—which one critic alluded to—and they obstinately remained just that, whether she was thin or fat. When Maria went into a flash Milan boutique, overweight, wearing flat shoes, a shapeless dress, and plastic earrings, one woman working there muttered

to another that Maria looked like "a peasant on her Sunday outing." Maria, dis-
tressed, left with her aging husband but told the staff, "I'll be back." A year later
she turned up and they didn't recognize her. She had shed all her weight, as if she
had slipped off her heavy frame like an unwanted coat to allow this slim, svelte
"other" to step out.

So how did Maria do it? She had tried all sorts of medications, vials, powders,
salads, and programs to lose weight. This remarkable reforging of her physical
self only piqued curiosity: a pasta company persuaded Maria's brother-in-law
Dr. Giovanni Cazzarolli to write a testimonial—which he did with literary
flourish—claiming that he had treated Maria himself by encouraging her to eat
their remarkable physiological, dietetic pasta from the Patanella Mills. How wonderful life would be for all of us were Dr. Cazzaolli's magnificent claims true!
But alas no: the singer's version of her weight loss has Maria, ever the carnivore,
scoffing a mouthful too many of rare meat. One of those mouthfuls contained a
tapeworm, which happily set up home in Maria's gastric tract. Fortunately for her,
its larvae didn't decide to migrate to her muscles or brain. She had, in effect, been
eating for one when she should have been eating for two. After the removal of the
worm, Maria claimed, she lost weight. Other, more incredulous forces attested that
Maria deliberately ingested tapeworms in a desperate bid to lose weight—but at
what cost to the timbre of her voice?

Cupid, though, was on his way to strike an arrow through Maria's heart—Cupid
in the whale-like form of the hostess, wit, and bon vivant rheumy-eyed Miss Elsa
Maxwell, who decided to throw a ball in watery, greening Venice at the palatial
Hotel Danieli. It was September 3, 1957. Tina and Ari Onassis were there; she
twenty-eight and lovely, Ari a paunchy fifty-three. After a breakfast of spaghetti,
Elsa started tinkering on the piano, and Maria joined in, humming "Stormy
Weather" through the fog of tobacco smoke and over the half-drained drinks. Battista listened fondly to her voice. Ari Onassis listened, too, but with less interest in
her voice and more in Callas's charisma and magnetism; she enchanted him. By
1958, Maria was firmly in Ari's sights, and he invited her and Battista to join him
and Tina (plus Winston and Clementine "Clemmie" Churchill and their wide-eyed
granddaughter Celia) on the *Christina* for a leisurely summer tour of the Mediterranean coast, winding up in Venice for the film festival. Innocently abetting her
husband's future seduction of Maria, Tina pored over the yacht's menus with the
Onassises' French chef.

This chaotic, befuddling, and romantic cruise spelled the end of Callas's
marriage.

Life on the *Christina* was both charming and hilariously confusing. Lunch was
in tiny fishing villages, pocket-size and tucked into the crenellated shoreline. Ari
liked to row across to the shore and eat local Greek food or steak and salad. Maria

would eat similarly, still dieting, but with her fork darting out for a taste of what was on everyone else's plate. Battista, meanwhile, was green with seasickness. His envy curdled with dyspepsia and the jogging about of the yacht.

Docked in Lilliputian harbors come the sultry evening, the sea rocked the party's little shore-to-yacht boats as they pushed off from the *Christina*, heading for the twinkly bunting of the lights and restaurants of Portofino and Capri—though Winston's doddery, painful walk meant he and Clemmie couldn't join them on these outings. Onboard every attempt was made by Ari to serve his guests lavishly: at sunset angular, witty cocktails and caviar were served, the caviar in a four-pound tin, guests digging into the sooty, shining eggs with spoons. Ari knelt by Winston's side, maternally spoon-feeding caviar to him. This ritualized taking of champagne and appetizers stretched out lazily for a balmy hour or two. Ari loved brick-red sea urchin eggs, the spiked urchins dredged from the sea bed when the moon was full. His sister Artemis Grarafoulias sent dark homemade bread to the *Christina* as a special treat for Ari. Baklava was flown into the yacht, as was the caviar from Iran and fish from the cold waters of Northern Europe. Ari even had marinated camel meat flown in from Capadocia in Turkey.

The pale green and white dining room was immaculately polished. Ari always planned the seating arrangements: Clementine Churchill on his right, Maria to his left, Tina somewhere appropriately mute and subdued while Maria and Ari cast smoldering glances at each other. Maria loved having octogenarian Winston alongside her. Determined to charm him, she would try to tempt him with noisome morsels from her plate, trembling spoonfuls of ice cream—one might ask why Winston brought out this propensity to spoon-feed. Humble though she may have been with Winston himself, Maria grandly confided in another guest, "I like travelling with Winston Churchill. It relieves me of my popularity." Winston, delighted, was always rather foggy about what Maria actually did for a living—he wasn't much of an opera lover. His granddaughter, sixteen-year-old Celia, staring out through wise young eyes, took a rather bleak view of the diva: "Maria always wanted to sit next to my grandfather, I don't suppose she got terribly good vibes from the rest of us. We all hated her. We were all sort of revolted by her trying to feed him ice cream from her plate, but he was enchanted by her. He loved glamorous women. Every time we sat down to dinner she would do something to aggravate everyone else." Winston, however, had less fun when Gracie Fields piled onto the boat and began serenading him through sulky red lips, the piano jangling a ceaseless tirade of wartime songs—cheered on by winks, nods, and smiles and finger tapping. He bleated a little too loudly to his private secretary Anthony Montague Browne, "God's teeth! How long is this going on?"

Before you feel sorry for Battista, in an attempt at one-upmanship he kept inexpertly trying to play footsie with Anthony's wife under the table at dinner, ruining the very patient Noni Montague Brown's shoes. Finding Noni too British to flirt, Battista took to trotting off to bed early, having to sleep without air-conditioning so that Maria's voice was not damaged. At the Bay of Naples, he tried to jump ship but was apprehended by Maria, who scolded him back on deck.

While Battista rolled about in his suffocating cabin, Maria and Ari would stay up for much of the night, talking in Greek under the luminescent stars and the flare from Ari's glowing cigar when he pulled on it (they were chaperoned by some shortsighted guest swimming in the saltwater darkness), sipping champagne, and eating saletés grecs. Winsomely, Ari trailed his fingers in the bespangled waters and told Maria wonderful stories. If the *Christina* was near land, you could hear the chirp of crickets.

The lovers' infidelity seemed in part to coalesce about a shared sensuous pleasure in Greek food. Usually, there was more formal, sophisticated French fare at dinner (though one morning Ari flew a plane several hundred miles to Athens to fetch baklava for Winston because he said he'd like to try it—this meant its cost came in at a tidy $1,000 per slice). Tina, educated abroad, was not Greek in the same way as Ari—only Maria was. One evening, after a visit to the ebony volcanic island of Santorini, the Sandys and the Churchills and the Montague Browns traipsed into the yacht's dining room to be greeted by partner-less Tina and Battista, ready for dinner. Ari and Maria were missing. Tina mumbled, "Oh, they've already eaten. Maria ordered a special Greek meal, just for them."

Greek Salad

INGREDIENTS

1 clove garlic	14 black Kalamata olives
Pinch of sea salt	A generous slab of feta cheese
6 ripe, sweet tomatoes (smell them—	(about 150 g)
they should give off a metallic	1 tbsp. fresh, finely chopped
tang), roughly chopped	oregano
¾ of a cucumber, peeled and	Freshly ground black pepper
roughly chopped	1 tbsp. freshly squeezed lemon juice
½ red onion, peeled and very	½ tsp. sugar
finely sliced	2 tbsp. olive oil

METHOD

Slice the onions and place them in the olive oil for about 20 minutes. Sprinkle a pinch of sea salt into the base of your salad bowl and rub the peeled garlic clove against the bowl, using the salt as grist; keep pressing down on the garlic with your thumb and rubbing it around the bowl. Remove the tousled, tuft of garlic that's left and discard, leaving behind a salty, garlicky slick, which your salad will pick up.

Greek Salad (*continued*)

Now add the cucumber, tomatoes, olives, and oregano to the bowl. Toss them around the bowl, picking up the garlic oil. Pepper the salad. Now remove the onions from the olive oil and add them. Retain the olive oil and, in a smaller bowl, mix it with the sugar and lemon juice to make a dressing. Drizzle the salad dressing over the salad, retaining a teaspoonful. Finally, place the slice of feta on the top of the salad and drizzle with the remaining salad dressing.

A Thousand-Dollar Baklava

INGREDIENTS
1 cup butter
2½ cups walnuts, roughly chopped
½ cup pistachio nuts, roughly
    chopped
1½ cups ground almonds

1 tsp. ground cinnamon
1 tsp. ground cardamom
Grated zest of a lemon
Grated zest of an orange
12 sheets of filo pastry

FOR THE SYRUP . . .
1⅓ cups granulated sugar
Juice of a lemon
½ cup water

1 stick of cinnamon
1 tsp. rich honey
1 tbsp. orange blossom water

METHOD
Preheat the oven to 160°C. Butter a square or rectangular baking tin.

Now melt the butter. Place the walnuts, pistachios, and ground almonds in a bowl. Add 5 tablespoons of the melted butter (reserve the rest for buttering the filo pastry).

Mix the nuts and butter with the cinnamon, cardamom, and lemon and orange zest. I use a coffee grinder to grind spices fresh, as they are beautifully aromatic: a small handful of cardamom pods will give you a teaspoon, and one 2-inch cinnamon stick will suffice for a teaspoon of cinnamon.

Now for building the baklava. Melt the remaining butter. Lay the filo pastry sheets beside the baking tin. Cover the filo with a damp cloth to prevent them from drying out. One sheet at a time, brush the filo with butter and lay it flat in the baking tin. Build up 5 layers. Now spoon the filling over the filo. Use a light touch. Cover with the remaining 7 sheets of filo, each buttered and laid flat, one after the other.

A Thousand-Dollar Baklava (*continued*)

Brush the top with melted butter, and then, using a very sharp knife, slice down through the layers diagonally to make a counterpane of smallish diamond shapes; you may need to hold the pastry in place with your fingertips, as the knife has a tendency to drag the pastry. Bake in the oven for an hour. Now make the baklava syrup. Into a saucepan place the sugar, lemon juice, cinnamon stick, honey, and water. Stirring over a medium heat, bring to a boil—you want to give the cinnamon the chance to really infuse the syrup—and then simmer for 10 minutes until the mix has a syrupy consistency. Cool and then add the orange blossom water.

After an hour, the baklava should be a lovely golden color. Remove but do not turn off the oven; raise its temperature to 180°C. Carefully pour the syrup over the baklava, letting it roll down into the incisions. Return the baklava to the oven for 5 minutes; then remove and cool. Plate up the small, diamond-shaped baklava. If you wish, scatter them with some more crushed pistachio.

But it wasn't until the group trooped up to Mount Athos in early August that Battista truly saw the writing on the wall. Ancient patriarch Athengoras took Ari and Maria's hands in his own (as good Greek children) and blessed them together. Green-eyed, Battista watched this, fuming that it looked a bit too much like a wedding ceremony. And it certainly was the prelude to one union—as Maria told a friend later, it was in the heat of that same evening that she and Ari first became lovers. Hopping mad, Battista stared as the amorous couple exchanged intimate toasts and glances: Winston, Clemmie, and company decided to take refuge in their cabin while Battista wailed. Their cabin was a hotbed of gossip.

Soon after the doomed cruise, Maria demanded a divorce, telling Battista with her usual tact and tenderness that he was "a country bumpkin who had fulfilled his ambitions through her glory." Having secured custody of their toy poodles, Toy and Thea, Maria never looked back. Ari left with Battista's curse in his ears: "May you never find peace for the rest of your days." Ironically, Battista was far more capable than Ari of appreciating Maria's voice. Nadia Stancioff, Maria's biographer, recounts that after Maria's brilliant 1960 performance in *Norma* in Epidaurus, Greece, Ari was left quite indifferent: it wasn't Greek music, after all. Instead, at the post-performance party, Ari worried about the freshness of the shrimps they were serving and whether the steaks were overdone. Rough, crude, swearing like a trooper, he wanted Maria to practice out of earshot and didn't appreciate her singing to their guests. Ari's idea of musical fun was to use the street organ he kept on the *Christina* to grind out special ditties. Maria, meanwhile, frantically crammed herself with diuretics if she gained so much as a pound; Ari came to detest any mention of her dieting. If Maria tried to refuse food on the *Christina*, Ari scolded,

"The chef is killing himself all day in the kitchen to please us, you can't ignore these people."

Tina divorced Ari and moved on through another two marriages toward a graceless, sad, and untimely death in her forties. Maria, meanwhile, had her hopes of being the next Mrs. Onassis disappointed. That auspicious title was to be stolen from her by none other than Jackie Kennedy, widow of President John F. Kennedy. This terrible, unbearable news was recounted to Maria over the phone by none other than Ari's butler. Her power had waned; her voice had become enfeebled. Some blamed this on weight loss, others on her painful shenanigans with Ari.

Jackie Kennedy, meanwhile, had not a single qualm about Maria. Jackie, some wit noted, had "the social conscience of Louis XIV"; she loved presents—preferably twenty-four-carat ones—and who better to provide them than a Greek tycoon? Caroline Kennedy named Ari "Santa Claus," he showered so many gifts on them. As a dining companion for Jackie, Ari must have been a light relief after dinners with JFK. White House staff claimed that the president liked to whine all through dinner about social issues. When a delicious roast had just been carved at the table, he groaned to Jackie, "What in hell am I going to do about air pollution?" Jackie suggested that the air force spray U.S. industrial centers with Chanel Number Five. How droll.

Post-Dallas it was easy to slip into a romance with Ari Onassis: there was already a family precedent for sleeping with him—Jackie's whippet-thin sister, Lee Radziwill, had often been in his bed. Jackie and Ari had crossed paths several times over the years, regarding each other with mild, mutual good-will, which was to become impassioned following the assassination of JFK. Maria was no match for Jackie, who did all she could to snub Maria in the winter of 1964 when she had set her sights on Ari. Inviting him to one of her brunches in her spanking-new fifteen-room apartment on 1040 Fifth Avenue, New York, she limited the invitation to one place. When he got there, there could be no other female distractions—she was the only woman in a pool of circling men.

Maria, broken, left the *Christina* in a hurry, her jewels scattered behind her, some of which came to adorn Jackie's throat and wrists. She damaged her ribs and ended up in the hospital. When flowers arrived at her bedside, she pretended they were from her beloved Ari. The phone had to be kept by her side in case he should call her. He didn't.

When Teddy Kennedy and Jackie joined Ari on the yacht to negotiate marriage terms, Jackie dwarfing her husband-to-be (one of her friends quipped, "A woman needs a man, not a radiator cap"), he made sure there were some gamesome blondes on board for Teddy and set up a Greek bouzouki party for the guests. One enterprising journalist, Nicos Mastorakis, masqueraded as a member of the band with a camera hidden behind his guitar strings. He recalled, "The musical evening begins with red pepper tips, red ripe tomatoes, spinach puree, black caviar and liquor. Teddy drinks ouzo, permanently. Jackie prefers vodka at first. . . . A crooner sings and Jackie is rapt with fascination. From time to time Onassis . . . translates with whispers in her ear the words of the song and she stares with those big eyes. The bouzouki music reaches its peak and Teddy gets up to dance. . . . Teddy returns to his ouzo." Unfortunately, Nicos's cover was blown, his Minox camera was taken, and he had to cozy up in police custody that night.

The negotiations proved fruitful, and the two were married on Ari's private island, Skorpio, both dressed in turtlenecks, by a Greek priest who met Ari's blunt stipulations that he "understands English and doesn't look like Rasputin." The wedding feast was packed with the finest delicacies—but delicacies Ari had to explain to Jackie: Cypriot beccafico (fig peckers); tiny-boned songbirds preserved in vinegar and eaten, bones and all, with your fingers; olives; chestnuts; braised lamb; milky feta cheese; vegetables; pheasant; and champagne (Jackie stuck to martinis). Years later, in far less romantic times once pragmatism and mutually induced misery had set in, they were to eat BLTs together while Ari drafted his will.

According to biographer Nicholas Gage, just some forty-eight hours before the wedding, Maria's phone finally rang. It was Ari, pleading with her to save him from his engagement. He had it worked out. If Maria would just be so kind as to pop up in Athens, then Jackie would be so enraged that she'd storm back to America. Maria refused outright (though she did accept delivery of the cheese pies he sent her regularly). Despite all this, after what was—at least for Maria—a long, painful separation, she and Ari were reconciled at a party held in Maria's Parisian apartment at 36 Avenue Georges Mandel. Maria was docile, still deeply in love despite Ari's faithless marriage. Again there was the obligatory audience who watched after dinner as Ari settled down beside Maria, clapped his hand on her thigh, and announced, "Ah, that feels good! It's great to feel Maria's big fat thighs again. I've really missed them. Jackie is nothing but a bag of bones."

But nothing was ever to be the same again; it was as if Battista's curse had struck its mark. Plus *e Hira*—"the widow," as Maria and Ari refereed to Jackie—was jinxed. Death took from Ari the one thing he could not bear to lose, the one person his treasures could not return: his twenty-four-year-old son Alexander was killed in an airplane crash. Ari was bereft. Not even the Anatolian dainties made by his sister Artemis could tempt his appetite. While his trademark dark glasses (he even wore them to swim) seemed to symbolize his withdrawal from life, in truth they concealed the myasthenia gravis that was to plague him. Alexander's body was buried on Skorpios, and Ari took to wandering the island, his mongrel dog Vana at his heels, talking to the dog and forever wandering closer to Alexander's tomb. There, wearily, Ari would place two tumblers on the grass, crack open a bottle of ouzo, and talk to his dead son, sitting on the blanket employees began to leave out for him. Sometimes he would bring food and a plate for Alexander, too. Finally, two years after Alexander's death, when Ari succumbed to illness and conceded he would go to the hospital, there was only one thing he insisted on taking with him: a small, bright red blanket that Maria had once given him. In this sense, Maria was by him when he died.

Maria herself died, all too young, aged fifty-three, in her Paris apartment, a recluse, still heartbroken at Ari's death, endlessly watching westerns on TV. She had made one last visit to Greece only to be caught by the press eating ipovrihio, a dessert of rose-flavored mastic served on a spoon and submerged in a tall glass of ice-cold water. Addicted to Mandrax sleeping pills, with a few of the diuretics Ari used to nag her about perhaps thrown in, Maria's heart gave way, leaving her maid Bruni to weep for her. Her long-estranged sister Jackie, despite Maria's cruel snubs, turned up to pay her respects. In her *Memoirs*, Jackie Callas recounts the small, private ceremony of friends and well-wishers when they scattered Maria's ashes at sea. The Greek minister of culture Dimitri Nanias stepped up to the ship's rail and poured the ashes of Maria Callas over the side. But it was just at that moment that a sudden gust of wind whipped up, flinging the ashes back in the faces of the mourners. Vasso Devetzi, the pianist and a friend of Maria's, got a mouthful: "A great deal went straight down her throat. She began to splutter and retch. Indeed we all got some in the face and mouth and were forced to spit and cough it up. . . . Rubbing my lips with my handkerchief I looked around at the illustrious party and realized that we were all swallowing Maria's remains. We were helplessly eating my sister; the greatest diva of the century was being consumed by those who had thought to placate her spirit."

ALLIGATOR LOVE CALLS WITH HOWARD HUGHES

Howard Hughes was very keen on physical ailments, especially constipation and ear ailments. He'd have you popping your ears, yawning, and holding your nose and blowing sharply down it. His bodyguards knew they only had to hint at trouble with their poo and Howard would look at them solicitously and give them a day off. Obsessive hypochondria governed Hughes's life thanks to his hygiene-mad mother, Allene Gano. Mother and son occupied their own world, scrubbed clean but always in danger of bacterial invasion—from cats, cockroaches, beetles, and legions of winged creatures in general. Every night Allene dosed little Howard with Russian mineral oil, warding off rumors of polio, infantile paralysis, and, she hinted, untoward things that might happen to the soles of Howard's feet. Howard, hard of hearing and smothered by Allene, was isolated from other children by maternal instructions that followed him into the outside world: he was not to eat flapjacks at scout camp; he must be cautious in group activities. Allene scoured her pans vigorously and scrubbed down the family's fruit, vegetables, and meat. Life must have seemed very precarious.

And indeed it was. Allene died an early death, leaving Howard and his father, Bo—the founder of their fortunes, the Hughes Tool Company—alone together in Los Angeles. There were hints of Howard's future life in the film industry. Bo loved movies and his brother, Rupert, wrote plots for silent movies. Family Sunday brunches at Rupert's house were perfumed, glitzy events with svelte, sassy actresses. Then Bo had a crushing heart attack—he was only fifty-four—leaving eighteen-year-old Howard the fortune from Hughes Tools Inc. that was to fuel his maverick passions. Although he was young and goofy, Howard's future was already set in the stone of wealth and obsession. His diet throughout his life was salted with an indefatigable boyishness. He had a passion for ice cream and loved ice-cream-eating challenges with pretty girls.

When it came to flying, Howard was magnificent, fearless. Not only did he own Trans World Airlines (TWA), but he was also a gifted pilot. He flew around the world in record time in 1938. When he landed in Russia, the Russians had gone to all the trouble of finding him Cornflakes for breakfast, but Hughes feigned indifference and cunningly turned down the Russians' offer of a parting gift of caviar. They were trying to spoil his chances; caviar would have weighed his craft down. Plummeting down from the sky never put him off. Wild crashes only made his ambitions rocket. Until, that is, the catastrophic crash of July 1946, which almost cost him his life. Perhaps his luck failed him, he might have reasoned, because he had behaved out of character. That very morning he went all-out and fell for the temptations of banana cream pie for breakfast. A break in ritual. No doubt when Howard had the chance to contemplate his actions in the lead up to his crash, he took account of the contribution of such loopy, intemperate, out-of-habit eating.

Banana Cream Pie (only for the reckless)

FOR THE CRUST . . .

3 tbsp. melted butter
1 tbsp. demerara sugar
1 tbsp. maple syrup

½ tsp. ground cinnamon
2 cups crushed graham crackers

FOR THE CREAMY FILLING . . .

3 cups heavy cream
1 tbsp. granulated sugar
1 tsp. vanilla essence
1 cup cream cheese

1½ cups sweetened condensed milk
6 bananas
½ cup shredded coconut

METHOD

In a frying pan, melt the butter, then stir in the demerara sugar until it dissolves. Add the maple syrup, cinnamon, and the crushed graham crackers. Warm through, mixing the crust together. Butter a deep pie pan and line with the crust. Put into the fridge to firm up and set.

Now make the filling. Pour the cream into a large mixing bowl. Add the sugar and vanilla. Using an electric mixer, work the cream up to a soft, cloudy mass. In another bowl, beat the cream cheese until it is fluffy. Now add the condensed milk and combine thoroughly. Using a metal spoon, gently fold half the whipped vanilla cream into the cream cheese mix.

Now you can begin to assemble the pie. Take the cooled crust out of the fridge. Scoop up a few generous blobs of the cream cheese filling and gently spread this as a modest base layer. Take 4 of the bananas, peel them, and cut them into chunks. Place these randomly on top of the cream cheese and line the sides. Empty the rest of the filling over the bananas. Scoop up the remaining mass of vanilla cream and put this on top. Chill in the fridge for 1 hour. In a dry frying pan, toast the shredded coconut to release its lovely aromas; let it turn golden brown. Cool. Finally, remove the chilled banana cream pie from the fridge and decorate with the remaining newly chopped bananas and toasted coconut. You are now capable of anything; avoid flight.

Banana cream pie had caused Howard to suffer agonizing third-degree burns, a shift in the position of his heart, and a deflated lung. But fresh orange juice was the cure, and he began drinking it daily, without fail. If only immortality were so easy. Unfortunately, orange juice couldn't dull the pain, and from then onward, Howard was usually pumped full of medications.

Clearly, Howard suffered from obsessive-compulsive disorder, which, unchecked and untreated, slowly consumed his life. Compulsion was made worse by his enormous wealth. He was surrounded by a shoal of employees and acquaintances very

willing to indulge his every eccentricity, pandering to Howard's illness but never
helping Howard. Marriage to lanky, finickity Howard in 1925 proved too much for
Ella Rice: by the time their honeymoon was over, their relationship was a quiv-
ering mess. Part of Howard's strange life pattern was to live in hotels, where he
could micromanage his existence—in this case, with Ella in the Ambassador Hotel,
Houston, Texas. When they went to parties, Howard wouldn't swallow any alcohol, smuggling his drink into the bathroom to throw away. Breakfast had to be three
eggs scrambled with milk, and dinner was steak, medium rare, with exactly twelve
peas of the same size; if one was tubbier than the rest, it was *returned* to the hotel
kitchens to be replaced by an alternative, more suitable and comely pea. Any other
vegetable was an illegal migrant onto Howard's plate, leading to him spending his
lifetime on the toilet for hours on end with constipation. Howard spent hours in the
bathroom poring over the *Wall Street Journal* and felt completely carefree about
holding the odd business conference in there with his white-faced assistants. To
complete the package, Howard also had telephones installed there. When he wasn't
on the toilet, he spent hours golfing. That means *hours*. Ella stormed out, then was
persuaded to return to him again, only to catch sight of Carole Lombard being
whisked out the back door. That put an end to any soft-heartedness.

Owning RKO Radio Studios gave Howard access to alluring actresses of
all shapes and sizes and also allowed his OCD free rein as he pored over film
sequences for hours at a time and was able to shape and direct his fantasies. Famously, entranced by her breasts, he spent hours designing what proved to be very
painful bras for Jane Russell so that her breasts were shown to their best advantage
on-screen. His aide Walter Kane was supposed to screen nubile girls for Howard,
and they set up an apartment at 8484 Sunset Boulevard for "photographic tests."
Mamie Van Doren was just such a young hopeful and, aged fifteen, met Walter
Kane with the vague promise of getting work in RKO Studios. Walter's opening
line was "Do you have any black stockings?" Mamie didn't, so Walter bought her
some and got her to strut about in them, his watery blue eyes on her and his voice
thickening. It must have worked, as Walter invited her for lunch with Howard,
saying, "Oh . . . one more thing. Make sure you wear a white sweater . . . with no
bra." At RKO she met Walter "and a tall, dishevelled man who looked as though
he hadn't shaved in several days: Howard Hughes. Hughes . . . wore one of those
hounds-tooth jackets with sleeves made of different material that were popular in
the forties, baggy brown slacks, a nondescript shirt, and no tie. His shoes were a
pair of scuffed tennis sneakers. Except for the shoes, his clothes were clean but
rumpled, as if he had slept in them." Howard and Mamie sat down for lunch, and
Howard thought it was a bright idea to break the conversational ice with "Are
you a virgin?" Mamie had entered the circumspect, fantastical world of Howard
Hughes. He asked her to use the pseudonym "Mr. Murphy" for him. One time he

drove Mamie and her mother to Palm Springs in his Chevy. When Mamie said she couldn't have lunch with him because of an important commitment, Howard went into a huff and abandoned them, leaving Mamie and her mother to hoof it back home on the Greyhound bus, dusty heeled.

The next time Mamie met him, a few years later, he was still dressed in the same outfit but spoke to her through a "mouth mask" of Kleenex. As she recalls in her memoirs, "I saw he was carrying a box of Kleenex in his other hand. He pulled one from the box and held it over his nose and mouth. He leaned forward and cupped his ear with his free hand. 'How've you been Mamie?' Hughes asked, muffled through the tissue." They did what she comically described as a "stiff dance" around the room, Howard moving away from her, she following. Then he sat down and gestured for her to sit in the chair opposite from him, moving it away from him with his foot. After chatting, Mamie "stood up and he took a step toward me. He looked down at my breasts with widened eyes. I could hear his breathing. After a moment more, he appeared to remember something and took several steps away from me."

An early girlfriend was Katharine Hepburn. She seemed to fit well with Howard's interests. She was horseyish, aeronautical, and posh. She even liked golf but wasn't so sure about Howard, at least at the start. The Hepburn family were exasperated by Howard's determination to start eating after everyone else was finished. Intrigued by Cary Grant's tales about Katharine's boyishness on the set of *Sylvia Scarlett*, Howard decided he had to meet her and gate-crashed a picnic they were having on the film set. In the manner of a daredevil, Howard decided his best entrance would be if he flew low in over the picnickers, but his stunt mangled the scene they were filming, much to Katharine's ire. Howard had brought hampers of goodies with him, but this did nothing to sweeten Katharine's mood. She knew Howard was deaf and, evilly, persuaded her fellow actors to whisper all through lunch. Howard, blushing with anxiety and irritation, asked them to speak up a little, at which point Katharine would open her mouth wide as if shouting but in truth remaining mute. Howard left, mortified. Who could blame him? Eventually, Howard lived with Katharine, taught her to fly, and made her so jealous of his closeness to Ginger Rogers that when, at the RKO Studios, Katharine spotted Ginger down below on the studio floor, looking all glossy and smug in a mink coat, she grabbed a jug of water and poured it onto Ginger's coiffed head. The Hughes-Hepburn home was a battle of contrasts: Katharine had an enormous appetite; Howard stuck to his steak and peas. Howard stayed in bed; Katharine rose early. Howard refused to use chemical-rich toothpaste, opting instead for mouthwash and what Katharine only identified as small, black seeds, the scourge of both bugs and constipation. If guests came around, Howard used cheap crockery that he could destroy afterward. He had periods when he would mysteriously vanish for a few months at a time. Whenever he turned up, he seemed to have douche bags stowed away on his person. Howard, ever the womanizer, allegedly managed to dally with Cary Grant *and* Bette Davis while also proposing to Joan Fontaine *and* her sister, Olivia de Havilland. Hughes had the amazing ability to relentlessly pursue several starlets all at the same time thanks to his troupe of Mormon employees (he thought only Mormons were trustworthy), who were forever whisking him out of beds and buildings.

On her first meeting with Howard Hughes, starlet Terry Moore (her original name was Helen Koford) was not long out of her braces. When they went out for dinner, young men kept springing up by their table, asking Howard if they could dance with his daughter. Not that this put Howard off. Terry's Mormon parents advised her that an invite to their family home in Glendale would set Howard on the straight and narrow about what a respectable girl she was. Besides, her mother, Mrs. Luella Koford, added, "Poor thing, nothing but restaurant food for months on end. Well, he'll get a real home-cooked meal from me." Undeterred, Howard agreed. Terry recounted in her memoirs that Mrs. Koford was dressed in gamesome red and black as she awaited the "coming of Howard," while Terry looked staunchly virginal in her bobby socks. Howard swung into the kitchen and, in that split second, Terry realized he was the perfect age for her mother. Terry's father was cross with Howard for being late, but soon they were all tucked up around the kitchen table with Stormy, the mongrel dog, browsing the floor for snacks. It was the most unhygienic environment Howard could be in; yet love meant he mastered all. Mr. Koford announced, "We're having Luella's company dinner: Swiss Steak, smothered in onions, baked stuffed tomatoes and potatoes." Then someone cheerfully piped, "Try one of the biscuits while they're hot . . . made right from the beginning. Help yourself to some more salad. You'd better like garlic!"

Unbeknownst to anyone present, Howard was prey to a garlic and onions phobia, thinking that the human body sweated out their sulfurous odors for weeks after eating. Terry tells us, "That night, Howard wolfed down his food. Looking back, I realised he probably swallowed it whole so as to not taste it." Moore comically recounts that after he left, Mrs. Koford mused that Howard "was kind, considerate, boyish." Mr. Koford snorted: "What did he do that was kind and considerate? I thought he was a bore." When Howard called Terry later that night, it sounded as though he were eating. Nevertheless, Terry's Mormon family wowed him, so much so that he began hiring more and more Mormons to work for him. In the later, glummer years of their relationship, Terry liked nothing better than eating lots of garlic and burgers smothered in raw onions—and once when Howard was sneaking a dessert date with another starlet behind her back, Terry phoned the restaurant and asked that the starlet's steak be smothered in onions and garlic before she met Howard.

A COMPANY DINNER
Swiss Steak, Smothered in Onions

INGREDIENTS

4 sirloin steaks, ½ lb. each
3 tbsp. olive oil
2 tbsp. all-purpose flour
2 onions, chopped
1 lb. fresh tomatoes
3 cloves of garlic, finely chopped
1 bell pepper, chopped
1 rib of celery, chopped

8 medium-size mushrooms, sliced
1 tbsp. fresh oregano, chopped
1 tsp. smoked paprika
1 bay leaf
1 tbsp. Worcestershire sauce
1 cup beef bouillon
Sea salt
Freshly ground black pepper

METHOD

Wash your hands. Preheat the oven to 190°C. Put the steaks in a plastic bag and beat with a mallet for a minute. Think about how damned angry you are that you are not a starlet. Put the flour on a plate and salt and pepper it. Now coat the steak on each side with the flour. Heat the olive oil in the base of a Dutch oven and quickly brown the steak in this (you may have to do one steak at a time). Remove and set to one side. Fry the onions until soft, and then add the steaks. Add the tomatoes, garlic, bell pepper, celery, mushrooms, oregano, smoked paprika, and bay leaf. Pour on the beef stock and Worcestershire sauce.

Cover the Dutch oven and cook for 1–2 hours, checking every so often, until the steak is very tender. Serve with extra fried onions, stuffed tomatoes, and mashed potatoes.

Baked, Stuffed Tomatoes

INGREDIENTS

6 medium-size tomatoes, halved,
  with the seeds removed
½ cup breadcrumbs
1 scallion, finely chopped

1 tsp. fresh thyme leaves
1 clove of garlic, crushed
1 tbsp. olive oil
1 tbsp. Dijon mustard

METHOD

Wash your hands very carefully. Preheat the oven to 180°C. Lay the tomatoes on a lightly buttered ovenproof dish. In a bowl, mix together the breadcrumbs, scallion, thyme, garlic, and olive oil. Smear each tomato with a little Dijon mustard and then put a teaspoonful or two of stuffing on top. Bake in the oven for about 15 minutes. Dish tissues out to all your guests.

Howard spent the next year or two ducking and diving about marrying Terry, always trying to get her into bed while promising marriage. After a hot fudge sundae or two too many with Terry, Howard took her to a hilltop overlooking the panorama of Los Angeles. Nobly, he suggested that they kneel right there and then and wed themselves in the eyes of God, beneath the stars (it turns out he did the same thing in the same place with Jean Peters). But Terry had no problem seeing the difference between spiritual and physical marriage, and when Howard gaily suggested they consummate their union in his bedroom that night, she drew the line. Next, Howard tried out a fishy marriage ceremony on board a boat, conducted in utter secrecy and officiated over by one Captain Flynn, who had a bulbous, red nose. Instead of the expected wedding feast—Howard grandly announced food was being flown in on his own airline from New York—it was hot dogs and French fries from Long Island. Terry recalled, "Everyone wolfed them down. Howard said they were very special and ate six of them. I thought they'd be more special if they'd been left back in Coney Island. The fish devoured my French fries."

When he was in really hot water, Howard would make a preposterous "Alligator Love Call" on the phone, a reptilian yowl that meant he loved her beyond all else. It melted Terry's heart, and she'd alligator it right back over the line. Quickly, the couple slipped into the ritualized controlled behavior Howard liked best. He liked to cauterize her teenage pimples and wash any lipstick from her lips. They would spend their nights watching movies, then head up to the Beverly Hills Hotel for Howard's nightly steak with hearts of lettuce in a Roquefort cheese dressing. Howard issued the same edicts every night: the steaks had to be rare but charred on the outside, and the lettuce cut into one-inch pieces, using the sharpest of knives; the lettuce sections must not fall apart. Meanwhile, "the dressing must have the Roquefort crumbled in the bottom of the bowl. Pour in the oil and add one teaspoon French's mustard and Worcestershire sauce with a dash of salt and pepper, one teaspoon sugar and one tablespoon wine vinegar. Stir it well." Then it was time to tuck into cherries jubilee made with Howard's beloved ice cream. He would wipe the creamy dribbles off Terry's chin.

Incredibly, Howard cooked for Terry, making food he remembered from those boyhood summer camps his mother had sent him to: scrambled eggs; very thin pork chops dipped in apple sauce; a concoction he called Welsh goulash, which was a mix of sliced hot dogs stirred through tinned pork and beans; a poached egg popped on top of tinned corned beef hash. He donned an apron and shopped for tins of food, which was very exciting. Howard discovered anonymity in supermarkets and particularly liked to linger in the cookies section.

Terry experienced frequent loneliness in her secret "marriage" to Howard. For a start, she was never allowed to tell anyone they had married and had to listen to gossip about him and starlets. Victor Mature tried to dry Terry's tears with his own

Cherries Jubilee

INGREDIENTS

2 tbsp. butter
½ cup demerara sugar
1 lb. fresh black cherries, pips
  removed

1 tbsp. brandy
A tub of very good vanilla
  ice cream

METHOD

Wash your hands very carefully. In a large skillet, melt the butter, then add the demerara sugar and stir until the sugar has dissolved. Add the black cherries and cook for 8 minutes, until the skins begin to pop and ooze delicious cherry juice. Remove from the heat and pour on the brandy. Line up two glass ice-cream sundae dishes; put a scoop or two of vanilla ice cream in the base and then pour over the hot, mildly alcoholic cherries.

special invention, coke and root beer, or he would offer her a share of his breakfast of hot dogs and chili. Terry wanted children, but Howard really wasn't interested: he couldn't bear the saggy breasts or brown nipples he claimed pregnant and breast-feeding women developed. Finally, Terry moved on to better things and learned to hang up the moment she heard the opening yowl of the "Alligator Love Call."

Some of Howard's love interests were far less tolerant of him: Ava Gardner didn't really know what to make of Howard. Again, like many of his other love interests (all running concurrently), his focus on her was intense, spanning several years, and, to Ava, very far from seductive or glamorous. First, he was a terrible dancer, grabbing her in a tentacled embrace so tight that her beautifully made-up face was buried in the front of his shirt. Next, she tired of watching him eat nothing but steak, peas, and ice cream with caramel sauce for years and years. Even worse, he took her to flyblown greasy spoons for dinner, just so his steak and green pea fetish could be satisfied. When he drove her home, they swept up the driveway, but he wouldn't let her open the car door until the dust grew still. He couldn't have any of that nasty, dangerous stuff blowing in on him, could he? Once, when sweeping her off her feet by supposedly helping her catch a train to San Francisco, he borrowed his cook's car, "an old jalopy" with no hood. Feet on the pedals, his trousers were held up by a tie and his shoelaces were undone. No sooner had Ava settled in the train's bar car later that day—a stylish space with waiters smart in gleaming black uniforms—than a large white cardboard box materialized before her (Howard was very keen on using large white cardboard boxes for his luggage). The svelte waiter dragged wads of newspaper out of the box only to reveal from the box's core a scrumptious bottle of champagne. Cue Howard, who, having shed his mad trousers for an equally mad ice-cream-colored suit too short in the arms and legs by four to six inches, came mincing toward Ava, all set for romance. And when he was away from her, he jealously instructed his Mormon bodyguards to escort Ava everywhere.

By the 1950s, Howard's passion for secrecy was intense. When he finally married Jean Peters (whom his bodyguards referred to by the code name "the Major"), she was incarcerated in a bungalow called BHH Number 9 (he was in BHH Number 4, with blacked-out windows) at the Palm Springs Hotel. There was a generous supply of fruit juice, fruit, and chocolate delivered to Jean's bungalow, but all meat and fish were banned. Nor were Howard's staff free to eat what they wished. A decree was issued: the eating of all "breath destroyers" of pork, garlic, and onions was forbidden. Speech was forbidden; communication must be in note form. Howard, deep in his obsessive-compulsive world, prepared an intricate manual on food preparation and hygiene for his staff, including a nine-step guide written on ruled yellow paper detailing how a fruit tin should be opened. It was exhausting, encyclopedic—from washing the can to drying it with "six thicknesses of paper towels." On no account "should fingers break through the towels, thereby touching the can." Removing fruit from the can was a herculean task. There should be as little contact as possible between the can and the fruit; also the can-handler must "be very sure that no part of the body, including the hands, be directly over the can or the plate at any time" and "there must be absolutely no talking, coughing, clearing of the throat." When the fruit is handed to the baker (to make the pie—at last), the exchange must happen "without any words being spoken or signs with the hands."

If you think that was weird, Howard's bungalow was also stacked with facial tissues and golden jars piled up, filled with his own stored urine. Howard was lost in a world of his own making. Jean spent her time smoking and dressmaking, her diet and movements controlled by Howard. She was not permitted to eat anything cooked on a frying pan or grill. Howard stipulated, "Now waffles are OK provided they are cooked on a waffle iron where only waffles are cooked. Now it is not alright to have French toast, fried eggs, pancakes, wheat cakes, or anything like that because they are usually cooked in a frying pan or skillet in which sausage or bacon has been cooked. Now they might say that the former has not been cooked in them, but I don't believe them so it is best not even to question them."

It was a terrible kind of love. Just in case she cheated, Jean's food consumption was under surveillance day and night; for example:

Wed, 6/19/57
Info   At 8:52 a.m. JP ordered 1 coffee, 2 milk and papers for 10A.
Info   At 10:18 a.m. JP ordered breakfast for 3 in Bung: eggs benedict, 2 large orange juice, 4 bottles of milk packed in ice, 2 orders of sweet rolls, 2 large pots of coffee, 3 bottles of Poland water, 1 packed in ice.

Howard's teeth were getting worse, rotting slowly, in part as a result of all that orange juice he thought he owed his life to. He was moving, gradually, away from steak and toward beef stew. Stew, one imagines, is a messy affair, but Howard kept special rules for measuring the length of his carrots: they had to be in exact, beautiful half-inch pieces. That way they were safe. The couple finally decamped from the bungalows in 1960 thanks to a pineapple upside-down cake. Hughes had ordered it and then, cutting into the cake, noticed a bill of $3.75 for the cake: Did the hotel think he was made of money? He promptly departed.

An alternative haunt was the Desert Inn. There a specialized little cadre checked and rechecked his meals: his charbroiled, rare steaks were cut into small chunks; Campbell's chicken soup was a winner, but then Howard began to worry about the dark meat in it and eventually insisted on his own, personalized chicken brew. He had a special spoon and wanted to use the same cutlery every day. He was shaken to the core by the deliciousness of Baskin and Robbins' Flavor-of-the-Month banana nut ice cream when he first tried it (remember, in the world of Hughes, this is exotic novelty of a kind never swallowed before). When it stopped being the flavor of the month and was withdrawn, he was traumatized. Would Baskin and Robbins be so kind as to make him a batch? he inquired. Unfortunately, they replied, they only made ice cream in batches of three hundred gallons a time. "Get it!" ordered Howard, panicking. Of course, it had to be secret, so the three hundred gallons were smuggled into the Desert Inn. A small bowlful (wrapped in facial tissues, of course) was placed in Howard's tissue-wrapped hands. He tasted, ruminated, and then said petulantly, "I don't want any more. I want to go back to vanilla." The hotel staff spent many days on a diet of banana nut ice cream. It was offered on special promotion, and Howard's biographers Brown and Broeske say, "Casino customers who hit jackpots were sometimes given unexpected bonuses—pints of Baskin-Robbins banana-nut ice cream. It took the Desert Inn a year to unload Hughes' frozen folly."

Arby's roast beef sandwiches awoke a similarly transient passion, until Arby's turned down Howard's request for a personalized, sterilized roast beef cutter. And then there was the Swanson's Turkey TV Dinners incident. The Swanson's advert was black and white. The cleanness of the tray, its dinky secure compartments, and the shapeliness of the meal lured Howard. In the rectangular, three-compartment TV dinner tray were virginal mashed potatoes, pre-sliced turkey (in accommodatingly even slices), gravy and stuffing, and a cheeky little apple and cranberry dessert to follow. It was perfect for Howard—no one could touch the food as it was sealed in foil; it was sterile because it had been frozen. Then it all went wrong: Howard discovered that *other* types of TV dinners offered a peach cobbler.

"Contact Swanson's immediately," he commanded his Mormons. "Tell them I need peach cobblers." In return, he hoped to woo Swanson's by buying as many as thirty-six turkey dinners a month. Now, that's going to sway a vast capitalist enterprise, isn't it? He also recommended they use all white turkey meat, and instead of putting the dressing under the meat, it would be far more helpful if it were in a separate compartment. This, he pointed out to Swanson's, would prevent the dressing and meat from sticking together. His final act was to request the reorganized meals be sent to "R. M. Johnson in care of the Desert Inn." Somehow, it didn't work out.

That Howard Hughes would die a lonely death seems obvious and rather tragic. Poor Howard. As he aged, his constant pain became more piquant, and more insistent. He had an anal fissure after years of constipation. The Californian orange juice he had flown in daily had burned its way down his esophagus. His weight plummeted with grim regularity, and he underwent numerous blood transfusions—losing forty pounds after a spate of them. His immune system was compromised, the cause of his illnesses inexplicable. Pneumonia kept revisiting his lungs. He was emaciated. Tumors grew. His kidneys failed. He took up to thirty aspirin daily, causing his kidneys to become necrotic. Sudden blindness engulfed him. The codeine he took was self-injected, and, fumbling, he was always breaking needles. In one attempt, he might have a few needle points bristling out of the needle site. Codeine also caused constipation; yet Howard refused to allow doctors to examine his back passage. He found walking difficult but was still storing urine in Mason jars. His teeth and gums were a morass of decay. His teeth were so loose that he could easily have swallowed one, and it was suspected this did indeed happen. Apart from the occasional brief obsession with apple strudel, his eating range dangerously narrowed more and more. On Christmas Day 1971, the Hughes logbook records, "Wants to start orange tarts again. Also wants to change the Napoleons so there is cake between custard rather than the flaky pie crust material they now have." His rotting teeth meant he had to take up very soft chicken, preferably boiled, followed by a Napoleon cake or two. Bedridden, tended to by his muscular guards, those big, dispassionate nurses, Howard slowly slipped away in his room in the Acapulco Princess Hotel.

I would give you a Napoleon cake recipe here, but I don't have a ruler to make each one perfectly square. Did I ask if you'd washed your hands?

IT WASN'T ALL SHOES: IMELDA MARCOS

She began life as Imelda Romualdez and monstrously metamorphosed into the bouffant spendthrift Imelda Marcos, owner of a thousand pairs of heels and wife of Ferdinand Marcos, the great dictator of the Philippines.

For Imelda, family life began in a prosperous and well-appointed house on leafy General Solano Street in the collegiate San Miguel district of Manila near the Pasig River (but far from the peg-legged shanty houses of the river's poor). Imelda's was a luckless branch of the wealthy and powerful Romualdez family. And that bad luck came from her father, Don Vicente Romualdez. Vicente was a lawyer, one of three able sons born to the Romualdez family. But there was a catch: Vicente had none of the flair, brilliance, or ambition of his brothers, and almost annually, his wealth and status dissipated. Imelda's admirable mother, Remedios, also didn't score high on the luck stakes: she was an orphanage girl, sought out to be lowly wife number two by Don Vicente's formidable mother, Doña Trinidad.

After the death of Vicente's first wife, Juanita Acerada, Doña Trinidad was on a mission to find her son a suitable replacement wife, having discovered Vicente canoodling with his very unsuitable housekeeper, and where better to look for a wife than in one of Manila's Catholic orphanages? In these, nuns trained young girls (some of whom were not actually orphans themselves) in homely duties—cooking, cleaning, childcare, obedience—the perfect prototype to manage Don Vicente's house on General Soldano Street and his five children. After scouring three orphanages, Doña Trinidad decided on two candidates: the Moorish beauty Alice Burcher and the willowy Remedios Trinidad (the shared last name was coincidental). Now it was for Don Vicente to choose between the girls—without embarrassing them. Doña Trinidad prepared a *merienda* at home (in the Philippines, a *merienda* is a moveable, small meal coming between breakfast and lunch or lunch and dinner) of the delicious spiral and sugared ensaimada bread, larded with pork fat and sometimes stuffed with cream or almond nougat; savory tamales; and hot chocolate on the polished dining table. Meanwhile, a nun at the orphanage instructed the two girls to take a note to a very fine gentleman, one Don Vicente, and to wait at the Romualdez house until he had penned his reply.

Both girls hovered on the doorstep, Alice in a pretty dress that set off her lovely coloring and Remedios in a sober native *saya*. Come in for *merienda*, they were urged, and when it came to the girls' turn to contribute to in-house entertainment, Alice demurred—she had never learned to sing. Remedios, in contrast, gathering her *saya* about her and, with the children watching through the stairs, beautifully and soulfully sang a song about misfortune. It was enchanting but, in hindsight, perhaps a bad omen. Doña Trinidad clucked in approval. This was the one: Remedios Trinidad, a kind, gentle girl to marry Vicente. And so it was that the very existence of Imelda Marcos depended on a song and a mouthful of sugared bread.

Ensaimada

INGREDIENTS

4½ cups all-purpose flour
3 tbsp. sugar
A generous pinch of sea salt
2½ tsp. yeast
A generous cup of warm milk

2 eggs, beaten
2 tbsp. olive oil
5 tbsp. melted pork lard
Powdered sugar for dusting

METHOD

In a large bowl, combine the sieved flour, sugar, and sea salt. Make a well in the center and crumble the yeast into it. Add a pinch of sugar and some of the lukewarm milk to cover the yeast. Agitate the milk-yeast mixture gently. Cover the bowl with a dishcloth and leave to rest in a warm place for 15 minutes; the yeast will develop a frothy head.

Now add the rest of the milk, the eggs, and the olive oil and knead well; add extra flour, kneading in a little at a time, if the dough seems too wet. Place the dough in its bowl in a warm place, covered, for 30 minutes, until the dough has doubled in size.

Flour the work surface. Remove the dough from its bowl and punch it down. Separate into 10 balls. Sprinkle these with flour and leave, covered, to rise once more for 30 minutes.

Melt the pork lard. Line a baking tray with parchment paper. Roll each ball into a circle and then brush with pork lard. Roll the circle up into a loose cigar shape. Repeat with all 10 balls. Coil each cigar of dough into the loose shape of a snail's shell, tucking in the outer end. Now brush the ensaimadas with pork lard again and cover. Leave these to rise once more overnight—they will be giants by the morning.

The next day, preheat the oven to 200°C. Bake the ensaimadas for about 10–15 minutes, until they are golden brown (keep a close eye on them, as they brown very easily). Let them cool on a wire rack and dust with powdered sugar.

Philippine Tamales

Distinctively, the Philippine tamale consists of rice and meat, partly colored with annatto, wrapped together in banana leaves.

INGREDIENTS

3 cups short-grain rice
1 cup roasted peanuts
½ cup brown sugar
5 cups coconut milk
Salt and pepper to taste
Annatto powder, dissolved in
  ¼ cup water

1 cup shredded chicken
6 scallions, shredded and roughly
  chopped
A handful of cashew nuts
2 boiled eggs, roughly chopped
½ cup shelled tiny shrimp
Banana leaves, about 13

Philippine Tamales *(continued)*

METHOD

Begin by toasting the rice in a dry frying pan until it is a golden color. Now grind the roasted peanuts and rice together until you have a fine blend. In a saucepan, combine the coconut milk, pinch of salt, black pepper, and brown sugar. Now add the powdered rice and peanut, stirring regularly over a low heat. The mixture will become increasingly paste-like and when it begins to come away from the edges of the pan, should be removed from the heat. Divide the paste into two equal amounts. Reserve one half for later.

Now take half the paste and add the annatto water to it. Return to heat and stir; the paste will become red. On the work surface, lay 2 banana leaves flat. At the center, put 2 tablespoons of the plain tamale paste. On top, place a little shredded chicken, a couple of cashews, some scallions, a shard or two of chopped egg, and some shrimp. Now top with 2 tablespoons of the red paste. Take another banana leaf and tear it into strips; you will use these to secure your tamale parcels. Fold the banana leaves into a parcel; tie up and then steam for about 12 minutes.

Remedios had her work cut out for her. First, she was shaken awake in the middle of the night—at 3 a.m. exactly—to marry Vicente, only to be met by the Romualdez clan standing in the gloom of the church. This subterfuge was because they wanted to avoid a disagreeable scene with Vicente's housekeeper-lover by marrying at dawn.

Even Remedios's nun-trained diligence was tested when she arrived at the house on General Soldano Street, fresh out of her wedding dress. The floors were dirty and smeared; stacks of dirty dishes had piled up unwashed. Her unambitious, lackluster bridegroom had panicked while trying to manage his five children, and disorganization had crept over the house like ivy. Pictures of the deceased first wife, Juanita Acerada, glowered down at Remedios, and her five stepchildren stood openmouthed in astonishment at her arrival. Perhaps fearfully, Don Vicente had not even told them he was bringing home a new wife. Remedios set to work, but the stepchildren rebelled, mocking her, particularly the oldest child, Lourdes, who showed nothing of the saintliness suggested by her name toward her gentle stepmother. Remedios, an excellent cook, found that even her galatina did not warm their hearts.

Galatina

INGREDIENTS

1 whole chicken, deboned
¾ cup light soy sauce
Juice of 1 lemon
¾ lb. minced, lean pork
¾ cup ham, chopped
½ cup raisins
½ cup onion, minced

5 tbsp. fresh, homemade breadcrumbs
2 carrots, minced
3 tbsp. sweet pickle relish
4 Chinese sausages, quartered
  lengthwise
3 small hard-boiled eggs
3 pint water

METHOD

Combine the soy sauce and lemon juice in a bowl big enough to fit the chicken. Marinate the chicken in this mixture for 1 hour. In a mixing bowl, combine the minced pork, ham, raisins, onion, breadcrumbs, carrots, and sweet pickle relish. Remove the chicken from its marinade and stuff it. Finally, push the lengths of Chinese sausage and three small eggs into the stuffing (the trick being that when you slice through the chicken, these give a lovely, surprise patterning to the stuffing). Close up the chicken and wrap it in a muslin or cheesecloth, tying both ends. Bring about 3 pints of water to a boil in a steamer. Steam the chicken for 90 minutes, then remove. Cool for 2 hours and then serve.

Vicente, desperate to placate Lourdes, increasingly favored her, shoving his quiet wife aside. Misery washed over the marriage, but a further six children still appeared. The first was Imelda, small, soft, beautiful, and moonfaced. Doctors at the delivery noticed that Don Vicente seemed unusually nervous; he told them prophetically, "This child will be important." Important as Imelda may have been, she, her five siblings, and Remedios ended up living in the garage at the house on General Soldano Street when the war between Remedios and Vicente became open. Remedios, eventually worn down by despair at her situation, seemed to decide to slip out of life, dying quietly of double pneumonia.

Vicente's personal fortune was ever dwindling—he could never quite rouse himself to do very much—and, never at ease with the cosmopolitan hurly-burly of Manila, decided to move back to Tacloban in the region of Leyte (where the Romualdez family had some property that he could squat on with his eleven children). But this wasn't to last: the property was reappropriated by its rightful owner, and the family ended up in a Quonset hut constructed of American surplus materials. Food was always short, and Imelda, growing up fast, always asked for a little more to feed her many siblings when buying food in the local shop. She envied her neighbors who had fancy American-style bread, slippery with margarine, for their breakfast. Vicente's children filled their mouths with pillowy Filipino pan del sal (salted bread rolls) and tar-black coffee in the morning—and if you were late to breakfast, it would be gone. Vicente used to squirrel away coins in a bamboo pole (his version of a piggy bank) in order to be able to buy a leg of ham come Christmas. "I remember how Papa loved picnics," recalled Conchita, Imelda's youngest sister. "Almost every weekend we would take a jeep and go to the family beach in Tolosa [a seaside resort]. We were always a big group of girls with the inevitable train of admirers. Papa would ask the caretaker to broil fish. We swam all day and feasted on fish, Palawan [tuber] and silot [young coconuts]. We sang our voices hoarse. We slept in a nipa hut by the beach and returned to Tacloban the following day." As First Lady of the Philippines, Imelda built a palatial summer home on the same beach to which Vicente Romualdez had brought his children.

Imelda bloomed as a teenager, becoming known as the Rose of Tacloban. Famed for her beauty, she was chosen by the townspeople to present visiting dignitaries with a garland and to sing to them. A local celebrity, she scrawled in the autograph book of her friend an innocent list of her favorite things: her love of blue and pink; her favorite subject, which she schoolgirlishly listed as "lovemaking"; and her delight in ice cream and fried chicken.

Minor celebrity only made the pull of Manila all the stronger; Tacloban was a provincial dump in comparison. Imelda arrived at her destiny on a Philippine Airline flight, which rolled into the Manila domestic airport. She was going to be an opera singer.

Imelda had influential relatives in Manila. Her cousin Danieling Romualdez, an up-and-coming politician, had paid for her flight, and another cousin, Loreto Romualdez Ramos, arranged singing tuition for her. Imelda stayed in Danieling's house, and although she was in the same room as the maid, Danieling's home placed Imelda at the center of political life in Manila. She had a music scholarship to the Philippine Women's University but had to supplement her scholarship by working in the hip P. E. Domingo's music store as a salesgirl who played the piano and sang songs to customers. She went over well, but when Vicente found out, he demanded that she stop parading herself. Obediently, Imelda found alternative work in the Central Bank. There she sang to her coworkers at break time in exchange for snacks. Inevitably, though, she was talent-spotted for her beauty and appeared in the *Week* magazine, a supplement of the *Manila Chronicle*. Next, she entered the Miss Manila competition and, after a bit of a tussle about who was the real winner of the title, persevered to be declared the Muse of Manila.

Ambitious, clever politician Ferdinand Marcos met Imelda in April 1954 and proposed to her within eleven days. She was twenty-four and he was thirty-seven. Drawn to her by both her beauty and the power of her name (he didn't know at the time that there were any down-at-heel Romualdezes around), he knew he could also make political capital out of Imelda being the niece of Danieling Romualdez. They met for the first time in a cafeteria at the Congress in Manila when she turned up to collect her cousin Danieling. She was cracking dried watermelon seeds between her teeth, dressed in a scruffy housedress and slippers. Although she wasn't much impressed by him, she offered him a watermelon seed. "There must have been some magic drug in those watermelon seeds," Ferdinand recalled, "because they made me feel as I have never felt before."

Ferdinand was a real political hustler and showed Imelda all sorts of hidey-holes about his bungalow on Ortega Street, usually stuffed with $100 bills. He already had a mistress with whom he had three children, but, regardless, newly married life was exhilarating for Imelda. Did she care about Marcos's litter of fur-bikini-ed, blonde mistresses? Probably not very much. Gone was the hard-up, pretty girl from Tacloban; now Imelda was a well-heeled, distinguished, and beautiful politician's wife, living in a prosperous suburb of Manila. Imelda couldn't cook. When they dined together in restaurants and Ferdinand ate one of his favorites, such as sate babi (pork BBQ), he'd tease her that she needed to master the arts of the pan. She was tempted, being aghast at the amount of money Ferdinand paid the cook, which was substantially more than she'd earned at the Central Bank. The spirit of Remedios burned (temporarily) within her. *Save the money you pay the cook; pay it to me instead and I will do the cook's job*, she challenged her husband. However, greed on a far grander scale grew as rapidly within Imelda, spurred in part by a late-night visit from one of Ferdinand's political supporters and agitators. Ferdinand asked Imelda to fetch five thousand pesos to give to the visitor. The next day, Imelda said to her husband, "Gosh, I have such a hard time cooking. My nails are all broken, and I only get a hundred and twenty pesos a month. A man comes along from out of the blue and you give him five thousand pesos just like that."

"It's your fault," Ferdinand laughed. "Who told you to work hard for only a hundred and twenty pesos?" From that moment on, Imelda decided to save her nails, abandon the saucepans, and live the life of a rich socialite in Manila—with all of her husband's money to spend.

Ferdinand was inaugurated president of the Philippines in December 1965. Imelda, sheathed in plain Philippine embroidered cloth, had been the driving, dogged force behind Ferdinand's political campaign for the presidency. He hung on to the bungalow as his campaign headquarters, but the couple settled into the luxuries of the opulent, chandeliered Malacañan Palace, which seemed almost to hover over the waters of the Pasig River. The Marcos held Manila in their parasitic embrace for the next twenty years. By then, they already had three children together, and lustrous, limpid-eyed Imelda had shaped up to be one of Ferdinand's prime political assets. She caused hearts to flutter when she serenaded Lyndon and Lady Bird Johnson in Washington, DC, with a woozy soprano version of a Filipino love song.

Sate Babi

INGREDIENTS
1 lb. pork fillet, cut into ½ in. pieces
2 cloves of garlic, crushed
2 tsp. ground cilantro
½ tsp. ground cumin
5 tbsp. light soy sauce

3 tbsp. dark soy sauce
Juice of 2 limes
2 tbsp. peanut oil
4 tbsp. palm sugar

FOR THE SPICE PASTE . . .
8 shallots, finely chopped
4 cloves of garlic
2 red chilies
2 tsp. fresh, chopped cilantro root

2 tbsp. candle nuts
1 in. galangal
½ in. fresh turmeric
Juice and zest of 1 lime

FOR THE CHILI DIPPING SAUCE . . .
1 shallot, finely sliced
1 large red chili, sliced

Juice of 1 lime

METHOD
In a mortar and pestle or food processor, grind together the ingredients for the spice paste. In a bowl, combine the garlic, cilantro, cumin, light soy sauce, dark soy sauce, lime juice, oil, and palm sugar. Add the spice paste. Stir together and then add the pork; mix well. Cover and refrigerate overnight.

The next day, soak about 30 wooden skewers in water. Drain the marinade from the pork; keep the marinade. Heat up a charcoal grill. Thread the pork onto the damp skewers. Pour the marinade into a saucepan and bring to a boil; allow this to simmer away until it is reduced and thickened. Remove from the heat and add the shallot, chili, and lime. Grill the pork skewers. When they are cooked, lay them on a platter and serve the dipping sauce alongside.

Beneath the veneer of their marriage, sanctified by the vows of complicity, avarice, and greed, power was doing its usual business of corrupting those who hold it. Stories abound of the excesses and dishonesties of the Marcos. There was the dodgy fund-raiser Imelda ran in a Christmas drive for the poor. All checks were made out to Imelda and deposited in her name. When it came time to send the food parcels out to the starving poor, Imelda didn't distribute them until they could be tagged "A Gift from the First Lady." Then she went into a huff with the Beatles when they performed in the Philippines, as they turned down a palace invite. Imelda removed their place tags from the table and had them roughed up at the airport. They were never paid for their concert.

Imelda's chauffeur-driven car was swarmed by crowds of admirers. Imelda leaned over her fellow passengers, bulletproof brassiere solid against them, and urged them on: "Smile, smile at the fools. That is what they want." Richard Nixon called her "the Angel from Asia," and she endlessly replayed a video of her having dinner with Nixon in order to intimidate and awe political friends and enemies. Dinner with President Marcos seemed to offer the prospect of lots of alcohol, but it was poured very parsimoniously by the waiters, who would then vanish, leaving guests with empty glasses—a cunning ruse, as the waiters resold the unused wine on the black market. Diners in the know had a couple of drinks before turning up. It was also wise to have a snack or three before dinner, as the quality of the food on offer was capricious to say the least. Imelda shifted loyalties between different caterers and restaurants, according to her whim, so visitors never knew whether they were in for a good time or a bad one. One shocked chef from Europe wandered into the palace kitchen only to find a cat fast asleep on the work surface. Filipinos usually combine a spoon with a fork, but the Marcos naturally shunted off local, "low" traditions and sought to impress with gleaming European knives.

Imelda's contempt for those she should have sought to protect—the Filipino poor living in shacks and huts with primitive toilets—is apparent in her buying up of penthouses in Kensington, London, her identity hidden. When a would-be assassin slashed her arm, Imelda used a double strand of pearls as a sling. In the meantime, Ferdinand was double-dealing Imelda, as revealed in his much publicized love affair with Dovie Beams in the late 1960s. Dovie was introduced to one "Fred," who turned out to be the president—he called her "Big Eyes." She secretly tape-recorded Ferdinand in her bed. How did Imelda take the news? She announced that Dovie must be either bought or killed. When she managed to see Dovie off on a flight out of the Philippines, she made sure that one of her husband's most notorious henchmen was seated quietly a seat or two away from the actress, just enough to make Dovie sweat for the hours of the flight. Bribery, constitutional fiddling, even kidnapping was the name of the game, reaching a crescendo in 1972 when Ferdinand declared martial law and sought presidency for life.

Imelda's Blue Ladies, her ladies-in-waiting, also emerged during her reign: these were posh Filipino ladies-who-lunch—the Real Housewives of Manila—and who, Imelda determined, would wear blue (remember that teenage autograph book?). Imelda issued decrees daily about what would be worn by her posse, along the lines of "Today we wear silk, wool, cashmere." Imelda's Blue Ladies traveled with her, eating Indian food for the first time on a visit to Indira Gandhi. They were surprised by the intense chili heat of some of the dishes and learned to slap yogurt onto each mouthful. More eating fun was had in Burma, where they ate a delicious lunch of chicken soup, slippery with soft noodles but also crunchy with fried noodles. They were surprised, though, by the Burmese offering of pastry boats filled with cold baked beans.

Imelda liked late-evening suppers at the Manila Hotel, where ashen-faced, dog-tired musicians awaited her arrival for perhaps a few hours. Eventually, she'd show up, sweep along the red carpets, a bouquet of orchids in her arms, to enjoy a bite of capelli d'angelo with crab at the Manila Hotel until 2 or 3 a.m.

Capelli d'Angelo with Crab

INGREDIENTS

3 cups or 300 g capelli d'angelo pasta
Brown and white meat of 1 whole cooked crab
3 tbsp. olive oil
1 red chili, finely chopped

2 cloves of garlic, finely chopped
½ glass of dry white wine
Large handful of flat-leaf parsley, finely chopped
1 tbsp. softened butter
½ lemon

METHOD

Put on a deep pan of boiling, salted water. In a frying pan, warm the olive oil, then add the chili and garlic. When these are softened, turn up the heat and add the white wine. Let this reduce, bubbling. Meanwhile drop the capelli d'angelo pasta into the boiling water and stir. Remove the frying pan from the heat and add the crab meat and parsley. Drain the pasta after 3 minutes, stir the butter through it, and then plate up, forming a nest shape. Place the crab meat in the center and drizzle a little fresh lemon juice onto it. Wear blue to eat.

Money was leaving the Philippines as Imelda and Ferdinand snapped up properties in Manhattan, New Jersey, Long Island. Meanwhile, they had no qualms about building opulent "pop-up" conveniences for the visiting rich and royal, such as when they built a remarkable "Coconut Palace" for Pope John Paul II. The papal visit went rather awry, though. First, Imelda tried to bundle him into a monster-size maroon stretch limo when he landed; he declined. Then he declined her hospitality at the Coconut Palace and sternly headed off to a nunciature. Good for the pope! The likes of Colonel Gaddafi and Brooke Shields were happy enough to snuggle up at the Coconut Palace, though. Imelda also erected a mosque (as one does) for Colonel Gaddafi's visit. All this talk of building brings us to Imelda's plans for an international film festival and a Parthenon-inspired edifice to host it. Imelda was in a rush to complete the project, and building continued without the cement being allowed to set. Tragically, a whole floor collapsed, killing scores of poor Filipino construction workers, impaling others, and burying some alive. The grieving families gathered to collect the bodies of their loved ones or to search for the missing. What did Imelda do? Orders came from above—"Pour the cement!"—and the bodies were encased forever. After all, what was more important, these dead workers or Imelda's international film festival?

Imelda and Ferdinand fled the Philippines in 1986 with about $1.6 billion in their pockets.

THE TASTE OF FREEDOM AND CONSUELO VANDERBILT

Wealthy, sensitive, and lovely, American heiress Consuelo Vanderbilt was forced into a stuffy, starchily arranged marriage to a British aristocrat, the Duke of Marlborough, occupant of Blenheim Palace. Both of them were in love with other people, but "Sunny" Marlborough (the name is no reflection of his nature, but rather an abbreviation of another of his titles, the Earl of Sunderland) was more pragmatic than Consuelo. He was prepared to sacrifice his heart and the girl he loved for the upkeep of the ancestral pile, Blenheim Palace. The Marlboroughs were hungry for Vanderbilt money.

Determined to escape Sunny's clutches, Consuelo's heart was set on another love, one Winthrop Rutherfurd, who had chased after Consuelo on a bicycle outing in order to hurriedly propose to her; all the while, her stern mother, Alva Vanderbilt, was cycling madly toward them, determined to thwart the lovers. Consuelo was not to be Winthrop's. She was locked up in Marble House, the family's fifty-room "cottage" in Newport, Rhode Island, and Winthrop's letters were hidden from her—which wouldn't be hard with fifty rooms to choose from. Alva would go to any means to thwart the union, variously claiming that madness ran wild in the Rutherfurd line, that Winthrop was infertile, and that, if all else failed, she was prepared to take a shot at him. And in case none of that worked, Alva took to her bed and claimed she had been struck by a heart attack; any agitation or upset might tip the balance and cause another. Winthrop backed off and afterward was only ever to be glimpsed on golf courses—as good a way as any to mend a broken heart.

Alva had set her sights on a brilliant social coup: to marry Consuelo off to British aristocracy. It didn't matter that Sunny was short, dull, and dissipated; he had a title. He was a duke! American dollars could buy British titles. The Vanderbilts had, unglamorously, made their money in transportation, first in shipping and then in rail, mostly as a result of the labors of one Cornelius Vanderbilt, who was very keen on contacting the spirit world so that he could ask about stock fluctuations. Now it was the Vanderbilts' time to become aristocrats. Alva and Consuelo headed off for a tour of Europe, and who should they meet but boggle-eyed Sunny, who invited them to Blenheim Palace for a visit. An earlier marriage by his father to an American heiress had already given Blenheim its heating and lighting, and it was expensive to maintain, having been built to rival Versailles. Alva's ferocious chaperonage completely vanished. Consuelo must have wanted to kick her when she invited Sunny to visit them in America. When he did so, even the porter was instructed not to let Consuelo out. Having popped the question and been accepted by a miserable Consuelo, who must have decided this was her only means of escape from Alva and Marble House, Sunny went off to tour the United States briefly. He said he never intended to visit again and so had decided he'd get all his sightseeing over and done with.

The wedding took place in 1895 and was held at St. Thomas Church, New York. Nary a Vanderbilt was in sight—none had been invited (except, of course, immediate family). Fabulous wealth was evident, seated at every pew. Even the bride's stocking clasps were made of gold, reported the press—though Consuelo said, "I read to my stupefaction that my garters had gold clasps studded with diamonds . . . and wondered how I should live down such vulgarities." Alva, smug in blue satin and sable, flanked by her sons, marched through the asparagus fern to take her place among the crème de la crème.

Weeping her way to the altar, Consuelo, blanched and pale in the bridal clothes Alva had picked out and with Alva's choice of bridesmaids (probably to ensure that Winthrop didn't disguise himself as one), had never felt more alone. She glanced down at her groom; she was six inches taller than him (he was a mere five feet, two inches). Perhaps this was a moment for a reconciliatory, understanding glance? But no, Sunny was staring vacantly into space, no doubt thinking about the substantial amount of railway stock he was about to get his hands on. No wonder the American press was suspicious of him: he liked more than a drop of Kentucky whiskey, had a weedy chest, wore "queer hats," and had been arrested in Central Park for cycling at great speed with his feet on the handlebars.

The newlyweds set off for a honeymoon in Europe, which was an eye-opener for eighteen-year-old Consuelo, who was startled by the sexual hypocrisies of the wealthy European and transatlantic male travelers. At the Hôtel de Paris in Monte Carlo, over dinner, as smartly dressed gentlemen and their beautiful female companions greeted Sunny with great familiarity, Consuelo quite naturally asked him who all these charming people were. Sunny became very prim and shifty, telling Consuelo not to look at the gorgeous women. Bewildered, she then saw several former suitors of hers also in company with the ladies. On no account, Sunny stipulated, was Consuelo to say hello or in any other way recognize the physical materiality of any of the men she knew; the cultured, clever beauties she so admired were high-class prostitutes. Sunny next began to get very snooty about food, making lots of demands about provenance, temperature, and so on. Consuelo's memoirs tell of Sunny expounding on the importance of food: "'Considering,' I was told, 'that it is the only pleasure one can count on having three times a day every day of one's life, a well-ordered meal is of prime importance.'" Sunny's snobbery, the petty demands he placed on the serving staff, and his self-importance were, Consuelo considered retrospectively, a clear signal: "Perhaps one of the most ominous signs during those first few weeks was that mealtimes began to assume enormous importance. . . . We seemed to spend hours discussing the merit of a dish or the bouquet of a vintage. The maître d'hôtel had become an important person to whom at meals most of my husband's conversation was addressed."

European exploration proved limiting. Consuelo fumed in Pompeii. As a lady, she was banned from seeing most of it and had to countenance Sunny hotfooting it off with the guide to see the statues and paintwork in worship of the god Priapus while she lingered in the hot dust. Next, she was less than impressed by the dancing girls on their steamer on the Nile. Sunny seemed to be hugely impressed, so Consuelo took herself off to bed and was not unhappy to hear the next day that one of the girls had fallen off the steamer (she was safely fished out).

Consuelo's fate lay across the North Sea in the huge halls, corridors, and parklands of Blenheim Palace, deep in the Oxfordshire countryside and packed to the brim with Sunny's relatives, the Churchills. The Churchills thought Consuelo a queer sort and were forever looking her up and down, glancing covertly at her stomach or directly demanding whether she and Sunny were going to have a baby. Particularly anxious on this count was the venerable Dowager Duchess Marlborough (Sunny's grandmother), who thought they'd better make haste else "that upstart Winston" got his hands on Blenheim. Yes, Winston Churchill, as Sunny's cousin (the resemblance stops there), was in line to succeed to the dukedom should Consuelo not conceive a boy. When Consuelo and Sunny arrived at Blenheim on a raw and rainy March day, she met and immediately liked young, red-haired Winston. He was witty and kind, and his mother, the luminescent, lovely Jennie Churchill, was adorable and, heaven of heavens, an American! Over dinner it emerged that Consuelo's mother-in-law, Lady Blandford, "thought we [rich, white Americans] all lived on plantations with negro slaves and that there were Red Indians ready to scalp us just round the corner." Dinner at Blenheim stretched out over half a dozen courses: two soups were offered, one hot, the other cold; this was followed by a similar choice of fish, one hot, one cold, with accompanying sauces. Then the Churchills cleansed their palates with a sorbet; maraschino was a favorite at the time. A main course would be served next: game such as woodcock, pheasant, grouse, or duck, often shot on the grounds of Blenheim in the winter, and more exotic small birds such as Parisian ortolan or Egyptian quail in the summer. A grand dessert followed, and then some delicious hot savory came with the port (which Consuelo always found seemed of great comfort to the British). Finally, the diners would finish with a little fruit, taken from the pyramids of peaches, apricots, strawberries, and plums that rested between the crumpled paper heads of orange-pink Gloire de Dijon roses and Malmaison.

Sunny himself seemed hardly up to the business of making anyone conceive. He spent a great deal of time having his hands manicured and, when he spotted Consuelo's Russian sable-lined coat, squealed, "What a wonderful coat, what priceless furs! . . . I must send for my sables to compare them." He did so and found that his were very second class. Consuelo had so far led a fairly choiceless life, and this continued. Sunny took over from Alva in dressing her up; his aim was for her to appear as magnificent as possible. Weighed down by a heavy dog collar of diamonds, clad in pink velvet, a diamond tiara with puffs and nests of ostrich feathers attached, and with a diamond belt about her waist, Consuelo's heart was as heavy as her purse. Lady Blandford, meanwhile, worried that Consuelo was too American, hinting at it as if it were a vulgarity. When Consuelo was to be introduced at court, Lady Blandford said approvingly that no one could possibly take her for an American. Consuelo found Queen Victoria so small that she had to go down on her knees to kiss Victoria's hand. Lady Blandford's snootiness aside, American dollars were considered good enough for the installation of bathrooms at Blenheim, which were very rare, adding to the workload of the limp-haired housemaids, who had to run around the corridors with steaming, heavy jugs of hot water to accommodate the bathing rituals of often more than thirty guests at Blenheim weekend parties. Consuelo was not impressed by the glut of wretched "toilet aids" in the bathroomless rooms. The words carved over the chimney piece in her room in Blenheim, "Dust and ashes," a cheerless and skeletal motto put there by Sunny's sepulchral father, the previous Duke of Marlborough, did as little to welcome Consuelo as the cockroaches and long, chilly corridors. From her window in Blenheim, Consuelo "overlooked a pond in which a former butler had drowned himself. As one gloomy day succeeded another I began to feel a deep sympathy for him."

Consuelo's style as a hostess was zephyr-like and gentle. With poise, intelligence, and quiet grace—made more pronounced by her unusual appearance—she drifted through the diplomats, blue bloods, politicians, and great wits of the day who visited Blenheim. Consuelo had a long swanlike neck, as she had spent hours as a girl strapped into a neck brace to ensure that her posture was perfect (Alva's doing again). Her hair was dark and massy; her face, hands, and feet narrow, delicate, and slender. Lord Curzon said she was like "a black soundless swan, aloof in soundless waters." In this, Curzon tuned into her essential privacy of soul. She had long since emotionally withdrawn from her husband, and the acoustics in the dining room, combined with a slight deafness she had developed as a child, meant she found it hard to hear conversations—a problem that fired Sunny's irritation. In the beginning, Consuelo found it particularly perplexing working out the order of precedence at dinner, as getting it wrong caused great commotion and offense, while if she just opted for social standing without a tempering of wits, dinners could leave people yawning into their napkins. The discovery of a booklet advising on the "Table of Precedence" was a godsend. Consuelo riffled through it, delighted to work out where she fit in too, as she recalls in her memoirs: "I was glad to know my own number, for, after waiting at the door of the dining room for older women to pass through, I one day received a furious push from an irate Marchioness who loudly proclaimed it was just as vulgar to hang back as to leave before one's turn."

Alone together, Consuelo and Sunny sat stiff as mannequins over dinner. In her memoirs, she recalled, "How I learned to dread and hate those dinners, how ominous and wearisome they loomed at the end of a long day. They were served with all the accustomed ceremony, but once a course had been passed the servants retired to the hall; the door was closed and only a ring of the bell placed before Marlborough summoned them. He had a way of piling food on his plate, the next move was to push the plate away, together with knives, forks, spoons and glasses— all this in considered gestures which took a long time; then he backed his chair away from the table, crossed one leg over the other and endlessly twirled the ring on his little finger." In every tiny movement Sunny made, you can feel Consuelo's gathering anger. It was just like being at the altar again. Sunny, quite indifferent to her, sat in dreamy, dull reflection. Then, after about fifteen minutes, he would shake himself, begin to eat, and then complain how very cold the food was. Consuelo decided to take up knitting at the dinner table and, she claimed, the butler settled down to some arresting detective stories in the hall.

Sunny loathed what he deemed the "lower orders" and venerated the British class system, but Consuelo had different views and nursed a secret radicalism. One pastime that was allowable for respectable Victorian ladies was philanthropy. Whatever was left of Consuelo and Sunny's lunch was shoveled into tins on a side table in the dining room to be carried down to the poorest and most miserable tenants occupying one or other of the villages on Sunny's estates. On closer inspection, Consuelo realized that sweet and savory, fish, gravy, bone, and dessert were being slopped together in the same tin with little consideration for the taste buds and appetites of the poor. Appetite, it was assumed, would add enough piquancy to such charity. Incensed, Consuelo ensured they were separated into savory and sweet. Sunny cared not a hoot for his tenants, dependents, or servants. Like any imperialist worth his salt, he had "acquired" an Egyptian boy on his travels and relished the show of the child dressed up in exotic cloths, serving him lemonade. The boy was hastily returned to Egypt when he pulled a knife in the village toy shop, roaring that he would kill the grandmotherly lady who worked there unless she reimbursed him for toys (now broken) that he was returning.

Other than the consolation of knowing that the poor of the Blenheim estates would get some decent grub from their master's table, Consuelo was also consoled by her friendships. She loved that cousin Winston was not stuffy and self-important like her husband. They could discuss wide and varied topics together, as both loved reading. In warmer weather, they might sit in the Indian tent that had been erected under the cedars and, with the newspapers lying around them, talk not just about politics but also about Edith Wharton and Henry James—in other words, American authors writing about English manners. They might stroll down and row together on the mirrored lake and then have tea under the green cluster of a tree. Diets were unheard of, Consuelo claimed, so she and Winston ate their way through hilly scones plastered with thick Devonshire cream and homemade jams washed down with iced coffee and strawberries, sugared icing on their lips.

Another friend whom both Consuelo *and* Sunny found most diverting was the ravishing, clever, and magnetizing American beauty Gladys Deacon, who, unbeknownst to all three of them, was to be the next Duchess of Marlborough. Consuelo and Sunny felt equally passionate about Gladys, who was in the habit of staying for several months in the summer at Blenheim with them. Consuelo confessed, "I was soon subjugated by the charm of her companionship and we began a friendship which only ended years later." Gladys was a charmer; she even enchanted Prince Wilhelm of Germany (the kaiser's son), who spent so long staring at her that he almost drove his horse and trap off the road. Gladys, though, restlessly discontented with her own beauty, experimented with plastic surgery and had paraffin wax injected into the bridge of her nose in Rome.

After Sunny and Consuelo's children had followed the fate of all rich children and been sent to distant, badly plumbed, and bullish British boarding schools, their marriage shriveled further. After years of spiritless matrimony, separation was in the cards for Consuelo and Sunny. Friends took sides—Theodore Roosevelt hotly called Sunny "a cad." Sunny took a motor trip to France to take the measure of his existence so far, but at dinner he tripped over the dinner table and its contents by accident. It was all tossed about into the corner of the room. A friend mulled, "The Duke was miserable; by the way he looked at the debris one might have thought he was peering at his own life, which, at the moment is in much the same state."

Despite such lugubriousness, Sunny was pressing his attentions on Gladys. She had, he described in a leaden-winged "flight" of romance, "a heart kinder and more sensitive than any I have known." Finally, the Marlboroughs separated, to the relief of almost all, in 1907. Consuelo went off to live in their house in London, called Sunderland House and built with Vanderbilt money. A decade or so later she would fall in love again.

Meanwhile, Gladys was starstruck: Sunny was in love with her! They had to wait to marry until Sunny and Consuelo finally divorced in 1921. Gladys's childhood dream had been of marrying a duke, and apparently she'd even thought that the Duke of Marlborough sounded the most sublime. But even as they notched up their first wedding anniversary, Gladys reported that Sunny was cross because their anniversary picnic was not up to standard and that he read a book on Napoleon before dinner, after dinner, and in bed. When he gave her a foot muff for Christmas, she noted in her diary, "Most interesting to me is Sunny's rudeness to me. Not very marked in public yet—but that will come." Causticity laced their union. Should she and Sunny have a daughter, Gladys said, "We shall call her 'Syphilis.' Lady Syphilis Churchill is such a pretty sounding name." Sunny's light was dimming, and rightly so—he was an arse. When the sculptor Jacob Epstein came to stay to do Sunny's bust, Sunny showed him around Blenheim's chapel. Epstein remarked on how little Christian paraphernalia there was, and Sunny defensively barked, "The Marlboroughs are worshipped here."

Sunny's loathing of Americans became increasingly pointed as the years of his marriage to Gladys ticked by. He embraced Roman Catholicism. Blenheim was always full of heavy, bloodthirsty people with guns who went tramping past Gladys's precious statue by Auguste Rodin without so much as a thoughtful glance. Gladys was used to the attentions of the likes of Proust and found little bright conversation among the denizens of the horsey country aristocracy.

Then, like a blight in a fairy tale, something terrible began to happen to Gladys's face. Cruelly, the wax melted in the bridge of her nose. Strange discolorations appeared; her cheeks puffed and her mouth twisted. Men looked away from her quickly; former lovers winced; one said she looked "mannequin-like and repellent." The marks became two long whorls, at each side of her nose, and traveling all the way to her chin, where there grew two small horns of wax. Sunny gave Gladys a black eye; her spoiled looks were not fit for the beauty of Blenheim. Poor, lovely, clever Gladys must have rued her childhood dream of marrying a duke. She took to breeding Blenheim spaniels. Like Consuelo before her, she realized the measure of the man she had married. At one dinner party, Sunny was rumbling on about politics when Gladys suddenly shouted over the table, "Shut up! You know nothing about politics. I've slept with every prime minister in Europe and most kings. You are not qualified to speak." Sunny concentrated on his food.

At another meal, Gladys quietly placed a revolver by her table setting. "What's that for?" piped a guest.

"Oh, I don't know," Gladys smiled toothily. "I might just shoot Marlborough!"

With that, Sunny took fright, fled Blenheim for two years, and then he returned to forcibly evict Gladys. She was more interested in her dogs than in him.

There is a happy end to this tale, however—at least for one of our ménage à trois. Consuelo married her one true love, the dashing, sensitive French aviator Jacques Balsan, on July 4, 1921. Being Madame Jacques Balsan, finally liberated of her great name, of the heavy diamonds and titles of the Marlboroughs, made up for all those stuffy, dreary dinners at Blenheim. Even her mother, Alva, was a reformed character, and she and Consuelo became dear companions. They were both keen on social work and the rights of sweated women (Alva struck up a fierce friendship with Christabel Pankhurst on the basis of a shared detestation of men). Life was golden in Paris and, in the winter months, on the Riviera, where Consuelo and Jacques built a house, Lou Sueil, by the fortress town of Èze, France. They had to negotiate with fifty peasants who all owned sections of the land they wanted to buy and "seated at their kitchen tables, we sealed the contracts in the strong, bitter wines they brewed." Consuelo was in her element: "Pouring with lavish hand into polished tumblers, they drank without drawing breath, and rather than offend I sipped the potent vintage and suffered the inevitable headache." They could go to the opera in Nice and the theater in Monaco. But one of the best things of all was the companionship Consuelo and Jacques found in eating. Gone was the snootiness of Sunny, the terrible minute stipulations and demands. Together, she and Jacques lunched in the open air, sampling the delicious fresh food of Provence with friends. Consuelo recalled:

We each brought a dish—cold curried chicken—potato salad—the little artichokes that are so tender and flavourful—cheese and light pastries with the purple figs—or cherries just picked from our trees. A *vin de pays* and steaming coffee ended each meal. The dogs that accompanied us had their own specially prepared bowls. Sometimes instead of picnicking we went to an inn renowned for mountain trout—a fish that when grilled on the cinders of aromatic herbs is no longer a fish, but a dish for the gods. We grew to know *toutes les specialities de la maison*, from the *bouillabaisse* with its saffron flavour to the meringues with a pastry as light as thistledown and a cream whipped to a bubble. The *vin de pays—bellet*, iced to a rosy glow—added the headiness which in America is supplied by the cocktail; but it was a headiness founded on a perfectly cooked meal, not on the yearnings of an empty stomach, a headiness, moreover, whose ebullience is flavoured by wit and gaiety, like the warm sparkle of the sun.

THE FOOD OF SECOND CHANCES
Cold Curried Chicken

INGREDIENTS

A handful of cashew nuts
2 tbsp. mild curry powder
½ tsp. cinnamon
2 cm piece of fresh ginger, finely chopped
⅓ cup dried apricot, finely chopped
3 tbsp. Major Grey mango chutney

3 scallions, finely chopped
¾ cup mayonnaise
¾ cup Greek yogurt
2 tsp. Worcestershire sauce
3 roasted chicken breasts, diced
2 tbsp. minced fresh cilantro
Slivered almonds, toasted

METHOD

Warm a skillet and toast the cashew nuts over a medium-high heat until they are brown. Remove and set aside. Now warm the curry powder and cinnamon in the pan. Add the chopped ginger. In a large bowl, combine the mango chutney and apricots. Now add to this the curry powder and ginger from the skillet. Add the cashew nuts and the scallions. Combine the mayonnaise, yogurt, and Worcestershire sauce. Add the chicken breast, season with sea salt and black pepper, and refrigerate for 2 hours. Finally, stir through the cilantro and decorate with toasted almonds.

Meringues

INGREDIENTS
5 egg whites, at room temperature
A pinch of salt
1 ¼ cups vanilla castor sugar
  (made by keeping a vanilla
pod or two embedded in a pot of
sugar)
4 tsp. cornstarch
2 tsp. white wine vinegar

METHOD
Heat the oven to 120°C. Meanwhile, get a large, very clean bowl and add the egg whites and salt. Using an electric mixer, whisk the egg whites until stiff. Add the sugar slowly, spoonful by spoonful, whisking in; then beat in the cornstarch and vinegar: now you have a lovely, snow-white mass of meringue.

Line a baking tray with parchment paper and transfer the meringue mix onto the parchment, building your meringues into towering, glossy individual peaks. Slide them into the oven and cook for about 1 hour and 15 minutes. Turn off the oven and leave the meringues in there to cool. Serve with raspberries, strawberries, cream, and, perhaps in honor of Consuelo, some passion fruit.

Lou Sueil had hanging gardens, full of scented yellow mimosa. It was so beautiful it pulled in visitors. Edith Wharton showed up—she had very good teeth but was ferociously puritanical in her tailoring—as did the emperor of Japan, who took ten minutes to sign the visitors' book in perfect, divine Japanese characters. The Polish ambassador regaled Consuelo and Jacques with tales of the Nazi Hermann Goering. Goering, passionate about shooting, was commiserating with a Polish count about his problems with poachers and advised, "Poachers! Take it from me, Excellency, you have only to shoot two or three as I have done and you will have no more trouble!" Sound advice, indeed. The king and queen of Denmark, a pair of giants who took to sedately bicycling everywhere, lived nearby. The Hindu maharajah of Karurthna was deeply thankful when Consuelo served him lobster and chicken. "I am so often given nothing else [but beef]," he explained, "and once as an alternative tongue was served, my hostess not seeming to realise that tongue came from the cow." Cousin Winston Churchill and his wife, Clementine, showed up and had great fun. Lord Curzon, a loved guest, peaceably admired the beautiful, light-dappled landscape with Consuelo at his side. "Then it has been worth the sacrifice?" he asked her.

"Sacrifice?"

"Yes—to give up being the beautiful Duchess of Marlborough and all it meant?" Madame Balsan must have smiled wisely.

BUNNY CHOW WITH HUGH HEFNER

To any bright-eyed blonde ingénue, an invitation to Hugh Hefner's Midsummer Night's Dream Party at either of his Playboy mansions in Chicago or Los Angeles is a ticket to ride (did I just *say* that?). Contact with Hefner is gold dust for those beguiling girls hungry for fame, to be a centerfold, a Playmate . . . a Bunny. Either Playboy Mansion seems like a timeless emporium of slap and tickle, the glowing mansion windows offering access to one of the great gurus of porn. Hef's parties, even if he is a wobbly-legged eighty-year-old in pajamas, have all the attendant flashes of Botox glamour, the twinkle of whitened teeth, lights, and celebrity tans.

And, always, there is a buffet of every imaginable glory laid out at stations, from cheeky little sushi numbers through to buxom seafood, surprised on their skewers. Carts wobble with desserts. Indeed, at one point, a stay at the Playboy Mansion was uber-cool; even the Rolling Stones requested a visit. Mick Jagger wandered around the mansion, looking for sex, and meandered into the bedroom of Bobby Arnstein. She would, perhaps, have had sex with him but then remembered she'd eaten a lot of cheese and would have smelly breath. Jagger, meanwhile, staggered back into a chair, on which a birthday cake just so happened to rest. Quelled by Bobby's rejection, he then slid out of the room, and the last she saw of Mick was his nimble, leather-clad bottom, decorated with soft, sticky icing, leaving the room.

So how do you go about getting into bed with Hef? If Hef and his girlfriends like the look of you, you are gradually invited to more events: Sunday Fundays or biweekly clubbing nights (though at club nights Hef's ladies have to sit cordoned off in a sort of pen). Then there will be homely "dinner and movie" nights at home with Hef (before you opt for that one, Hef manages to suck the life out of it by reading his notes about the film to the assembled company in advance). For some of us, the prospect of life with Hugh Hefner in a pink-and-white striped room sprinkled with dull-eyed Disney soft toys, the white carpets stained a little yellow by dog pee, and Hef shambling about in his silk PJs with Viagra pills rattling in his pocket may not appeal, but for the ambitious Playmate, the greatest accolade is to become one of Hef's posse of girlfriends and move into the mansion. Then you are only a rhinestone bustier away from heaven and the recipient of a $1,000-a-week clothing allowance. Life seems simple: all you have to do is stay permanently waxed and perhaps lick somebody's nether regions occasionally. A convincing squeal helps too. Then it all starts to give way. Sisterhood isn't possible, as all the girls elbow each other aside for Hef's attention. The bunny pendant that everyone thought was diamond is only made with crummy zirconia. The nine o'clock curfew jars.

Playboy Penthouse was Hef's first TV show and was set up as a party. Afterward, sweaty from the camera lights, guests would slope off to the Chicago Playboy Mansion or jive at the Playboy Club and then end up going back to the mansion for a lavish buffet. There was always, according to comedian and radical vegetarian Dick Gregory, "so much food. I never realised that meat came this large. There was no such thing as you get there at four o'clock in the morning and the plates were empty." At one point, Hef's party guests could order whatever they dreamed of from the mansion's kitchens—apparently, in the 1970s, Jack Nicolson would just roll up on his way to somewhere else and collect Playboy takeout (having called ahead of time to place his order). This put a damper on Hef's hospitality. Neighborhood binoculars were focused on the rooftop sundeck, particularly in the daytime, when voluptuous Bunnies teetered about on high heels, their nipple tassels swaying. Why any woman in her right mind ever expected an inch of fidelity from Hugh Hefner is beyond knowing—but they did. Joni Mattis, a very demure Miss November in 1960—she got one fan letter from a clergyman trying to rescue her—and a girlfriend of Hef's, had romantic expectations of him (unlike modern jaded Bunnies). When she caught him canoodling with one of the other girls, she pushed the girl into the swimming pool. Personally, I think it was Hef who deserved the cold shower. He bumped into elfin eighteen-year-old Barbie Benton on the set of *Playboy After Dark* and asked her out. Bearing in mind that Hef was forty-two, she said, "I've never gone out with anyone older than twenty-four." Hef smirked and said, "That's all right. Neither have I."

The Playboy world enabled Hef to shake off the traces of his first doomed marriage to Mildred Williams, an experience that sounds as if he'd been briefly miscast in the wrong life. At the start of their marriage, Hugh and Mildred lived in the family home with his doughty Methodist parents and slept in the bed that had been his parents'—not exactly a situation to arouse the sensualist. All of which helped to compound the terrible foreboding he felt about life: that he would live the life his parents had lived. He says, "And I hated it." When he managed to extricate himself from Mildred's clutches, Hugh renamed himself "Hef"—it sounded much cooler. Even now, in a mockery of their parents' strictures about not going to the movies on Sundays, he and his brother, Keith, get together on Sundays to watch movies. "Naturally," Hef chortles, "Sunday became movie night at the mansion."

Girlfriends at the mansion have to make way for Hef's "Manly Nights," when he and the boys—his increasingly elderly pack of male friends—take in a movie together at the mansion. Just the mention of a "Manly Night" would give Hefner's second wife, Kimberly Conran, a headache. While the day of the week may change, the boys are pretty much devoted to a manly dinner of roast turkey, corn on the cob, peas, gravy, and—wait for it—mashed potatoes. The year 1989 saw Hef marry Kimberley, but he managed to forget the wedding ring (think Freud), and as he stood beneath the large, billowing white wedding tent, he smirked winsomely, bit into a slice of apple pie topped with whipped cream, and declared, "This is what passes for sin at the Playboy Mansion West these days." It wasn't to last, though. Kimberley got increasingly fed up with finding strange people, whom Hef had scooped up, at the table at breakfast—some topless. She pinned a sign meaningfully by the kitchen: "When mama ain't happy, ain't nobody happy."

With Kimberley gone, the Playboy Mansion was overrun by girlfriends and their dogs: Hef is very tolerant of these, perhaps going back to his childhood and his pet dog, Brows, who was poorly and slept on Hef's special "bunny blanket." Hef, by now in his eighties, lies palely masturbating on his rotating bed within a circle of frazzled girlfriends, all hoping to avoid having sex with him. If you're lucky, he'll only massage you with lots of baby oil.

For the hungry, the unlimited free food in the twenty-four-hour kitchen offers some compensation for the mansion's shortcomings. Simply press zero on your bedroom phone for food and have what you will. Girlfriend Isabella St. James used to order half of one meal and half of the other to be delivered to her room. Lillian Muller piled on weight in the mansion; she'd lived in an orphanage as a child, where access to food was strictly limited. At the mansion, however, Lillian could just pull a chair into the walk-in refrigerator and eat from the buckets of crab, lobster, and cold roast chicken. Hef knew just to take a peek in the refrigerator when he wanted to track her down. One girlfriend regularly breakfasted on chocolate cake and chocolate milk, brought straight to her widening lap on a tray. Golden French toast with fresh berries is a favorite among girlfriends, eating breakfast in what's called the "Mediterranean room," a leafy room near the kitchen and the butler's pantry. Dinner can be homemade chips and guacamole; chicken fajitas; penne with buttery, Parmesan-rich Alfredo sauce; cheeseburgers. Dieting isn't necessary, as Hef pays for nips, tucks, liposuctions, and breast enhancements; he likes well-rounded girls anyway. Girlfriends, though, are banned from making their own food and from putting a foot inside the butler's pantry—butlers are to be watched.

The *Playboy* magazine prided itself on gourmandizing, wheeling out a food and drinks editor in 1954 so that when the *Playboy* reader had laid aside his volume of Nietzsche, he knew how to shuck an oyster and cook the pants off any young lady who made it to his lair. It was sheer escapism and reached its high point when *Playboy*'s food editor, Thomas Mario, produced *The Playboy Gourmet* in 1961. Housewives had invaded the inviolably masculine terrain of the chef. Now the time was ripe for the bachelor to reclaim the kitchen. He'd sweep away creepy baby blue colors and throw the forget-me-not pans in the bin. Copper implements were the name of the game. But does our bachelor do the cooking himself? No. Along comes some amiable hired hand—male or female—to do all the actual food preparation and the washing up. The bachelor, meanwhile, gets in at the end to add a flounce of sherry to the lobster or to strip down a meat kebab. All will be served in his "kitchenless kitchen," a food bar at which he'll stand before his admiring female audience with all his flashing gadgets. And if that doesn't get her into bed, then his detailed understanding of the mating rituals of king crabs certainly will.

To cast Hef himself as the "kitchenless kitchen" bachelor would be sheer folly: when our white-socked, pipe-smoking editor wasn't working around the clock penning long, tedious essays setting out his personal philosophies, drinking twenty-plus Pepsis a day, or cutting and pasting pictures into his many, many scrapbooks, he would occasionally remember to eat a plate of his interminably favorite dish of fried chicken. The Playboy publishing offices never knew when to expect him: he would squirrel himself away working, then only show up at the offices in the late afternoon. But before you imagine this sounds like the perfect boss, Hef liked to hold meetings until 2 a.m.

All that hard work paid off as the Playboy dream expanded. Hef bought a corporate jet, christened it the "Big Bunny," painted it black, and filled it with Jet Bunnies in thigh-length leather boots, as well as its own furred, round bed for Hef (plus a disco section). The winsome Jet Bunnies were in charge of feeding Hef's guests on the flight, often meals of up to four courses and always including a Hef treat. On one fateful day, this was fried chicken legs, but Hef, tired, said he wasn't hungry and retreated into his bedroom for a rest. The guests ate, and the Jet Bunnies polished off some and then threw the rest into the garbage. They were due to land when Hef's blue service light winked at them. Hef was hungry, ready for his dinner. Aghast, at their wits' end, the leather-clad Jet Bunnies dove into the garbage, dragging out gravy-covered clots of mashed potatoes and peas and detangling chicken legs from the bin liner. They rearranged it, reheated it, and presented it on a spanking-clean tray. Before the flight was done, Hef thanked the Jet Bunnies for the best fried chicken he'd ever had from them. So much for the Mile High Club.

If anything, one could expect Hef's food tastes to be as eclectic as his taste in ladies. How wrong that would be, though, as a former Bunny and live-in lover at the Playboy Mansion recalled, "I used to laugh at the kind of food Hef liked, fried chicken and meat loaf." He was fizzy with Coca-Cola, the caffeine from this perhaps being dulled by the whack of nicotine he got from his pipes of Mixture 79 tobacco, and snacked on all-American peanut- and toffee-style candies like Butterfingers and Clarks Bars or milder, peanutless puffy little Twinkies. Once that all got digested and his tummy really rumbled, he could simply press a button and a cook would prepare him one of his more solid favorite dishes, like fried chicken, lamb chops, or pot roast, with a pile of creamy mashed potatoes, some steaming corn on the cob, and gravy. Beware she who interferes with this: Hef kicked up a fuss when too many girlfriends at the mansion ordered lamb chops for their dogs, depriving Hef of his hoard.

Daily, Hef eats one muffin for breakfast (in bed), accompanied by butter and strawberry jam. This can be varied by a jelly donut and half a grapefruit: this he has eaten for about two decades. At about 5 p.m. (back in bed), he sups on instant chicken noodle soup (Lipton's) with some saltine crackers. Dinner (back to bed again) will be late at night. But that's not all. The kitchen has a complete set of diagrams on not just how to prepare his endlessly repeated diet but also where—and this is *crucial*—each item of a meal should be set out on his tray. Apart from the lamb chops and fried chicken with his mother's recipe for mashed potatoes (two creamy blobs of mashed potatoes, each with a poached egg slipped inside), he may occasionally delve into the avant-garde world of a cheeseburger and fries, but irrespective of the dish it must be served with applesauce and a glass of cool milk. Oatmeal raisin cookies ease his sweet tooth. Indeed, on nights out in restaurants with his girlfriends, not a crumb of the restaurant food passes his lips. His food will have been delivered from home to the restaurant kitchens, and while his girlfriends nibble on sushi, he'll smile indulgently over a lamb chop, safe from the vagaries of wasabi and ginger. The only exceptions are edamame and a thin-crust cheese pizza he likes in a haunt of his, Barfly. He does deviate from the cold milk at times but only with Jack Daniels and coke or the rare Mai Tai. If he gets tipsy, his shirt comes unbuttoned and—like the rest of us—he's convinced he can dance. When Hef was due to dine in Maxim's in Paris, his valet was sent to Paris at considerable expense to train Maxim's chef in the intricacies of making Hef's fried chicken. As one girlfriend recalled, "He didn't want any of that fancy food. . . . We all ordered our French food with the fancy sauces. Hef's chicken came . . . they had it under glass and he drank a glass of milk with it—and he devoured it."

Fried Chicken

INGREDIENTS

6 cups lard	1 egg
1 chicken, cut into 8 sections	½ cup milk
2 tsp. sea salt	1 cup all-purpose flour
Freshly ground black pepper	

METHOD

Preheat the oven to 50°C. Line a baking tray with paper towels and put this in the center of the oven.

Pat the chicken pieces dry. Put the flour on a flat plate and season with sea salt and black pepper. Beat the egg and mix it with the milk. Dip the chicken pieces in the egg-milk mixture and then dip them in the flour.

In a large, heavy, deep pan, melt the lard (about 4 cups of it). Melted, it should be 2 inches deep; if not, add additional lard. Now heat the lard until it is hot but not smoking. Fry the chicken, legs and drumsticks first, skin side down, in the lard in batches. Allow 12 minutes per piece. Transfer them onto the tray in the oven to keep warm. Now cook the chicken breasts and wings. The chicken breasts should take about 8 minutes.

Serve with applesauce, a glass of ice-cold milk, and two breast-like mounds of creamy mashed potatoes—slip a poached egg inside each of them.

Oatmeal Raisin Cookies

INGREDIENTS

¾ cup all-purpose flour
½ tsp. ground cinnamon
1 tsp. bicarbonate of soda
Pinch of sea salt
½ cup butter, slightly softened

¾ cup light brown sugar
1 cup rolled oats
½ cup raisins
Scant tsp. vanilla extract
1 egg, beaten

METHOD

Sieve the flour, cinnamon, bicarbonate of soda, and pinch of sea salt into a bowl. Next, whisk together the butter and sugar until they are light and fluffy. Now add the flour mixture and combine. Add the rolled oats, raisins, and vanilla extract. Add the beaten egg and combine. Cover with plastic wrap and chill in the fridge for an hour. Preheat the oven to 190°C. Butter and then lightly flour a very cold baking tray and measure the cookie dough into lumps of about 2 tablespoons each; flatten, and then place 5 centimeters apart on the baking tray. Bake until the oatmeal raisin cookies are a golden brown color—for just over 10 minutes. Remove from the oven, let them sit on the baking tray for 5 minutes, and then transfer to a wire rack.

THE ASTORS; OR, THE CLIVEDEN SET FOR DINNER

The turn-of-the-century American New York Astor ladies with their ostrich feathers and jeweled hairpins seem a far cry from the parsimony and filth of the founding father of the Astor fortunes: John Jacob Astor. Before he was heralded as the richest man in America, pioneering Lutheran John Jacob left the village of Walldorf, Germany, aged sixteen, traveled first to London, and then made his way across the washy Atlantic in 1783, carrying the flutes he hoped to trade. He paid five pounds for fare—including a daily meal of biscuits and salt beef. Delicious. He made most of his money, though, not in flutes but in the skin and fur of the humble beaver, whose coat he was very keen on caressing apparently. Fortunately for him, the Chinese were also dead keen on dead beavers, and between the beavers and the Chinese the Astors came to realize what seemed like limitless wealth. The Astors went on from beavers to shipping to banking to real estate in New York. How much of New York City could they buy? One Astor decided to line the floor of one room in his house with nothing but silver dollars. Another, Alice Astor, bloomed into a diverting eccentric who insisted she was the reincarnation of an Egyptian princess—the daughter of the high priest of Heliopolis, nonetheless. Alice was one of the first four people to set foot in Tutankhamen's tomb and always wore a rather disturbing necklace of gold rams' heads, taken from the tomb. When dancing one evening with Serge Obolensky, Serge claimed the necklace vibrated alarmingly— it must have done it for him, as he proposed to Alice that night (though by then she had managed to dress up as a Chinese princess). Endearingly or annoyingly, Alice was always late for dinner parties—who needs to worry about the time when they're a princess?—but put all the clocks in her house forty minutes ahead of time and kept her makeup kit in her Rolls.

One thing that the American Astors were famous for was their parties. Before you could do so much as shake the dust from your beaver-skin hat, it was time for fun. But it wasn't enough to simply *like* a party to be able to shimmy into one of the New York Astors' parties. No less than social magnitude was required. These were no cheerful, idling romps but the battlefields of those heavy-breasted arbiters of social standing, Mrs. Alice Vanderbilt (more of the Vanderbilts later) and Mrs. Caroline Astor (an heiress in her own right as a product of the Knickerbocker dynasty). Each was trying to outdo the other in their magnificence. Like rutting stags, they went at each other. Who was the more prominent; the more elegant; the more vogueish? Along with her stylish sidekick, Ward McAllister, Mrs. Astor drew up her list of the Four Hundred—the four hundred most prominent New Yorkers who could be invited to parties. Thus Mrs. Astor sailed into the tradition of the New York grand hostess, introducing such delights as *service à la Russe* (i.e., to be served at table rather than the friendly jostle and intermingling of buffet style), and a very useful symbol of personal wealth, as it required more servants—in this case, clad in blue Windsor Castle–style livery.

Mrs. Astor's house was at 350 Fifth Avenue (the Empire State Building has now risen from the ashes of Mrs. Astor's house; no doubt she would see it as a fitting tribute). It was the site of her glories, with Ward McAllister as her Rasputin. She supplied the money, McAllister the ideas (such as, perhaps, the drugged, moony-winged swans who glided over the indoor pond). Ward McAllister was polished, pompous, solicitous, and quick at sizing people up: if his eyes moved past you, you were nobody. He loved to refer obliquely to "the Four Hundred" of New York society—the press dubbed him Make-a-Lister—and had laid down a near-Mosaic set of laws about appropriate social behavior. The press trounced him as "the Lord High Separator of the Sheep from the Goats." Caroline Astor's husband, William, was often absent. He could be a bit of a liability, as he had been known to chuck guests out, and he was much happier bobbing about on his yacht, *Nourmahal* (Light of the Harem), with a lady or two. Caroline had a slight cast in her eye, was tall with solid jowls, and was dark-haired (which was thinning, so she wore a coal-black wig), all of which worked for Ward McAllister, as he reverentially noted her dignity was "a great restraining influence on the more frivolously inclined in her own set." Veiled often, she would glower from beneath her veils, thus leading to the satirical description of her as "Astorperious." She also had so many jewels that, according to witnesses, her appearance in a room was meteoric; her chest was a galaxy of diamonds. Fun was to be had, though, at an Astor party. In contrast, while an invitation to Alice Vanderbilt's was to be envied, no one went there to actually *enjoy* themselves. Their hostess was reputedly frosty and thin-lipped with, apparently, little to say.

Dinner at Caroline Astor's table was on heavy gold plates. She also was always keen on a prompt hot dinner—latecomers and laggards were not appreciated. Lucy Kavaler, the biographer of the Astors, mentions that French cuisine was the order of the day, and the menu at Mrs. Astor's often tended to be turtle consommé, ham mousse, salmon in the summer, terrapin in the winter, beef with truffles, calf's sweetbreads, pâté de foie gras and artichoke sauce, maraschino sorbet (rum was far too *common*), Camembert, and Nesselrode Pudding. All seasoned with snobbery.

Maraschino Sorbet

Unlike Mrs. Astor, most of us do not have servants, and therefore we will use the humble ice-cream machine for this one. Maraschino liqueur is required; it is delicious, tart, and has a magnificent bitter almond taste derived from the Croatian Marasca cherry. If you're really stuck, though, just use cherry brandy.

INGREDIENTS
¾ cup fine sugar
1 cup water
2 tbsp. maraschino liqueur

METHOD
In a small saucepan, heat the sugar and water until the sugar dissolves completely. Add the maraschino liqueur. Process in an ice-cream machine until the sorbet is nearly set. Serve with a teaspoon more of maraschino poured over it.

Nesselrode Pudding

INGREDIENTS
40 peeled, cooked chestnuts
2¼ cups sugar syrup
1 vanilla pod, split open
10 egg yolks
1 cup sugar
2½ cups heavy cream
¼ pint maraschino liqueur,
    plus some for macerating
    the dried fruit

¾ cup currants
¾ cup raisins
1 tbsp. candied lemon peel,
    finely chopped
2 cups heavy cream, whipped
4 egg whites

METHOD
Put the currants and raisins in a small bowl, add enough maraschino liqueur to cover them and leave to macerate for a couple of hours. In a pan, warm the sugar syrup with the vanilla pod. Add the chestnuts and simmer gently. Cool, remove the vanilla pod, and then in a blender, process the chestnuts and sugar syrup until smooth. Beat the egg yolks and add the cup of sugar, mixing until the mixture is thick and ribbon-like. In a saucepan, heat up the cream, and once it begins to steam, whisk it, in a thin trickle, into the egg yolks. Now return this warm egg-and-cream mixture to the heat and, stirring constantly, bring to a simmer or until a custard has formed. Remove from the heat and add the chestnut puree and macerated dried fruit, maraschino liqueur, and candied lemon peel. Cool and then fold in the whipped cream. Whisk the egg whites until they are stiff, and fold in also. Pour the pudding mix into a sparkly bowl and leave it to set in the freezer—this will take a couple of hours.

Another party organizer for Caroline Astor was Harry Lehr, whose trademark braying laugh heehawed through the perfumed halls. Among his feats (not at Caroline's but for the wild Mrs. Mamie Fish, who was hell-bent on having a good time) was one party where the invited gentlemen came costumed as cats and offered little, wriggling mice to the female guests. An enormous, puffing, performing elephant was the centerpiece—guests laughed and squealed as they held out handfuls of peanuts to its snuffling trunk. Caroline huffily disapproved of such excesses and made her disapproval crystal clear, to which Mamie Fish acidly rejoined, "Mrs. Astor is an elderly woman." And indeed Caroline had been known to don her "voluminous frilled white nightgown" and slip into bed while her guests caroused downstairs.

Across the Atlantic, meanwhile, the British wing of the Astors had their own social mark to make. In 1893, the press rippled with the news that the fastidious, solitary William Waldorf Astor, an American billionaire, had settled upon late Victorian England as his European home, buying the grand stately home of Cliveden as the repository for the magnificent paintings and objects he collected. Equally collectable were British newspapers like the *Observer* and the *Times*, and William also snapped up the ownership of journals and periodicals galore. Meanwhile, in New York he razed his house and in its place built the Waldorf Hotel, which was to merge eventually with his cousin's hotel, the Astoria. London society didn't quite know what to make of William Waldorf. Cliveden was idyllic, with swifts nesting above the nursery windows and long, green-shaded gardens. William Waldorf served the most superb food (this was a fellow who favored artichokes and prawns as a pre-breakfast snack), but there was a darker, contrary side to his personality. It was expected that his daughter Pauline should read aloud to him at all meals—all extracts from the Borgias or accounts of Napoleon. His ways were so set as to alienate wearied guests, and his rather bitter, snarling opinions did not endear him to London society. He called Alice Keppel a strumpet and claimed Edward VII was impotent. Given that Alice was the king's mistress, he seems to have confused the terms of their engagement!

William kept a pair of revolvers nestled in his bed in case of attack by intruders and had rigged all the doors in Cliveden so that they automatically locked as soon as you entered the room, having innocently flung the door closed behind you. People were left scratching at the paneling until William activated a secret panel to allow them out. He was scared of being murdered, but why? Was there a vengeful footman in the background? A wronged maid? A furious business adversary? A scorned butler? One apocryphal tale was that he had to sack his long-standing butler Pooley for repeated drunkenness but handed him £1,000 in gratitude. Mr. Pooley immediately bought drinks for the patrons in the local pub, toasting all with "That's something worth getting drunk for." Responsibility for the wine often fell to the butler. This meant that some became alcoholics and had to be gently retired on those grounds.

William's terrible, stiff dinner parties and soirees for music lovers were dry and fractious. He had all his guests drilled about when mealtimes were and proved endlessly bossy about timed activities, scolding others for being out of synch—even sleep, alarmingly, had an allotted slot. Epicure or not, William Waldorf's charms quickly wore thin. As soon as possible, William became a naturalized British subject. Someone objected—an effigy of him was set alight in Times Square, New York, daubed with scurrilous words: "Astor the Traitor." Keen on a peerage, William eventually bought his title from Lloyd George, becoming a baron and then a viscount, much to the ire of his son Waldorf, who had to resign his Commons Conservative seat and join the Lords with the death of his father—thus paving the way for Nancy Astor to become a member of Parliament (MP).

Finally, William left Cliveden to Waldorf and his sparky, opinionated American wife, Nancy, before retiring to Brighton, where he ended his years eating and drinking a great deal. Incidentally, he died in the lavatory "after a favourite dinner of mutton, macaroni and Beaune"—perhaps trapped behind one of his automatic-locking doors?

Waldorf Astor's wife-to-be, Nancy Langhorne, first sailed across to Britain in 1904, looking to do a bit of fox hunting. One of her first suitors on arrival in England was John Baring, to be Lord Revelstoke, a brilliant banker who completely reinvigorated the family bank, Baring Brothers. He was a charmer, and how Nancy resisted him is testimony to her unerring primness (later in life she told her daughter that shoe shops were to be avoided, as the fingers of male assistants might linger over their ankles). Revelstoke had the good fortune to have Rosa Lewis as his chef, crowned by Escoffier as the "Queen of Cooks." She famously chased a young Winston Churchill from her kitchen, shouting, "Hop it, copper knob!" A bachelor of forty-one years, Revelstoke was keenest on winning Nancy Langhorne. On her way to meet him for dinner in London, Nancy's train had been beset by terrible weather. Romantically, Revelstoke sent a servant through the deep snow with a pot of caviar to meet Nancy's train (she tended to have a rather exciting time on trains—Lord Elphinstone, another admirer, dramatically leaped onto a train she was on and, flinging open the doors of her compartment, begged for her hand in marriage). Most of us would have fallen into the arms of either man there and then, but Nancy's heart was hard as flint after her unhappy first marriage. It was not until her return journey to England in December 1905, on the *Cedric*, that she met Waldorf Astor.

Nancy had deep Virginian roots: she was a southern belle along with her four sisters. Her father, Chillie, was a railway boomer and had owned a tobacco plantation worked by slaves in Virginia, which he lost with the victory of the North in the Civil War. His fortunes restored, Chillie and his daughters lived in the palatial

Mirador, at the foot of the Blue Ridge Mountains. Unreconstructed in every other way, Chillie rolled up to Cliveden, startling the urbane, differential British staff there. Chillie had a pug of tobacco permanently lodged in his jaw and liked to spit out sudden bronzed shots of nicotine saliva, causing great consternation among others, including the Astors' chauffeur. Archduke Franz Ferdinand was to be collected from the train station (his visit was two weeks before his assassination). Chillie, as representative of the Astors, had settled into the backseat, chewing away. Thinking the (beautifully clean) back window was open, Chillie spat out a long, brown, and rheumy gob of saliva onto the window. Slowly, it tricked down the inside.

Perhaps Chillie should have stayed at home in Cliveden, making Archduke Ferdinand one of his breathtaking mint juleps. The famous butler, Edwin Lee, recalled Chillie's cocktail skills: "Mrs Astor's father was a great old character, real tough American, used to chew pug tobacco and was very fond of a drink. He loved to make Egg Nog and Rum Punch and got most of the guests tight, much to the disgust of Mrs Astor whose views were very much against drink of any kind, although it was always served at lunch and dinner." Having said this, Nancy had certainly picked up how to make a mint julep. During World War I, the Astors set up a lodge on the grounds of Cliveden as a hospital for the Canadian armed forces. Nancy admired the devotion of one Canadian, Colonel Newbourne, a skilled surgeon who worked there and who visited his patients two or three times a night. He was married and permanently harassed by his empty-headed wife, who once telephoned him during a tricky operation. He left the operating theater to take the call and, realizing it was her, blasted, "Is that you, Louise? Go to Hell!" Such was Nancy's admiration for him that she said, "Colonel Newbourne was the only living man for whom I ever made mint juleps. . . . When he was completely exhausted [I used to] sit him down on the terrace at Cliveden, and make him a mint julep like Father used to make in Virginia, long ago."

Mint Juleps for Weary Surgeons

INGREDIENTS
A palmful of fresh mint leaves
1 tsp. sugar
2 shots of bourbon

METHOD
Put the mint leaves and the sugar at the base of a prechilled glass. Using a muddler (or pestle), lightly crush the mint using the sugar as grist, releasing the sharp sweetness of the mint. Now pack a layer of crushed ice on top and pour the bourbon over the ice. Stir and serve with a sprig of mint by way of decoration.

Nancy's mint julep creation is even more impressive when one considers that both she and Waldorf were staunch teetotalers, and Christian Scientists to boot (she took some time to convert Waldorf, though). Waldorf had always felt a deep sense of public duty—when he traveled on family holidays by train he attached an additional carriage to the back of the train so he could transport a cow (and cowman) about the country with him, supplying children along the way with fresh milk.

True to the Astor style, Nancy's parties at Cliveden and at their house in St. James's Square, London, were awash with footmen, their hair powdered and their legs bright in yellow stockings, pandering to the American/British aristocracy such as Lord Curzon, Asquith, and Prince Arthur (Queen Victoria's third son) and American ladies like Consuelo Vanderbilt, Consuelo Yznaga de Valle, Mary Goelet, the Duchess of Roxburghe, and the Duchess of Manchester, all of whom had married into the British aristocracy and came with their own soft furnishings. Ladies traveling to a country house such as Cliveden would often take their own pillow and even bed linen. Writers like Rudyard Kipling, Henry James, George Bernard Shaw, and John Buchan might be on the guest list, traipsing over the animal skins flung before the fire in the great hall, along with the queen of Rumania, Charles Lindberg, and Henry Ford. When Mohandas Gandhi came to visit Cliveden, he presented a diverting figure, looking small, bright, and homespun among its opulence; he even continued working on his spinning wheel. Bossily, Nancy told him off for causing so much trouble abroad. Gandhi's diet, with its many vegan stipulations, caused similar consternation in the minor fiefdom of Cliveden. Nancy thought he might like some American pecans. To which he replied, "Oh, Lady Astor, be British and buy British." Whiskery Kitchener rolled up for weekends with the Astors too but made a nuisance of himself eyeing pieces of art, braying loudly about their beauty, and then hoping that the owner would hand a piece over as a gift. Nancy wasn't falling for it.

Lee the butler struck a sonorous gong every morning at eight to waken the guests in all twenty-five of Cliveden's bedrooms. Nancy would always have coffee and fruit in bed, casting an approving eye over the Christian Scientist publication *Science and Health*, plus a passage or two from the Bible. The guests drifted downstairs, languid and elegant, to a breakfast of scrumptious country house fare: hot dishes on one side of the dining room with crisp bacon, scrambled and fried eggs, brown mushrooms, kippers, and poached haddock; cold dishes on the other side of hams, handsome galantines, brawns, and pavilions of game pies. In her boudoir, Nancy discussed the menus for the day with her chef. The French chef Monsieur Papillion cooked for the Astors from 1909 until his death in 1914, when he was succeeded by a Monsieur Gilbert (between you and me, Mr. Lee thought Papillion was the superior chef). True to form, Nancy would tartly condemn the efforts of Papillion or Gilbert with the words "I don't think that went too well yesterday," the sourness of which was intended to spur their ambitions. Then she would grill Mr. Lee and various other acolytes in close succession. Nancy never showed her servants pleasure in their services; she assumed it was their duty to her. Back in Virginia, the Langhornes' servants were all former black slaves and treated with a casual contempt. Bee Wilson records, "The Langhorne family's meals were prepared by a Negro cook and butler. 'Don't kill him, Dab,' Nancy's mother cajoled, to save the butler from an act of violence when he tripped one day while carrying a tureen of oyster stew." Thus it was the British counterpart's duty to mildly stand tall against the gust of Nancy's rages. Her personal maid, Rosina Harrison, always knew a conversation was over when Nancy said, "Shut up, Rose!" Nancy also liked to mimic Rose cruelly. Thus it is refreshing to discover moments of servant rebellion, however well intentioned. A teetotaler to the grave, Nancy tossed back a pick-me-up blackcurrant essence Ribena every day at eleven, although, unbeknownst to her, the underbutler, Charles, always added a tot of Dubonnet to it if he thought she looked a bit down in the dumps.

Post-breakfast, guests could partake of fishing, hunting, shooting, squash, golf, and tennis. Nancy was always exercising, being lively, bustling and astringent. Even in her seventies she liked to throw herself into a cartwheel and, in younger years, loved going motorcycling with Lawrence of Arabia, notching up speeds of a hundred miles an hour.

If it was wintertime, afternoon tea was served in Cliveden's eighty-two-foot-long Great Hall; in the warm, balmy summer months, tea was served outside under a pavilion. One guest likened it to a Bedouin encampment, with children tumbling over cushions, open newspapers lying about, and a selection of specially designated tables. Children, for instance, were corralled to their own table, which Nancy's niece, the actress Joyce Grenfell, recalled in her memoirs: "We . . . sat at the children's table near the fire, where Uncle Waldorf chose to join us. He poured out our milk and sliced the wholesome loaf and plain cake baked for us to eat. At the grown-up table, where Aunt Nancy presided, there were delectable little scones in a lidded silver dish, kept hot over a spirit lamp. There was also a special, almost black, rich fruitcake topped with marzipan, chocolate eclairs and very short crisp shortbreads, all made in the still-room by two full-time cake-and-pastry cooks. Sometimes we were allowed special treats from the grown-ups' table, but Aunt Nancy kept an eye on the goodies, and we were strictly rationed." Joyce did no more than fantasize about another slice of fruitcake; nevertheless, Nancy always left her with the lingering sense that she'd done something wrong. Aunt Nancy, though, had a sweet side: a permanent supply of chewing gum was lodged in her pocket, as she received boxes and boxes of the stuff (plus pecans, sourballs, and Virginian ham) from America, all stashed in what was called her "present room," a small study adjacent to her boudoir. One such gift, roe herrings, dolefully pickled in brine and all the way from the James River, Virginia, materialized at Cliveden only to be used in an experiment: as a lure during a drag hunt. This is when a pack of dogs chase a scented sack (often of aniseed and sometimes dripping with urine and meat) that has been dragged over the ground in preparation for the real fox hunt later in the day. Michael Astor recalled, "The drag was a roaring success that morning; the scent was blinding, the beagles ran like dogs possessed, chasing they knew not what, but something rare and pungent."

Scones

INGREDIENTS

4½ cups all-purpose flour,
    plus extra for work surface
3 tbsp. softened butter,
    cut into small cubes
½ cup sugar
½ tbsp. baking powder

A generous pinch of sea salt
1 cup milk
2 large eggs, beaten, plus
    1 smaller egg, beaten with
    a pinch of salt, for glazing
    the scones

METHOD

Preheat the oven to 200°C. Sieve the flour into a large mixing bowl. Add the cubed butter, and rub together between your fingertips until the mixture has the texture of breadcrumbs. Now add the sugar, baking powder, eggs, and sea salt. Work through with a wooden spoon. Add half the milk, combine thoroughly, and then, a little at a time, add the rest of the milk, stopping when you have a soft, moist dough.

Flour the work surface. Sift a layer of flour on top of the dough. Roll up your sleeves; you are now going to do some "chaffing." Fold the scone dough in half, turn it 90 degrees, and fold again. This process adds air to the scone mix. Repeat until your dough is smooth—but only a couple of times; do not overwork the dough or your scones will not have the same rise.

Flour the work surface again. Sift another very light layer of flour on top of the dough. With a rolling pin, roll up from the middle and down from the middle, turning the dough gently by 90 degrees each time, until it is 1¼ inches thick. Using a pastry cutter, cut out scones. Cut each scone as close to the next as possible. If you are tempted to reuse dough, then do so, but beware: scones made from reworked pastry will never rise as high in baking.

Butter a baking tray and line it with baking paper. Place the scones on the tray. Let them sit for 5 minutes. Brush them with egg wash, slide the tray into the oven, and let them bake for about 15 minutes.

Cool on a wire rack and then serve with clotted cream and homemade strawberry jam.

Special Treat Fruitcake

INGREDIENTS

1½ cups currants
1½ cups sultanas
1½ cups glacé cherries
½ cup mixed peel
½ cup brandy
½ cup softened butter—also have
about a dessertspoonful extra
for buttering
½ cup muscovado sugar

4 eggs, beaten
1⅓ cups all-purpose flour
1 tsp. baking powder
Pinch of sea salt
1 tsp. mixed spice
1 cup ground almonds
Grated zest of 1 unwaxed lemon
½ cup whole almonds

METHOD

Pour the currants, sultanas, cherries, and dried peel into a bowl with the brandy. Cover and leave to marinate overnight.

Butter a cake tin; line it with baking parchment. Preheat the oven to 140°C. In a bowl, cream together the softened butter and muscovado sugar until they are of a fluffy and light consistency. Now gradually add the eggs, beating each in.

Sieve the flour into another bowl; add the baking powder, salt, mixed spice, and ground almonds. Fold this into the sugary, buttery, eggy fluff. Now add the macerated fruit, lemon zest, and chopped almonds. Combine.

Pour the mixture into the buttered and lined baking tin. Bake in the oven for an hour, then cover with foil and bake for a further 30 minutes. Check the cake is cooked through by testing with a skewer; when it comes out clean, the fruitcake is ready.

Shortbread

INGREDIENTS

8 tbsp. butter, softened
2 tbsp. granulated sugar
A generous pinch of sea salt

1¼ cups all-purpose flour
4½ tbsp. ground rice
2 tbsp. demerara sugar, for sprinkling

METHOD

Preheat the oven to 150°C. Beat the butter in a mixing bowl, then cream with the granulated sugar and sea salt. Add the flour and ground rice and mix until the buttery dough becomes a whole. If it doesn't adhere together properly, add a little more butter and mix again. Butter a square 17- to 18-centimeter baking tin. Put the mixture in and smooth out with your fingertips. Prick the surface all over with a fork and make light cuts, separating the dough into fingers. Chill in the fridge for about 15 minutes. Now bake in the oven for an hour or until the shortbread has become a deliciously pale gold color. Remove from the oven and, while it is still warm, divide it completely into fingers. Sprinkle the tops with demerara sugar.

Then there was the moonlight and the moonshine of dinner. Astor dinners glimmered with beauty, the food rich and luxurious for the forty or so oiled, scented, rustling, silken guests. Over the endless chatter were served two soups, a choice of fish, an entrée, game of all sorts when the shooting season was on, a joint of beef, savories, and some diaphanous dessert. Liqueurs followed for the men, and tiny silver bowls were laid alongside, with pink attar of rose pastilles in them, their strong flowery tones intended to make even the most pungent of alcoholic breaths smell sweet. The hothouses and vegetable gardens of Cliveden supplied the table with luscious fruit and vegetables all year round. Nancy's son, Michael Astor, noticed that their Christian Scientist visitors would fall silent when the talk was political but were "the real enthusiasts at eating. It was their only vice." Other guests were always welcome to drink—hock, port, brandy, claret—drawn from the deep, fine cellars of Cliveden. The staff would sometimes sneak funny, ironic moments at the expense of the tipsy toffs—not the ladies, though, who were expected to sip on one glass of champagne before moving on to the soberer joys of Apollinaris water. When one footman, Arthur, was serving vegetables, a very posh lady demanded, "What kind of beans are those?"

"Farting beans, madam," Arthur answered, without the ghost of a smile.

"Where do they come from?"

"Down under, madam."

"I'll have some of them," she said eagerly, forked a bean and, holding it aloft, honked down the table to her husband, "Harry, darling, you must try these, they're fahtin' beans, they come from Australia!"

After the rows, arguments, and hot debates over dinner, Nancy liked nothing better than a game of charades or some serious dressing up. It took no encouragement whatsoever for her to delve into her extensive array of costumes and masks, which she kept in a vast Chinese chest: shoes, ugly sister masks, Chinese villain masks, a Pierette costume, mandarin coats, and eye patches. Nancy was a hilarious mimic. She had a set of celluloid false teeth she'd use to caricature the Countess of Oxford. Or, dressing up in Waldorf's clothes, she would pretend to be a social climber, a huntsman in a pink coat with a wife he would incessantly refer to as "my Rosie."

When 10 o'clock struck, all fun and games were over for Nancy. A footman brought a "grog" tray to Nancy's room, balancing sliced lemons in tumblers with silver holders, while the ever-patient Mr. Lee followed heavily behind in his navy tailcoat with hot water in a silver jug to complete Lady Astor's digestive drink.

Cliveden, however, was not to remain far from scandal. By the early 1930s, several of the British aristocracy had taken a shine to Hitler. The British newspapers found him a fine chap; he appeared to be reinvigorating Germany as its chancellor. Many of the wealthiest in British society were anti-Semitic themselves and, at best, indifferent to Hitler's anti-Semitism; at worst, they cheered him on. Nancy's own uneasy prejudices soured her: she associated Jews with that horrible thing called Communism and was staunchly anti-Catholic to boot—she refused to employ any Catholic servants. Good old Hitler she thought of as a vaguely heroic lone Protestant bobbing about in a sea of hostile, incense-peddling Catholics. In fact, Catholics and cats were both an anathema to Nancy: she ordered all stray felines to be destroyed at Cliveden and used to hurl lumps of coal at caterwaulers in St. James's Square. While she might be friendly toward Fascists, the mere thought of brushing against a cat filled her with horror.

Increasingly, despite Nancy's love of a good row with the opposition, the Astors sought the company of other like-minded individuals, and so the notorious, much-mythologized Cliveden Set (a term coined in 1937) came to be. This was a far cry from Mrs. Caroline Astor's four hundred. These were, according to rumor, a posh secret cadre with a pro-Nazi agenda; an influential group of diners willing to make any sort of concession to Hitler in return for peace. Were they capable, their opponents wondered, of bending foreign policy to suit the Fascists? There were wild stories about their machinations. Could Berlin be Nancy's spiritual home? Didn't the Astors have "Germanic hearts"? The Cliveden Set met either at Cliveden or in the Astors' London home at St. James's Square. Nancy did herself no favors. When the Zionist leader, Chaim Weizmann, came for dinner at Cliveden during World War I, Nancy alerted her guests, "He's a great charmer. He will convert you to his point of view. He is the only decent Jew I have ever met." The assembled company stared in mortification down at their dinner plates. Nancy guffawed with delight when she discovered that her name was on the Gestapo's "Black List," as she thought this would put an end to all rumormongering about the Cliveden Set. When World War II finally broke out, Nancy set up Cliveden as a hospital again and, when at St. James's Square, wore a Jaeger dressing gown during air raids and carried copies of *Science and Health* and *Miscellaneous Writings* into the cellars.

One dinner guest, however, proved indifferent to Nancy's charms and took great umbrage to her odious views on Hitler: no less than Winston Churchill. Nancy and Winston bristled with animosity in each other's company. Woe betide the friendly fool who invited them both to dinner. Consuelo Vanderbilt, the one-time Duchess of Marlborough, vividly recalled their antipathy: "It was therefore unfortunate that on one of Lady Astor's visits to Blenheim . . . Winston should have chosen to appear. The expected result of their encounter was not long in coming; after a heated argument on some trivial matter Nancy, with a fervor whose sincerity could not be doubted, shouted, 'If I were your wife I would put poison in your coffee!' Whereupon Winston, with equal heat and sincerity answered, 'And if I were your husband I would drink it!'"

Winston wasn't even safe in the House of Commons. Nancy became the MP for Plymouth in 1919. She was the first woman ever to sit in the House of Commons.

Lloyd George winced as he watched chatterbox Nancy break the parliamentary rules by talking interminably during every inch of her progress up the floor of the House of Commons. Then she was in the thick of a conversation with Bonar Law and almost forgot to sign the register. And after all that, she wanted to stop for a chat with the Speaker. With her new duties in the House of Commons, St. James's Square became the site for what Nancy called her "town style party," as opposed to her "country style party." These "town parties" daunted some; the historian Lytton Strachey called them Nancy's "hectic frenzies" with hundreds of guests. Mr. Lee kept a list of party attendees in a small black book. Rosina Harrison, Nancy's maid, said in her memoirs that to read Mr. Lee's black book was "like dipping into history." An immense task faced Mr. Lee and his men as they prepared for parties at St. James's Square. For a start, they had to remove the silver from the commodious, room-size safe at Cliveden, a cache worth over £100,000 in the 1920s. Then this glittering hoard was driven to London in a car the staff called the "Black Maria." After that, it had to be polished until it flashed.

The London police were alerted that a dinner party was to be held at St. James's Square and, helmets on, patrolled the square, burbling at the traffic—mostly horse-drawn carriages, which jostled with boxy early motorcars. Before the grand house stood "Oppy" the linkman, doused in torchlight. Oppy's scarlet livery was at odds with his gnome-like frame, calling up the carriages to the front of the house. According to Rosina, Oppy had a whopping appetite, could take a pint of beer in one gulp, and thought himself quite glorious. The other servants decided to give him a salutary warning about vanity and blackened the inside of his hat. Every time Oppy majestically raised it to his mighty clientele, a wreath of soot was revealed around his knobbly head.

Mr. Lee boomed every guest's name and title as they entered, as if he were calling out arrivals in Heaven. Just in case their Christian Scientist hostess had decided to run a dry reception, many gents had hip flasks stowed about their persons, and when King George V and Queen Mary rolled up, their equerry handed Mr. Lee their own decanters of sherry and port. Punctuality was never a problem when the royal family were guests, as the other diners had to be assembled fifteen minutes before the royal presence materialized.

For any sizeable dinner, the kitchens would be a place of frantic, steaming rage (mostly courtesy of Monsieur Gilbert and the additional chefs drafted in), and extra footmen were hired. There might be a chef for each key course, but there was always an additional sugar chef crafting spun sugar into "beehives, letterboxes and bird's nests" from boiling sugar syrup, all of which would hold petits fours. "Odd men," as they were called—they had to be strong but were not necessarily the brightest—lugged food from the kitchen to the dining room, their legs buckling. Next, the air-like, powdered footmen took control of the plates of food. When one dropped some savories because the plate was hot, Mr. Lee admonished, "You're hired to hold it and hold it you will in the future, even if it burns you to the bone, do you understand? Fingers heal, food doesn't." Mr. Lee, always suspicious of fridges, insisted that the champagne and white wines be chilled in broken ice. On the tables, filmy light from candles twinkled on the silver.

A precedence-based seating plan had been drafted by Nancy, who, after leafing through such august volumes of social distinction as *Debrett*, *Who's Who*, and *Burke's Peerage*, was able to shake out her dukes from her marquesses and bishops. Indian guests, however, caused a mix-up because of their caste system, which was most inconvenient. Nancy made sure she would be elbow to elbow with anyone she deemed worth knowing—she found Kipling a stuffed shirt who clung to his wife and would give him a wide berth but made sure Joachim von Ribbentrop was by her side. Despite her caution with precedence, Nancy had pretty odd opinions on seating arrangements: only eighteen inches of space was allotted to each person at the table. The butler was to make no allowances, much to the fury of some guests. When Mr. Lee offered Churchill a pudding, Winston was in a deep sulk: "Take the damned stuff off. I can't move." In the end, pushed to endure what he considered intolerable discomforts, Winston refused to eat anything but instead sat huffily counting the dishes served, concluding bleakly, "Thirty dishes served and no damn room to eat one." The governor of the Bank of England was also upset and grumbled to Mr. Lee. Embarrassed, Mr. Lee alerted the hostess to her guests' unease. "They can both afford to lose a little weight," Nancy snapped mercilessly. Finally, Mr. Lee managed to persuade Nancy to let him pop in on Buckingham Palace and inquire how much space they accorded guests. Only when she received word on royal authority that the Windsors allowed their guests a handsome two feet and six inches did Nancy give way. One furious member of the first Labour government declared attending Nancy's dinners was a waste of time. He had watched her use a dinner plate as a fan while shoving her tiara of diamonds back on her head as if it were "an old hat."

After dinner, Nancy loved playing musical chairs. On one occasion, she launched into musical chairs with the assembled delegates from the League of Nations, all charging for a chair. Stiffly, the German and Soviet ambassadors stood out the game. Behind their bow ties they were baffled, "thinking no doubt that the English were mad, quite mad." Finally, the guests danced to an orchestra all night until the tired moon set (Nancy didn't like music but understood most people did). When dawn broke pinkly over London, slanting over Westminster Bridge, everyone dined on bacon and eggs, sipping bubbly champagne cups with fresh lemonade.

Below stairs, in what was another world, stood the exhausted, red-eyed maids washing the piles and piles of dishes, their hands raw from the soda they used as detergent, shedding slow, tired tears from pain and weariness.

Champagne Cup (but not for the maids)

INGREDIENTS

6 mint leaves
2 tbsp. sugar
Juice of 3 lemons
¼ cup Cointreau

¼ cup cognac
1 bottle of Moet Chandon
3 handfuls of crushed ice

TO GARNISH . . .

Thin half-moon slices of orange
  and lemon

Thin slices of peeled cucumber
Mint leaves

METHOD

Grind the mint leaves and sugar together, then empty them into the base of a chilled, beautiful cut-glass crystal punch bowl. Add the lemon juice, Cointreau, and cognac. Allow to rest for 15 minutes. Now add the crushed ice and pour the champagne over this. Arrange the garnish over the top. The champagne cup is now ready to serve!

DIPSY DINING WITH DOG NOSE: PEGGY GUGGENHEIM

Before she opened her first Guggenheim art gallery, Guggenheim Jeune in London in 1937, Peggy Guggenheim said she had spent the last decade or so as a "wife." If this is so, then let us all be such wives.

Peggy Guggenheim, the millionairess and bohemian art collector, was never going to be dull. She came from the eccentric Seligmans—she had a maternal aunt who, hat pins springing from her hair, burst into arias at the bus stop and liked to wipe her furniture down with Lysol in between making excellent tomato jellies. Another aunt resembled an elephant. Grandmother Seligman liked to surprise musty shopkeepers by leaning in conspiratorially toward them and whispering, "When do you think my husband last slept with me?" Peggy Guggenheim was a result of the Seligmans marrying into the duller Guggenheims. The Guggenheims, meanwhile, spent a lot of their time producing as many offspring as possible—and the great patriarch, Grandpa Guggenheim, cut a magnificent figure when he rode around New York in his sleigh and horses. But even Guggenheims understood the power of a dramatic moment: having abandoned his family, when Peggy's feckless father, Benjamin Guggenheim, died with his mistress on the *Titanic*, he greeted the grim reaper by dressing for dinner.

After her father's watery end, Peggy's existence became a little more peripatetic. In mourning, the family summered by the Atlantic in Allenhurst, New Jersey. Allenhurst was a tiny blip of humanity just a few blocks above Asbury Park, but it was packed with Jewish families—despite the local hotel, which refused to admit Jews (they watched in delight as the hotel burned down that summer). Wealthy districts like Long Branch excluded Jews, so they went to Allenhurst and to Deal, which today are still largely Jewish. A short time later, when World War I erupted, the Guggenheims decided to visit damply green England. A precursor of things to come, Peggy's wild appetites shocked Sir Charles Seligman, a renowned ethnologist and cousin of her mother's, when she asked for extra roast beef to mop up her mustard.

After what Peggy counted a miserable childhood and a series of wild crushes and sexual experiments, she married into bohemia by accepting the hand of the golden-haired wild-child novelist Laurence Vail. This union was unpromising from the start: on their honeymoon in Capri, Laurence said he'd like to throw several of his new in-laws—Peggy's uncles—from the rocks of Emperor Tiberius's villa (this was Tiberius's popular method of getting rid of people who bored him). Peggy knew Laurence wasn't that keen on being married to her. As she recalled when he proposed to her on the Eiffel Tower, "Every time I saw him look as though he were trying to swallow his Adam's apple I knew he was regretting his proposal."

Laurence was very artistic and temperamental, throwing Peggy's shoe out of the window when he was cross. He liked to slap Peggy about, throw her down stairs, tear her clothes off in restaurants, tread on her stomach, or rub jam into her hair. Luckily for Laurence, Peggy was remarkably tolerant of his appalling behavior—she seemed almost to see these wild acts as crimes of passion to be viewed with bohemian leniency.

The couple settled in Pramousquier in the South of France, much to the dread fascination of the local villagers. Madame, it was rumored, starved her husband and servants. When the butler ate apples, Peggy calculated their worth and deducted the cost from his wages. Madame's house was empty of food, or what was there was inedible, as Peggy insisted that all food, whatever state it was in, had to be eaten before it was replaced. When she read Laurence's 1926 novel *Murder! Murder!* Peggy spotted the close resemblance between the narrator's wife and herself, her lips moving in her sleep as she "dreams of sums." Yet she was also remarkably generous—she footed the bill for the anarchist Emma Goldman to write her memoirs in St. Tropez. When they visited, Emma rustled up such delicious gefilte fish that Laurence said she should write about food rather than her memories.

Peggy and Laurence drank deep of Muscadet from a local estate and sipped on cloudy, yellowing Pernod in the evenings. Peggy would beetle out in her car every morning for fresh bread, ice, and milk. They liked to eat outdoors, watching the sea, surrounded by heavy-blooming orange trees, dipping into a ready supply of wild boar hunted in the Forêt du Dom. They decided to eat their loaf-like pig, Chuto, and gave their kitchen over to a "specialist" who made blood sausage from Chuto, but when they had to transport the ample remains of Chuto to Paris, all his meat turned green from the cold. One spoiled pig.

After an acrimonious divorce from Laurence, their son, Sindbad, remained with his father; their daughter, Pegeen, went with Peggy. Peggy retreated to Hayford Hall on the edge of wild Dartmoor in Britain with her alcoholic, melancholic genius lover, John Holms, who never finished his sentences, had—according to the poet Edwin Muir—"an Elizabethan" forehead (what *does* that look like?), and could deliver lengthy lectures on any subject. He was also a frustrated writer of fiction, penning some great literary criticism but only one short story, appropriately titled "A Death." He was great friends with Djuna Barnes, who liked to pop in for the weekend, swirling her black cape about her. Peggy and John loved to ride ponies and horses across the wind-raveled, blustery landscape of Dartmoor (in her memoirs, Peggy just *has* to mention that the horses were supplied by a one-armed epileptic). Gone were the days of wild boar, but Peggy still clung onto a French cook, whose absence on Thursdays meant that she and John ate British pies, steak and kidney and cottage.

Steak and Kidney Pie

FOR THE ROUGH PUFF PASTRY . . .

2½ cups all-purpose flour

A generous cup of butter

1 tsp. sea salt

½ cup water

FOR THE PIE FILLING . . .

2 lb. lean sirloin, cut into 1 in. cubes

¾ lb. calf kidneys, peeled, trimmed, and cut into 1 in. cubes

1½ tsp. sea salt

Freshly ground black pepper

1 tbsp. flour

2 tbsp. beef suet or lard

8 brown mushrooms, sliced

3 onions, coarsely chopped

1½ cups water

1 small glass of dry sherry

2 tbsp. freshly chopped parsley

1 tsp. fresh thyme

1 tsp. Worcestershire sauce

3 shallots, finely chopped

TO DECORATE THE PIE CRUST . . .

1 egg yolk mixed with 2½ tsp. heavy cream

METHOD

Begin by making the rough puff pastry. Sieve the flour and sea salt into a large mixing bowl. Chop the butter into little chunks; add these and loosely rub into the flour (you want to be left with rich little gobbets and freckles of butter lodged in the pastry). Now add about a scant half of the water, mixing by hand until you have a dough, adding a little extra flour or water if necessary.

Flour the board you intend to work the pastry on. Gently shape the pastry into a rectangle. Begin to roll, working in one direction until it is three times wider. Don't lose the clear straight lines of the rectangle. Take the bottom third of the pastry and fold it up to the center. Then take the top third and fold it down over that. Turn the dough by a quarter. Repeat as before, rolling out in one direction until the rectangle is three times wider. Once you have completed the folding for the second time around, cover with plastic wrap again and let it rest and cool in the fridge for 20 minutes before rolling to form the pie crust.

Preheat the oven to 240°C. Mix the flour with sea salt and black pepper, put on a plate, and coat the steak and kidney cubes in flour.

In a skillet, heat the beef suet or lard until it is bubbling and splattering. Brown the cubed meat in batches—if necessary, add more fat. The meat cubes should be browned quickly but not burned. Transfer the meat cubes to a deep casserole dish, leaving behind the fat in the skillet.

Add the mushrooms and onions to the fat in the skillet and cook for 2–3 minutes. Now put them in the casserole. Add water to the skillet, and while it comes to a boil, scrape off all the fatty and meaty particles into the water. Pour it over the casserole and add the sherry, parsley, thyme, and Worcestershire sauce. Season with sea salt and black pepper again.

Steak and Kidney Pie (*continued*)

Now you can begin to assemble your pie. Put a clay-pipe funnel or an upturned china or wooden egg cup in the center of the casserole. Sprinkle the stew with the raw, minced shallots.

Flour a work surface and roll out the pastry to form a rectangle about a quarter of an inch thick. Cut 2 strips off the ends of the pastry; these should be half an inch in width and 12 inches in length. Place these strips around the rim of the casserole and use your fingertips to wedge them firmly in place. Now put a pie vent in the center of your pie. Wrap the remaining pastry around your rolling pin and lift it onto the casserole, laying it over the top. Using the prongs of a fork, crimp the lid together, with the pastry ringing the casserole dish. Trim the pastry, and use excess shreds to shape leaves. Have your egg yolk beaten with cream handy to brush the underside of your pastry leaves, and then attach them to the raw pie crust. Pop a small vent hole just where the pie vent is. Brush the crust all over with the egg-cream wash.

Bake the pie in the center of the oven for 30 minutes at 240°C; then reduce the heat to 180°C and bake for another 30 minutes. Serve with mashed potatoes.

The fact the horse supplier was one-armed was a warning sign. John cracked his wrist falling from a pony and went on to die miserably, far from the moors and under anesthetic in the bedroom of a house Peggy had taken on Woburn Square, Bloomsbury. One wise expert on astral projection warned from his sofa that it was a very bad idea that John go under anesthetic, as he might very well feel inclined to leave his body behind. Did anyone listen? No. Regretfully, that is exactly what happened. And that was with an anesthetist who worked for the king. But before one imagines the Peggy-John relationship was perfect, John, in a jealous rage, once dashed whiskey into Peggy's eyes and made her stand naked before an open window in cold December weather. Mercifully, the residents of Bloomsbury were fast asleep. Peggy's various lovers also seemed to think it their right to punish her for her enormous wealth, while she generously handed over houses to them, post-relationship, and financed their artistic ventures.

Her next lover, publisher and poet Douglas Garman, was more enthralled by Communism than by Peggy. She became increasingly isolated as Douglas beetled about England in his car, giving lectures on Marx and Lenin. All manner of harried Communist comrades hurried their way toward the couple's home, Yew Tree Cottage. It didn't matter what they were like as long as they were working class— God-like in Douglas's eyes. Even Stalin was forgiven for the Moscow purges. Yew Tree Cottage was an ancient Elizabethan "cottage" (it had four bedrooms!) on the South Downs. Peggy was despondent, as they only had Kitty, the fiancée of their gardener, Jack, to cook for them, and Kitty's cooking repertoire was limited to roast pheasant and Yorkshire pudding—without salt and pepper. While most of us would get on very cheerfully with this diet, adding our own salt—and perhaps leading shorter lives—Peggy had other ideas. Who better to retrain Kitty, she decided, than John Holms's old friend Wahab? (She doesn't tell us anything else about him in her memoirs, as if she expects us to understand the reference.) Peggy summoned Wahab to teach her and Kitty for a week, and they tried out all sorts of food experiments on Douglas. From Yew Tree Cottage's kitchen came bursts of steaming coq au vin, Spanish omelets, chicken in a sherry sauce, cocksure onion soups, paellas, and boeuf en daubes. One visitor said, "Food, you never quite knew. The standard of cooking was not high. You might get a marvellous Château Haut-Brion and the next time something ghastly." And, typical of Peggy, "the fare at her dinner table was generally Spartan, and all during the meal she would monitor just how much was being eaten; if a guest did not finish his portion, Peggy would dash over and scrape it right back into the serving bowl, excusing herself with, 'It's too good to waste.'"

Paella

INGREDIENTS

6 cups strong homemade chicken stock
¾ tsp. saffron
1 onion, halved
½ cup olive oil
2 portioned 3 lb. rabbits
Sea salt
2 onions, finely chopped
¼ lb. raw chorizo, cut into chunks
¼ lb. ham, cut into chunks
6 scallions, finely chopped
4 cloves of garlic, crushed

3 pimientos (bottled are fine), diced
1 lb. small, raw shrimp
8 large shrimp, shells intact
3 cups short-grain Valencian rice
3 bay leaves, crushed
6 tbsp. flat-leaf parsley, finely chopped
¾ cup fresh peas
½ cup dry white wine
1 tbsp. freshly squeezed lemon juice
16 tiny clams, cleaned
16 tiny mussels, cleaned

TO GARNISH . . .

3 tbsp. flat-leaf parsley, finely chopped   3 lemons, cut into wedges

METHOD

Preheat the oven to 170°C. In a saucepan, warm the chicken stock with the peeled, halved onion and the saffron strands. Cover and allow to simmer for 20 minutes. Then remove from the heat, take out the onion, and measure out the 5½ cups of saffron-infused chicken stock you will need for the paella. In a large paella pan, heat the olive oil. Add the pieces of rabbit and fry over a high heat until they are golden. Remove, transfer to a warmed plate, and sprinkle with a

Paella (*continued*)

little sea salt. Now fry the chopped onion, chorizo, and ham in the oil for 10 minutes. Add the scallions, garlic, and pimentos and sauté for 3 minutes. Now sauté the large shrimp for 3 minutes until it turns slightly pink; after 2 minutes, add the small shrimp. Remove from the pan and put onto the plate with the rabbit. Heat the chicken stock in a saucepan—bring to a boil. Now add the Valencian rice to the pan. Stir thoroughly, coating each grain of rice with oil. Add the bay leaves and chopped parsley.

Pour the boiling chicken stock into the rice and then add the peas, wine, and lemon juice. Raise the heat beneath the paella pan so that the stock and rice bubble. Simmer, uncovered, and stirring every so often for 10 minutes. Take the rabbit and shrimp and push them into the rice; next add the clams and mussels. Drape the large, shell-on shrimp over the surface of the paella. Take the paella dish and place it uncovered in the oven for 20 minutes. Finally, remove from the oven. Cover it in aluminum foil and leave for 10 minutes.

To serve, pour whichever surrealists you have handy a large glass of ice-cold wine each and decorate the paella with parsley and lemon wedges.

Ever after, Peggy collected recipes for Kitty on her travels. Douglas, though, discarded Peggy, having fallen in love with a very pretty proletariat comrade called Jessie "Paddy" Ayriss. Defeated, Peggy ruefully conceded her rival had a very attractive "tip-tilted nose." The aestheticism of Jessie's nose must have hurt Peggy to the quick. Peggy had been nicknamed "Dog Nose" by John Holms—Jimmy Ernst, son of Max Ernst, brilliantly describes Peggy in his memoirs: "All the features of that face seemed to be intent on wanting to draw attention away from an unnaturally bulbous nose."

Just as she was planning to open the Guggenheim Jeune gallery in London in 1938, on one of her quick buying trips in Paris, Peggy bumped into the blue-eyed young playwright Samuel Beckett over dinner at James Joyce's house. Peggy and Beckett spent twelve days rolling around in bed, drinking limitless amounts of champagne between kisses. Thankfully, during this time Beckett did not stamp on her or rub jam in her hair. He said nothing about her nose. Beckett was an acolyte of James Joyce, and when he and Peggy went to a dinner party for Joyce's fifty-sixth birthday, at Beckett's urging, Peggy managed to hunt down and procure Joyce's favorite Swiss wine—the effects of this inspired Joyce to dance a private jig (to the delight of Joyce's devoted Paris circle). Beckett, however, was rather an idle lover, despite all the promise of the athletic twelve-day stint. He shirked commitment, telling Peggy a lurid tale of still being haunted and stifled by terrible early memories of occupying his mother's womb. When she asked him what his plans were for the two of them, he sulkily replied, "Nothing," and things went from bad to worse. Helen Joyce unhelpfully suggested that Peggy "rape" Beckett, and when she lunged at him, Beckett ran away from her into the night. This was one of a series of unsuccessful sexual overtures—Beckett hopped out of bed as soon as Peggy hopped in. Undefeated in her quest for love, Peggy spent several uncomfy nights with English surrealist painter Roland Penrose, who liked to lock her into a pair of chained ivory cuffs for sex. All well and good, but then he *insisted* she stay trussed this way if she was to sleep the night by his side.

Surrealists were an argumentative lot, crossing the street to avoid saying hello, giving their rivals dark stares. Peggy, however, as a buyer of surrealist art, generally received a warm welcome at any surrealist table. Intriguingly, in her memoirs she mentions that the British sculptor Henry Moore's wife, Irina, made delicious food (Irina knew good food when she got it—she was abandoned by her mother in Kiev when she was six and grew up eating from dustbins) and that scrumptious vegetarian food was always on offer at the table of the founder of cubism, Albert Gleizes—but that the Gleizeses liked to eat at very odd times, so delicious dishes might be presented in the middle of the night.

Peggy seems to have barely known there was a war on until after the Germans had invaded Norway and were closing in on Paris. Her one thought was that she had to save the art in her keeping. She hid Klees, a Kandinsky, some Miró in packing cases in a musty barn (the Germans missed them!), and three days before the Germans took the city, she fled Paris with her Persian cats, the air filled with soot and desperation and the road to Fontainebleau jammed with cars creeping along, each with a wobbling turret of suitcases, boxes, and furniture.

Marriage to surrealist painter Max Ernst and life in the United States lay ahead. Max Ernst had been in a concentration camp for German aliens in France, and Peggy was helping him flee France; however, he was—of course—irritatingly obsessed with one Leonora Carrington. And what do you bet, she had a tip-tilted nose! Fortunately for Peggy, Leonora was slightly unhinged and tended to wander off on her own adventures. Unfortunately for Peggy, she was adept at reappearing at inconvenient moments, setting a torch to Max Ernst's barely subdued love. What, then, was Peggy's allure when compared to the fascinating Leonora? In short, money, a safe passage out of France, and a substantial network of contacts in the United States.

The glamour of money that cocooned Peggy became apparent to Max's son, Jimmy Ernst, when he first entered the Guggenheim circle. Max was briefly incarcerated on Ellis Island when he came to the United States packed among Peggy's many bags. When Max's release was imminent, Peggy and Jimmy had a sumptuous celebratory dinner in New York. Jimmy realized the first of the many hazy surreal moments he was to have in the Guggenheim entourage when Peggy asked him to cross the restaurant and thank two men for helping her so kindly the day before when Max's hearing was held on Ellis Island. Jimmy, not long past twenty, weaved across to their table and sweatily conveyed Peggy's thanks. The two men denied any knowledge of the whole thing. They'd never even met Peggy.

"Waddaya talkin' about, kid?"

"Ellis island? Ya crazy or sump'n? . . . me and Sam wuz at de track all day yestiggy."

Bewildered for the first time but certainly not for the last, Jimmy returned to his table, where he and Peggy dined on cheese blintzes followed by a gooey, majestic black cherry cheesecake, which, Jimmy recalled, "came floating toward me like the castle in the Wizard of Oz." This Guggenheim feast was too potent and Jimmy had to dash to the toilet, the waiter telling him, "Turlette's over there, kid."

Ellis Island Cheese Blintzes

FOR THE BLINIS . . .

1 cup all-purpose flour	4 tbsp. melted butter
A pinch or two of sea salt	1 cup milk
4 eggs	1 or 2 tbsp. melted butter for frying

FOR THE CHEESE FILLING . . .

6 tbsp. sour cream	½ tbsp. lemon zest
2 cups ricotta cheese	2½ tbsp. granulated sugar
A few drops of vanilla essence	

METHOD

Sieve the flour into a large bowl; add 2 pinches of sea salt. Now whisk in the eggs, butter, and milk until you have a smooth batter. Cool this in the fridge for an hour. After the hour is up, have a look at the blini batter; it should be loose. If it seems to be too thick (remember, you are aiming for a nice, thin blini), then add a little extra milk.

In the meantime, make the delicious, creamy filling. In a bowl, combine the sour cream, ricotta, vanilla, lemon, and sugar.

Over a medium-high heat, warm the skillet. Brush it with melted butter. Take about 3–4 tablespoons of batter per blini and pour it ono the skillet until it forms an even layer. Don't touch it for 3 minutes; watch it blister and take on golden tones. Now it is time to turn the blini. Flip it in the air, or use a spatula to loosed it and flip. Give the blini only about 30 seconds on the reverse and then put it on a plate. Repeat, brushing the skillet with butter each time and letting those blinis stack up.

Now assemble your blintzes: Take 1 blini, spread it out flat, and put 2 or 3 tablespoons of creamy filling in the center. Gently fold the bottom part of the blini up and over the filling, then fold the sides in. You will now have a scrumptious parcel of cheese blintz; all that remains is to fry it.

Brush some more melted butter on the skillet and fry each blintz until it is browned on both sides. Put it on a plate and eat it either straight or with a blob of cherry or apple fruit compote or apricot jam on top.

Jimmy was ensnared in the Guggenheim-Ernst circus as they trawled America looking for a home, Peggy on high alert for a state that would marry her and Max, as they were both divorced and their divorce papers were in foreign languages. They explored the Grand Canyon; popped in on somewhere terrible called Wichita Falls in Texas (apologies to all its inhabitants!), which was a mecca for cockroaches (you could hear them crunch beneath your feet at night); and wound up in New Orleans in September, where they were crushed by the news that the cocktails on offer were still at the mercy of the seasons—this seems unimaginable now. They asked for a mint julep and were told that the summer and the mint had long gone.

Finally, Peggy and Max settled back in New York, in Hale House, while Peggy hunted for a spot for her museum and her smuggled paintings. There they threw dinner parties that, according to Peggy, were golden moments: Max made scrumptious, meticulous fish soup, which she followed up with her paella. He also made great curries and loved presiding over meals perched on an ex-theatrical prop: a roomy, high-backed throne. According to guests, though, these dinner parties were a lottery. Peggy thought herself a mistress of chocolate chicken, a recipe given to her by André Breton (the founder of surrealism) when he returned from Mexico. Given that Peggy barely noticed World War II, it seems unlikely that the attention she would give to the preparation of a dish would be greater—a guest could come to dread her dishes. Beyond that, Peggy still couldn't quite bring herself to splash out financially: one bottle of waspish wine would do for six, while other artists got thumping headaches from the Canadian Golden Wedding whiskey she offered them. Post-Ernst, things got even worse. Old, curling handkerchiefs of sandwiches were passed around. Dinner might be a rock of meatloaf, with cheerless endive salad and mashed potatoes. One wit quipped this was "not exactly a catered situation."

Peggy's abortive attempt at an affair with Samuel Beckett was almost preparation for her marriage to Max. She looked for romantic messages in the books that Max gave her or lent her. Instead, she would get the dull address of "To Peggy Guggenheim from Max Ernst," made all the more painful by the many books she'd seen inscribed passionately to Leonora. Max painted her stomach (she recognized it outright) onto a figure with two heads, and when she once, full of gratitude, thanked him for painting her face as a child, he later painted it out. Max's exhausted son, Jimmy, was privy to both their hearts, consoling Peggy when they argued and hunting Max down for her while providing alibis for Max's ever more regular "treasure hunts" about town for luscious young women. Max had lost interest in Peggy, as he had with all his previous wives (wife number two used to snuggle up next to the radiator and eat apples to stave off hunger pangs while Max dined with eligible, rich young ladies). Predictably, Peggy lost Max. He ran off with a Miss Dorothea Tanning, a skilled artist in her own right—but neither history nor Peggy make any mention of whether Miss Tanning had a tip-tilted nose.

Fortunately, the future proved kinder when Peggy finally settled, alone, in her beloved Venice and visitors turned up, like the wonderful, maverick writer Truman Capote (forever in carpet slippers), who made her laugh and eat fish every night in Harry's Bar. Writer John Brinnin recalled visiting Peggy with Truman one evening. Fresh from the ballet *Romeo and Juliet* and in company with the bright-faced dancers, their gondola slid up to the grassy edge of the Palazzo Venier dei Leoni. Peggy was waiting in her garden. She had never met either writer before but knew the other men. After dinner together, Brinnin discovered Truman sitting in Peggy's lap; the two began to fox-trot with slow, drunken grace. When Peggy waved goodbye that night, Truman said, "Poor dear. She's frightened of almost everything. I rather liked her. Didn't you?" When Truman holed up in Taormina, Sicily, to work on *The Glass Harp*, Peggy appeared and is described with beautifully unkind acidity by Pearl Kazin Bell, who was also trying to concentrate on her writing: "She really was an impossible woman with a kind of rich, worthless quality about her that I just found very disconcerting." Not only that, but "Peggy Guggenheim was just gallivanting around. She made it difficult for us to sit down and work because she talked incessantly. She also fancied herself a very great cook; so she would cook up things like chicken mole, which is chicken with chocolate sauce. It's apparently a great Mexican spicy dish, but I found it inedible, or maybe that was just the way she cooked it."

Despite the age difference, Peggy had in a way met her ideal man. Truman adored the way she rattled her false teeth, didn't give a damn about the quality of her chocolate chicken, and fantasized about marrying her, deliberately ignoring the fact that he was gay, but then Peggy would probably have found that no impediment. They drank stiff, dry martinis together and bobbed about the canals on Peggy's personal gondola with her gondolier, liveried in pearly white, an aquamarine sash about his chest. Later, when she reminisced with John Brinnin about her first evening with Truman Capote, he reminded her, "You and Truman were the only ones who seemed to know what a fox-trot was."

"All dead and gone," she sighed. "No one knows what *fun* is anymore."

Chocolate Chicken for Those Who Never Give Up

FOR THE CHIPOTLE PASTE . . .

1¼ cups water
⅓ cup muscovado sugar
2 tsp. blackstrap molasses
Sunflower oil

8 dried chipotle chilies
3 cloves of garlic, crushed
A pinch of sea salt

FOR THE MOLE . . .

3 ancho chilies
2 tbsp. olive oil
8 on-the-bone chicken thighs,
   stripped of their skin
3 onions, finely chopped
2 tsp. cinnamon
2 tsp. ground cumin
4 cloves of garlic

⅓ cup raisins
2 tbsp. unsweetened, crunchy
   peanut butter
2 tbsp. chipotle paste
1 lb. bottled tomatoes
1¾ cups chicken stock
2½ tbsp. dark chocolate
Juice of 1 lime

TO GARNISH . . .

1 red onion, sliced
2 limes cut into wedges

2 tbsp. finely chopped cilantro

METHOD

Begin by making the chipotle paste. In a medium-size saucepan, bring the water, muscovado sugar, and molasses to a boil. Turn the heat down to very low and, stirring, allow the sugar crystals to dissolve. Warm the sunflower oil in a skillet, and fry the garlic until it is golden. Transfer it to the sugar syrup. Turn the heat up under the skillet, and when the oil is sizzling hot, add the chipotle chilies in batches, cooking for about 1 minute per batch. Put the toasted/fried chipotles into the molasses-sugar syrup. Blitz the whole lot in a blender.

Add a little more oil to the skillet and fry the chipotle puree in this for about 15 minutes, stirring to prevent it from sticking, and letting it reduce in quantity and concentrate in flavor. Now it is ready to use. Season with sea salt.

Now you can start making the chocolate chicken. Place the ancho chilies in a bowl and cover with boiling water; leave this to soften for about 20 minutes. Get a casserole dish, place it on a medium-hot heat, and brown the chicken thighs in batches. Stack them on a plate. Now add the onion and cook it gently for about 8 minutes until it is soft and golden. Add the cinnamon and cumin and warm through for 1 minute. Taking care to reserve the chili water, drain the anchos and remove their stalks and seeds. Process the ancho chilies, garlic, and raisins in a food processor with 4 tablespoons of the chili water and the lime juice until a paste is formed. Add to the casserole dish along with the peanut paste, chipotle paste, tomatoes, and 1¾ cups of chicken stock. Place the chicken thighs in the casserole dish, cover with a lid, and cook for 1 hour. Add the grated chocolate and cook for a further 15 minutes. Now, if your name is Peggy Guggenheim, you will forget all about it and let it burn and dry out. Otherwise, sprinkle the chocolate chicken with the onion and cilantro. Serve with rice and the lime segments.

THOSE MAD, MARVELOUS MITFORDS

The famous, fabulous Mitford sisters, whose childhoods are enshrined in the novels of Nancy Mitford, managed to entangle themselves with a great deal of transatlantic history in their lives through Unity Mitford's passionate friendship with Adolf Hitler; Diana Mitford's marriage to the leader of the British Union of Fascists, Sir Oswald Mosley; and revolutionary Jessica Mitford's World War II escapades (she went on to contribute massively to the American civil rights movement).

Some of the sisters saw their British, aristocratic childhoods as stupendous; others as claustrophobic. The family rules of diet in deepest Oxfordshire meant that you never had to eat anything you didn't wish to. Brilliant: Unity ingested nothing other than mashed potatoes for two weeks. Deborah dined on bread sauce, eaten with a spoon. Their mother, Sydney Freeman-Mitford, Lady Redesdale, had strong opinions on dietary laws, so rabbits, shellfish, and anything remotely porky were the fare of the devil: only David Freeman-Mitford, Lord Redesdale, was allowed sausages and bacon, which he savored every morning, raising the sausage to an ambrosial, mythic status, a forbidden food, so much so that Tom, the only male child and the only one to receive a full formal education, wrote home from boarding school with the incredible news, "We have sossidges [*sic*] every Sunday." The girls, meanwhile, had a wild-eyed governess called Miss Pratt who showed not the slightest interest in teaching them, although she taught them the card game Racing Demon, which they played every morning for two hours.

Sydney's aversion to sausages was undermined by the squash-faced maid, Mabel, who kept a little leftover sausage aside for the children, and they danced about the kitchen with it in a porcine frolic of joy. Nanny Blor was also an excellent ally, introducing the children to the crisp seduction of brandy snaps when she took them on visits to her sister. The reason for Sydney's dietary stipulations was because her MP father noticed that Jewish children living in London looked particularly well nourished and decided to raise his children on the dietary laws as set out in the Old Testament. As her daughter Deborah Mitford, who went on to become the Duchess of Devonshire, recalled in her memoirs:

> Muv adopted these laws and we were fed accordingly. The language in which the Lord spoke to Moses is as threatening as a thunderstorm. We did not feel deprived of "eagle, ossifrage and osprey," which are an "abomination" and therefore banned from the table, but swine being "cloven-footed" but not chewers of the cud meant no bacon and the rule against eating anything without fins and scales but that lived in the water meant no shellfish. I did not taste lobster until I was eighteen.

Bovril was banned, as it was thick with preservatives. If the children wanted it, they had to buy it out of their pocket money. Tinned food was likely to be the end of you, with the peculiar exception of sardines and an odd delicacy David Freeman-Mitford favored called "glass tongue," a mystery that you could only just glimpse through the jar. Only stone-ground, whole grain wheat was to be used in bread making. Refrigerators, Sydney complained, made food too cold.

The food at the Mitford's home, perched above the muddled, pretty village at Swinbrook, Oxfordshire, was good, though. Sydney's father (the MP) had adored foreign food, so there were French influences on Sydney's table, delivered courtesy of the cook, Mrs. Stobie. Sydney had her own ideas about health. Even when three of their Guernsey cows tested positive for tuberculosis (a big killer of children), she insisted on the children drinking lots of fresh milk from the herd. When Jessica developed appendicitis, Sydney personally diagnosed it as Jessica overeating at breakfast. Jessica had to contact the doctor herself and, after this startlingly mature act, went on to sell her appendix to her little sister, who thought she was onto a fine thing until it started to smell. When a roast chicken turned up on the table, one or other of the children asked, "Is this Blackie or Whitey we're eating today?" without any loss of appetite when the chicken was identified, except perhaps for little Pamela, who had a love of animals and was nicknamed "the Woman" by the others on account of her caring nature. The Mitfords were very down-to-earth about food. When Sydney was at a posh dinner in Paris, she was explaining a special cut of pork to her neighbor and, determined to make her point clear, stood up in her shining dinner dress, slapped her thigh, and said, "Il faut le couper là"—you have to cut it *there*.

David was very particular about crumbs and stickiness. God forbid that any small person scrape their knife or spoon across their plate or bowl, he would either yawp or mutter "filthy beast" across the table. When beloved suet pudding (made with beef fat) was served and Lord Redesdale saw the familiar Tate and Lyle syrup tin, he stared, eagle-eyed, at poor Mabel to make sure she dished it up without crumbs or stickiness. The moment came for the children to pour their own syrup on the pudding; the fear and tension at the dining table was palpable (after twelve years of service, Mabel got engaged, and Lord Redesdale bellowed, "I would never have engaged you if I'd known you would leave at once"). A doer rather than a reader, David had only ever read *White Fang* until he married Sydney. She decided to educate him and read him *Tess of the D'Urbervilles*, by Thomas Hardy. When she reached the climax of Tess's death, he started crying. Sydney comforted him that it was only, after all, a story. Pushing her aside, he raged, "WHAT, do you mean to say the damn feller made it up?" Disarmingly blunt and old-fashioned, when he saw the painted red fingernails of one of his daughter Nancy's friends, he commiserated, "I am so sorry."

"Why?" she asked.

"I am so sorry to see you have been in a bus accident."

Delightfully, he mistook the ample bottom of one woman in the village of Swinbrook for a heifer calf when she was weeding her garden. As his older daughters,
Diana and Nancy, matured, various brainy, artistic, and literary young friends
turned up at the house; some he liked, and some he didn't. Either way, it was a
penance. Jessica Mitford told the story of one hapless youth, Mark, to whom Lord
Redesdale took a firm liking. In order to be even more deserving of the compliment, Mark made the brave attempt (after a rough night) to turn up for an 8 a.m.
breakfast with David. "Brains for breakfast, Mark!" thundered David. Mark had to
make a sharp exit to the bathroom.

Despite being part of the upper crust, there was a commonly held family percep-
tion that they lived very close to ruin, a misperception encouraged by David, who
decided to prospect for gold in America, and his daughter Unity, Hitler's future
confidant, was therefore usefully conceived in an outpost of gold prospecting
called Swastika and doubly blessed by having the middle name Valkyrie. Sydney,
trying to be a pioneer wife, bought a chicken, popped it in the oven, and then,
when it came to carving it, was nauseated by discovering its crop and gizzard were
packed with a last supper of corn. This then spilled into the gravy.

Although David did not strike it lucky prospecting for gold, the Mitfords still
hung on to their London residence at 26 Rutland Gate in Kensington, tugging open
its curtains for the London season. It was a great treat for the teenage Mitford girls
to be allowed to stay in a tiny flat there in the Mews with Nanny Blor. To feed
these budding aristocrats—as there was no permanent cook—Nanny Blor had to
call out of her memory great British working-class foods, which the girls adored
with all the reverence normally accorded to truffles and foie gras: there was prune
whip, tripe and onions, and bread pudding. They tasted extraordinary—of another
social class.

When the entire Mitford clan decamped to London, among the countless suitcases and hatboxes were a few loaves of Sydney's whole wheat homemade bread,
clad in white wax paper, to supply them until baking time was announced. As the
dust sheets were shaken out, the governess Miss Bunting (no doubt Miss Pratt was
lost to the gaming tables) told the girls chilling tales about white slavers who, apparently, stalked about London, a ripe territory for abducting fresh-faced young
maidens. On entering a London cinema alone, Miss Bunting claimed, a distant
acquaintance of hers was injected with morphine by a lady of grandmotherly appearance; she woke in Buenos Aires.

Although the oldest daughter, the great society beauty Diana Mitford, was to
find lasting love with the Fascist leader Oswald Mosley, she first married Bryan
Guinness. He was very impressed to hear she could fry an egg, and when he told
his mother, Lady Evelyn Guinness, of this, she said, "I've never *heard* of such a
thing. It's *too* clever." Diana married Bryan and escaped Swinbrook. Marking her

Tripe and Onions

Tripe is always sold cleaned and parboiled at the butcher's.

INGREDIENTS

1 lb. tripe	A blade of mace
2 tbsp. butter	A bay leaf
2 tbsp. all-purpose flour	Sea salt
4 onions, peeled and thinly sliced	Freshly ground black pepper
2½ cups milk	1 tbsp. fresh parsley, chopped

METHOD

Place the tripe in a saucepan; fill with water and bring to a boil. Drain and then allow the tripe to cool a little. Now rinse it under cold water and then cut into 1-inch pieces. Place the tripe, onions, milk, mace, and bay leaf back in the saucepan. Add a pinch of sea salt and some black pepper. Bring to a boil and then simmer for 2 hours, until the tripe is tender. Drain the tripe and onions, discard the mace and the bay leaf, while reserving 2½ cups of the liquid.

Melt the butter in a saucepan, remove from the heat, and stir in the flour to make a roux. Slowly add the reserved milk, incorporating it into the roux until you have a smooth, milky mix. Return the pan to the heat and, stirring constantly, bring to a boil. Add the tripe and onions to the white sauce again, adjust the seasoning, and sprinkle with parsley. You would normally eat tripe with a boiled potato or two.

Prune Whip

INGREDIENTS

1 cup prunes, pitted	½ cup granulated sugar
Juice of half a lemon	4 egg whites
1 tsp. lemon zest	

METHOD

Mash the prunes until they are smooth. Add the lemon juice, zest, and granulated sugar. In a large bowl, beat the egg whites until they are stiff and soft. Using a metal spoon, fold in the prune puree in a figure-eight pattern. Fill individual glass bowls with the whip, chill for 10 minutes, and then steel yourself!

flight, she sent her sisters delicious chocolates filled with rich, dark truffle, which seemed, to Jessica, to taste of Diana and Bryan's honeymoon. Unity (nicknamed "Boud"), meanwhile, was due to become a debutante. Standing at six foot one, she was a complicated rebel. She took her pet rat, Ratular, to dances; danced with her snake, Enid; and filched writing paper on a visit to Buckingham Palace. She could, single-handedly, crush her father; Jessica Mitford remembered. "She would sit silently stowing away quantities of mashed potatoes, her eyes fixed on Farve with a sombre, brooding glare. He would glare back, trying to make Boud drop her gaze, but she invariably won out. Crashing his fists on the table, he would roar, 'Stop looking at me, damn you!'"

Finally, it was also the turn of the youngest Mitford sister, Deborah, to come out at a debutantes' party her mother held for her at Rutland Gate. Guests feasted on kedgeree made with coral red wild salmon, followed by succulent black cherries and cream from Devon. Deborah was soon snapped up by Andrew Devonshire in 1941, at that point not yet heir to the Devonshire dukedom. Deborah's sister-in-law was Kick Kennedy, John F. Kennedy's sister, who, despite much opposition from her staunchly Catholic mother, Rose Kennedy, married Billy Devonshire, the Protestant heir to the dukedom. Tragically, Billy was killed in 1944, and Kick, left widowed at only twenty-four and still so much in love with him, was heartbroken (poor Kick was killed in a plane crash in 1948, while young Tom Mitford—of the "sossidges" fame—was killed in Burma in 1945). According to the laws of primogeniture, Billy's death made Andrew heir to the dukedom. Deborah's father-in-law, the Duke of Devonshire, was cut from the same cloth as Lord Redesdale. A lover of fly-fishing, the duke would gallantly beg feathers from the plumage worn by lovely ladies at balls and then, whenever picking up a fly to skewer a maggot onto, would whisper romantically something like "Delia Curzon, 1919." In order to test the lure of the flies, he lay submerged in the bath pretending to be a salmon while his butler trailed the lures over the bath's surface, the duke's eyes following him from the watery depths. Deborah and Andrew went on to manage the magnificent Chatsworth Estate and were visited by such luminaries as Wallis Simpson and the redoubtable Margaret Thatcher, of whom Deborah recalled, "When Mrs Thatcher left, as tidy as when she arrived, I gave her half a dozen of my best dark brown Welsummer eggs as a thank-you. She looked rather surprised and I wondered if she threw them out of the car window."

Unity, politicized by Diana's married lover, Sir Oswald Mosley (Diana had left Guinness, but Oswald remained married until his wife's death), joined the National Union of Fascists. Unity always loved being different, striking a radical pose, and what better way than by wearing the uniform of the Fascists—a black shirt—much to the surprise of the humble residents of the village of Swinbrook, to whom she insisted on issuing a Fascist salute when visiting the post office or dropping in on the grocer's. The postmistress didn't know what to make of it. Unity and her younger sister, Jessica, shared a bedroom and sparred with each other over politics: Jessica vowed she was a Communist and subscribed to the *Daily Worker*. To Jessica's contempt, Unity went with Diana to Germany in 1933. Diana had been lured to Germany by Hitler's then foreign press secretary, the tall, gangly, and charming Ernst "Putzi" Hanfstaengl, by the promise that he'd introduce her to the dynamic new chancellor. Putzi was to rue the day he ever met Unity. She later denounced him to Hitler, and Putzi was flown around over Germany in a small light aircraft by Hitler's henchmen, convinced they were about to throw him, wriggling, from the plane—Hitler's idea of a practical joke. In his memoirs, *The Missing Years*, Putzi vividly recalled his heart sinking when he clapped eyes on the sisters in Munich: "They were very attractive but made-up to the eyebrows in a manner that conflicted directly with the newly proclaimed Nazi idea of German womanhood. Their set purpose was to meet Hitler, and on the way to the Deutscher Hof Hotel, where he was staying, there were so many frank comments from passers-by that I had to duck behind a building with them." Exasperated, Putzi pulled out his large and very clean handkerchief and said, "My dears, it is no good, but to stand any hope of meeting him you will have to wipe some of that stuff from your faces." Meekly, the girls did so, but this didn't stop Joseph Goebbels and Hermann Goering from mocking Putzi for bringing "such painted hussies" to Hitler's hotel rooms. One can't help but wonder if the Mitfords would have been quite as enamored of Hitler had they known that he habitually picked his teeth and liked to sit soaking his yellowing feet in a footbath while Eva Braun read him tales of Alexander the Great—hardly a romantic hero.

The sisters had to settle for catching sight of Hitler at the 1934 Nuremberg Rally to celebrate the Year of Power (also called the Year of Unity—and it was to be her year!). For Unity, this proved too tantalizing: she had to meet him face-to-face. And the best way to do this, Unity divined, was by stalking him through his favorite tea parlors and restaurants.

Hitler himself claimed, "What I like best is to dine with a pretty woman. And rather than be left at home by myself, I'd go and dine at the Osteria." Cue Unity Mitford. She traveled to Munich again, booked a course of German lessons, and followed her plan of restaurant stalking for over a year. Friends in Munich knew of Unity's quest, acting as spies for her, watching places like the elegant, palm-lined Carlton tearooms for a glimpse of the chancellor. Albert Speer, Hitler's architect, recalled, "[Hitler] frequently visited Carlton's Tearooms, a bogus luxurious place with reproduction furniture and fake crystal chandeliers. He liked it because the people there left him undisturbed, did not bother him with applause or requests for autographs, as was generally the case elsewhere in Munich." Finally, in 1934, seventeen-year-old Derek Hill, a young artist and friend of Unity's, while having tea with his mother and aunt (who had also planted themselves there on the lookout for Hitler; Derek had heard he liked the Carlton on Monday evenings at about six), spotted Hitler marching into the swanky tearooms with Goebbels at his heels. Derek dashed to the phone and alerted Unity, who threw herself into a taxi and was seated by the Hills in the blink of an eye. She was too nervous to drink the hot chocolate she ordered; her hands shaking, she offered it to Derek to hold. Writing passionately to Diana of the event, Unity confides, "At about six last night Derek rang me up from the Carlton Teeraum & said He was there. . . . The aunt said 'You're trembling all over with excitement,' and sure enough I was, so much so that Derek had to drink my chocolate for me because I couldn't hold the cup. He [Hitler] sat there for 1½ hours. . . . When he went he gave me a special salute all to myself." Goodness knows what Mrs. Hill and her sister thought of all this, or perhaps they, too, were awed by Hitler—as they departed, these two misguided Scotswomen tried to give him a wavering Nazi salute. After Hitler had left, no doubt sweet-toothed Unity went back to her cooled hot chocolate or perhaps a celebratory slice of chocolate cake with rippled Schlagobers (whipped cream), sighing as she took her fork to it, "Noch ein Pfund"—meaning, in Unity's pidgin German, "Another pound . . ."

Unity scanned the papers daily for Hitler's appointments and appearances. Engaged in conversation with the sentries at the Brown House—the National Socialist Party's headquarters in Germany—through German contacts (namely, her hairdresser), Unity struck gold, discovering that Hitler very much liked to eat lunch at a restaurant called the Osteria Bavaria (its Bavarian owner, Herr Deutelmoser, had opened it in 1890). It was near the Brown House. He was most often there on Fridays, his black Mercedes drawing up outside. Osteria Bavaria was small and private. On entering, there was a recess to the right with a thick, long curtain that could be drawn across it. Hitler often chose to eat there, among the dark paneled walls, the curtain drawn, a small circle about him—his alcove table seated between eight and ten. Like guard dogs, black-clad SS guards sat on benches. Unity wasted no time. She turned up at 2:30 daily with a book, had a light lunch, and then put in the hours until 5 p.m. in the hope of seeing Hitler. She even took her father, Lord Redesdale, there for a sighting. In a bid to make eye contact with Hitler, Unity perched at a small table near the entrance every day, her coffee growing cold. He could be spotted, still wearing his brown mackintosh, among the tables, eating a plate of oven-baked cauliflower cheese or taking a forkful of Linzertorte or walnut cake, in the company of close associates like Albert Speer, his personal aide Julius Schaub, and his heavy-drinking court jester, the photographer Heinrich Hoffman. Most often Hitler would order ravioli, believing "Roman" food to be manly and invigorating. Albert Speers recalled that Hitler gave Herr Deutelmoser and his two waitresses a merry greeting: "'What's good today? Ravioli? If only you didn't make it so delicious. It's too tempting!' Hitler snapped his fingers: 'Everything would be perfect in your place, Herr Deutelmoser, if I did not have to think of my waistline. You forget that the Fuehrer cannot eat whatever he would like to.' Then he would study the menu for a long time and order ravioli."

Cauliflower Cheese

INGREDIENTS

A whole cauliflower, separated into
   medium-size florets, retain a
   few leaves
1 tbsp. butter
1 tbsp. all-purpose flour

1½ cups milk
1 tsp. Dijon mustard
Sea salt
Black pepper
1 cup freshly grated Parmesan cheese

METHOD

Preheat the oven to 180°C. In a small saucepan, melt the butter, then remove from the heat and stir in the flour to make a roux. Slowly add the milk, incorporating it into the roux until you have a smooth, milky mix. Add the Dijon mustard. Heat a shallow frying pan with a small amount of olive oil. Add the cauliflower florets and leaves and cover to allow them to steam. Turn down the heat and let the white sauce cook for 5 minutes. Test the cauliflower with a fork; as soon as it is tender enough for the fork to pierce it easily, remove the cauliflower from the frying pan, drain briefly in a colander, and then assemble it in a snug baking dish. Now add three-quarters of the Parmesan to the white sauce, stirring to incorporate the cheese. Salt and pepper to taste. Pour the cheesy sauce over the cauliflower, sprinkle the top with Parmesan, and then bake in the oven for 5 minutes or until the cauliflower cheese is golden on top.

Walnut Cake

INGREDIENTS

1 tbsp. espresso coffee
1 cup walnut halves
½ cup butter, very soft
¾ cup demerara sugar
2 eggs, beaten

1 generous cup all-purpose flour
1½ tsp. baking powder
Pinch of sea salt
A little milk, if necessary

METHOD

Preheat the oven to 180°C, and butter a cake tin. In a dry frying pan, toast the walnut pieces until they are a darker gold. Reserve. Cream together the butter and demerara sugar until this mixture is light and fluffed. Now add the beaten eggs, very gradually whisking them in. Sieve the flour, baking powder, and sea salt onto the egg/butter/sugar fluff and then fold together using a metal spoon. Now do the same with the coffee and toasted walnuts. You should have a batter with a dropping consistency (if you lift up your spoon, the batter will form a thick, gloopy drop that pauses for a moment and then falls). Fill the buttered tin with the cake batter. Bake in the oven for 25 minutes; check if it is ready with a skewer. Cool for ten minutes in the tin and then remove to a wire rack to cool completely.

Cheese Ravioli

INGREDIENTS

1 ½ cups Italian doppio zero flour
½ cup semolina flour
1 tsp. sea salt

2 eggs, beaten (plus 1 beaten egg
  in reserve)

FOR THE FILLING . . .

1 cup fresh ricotta
½ cup creamy goat's cheese
¾ cup Parmesan, freshly grated
2 tsp. grated onion

A generous pinch of nutmeg
3 egg yolks, plus 1 egg, beaten,
  to seal the ravioli edges

TO DRESS THE RAVIOLI . . .

6 tbsp. butter
18 fresh sage leaves
Sea salt

Freshly ground black pepper
A handful of freshly grated Parmesan

METHOD

First make your filling a couple of hours beforehand. In a bowl, combine the ricotta, goat's cheese, Parmesan, grated onion, nutmeg, and egg yolks. Cover and put in the fridge for a few hours.

After this, begin to make the ravioli. Sift the two flours and the salt together in a large, roomy mixing bowl. Make a well in the center and pour in the beaten eggs. Using your fingertips, incorporate the eggs, bringing the flour in until the dough forms a ball that is smooth and still slightly sticky. Add a little extra of your beaten egg reserve if necessary. Continue to knead the dough for 10 minutes; it should now be elastic and rubbery. Divide the ball in two and wrap each in plastic wrap (no, they wouldn't have had this in the Osteria!), and let them rest in the fridge for 1 hour; don't let it dry out.

Set up your pasta machine. Flour a work surface. Take the first lump of pasta (keep the other moist under a damp tea towel) and, using a rolling pin, roll out the pasta until it is about 1 centimeter thick. Now process the dough through the pasta machine at the widest setting; fold and then repeat this process. Now move through each setting twice, until the pasta dough is thin, elastic, and silky. When it gets too long, divide it and continue. If the dough is sticking too much, simply dust with a little flour. Your aim is to end up with several roughly rectangular sheets of pasta that are about 4 inches wide and 12 inches long (and it is fine if you have two of these!).

Flour a tray for your completed ravioli. Make sure the work surface is well floured and lay your sheets of pasta down on this. Don't flour the top of the ravioli dough, as its stickiness will help to seal the ravioli. Get the ravioli filling out of the fridge and, using 2 teaspoons or a piping bag, place small, teaspoon-size heaps of the filling on the ravioli dough sheet; allow for a 1-inch space between each

Cheese Ravioli (*continued*)

ravioli mound, and aim to place these little mounds slightly off center. Brush the beaten egg wash on the edges of the dough and between the mounds of filling.

Now carefully fold over the sheet of dough until the edges meet. Using your fingertips, gently press down on the edges of the dough, working out any air that is trapped. Press firmly on the points where there is no filling but only dough. No air should remain caught between the two layers of dough. Employ either a ravioli-cutting shape or a pastry wheel to cut out each ravioli. Place the ravioli one by one in a single layer on the preprepared floured tray.

Make the butter and sage dressing for the ravioli. In a frying pan, heat the butter until it bubbles, and then add the sage leaves. The butter must not burn, just turn light brown, and the sage leaves should just be slightly crispy. Salt and pepper.

Fill a pan with boiling salted water and cook the ravioli for 2 minutes. Remove them in small groups as fast as you can with a slotted spoon—pouring them into a colander will just break up the ravioli. Serve 4–6 ravioli on a warmed plate, and spoon sage and butter dressing over them. Finish with a sprinkle of Parmesan and some black pepper.

Finally, on February 9, 1935, some eight months after the Carlton tearooms incident, Hitler made contact with Unity. Hitler couldn't have failed to notice the determined presence of the tall, fierce young woman who stared at him every week, and he had discovered, through Herr Deutelmoser, that she was an English aristocrat who was allied to his cause. Delighted, he invited her to join his table. Unity and Hitler got on like a house on fire. Hitler called her "Kind," for child, while she called him "Wolf." Unity had a deep crush on Hitler. She wrote after one meal in the Osteria, "The Fuhrer was *heavenly*, in his best mood & very gay. There was a choice of two soups & he tossed a coin to see which one he would have, & he was *so* sweet doing it." An unlikely image indeed. Unity's inherent brutality and sexual longing made her very pliable. Lunches became suppers and shared teas. Unity loved popping into his flat in the Prinzregentenstrasse and cooed, "The greatest moment in my life was sitting at Hitler's feet and having him stroke my hair." His flat had flowers everywhere, and to please his guests, the Fuhrer ordered cream cakes, which he'd insist you eat, quelling his appetite with only a smidgen of knackebrod (rye crispbread). Unity lived for him, waiting in every day until 2 p.m. to see if he would call and invite her to lunch, followed either by a dulling, lonesome anticlimax or by the joy of dressing up.

In-jokes developed between the pair; they set each other off giggling. She delighted in his Fascism, his anti-Semitism, sniggered over dreadful cruelties. Always up for Jew bashing, Unity shamelessly and sadistically shouted with glee at the idea of starving Jews being forced to eat grass. Hitler found her a flat to live in, one requisitioned from Jews post-Kristallnacht. The erstwhile owners sobbed while Unity inspected their curtains. Unity, grotesquely romantic, used crimson ink to record her encounters with Hitler in her diary: these entries number 140 over five years. Without a doubt, Unity was in love. When a friend asked Diana, "What does Unity do when she doesn't see Hitler?" Diana replied, "She thinks of him." Eva Braun, who worked as a photographic assistant for Heinrich Hoffman, recalled wearily in her diary, "Herr Hoffmann lovingly and tactlessly informs me that he [Hitler] has found a replacement for me. She is known as Walküre and looks the part. But these are the dimensions he prefers. If it is true, though, he will soon make her lose thirty pounds, through worry, unless she has a gift for growing fat in adversity."

Unity sought to introduce Hitler to all the other Mitfords she could lure over to Germany; Diana visited frequently (Hitler came to her wedding to Oswald Mosley, who was finally wife free). Hitler couldn't speak English, but that didn't stop Lady Sydney Redesdale from holding forth for some time, in cut-glass English, on the dietary virtues of homemade whole wheat bread. Unity, blushing, had to translate every word. She later tried to force Sydney to salute Hitler, but that was a step too far for Sydney. Her sister Pam was also a less than satisfactory acolyte—she thought Hitler was like a "farmer in his old khaki suit" and forgot everything he said to her but remembered, according to biographer Mary Lovell, "every detail of the food they ate," particularly some excellent new potatoes. Jessica, meanwhile, secretly planned to go with Unity to meet Hitler. Then, she decided, she would pull out a gun and shoot him. It was to Jessica's everlasting regret that she did not assassinate Hitler over lunch.

Unity was woefully indiscreet, passing on information about the British position and foreign policy, their armed capabilities on land, air, and sea. The British Secret Service got wind of her carelessness but realized that Unity was so open that this could also work in their favor. Meanwhile, Hitler's table companions were rather shocked by Unity's inclusion. She not only listened to Hitler but also had the temerity to challenge and debate with him. Beyond that, she was privy to discussion about the Third Reich's policy and politics. For instance, Diana and Unity were at a hair-raising meal with Hitler during one crisis in the Spanish Civil War. Goebbels and Goring kept exploding into the room with urgent missives, and the sisters, idly, had to wait for their meal, listening to each fresh development. That her presence was treasonous never dawned on Unity. Britain and Germany were brothers-in-arms, she was sure; any war was untenable. Again, Albert Speer recalled, "Lady Mitford . . . even in the later years of international tension persistently spoke up for her country and often actually pleaded with Hitler to make a deal with England."

While Diana and Unity were at Hitler's side, egging on Fascist General Franco in the Spanish Civil War, their sister Jessica was busy running away with Esmond Romilly, her husband-to-be, to join Franco's enemies, the left-wing Republicans. Jessica went missing. Perhaps thanks to Miss Bunting's tales of white slavers, David Mitford decided Jessica had been ensnared by them. Then again, he conceded, she *might* have joined a Communist cell. In comparison to the notion that Jessica might have married one of the notorious, ne'er-do-well Romilly family, white slavers and Communists seemed a bit of a letdown, but bearable, to David. Esmond Romilly was Winston Churchill's nephew; nevertheless, he came from a queer lot: his mother, Nellie, was a terrible gambler who kept a vast carpetbag stuffed full of mysterious items. "With this bag," she explained, "I could leave for Peru tomorrow." It seems never to have occurred to anyone to ask what could necessitate such a departure or such a destination, but it was probably to do with gambling in Dieppe, France. Esmond and his brother ran wild. They drained the leftovers of adults' cocktails and precociously knew far too much about blackjack and roulette. Esmond ran away from the famous British public school Wellington College on account, perhaps, of one master (teacher) who used to pinch his nose "between an enormous pair of wooden compasses." Fifteen-year-old Esmond sported Muscovite "Red" views and a black Homberg when he visited the Churchills at Chartwell, coolly puffing on a Craven "A" cigarette. He was an out-and-out black sheep, having already cycled to Marseilles to join the International Brigade and fight Franco. Hs companions were killed in Spain, and Esmond, aged only about seventeen, was sent back home with dysentery.

Jessica, plowing a lonely revolutionary furrow in sleepy Swinbrook, had followed the mysterious and magnificent Esmond's adventures with admiration. She could hardly contain her joy when it turned out that this dangerous character might be at her willowy cousin Dorothy Allhusen's weekend party at Havering House (incidentally, Dorothy penned several cookbooks, including one called *Unusual Savouries*). It was while the assembled company was busily eating savories of hot stuffed mushrooms and tiny chicken livers wrapped in bacon that Jessica heard Esmond was on his way. Her future had landed on the doorstep!

Jessica almost fainted with delight.

More than anything, she wanted Esmond to help her get to Spain. In her memoirs, Jessica recounts their conversation:

> "Esmond, are you planning to go back to Spain?" I asked.
> "Yes. I think I'll be leaving again in a week or two."
> "Well—I was wondering if you could possibly take me with you."

Covertly, he agreed. They continued dinner, Esmond joking with Dorothy, the hostess, about the likelihood of his surviving the pudding.

Revolutionary Hot Stuffed Mushrooms

INGREDIENTS

8 medium-size portabello mushrooms
1 cup freshly made brown
   breadcrumbs
2 cloves of garlic, minced
1 shallot, minced
2 tbsp. freshly grated Parmesan
   cheese

1 tsp. fresh thyme leaves
½ tsp. fresh rosemary, minced
1 egg, beaten
Freshly ground black pepper
Sea salt
2 tbsp. olive oil

METHOD

Preheat the oven to 180°C, and lightly grease a baking tray. Clean the mushrooms and remove the stalk from the center of each mushroom. In a bowl, combine the breadcrumbs, garlic, shallot, Parmesan, thyme, rosemary, and beaten egg. Season with black pepper and sea salt. Using a spoon and your fingers, build a mound of stuffing to fill each mushroom. Drizzle with olive oil, and bake in the oven for 8–10 minutes.

A shared breakfast of sausages and eggs the next morning enabled the two to set out their cunning plans. Since realizing in childhood that she had the "misfortune" to be born into the aristocratic Mitford family, Jessica had been saving money in a "running away" fund, and now was the time to use it. She forged a letter from some twins the family knew, asking her to vacation with them in Dieppe. The escape was set.

First, Esmond and Jessica had to get to Spain. From France, they boarded a ship, *Urbi*, which was to take them to Bilbao, Spain, inching its way past Franco's armed submarines. Some dozen chickens were their companions on board the *Urbi*, looking rather seasick and bedraggled. The Spanish captain, who spoke no English, nevertheless invited the couple to join him and his fifteen-man crew for the evening meal. The sense of camaraderie was high on board the *Urbi* that night. The grinning crew toasted the engaged couple over the thin red wine. Enormous Spanish brandies appeared, and despite the language difficulties, the crew and the couple all yelled "Death to the Fascistas!" together over the befuddling brandy, the rich Basque soup, stewed beef, chicken, écrevisses, fruit, and cake. To Jessica, every sip and gulp tasted of revolution.

"DEATH TO THE FASCISTAS!" DINNER

Basque Soup

INGREDIENTS

3 tbsp. olive oil
8 cloves of garlic, peeled
8 slices of stale, Spanish-style bread, about ½ cm thick
8 cups rich homemade chicken stock
1 bay leaf

3 tbsp. dry Spanish sherry
3 eggs
2 tbsp. heavy cream
2 tbsp. flat-leaf parsley, finely chopped
Freshly ground black pepper

METHOD

Preheat a baking tray in the oven at 50°C. Warm the olive oil in a frying pan and gently sauté the garlic cloves until they are golden and soft. Remove, crush them lightly, and keep to the side. Now fry the bread, probably 3 or 4 slices at a time, until they are golden and crunchy. Keep them warm on the baking tray in the oven. Pour the strained chicken stock into a saucepan and add the lightly crushed garlic. Add the bay leaf and the sherry. Simmer for an hour.

In a large bowl, whisk the eggs thoroughly to incorporate as much air as possible. Add the cream. Now raise the heat of the soup so that it is bubbling away. Beat the boiling soup into the eggs and cream.

Put a piece of fried bread in each soup bowl and pour the hot soup in so that the bread is half submerged in the soup. Sprinkle with parsley and consume.

Beef Stew

INGREDIENTS

2 tbsp. olive oil
2 large onions, chopped
Head of garlic, separated and peeled
2 lb. stewing beef, cut into 2 in. chunks
1 tbsp. flour

1 cup dry white wine
1 tbsp. minced parsley
1 bay leaf
¼ tsp. fresh thyme
2 cloves
Freshly ground black pepper
Sea salt

METHOD

Warm the olive oil in a deep, heavy-bottomed pan. Gently cook the onions and garlic until they are soft and golden. Add the flour and mix it in. Now add the beef and brown it. Pour on the wine and add the parsley, bay leaf, thyme, cloves, black pepper, and a generous pinch of sea salt. Cover, turn to a low-to-moderate heat, and cook for 2 hours.

Eat with roast potatoes and chestnuts.

Écrevisses

INGREDIENTS

4 tbsp. olive oil
2 tbsp. butter
¾ lb. écrevisses, shell on
4 cloves of garlic, sliced
2 tbsp. freshly squeezed lemon juice
3 tbsp. dry sherry

1 tsp. paprika
1 tsp. dried red chili
Sea salt
Freshly ground pepper
1½ tbsp. flat-leaf parsley, finely
chopped

METHOD

In a bowl, mix together the lemon juice, sherry, paprika, chili, salt, and black pepper. Keep to the side. Next, in a frying pan, heat the olive oil and butter until they are bubbling. Add the écrevisses and garlic and flash fry for 3 minutes, constantly moving them around. The écrevisses will go from translucent to pink. Immediately add the lemon juice, sherry, paprika, chili, salt, and black pepper; these will bubble and hiss. Serve immediately and sprinkle with parsley.

News of the elopement broke. Jessica's old friend Nanny Blor fretted that Jessica didn't have suitable clothes to fight the Fascists in. Unity told Hitler, "My sister has run away to Spain with the reds." Hitler clasped his face with both hands: "Armes kind!" (poor child) he moaned. Newspaper headlines blared out "Jessica Mitford Feared Lost in Pyrenees!" False "friends" popped up in London to be interviewed by reporters, claiming the posh couple had had a farewell supper of foie gras and champagne in the West End of London.

In Bilbao, rationing was in full force; it was all garbanzo beans and rice. Thus it was that either the Mitfords or the Foreign Office set up a cunning ruse to recover Jessica: they would use her appetite against her. Jessica's novelist sister, Nancy, contacted her, saying that she and her husband, Peter, would simply like to meet and talk to Jessica. They would arrive on a British destroyer at the port of Bermeo. Jessica turned up. But there was no sign of Nancy, and Jessica felt famished after her journey. The captain of the destroyer cordially invited her aboard for lunch. Jessica recalled that he said, "'We'd really love to have you. Roast chicken, bread sauce, peas, mashed potatoes, chocolate cake, all that sort of thing you know.' He rolled the words slowly, with tantalising emphasis. 'As a matter of fact, the ship's cook really outdid himself in honour of your visit.'"

Her mouth watered; the thought of roast chicken, tender breasted with crackled, buttery skin, and the soft, sweet kindnesses of chocolate cake almost made her swoon. Faltering, she made her excuses to put a call through to Esmond, who understood the nature of temptation. "'Don't go,' said Esmond, 'It's obviously a plot, make him bring the roast chicken on shore—as a matter of fact, you might bring some of it back here for me.'"

Jessica returned to the destroyer and told the sweet captain she couldn't lunch with him—he looked terribly wounded, and so she didn't have the temerity to ask that he give her a chicken takeout. The plot had failed.

Jessica and Esmond eventually married and returned to London and a flat jammed between warehouses in the poor and run-down district of Rotherhithe, far from their stately antecedents. With an almost anthropological gaze, Jessica noticed that the poor inhabitants of Rotherhithe were shorter and paler than those of the wealthy West End. The couple were happy as larks but always short of cash. Jessica did not understand that electricity had to be paid for and so left their lights running. Someone gave her a recipe book by Marcel Boulestin, but the delicious recipes involved wads of butter, wineglasses of brandy, cream, a fresh lobster—all impossible. They settled for fish and chips.

Jessica and her older sister Diana were never to be reconciled. Jessica could never bring herself to visit Diana when she was imprisoned for Fascist activities by the British government in 1940—although Unity was very keen to visit! At first, Diana's husband, Mosley, was incarcerated in London's Brixton Prison, while Diana was in Holloway Prison, along with other Fascist women. For the very posh Diana, the quality of prison food was one of the great horrors to be faced. Instead of a plate, Diana was handed a greasy, smeared metal container, subdivided in two. The top part held potatoes, which could have done with a wash, in the embrace of straw—apparently it was once cabbage. When Diana lifted this lid, though, she discovered a swamp of some meat-based stew, with gristle emerging like the remains of a victim lost in the swamp. She decided instead to eat the pat of margarine the warder had given her—it had hints of gasoline about it but, spread on bread with some sugar, was palatable. Such torture was brief, though, as, believe it or not, Diana still had an account at Harrods and was able to continue ordering from there. Holloway's gates saw a bottle or two of Harrods' finest port sail past. Mosley, likewise a customer, sent a whole Stilton to Diana. Port and Stilton became her prison diet.

Eventually, for some two years until their release in 1943, the couple were allowed to share quarters in prison, and Mosley, calling himself "Old Sproots," established a kitchen garden, where he grew beans, eggplants, wild strawberries (a favorite of Diana's), onions, cabbages, and kohlrabi. He also built up a sizeable compost heap, which the prison authorities removed despite Diana's protests that "it [is] the breath of life to Sir Oswald!" To top it all, the couple had their prison rations delivered raw so that they could make their own meals from scratch. On one occasion, when Mosley's son, Nicholas, spent the day with them (he was an officer in the army) he smuggled in so much food that he resembled a grocer's van.

Delighted, he clanked through the prison gates with toothsome delicacies under his greatcoat: flasks of brandy and bottles of champagne; luxurious titbits from Fortnum and Mason; even a gramophone record or two. Ironically, it sounded as if Diana were more capable of executing Boulestin recipes as an imprisoned aristocrat than Jessica was as a revolutionary sharing the lives of the London poor. Diana wrote to her sister Pamela from Holloway in 1940, "The vegetables from last week are still lasting, they are heaven. I made saucisses au vin blanc today for tea." Lady Sydney brought in eggs and "some delicious brioche." Diana's furniture gave the rooms some elegance, and soon from the horned gramophone came the voice of Kirsten Flagstad singing Isolde. While Diana cooked one of her "legendary dishes," the Mosley men supped brandy. Once, when the prison governor popped in on their discussion of Nietzsche, he delightedly shared a brandy with them and, smacking his lips, declared, "Ah, you don't often see brandy like this nowadays!"

Prison-Style Saucisses au Vin Blanc

INGREDIENTS

6 Toulouse sausages, pricked
2 onions, finely sliced
1 tbsp. butter
½ tbsp. all-purpose flour

1 glass of dry white wine
1 tbsp. flat-leaf parsley, finely chopped
Black pepper
Sea salt

METHOD
Warm the butter in a frying pan. Prick the sausages, and then fry them with the onions in the pan. Once the sausages are golden, remove the pan from the heat and amalgamate the flour with the buttery sausage fat. Now add the white wine and return to the heat. Keep stirring as the wine sauce thickens a little. Now add the black pepper, pinch of salt, and parsley. Serve with either mashed potatoes or bread.

Although Diana rustled up delicious meals in prison and Jessica learned to make a fine chicken paprika later in life, it was the quietest of the Mitford sisters, the animal-loving Pamela, who was to excel at cooking on her blue Raeburn stove. It was in this she continued to make the whole wheat bread Lady Sydney had bored Hitler about (remember, Pamela was the one that only remembered the potatoes when she met Hitler). Anyone who dined with Pam remembered her tasty, simple food: mince braised with lemon and herbs; salad dressings spiced with curry powder; a dash of Worcestershire sauce added to the Yorkshire pudding. She kept her own chickens, a beautiful, punk-headed, black-spotted white Appenzeller Spitzhauben brood, whose eggs she'd smuggled into Britain in a Swiss chocolate box. Her obstreperous goat, Snowdrop, had little time for them though. A real feeder, Pamela gave her dachshunds a cranky miracle mix of brown bread, rice, and meat. She also made lovely Apple Charlotte, a painting by Hitler hanging from the wall.

Apple Charlotte

INGREDIENTS
2 lb. apples
2 tbsp. granulated sugar
1½ tsp. cinnamon
2 tsp. grated lemon zest

5 tbsp. butter
10–12 slices of brown bread
(¼ in. thick), crusts removed
2 egg yolks, beaten

METHOD
Clean, peel, core, and then slice all the apples. Put the apples, sugar, cinnamon, lemon zest, and 1 ounce of the butter in a saucepan. Over a low heat, stew the apples and sugar until you can crush them into a satisfying mush, though I prefer to keep soft, scrumptious chunks of apple. Cool in the fridge.

Melt the remaining butter in a small saucepan. Lay the slices of brown bread out, cut them into rectangles, and brush on both sides with the butter. Get a Pyrex pudding basin, butter it lightly, and then line it with three-quarters of the bread, leaving no gaps at all. Press the edges of the bread firmly together and aim to have the edges of bread slightly higher than the bowl.

Preheat the oven to 200°C. Combine the cooled apple puree with the beaten egg and then fill the Pyrex bowl with this. Finally, use the remaining slices of buttered bread to make a lid, overlapping the pieces. Place a heavy, ovenproof plate on top of this, and then further weigh it down with baking beans. Now let the raw Apple Charlotte sit for 30 minutes.

After this, remove the baking beans and the ovenproof plate. Place the Apple Charlotte in the oven and bake for 35 minutes. Let the buttered bread lid bake until it turns gold. Remove the Apple Charlotte from the oven and let it sit for 5 minutes. Carefully upend the warm, buttery Apple Charlotte onto a plate and served with thick, very cold cream.

Nothing scandalized Pam—except for food mistakes. Earlier in life, when married, she had instructed her cook on the intricacies of making game soup. All seemed well until the soup tureen appeared on the table. She told her sister Deborah of the terrible event: "You know . . . isn't Game Soup the loveliest and richest soup you ever *laid hands on*. Well, a *milky affair* came up." Diana wrote to Deborah of an impending visit to Pamela in 1982: "I'm longing for my visit to Woman, but also *terrified* because she suggests we cook every other day. First of all I can't, and second, imagine how I'd do every single thing WRONG, wrong times, wrong ingredients, wrong casseroles (the latter bound to be ruined if I cook them). Oh Debo do you think she would take me to Marks and Spencer and I could secretly buy all? Can't you picture Woman and Beetle back from a walk and Woman saying, 'I smell burning' or 'Nard, you should have put the potatoes on *long* ago.' It really will be the agony and the ecstasy because I love Woodfield [Pamela's house] and Woman and all but am not house trained."

Pamela also made delicious but formidably titled "Head Soup," which she dished out to her horror-struck nephews. But it was not made out of "ghoul," as she liked to call anything slightly creepy like real animal's heads, ears, noses, and brains. Instead, it was, she said, "soup out of my head"—whatever she had dreamed up. Young Max Mosley, son of Diana and Oswald, remembered his delight as a child when he and his cousins asked Pamela how she made something. She invariably answered, "'I made it out of my head' which used to mean that as children, none of us dared catch the other's eye for fear of starting to laugh. And of course, we always asked for the recipe just to get her to say that, even in later life."

Soup, of course, whatever deliciousness it was, was always accompanied by Lady Redesdale's bread, and the recipe for this dish still survives.

Lady Redesdale's Bread

INGREDIENTS

4½ cups whole wheat flour
1½ cups bread flour
2½ cups water

2 tbsp. sugar
2 packets dried yeast
1 tbsp. salt

METHOD

"Grease two baking tins. Place the water in a large bowl and add the other ingredients. Mix and knead the dough until it is thoroughly amalgamated. Leave in bowl to ferment for one hour. Remove dough from bowl, place on baking board and divide into two pieces. Shape the dough into rectangles the size of the tins and put into the tins. Heat the oven to 400F/205C. Cover the tins and let the dough rise for 30 minutes. Bake in the oven for 35 minutes. Remove loaves from oven and from tins and allow to cool on racks."

DON'T LEAVE A ROTHSCHILD ALONE IN THE KITCHEN

By reputation, the Rothschilds all had a passion for chocolate, and they could afford plenty of it, having made a fortune in banking, mining, fine art collecting, and in general being financial geniuses. If only we, too, were descended from Mayer Amschel. He had five sons who went on to open huge banking houses in Europe: Britain, France, Austria, Frankfurt, and the Kingdom of the Two Sicilies. It's almost biblical, or at least biblical capitalism. These banks all fared differently: The Kingdom of the Two Sicilies outfit closed its doors for business when the Bourbons had to hotfoot it out of Naples; then the Frankfurt bank closed when the Rothschild looking after it died, leaving *only* daughters. Hitler's invasion of Austria was the death knell for the Vienna branch (the Rothschilds are Jewish). All that remained were the banks in Paris and London.

The great-grandson of Mayer Amschel, Baron Ferdinand de Rothschild of the Austrian branch of the family, was left heartbroken at the tender age of nineteen when his beloved mother died. Then Ferdinand ("Ferdy") fell head over heels in love with his cousin Evelina—he had, in truth, felt great affection for her from childhood onward. Evelina ("Evy") was the cheery and robust-looking daughter of Baron Lionel de Rothschild (who was the first openly Jewish MP in Britain's Houses of Parliament). The cousins married to great social acclaim in London in July 1865 and honeymooned on one of the Rothschild estates in Schillersdorf. Evy and Ferdy reveled in deep, swooning marital bliss for eighteen months, until, eight months pregnant, Evy suffered horrifying convulsions and died giving birth to a stillborn son. Ferdinand wrote that he could "find no consolation in the future," only in the past and its memories.

Affairs of the heart were dead to Ferdinand, and he could find no more comforting home for his mourning than England. He commissioned a huge, beautiful house, Waddesdon Manor, to be built in Oxfordshire. Fortunately, though, for all who visited him in Waddesdon, whether in permanent mourning or not, Ferdinand always offered an excellent lunch. His house parties burgeoned. Inky signatures swelled the grand official visitors' book, and all of these visitors had to be fed. Ferdinand took his hosting duties pretty seriously—he added a stillroom to the kitchen. While stillrooms in grand, aristocratic British homes date back to the medieval period and were sort of in-house pharmacies, originally dedicated to distillation (sounds promising), making aromatic waters such as rose water, cosmetics, and ointments, by the late nineteenth and early twentieth century the stillroom was increasingly used as a working, productive pantry for baking, tea and coffee brewing, wobbly jelly making, and jam stewing—and came staffed by a floury, buttery stillroom maid. The Waddesdon stillroom must have smelled divine, its affable, toasty aromas wending their way down the corridors as it popped out floury, newly baked rolls and boldly fruited homemade marmalade. In yet another part of this Rothschild kitchen network, a baker worked pillows of dough and produced fresh bread daily. A little farther away, a cook crafted sweetmeats, stirred up puddings, and dreamed up sorbets and ice cream, all to be kept in the larders of the icehouse.

When it came to personal charm, though, Ferdinand made slips and could become confused about who was who and when they'd arrived. One guest, who had just arrived and was probably shaking the rain off his coat, was surprised by Ferdinand greeting him with "When are you leaving?" But he could also be the very essence of diplomacy, as when Bertie, the tubby Prince of Wales, fed up with trying to entertain the shah of Iran, suggested they get together at Waddesdon. Cunningly, Bertie ducked out of actually going himself, sending his two sons instead. The shah, deeply offended, went off to his room in a huff and refused to come down for dinner. Perplexed and dismayed, Ferdinand and company plotted how to winkle the shah out of his room. A message was sent to his chamber: a wonderful conjuror awaited the shah after his dinner. The ruse worked. The shah slunk back to the dinner table and, true to his word, Ferdinand enchanted the shah by introducing him to the conjuror: he wound up an enormous, musical, patinated bronze clockwork elephant, which rolled its eyes, swished its tail, and flapped its ears to entertain the shah. Mesmerized, the shah clapped his hands and, until his death less than a decade later, could never resist the gleam of a metal, mechanical toy. Considerable diplomacy was also needed when Queen Victoria came for lunch. She must have been an odd visitor, wishing to eat her lunch not with Ferdinand but in private with her daughters. Ever the gentleman, Ferdinand escorted her to the dining room, making slow, diplomatic progress on account of the queen's rheumatic knee. As he politely noted, "The royal appetite is proverbial, and it was not until about half past three that the Queen . . . reappeared." Given the menu, it is not surprising Victoria took her time. The meal began with consommé, then trout, then some scrumptiousness called Cailles en Caisses (quails in cases), and through beef and chicken onto Canetons Garnis d'Ortolans (ducklings garnished with ortolans, which reads like something out of a rather haunting children's fairy story), alongside asparagus, beignets à la Viennoise, and little soufflés. Ferdinand, meanwhile, had slunk off to smoke cigars on the terrace with fellow puffer Prince Henry of Battenberg until their pleasure was rudely interrupted: "[I] had to throw away the fragrant weed unfinished, being utterly railed at by my relations who said I should be reeking of smoke when Her Majesty came down." The butler worked as Ferdinand's "eyes" at the luncheon, reporting that Her Majesty had tasted every single dish offered and went back twice to the cold beef. Not only that, but she also "took away three copies from our bill of fare," and the royal cook was sent to Waddesdon to learn in Ferdinand's kitchens how to make three of the dishes. Ferdinand does not tell us which threes dishes were the queen's favorites, though, so it is up to our taste buds to decide.

Quails in Cases

INGREDIENTS

1 lb. puff pastry
1 egg, beaten
4 boned quails (bones retained)
Sea salt
Freshly ground black pepper
2 cups foie gras—cut most of it into
   8 slices, dice and reserve
   the rest

½ cup black truffles, sliced
1 tbsp. cognac
2 tbsp. butter
3 shallots, finely chopped
1 tbsp. cognac
½ cup homemade chicken stock
1 cup dry white wine
16 ripe purple figs, quartered

METHOD

Preheat the oven to 200°C. Flour a work surface, and roll out your slab of puff pastry. Now cut a series of four rounds, 5 inches in length, from the pastry. On each of these make a 3-inch inner circle—but go carefully, you must not pierce completely through the dough. Beat an egg, and brush the pastry cases. Place these on a parchment-lined baking tray and cook for about 20–25 minutes, until each pastry case is golden and puffed. Remove from the oven, and cool on a wire rack. Very gently, lift out the 3-inch "hat" of pastry from each case—each will be a "roof" of pastry over each quail.

Now increase the oven temperature to 230°C. Season the little quails inside and out with sea salt and black pepper. Place a slice of foie gras and at least three black truffle slices inside the cavity of each bird. Spoon some cognac over this, and then top with a second slice of foie gras. Truss the quails with kitchen string.

In a skillet, melt 1 tablespoon of butter until it bubbles and foams. Add the quail bones and brown them, then add the shallots, reduce the heat, and sauté for 3 minutes. Add the cognac and chicken stock, let them bubble, and then cook this on a gentle heat for about 30 minutes. Remove the quail bones.

Heat a second skillet, melt a tablespoon of butter in it, and brown each quail, allowing about 30 seconds to each side. Now place the quails, breasts facing downward, on a roasting tray, and roast for 8 minutes before turning the quails and roasting for another 5. Remove from the oven, and keep warm under a cozy towel.

Return to the heat the skillet in which you browned the quail, and the pour in the white wine. Let it bubble for a minute while you scrape the browned quail juices off the skillet. Now pour this into the cognac/stock sauce. Simmer for 3 minutes. Add the figs. Cook for 1 minute, and then add the remaining cubes of foie gras, stirring and melding the sauce together for a minute or two, until the sauce is reduced to about ⅔ cup.

Next, assemble the quails in cases. Place a pastry case on a warmed plate. Put the quail into the case, top with its "hat" of pastry, and drizzle with sauce. Place a few figs alongside, and try not to smoke strong cigars before serving.

Beignets à la Viennoise

INGREDIENTS

1 sachet of dried yeast	1 tsp. granulated sugar
A pinch of sugar	1 tsp. rum
2 tbsp. warm water	1 tsp. Cointreau
1½ cups all-purpose flour	1 tsp. grated orange zest
A pinch of salt	1 tsp. vanilla essence
4 egg yolks, whisked	A bottle of sunflower oil for deep frying
⅓ cup heavy cream, warmed slightly	2 tbsp. confectioners' sugar

METHOD

In a bowl, combine the yeast and a pinch of sugar with the warm water. Place somewhere warm for 15 minutes to allow the yeast to activate and froth. In a large bowl, sieve together the flour and sea salt. Make a well in the center, and then add the yeast, egg yolks, cream, sugar, rum, Cointreau, orange zest, and vanilla essence. Knead with hands to form a robust dough. Cover this with a cloth, put somewhere warm, and leave it to rise for 1 hour. It will double in size.

Lightly flour a work surface, empty the dough onto it, and work it again with your hands for a few minutes. Now form it into balls of about 4 inches in diameter. Place them on a floured baking sheet, with spaces between the raw beignets. Leave them to stand for 20 minutes.

In a deep, heavy-based pan, heat the sunflower oil until it grows silent. Test it is hot enough with a thread of dough; this will rise quickly to the surface with a "bubble wrap" of air about it. Cook 4–5 beignets at a time, removing them from the hot oil with a slotted spoon. Drain them on paper towels, dust with confectioners' sugar, and serve with Chantilly cream or ice cream or just plain cream. Think of Queen Victoria, and don't let your dignity slip.

The English Rothschilds were still going strong in World War I. Lady Battersea, better known as Constance Rothschild (a feisty feminist who did great work among Jewish prostitutes in London), possessed a butler who was the master of understatement. As bombs fell, he liked to wander languidly into the drawing room and, as biographer Frederic Morton puts it, "say boredly, as though announcing the arrival of a tedious ducal couple: 'The Zeppelins, my lady.'" Come autumn 1917, some nameless female Rothschild, it is told, clearly unaware of the fact that many of the men in her service had left to fight, asked the overworked gardener "how he'd been so clever as to sprinkle all these lovely leaves all along the garden paths and walkways?"

World War II called on the services of another fascinatingly curious British Rothschild: Victor, Lord Rothschild. While studying physiology and playing mild-mannered cricket in the English rain at Cambridge University, he befriended the future Soviet spies Guy Burgess and Anthony Blunt—he even shared a flat with them in London. He was recruited for MI5 and headed their bomb disposal division, but there was always a sinister edge to his activities, as he was suspected of being a double agent, covertly working for dark-browed, satanic Uncle Joe Stalin. Whether he was the "Fifth Man" or not, he lived a perfectly pleasant existence as a Labour MP, being cooked for by the very un-Russian Mrs. Ena Prentice (she began working as a scullery maid for the Rothschilds aged fifteen and packed in sixty-four years of service for them) and being driven around by his chauffeur, Wally. To really brush up her cookery skills, Victor Rothschild decided to send Mrs. Prentice to Paris, with Wally as her chaperone, in order to learn how to cook from a French master, the chef for Baron Alain de Rothschild. What fun the pair had: Mrs. Prentice and Wally went to see the Follies Bérgère of an evening, and when the French chef taught her to cook "Gigot de Sept Heures," Wally comically renamed it "'Gigolo' de Sept Heures." On her return, Mrs. Prentice's dishes delighted Victor Rothschild, and he compiled a list of fond and cherished favorites, titled "what Mrs P does better than anyone else in the world." Thanks to Sarah Daniels, editor of *Lord Rothschild's Favourite Recipes*, it is possible to see the list. Here is a taste of some of it: "Ouefs à l'aurore; Hot 'ouefs mimosa'; Egg cutlets; Poached eggs with brown sauce; Cold curried eggs; Cold scrambled egg and cold haddock; Haddock soufflé; crab soufflé; Cold sole Portugaise . . . Pancakes stuffed with chopped mushrooms; My special macaroni; Devilled grouse; Cold duck on mousse of duck; Turkey stuffing in patties; Gigot de sept heures; Shoulder of lamb with onion sauce . . . Hare steaks; Lettuce purée; Iced gooseberry soufflé; Iced chocolate soufflé; Special cold cherries; Coffee ice surrounded by cherries . . . Puff balls with apricot sauce."

"Gigolo" de Sept Heures, Courtesy of *Lord Rothschild's Favourite Recipes* (plus Mrs. Prentice and Wally)

INGREDIENTS

13 lb. leg of lamb	1 lb. onions
2 calves' feet	2 whited of leek
Veal bones	1 bouquet garni and garlic
1 lb. carrots	1 bottle of white wine

METHOD

"Prick the leg of lamb with garlic. Brown it on all sides in butter and oil in a large pot. Then brown the onions and carrots. Put the vegetables, leeks, the calves' feet, veal bones and bouquet garni round the meat. Moisten with the wine and good brown stock, well-seasoned, just to the height of the meat/bring to the boil and then lower the heat to a gentle simmer. Place in the oven for six to seven hours.

"After it is cooked, take out the meat and keep warm. Meanwhile degrease the gravy and reduce it to make a rich gravy. Serve the meat with well glazed carrots and the onions. When the meat is so well cooked it should be served with a spoon, not a knife."

Another English Rothschild, Lionel de Rothschild, had a house in London but was often drawn by his great interest in the properties of the rhododendrons to his estate in Exbury, where the said rhododendrons flourished. Nor were they Exbury's only allure. Lionel had managed to steal a wonderful French chef from the Ritz, one Monsieur Gallois, who cooked over the enormous black range in Exbury, which blasted the kitchen with its dragon-like, blistering breath every time its door was opened. If his hair was ever singed, Monsieur Gallois could cool off in his own sitting room and dining room at Exbury. Mahogany hatches slid open for the footmen, dressed in the traditional Rothschild livery of blue and yellow, to collect Gallois's delicious dishes. One of Lionel's favorites was Caneton Lamberty, which, according to his son Edmund de Rothschild, was a "cold roast duckling stuffed with foie gras and encased in a port jelly," while Lionel's guests often sighed in delight over mouthfuls of "Barbue Richemont, a dish of brill stuffed with a mixture of crab-meat and quenelle, garnished with crab claws." When King George came to dine, Lionel's brother Leo was told he should bow to the king and that he would recognize him by his beard, but it turned out everyone had beards, and Leo spent a long time bowing. A French pastry chef assisted Gallois, and the two made the Rothschild children incredible cakes. As Edmund recalled, "One of our favourites was a sponge and meringue cake in the shape of a house with a small bear standing in the doorway . . . he made a memorably delicious nougat birthday cake . . . in the form of a pony trap." Poor Gallois was too partial to a glass or two and, after Lionel found him prostrate and drunk under the kitchen table, having made dinner for a prestigious party of diners at Kensington Palace Gardens, Gallois was shipped back to France. Lionel, meanwhile, was so upset by the loss that he was found crying, his head in his hands.

While any exotic ingredient Gallois wished for was sent down from London, creamy milk and fresh eggs were delivered by the capable Mrs. Searle, who lived on a local farm. When Lionel left for London by train on Monday mornings, he always pocketed two of Mrs. Searle's eggs, which could then be boiled for him in the restaurant car of the early train. Lionel took to the high life on trains, as the Rothschilds had financed and directed the building of the Paris to Calais rail line and so benefited from reciprocal perks on British railways—for instance, the London "express" train had to screech to a halt at the Beaulieu station on Lionel's estate just to pick him up, with his eggs and briefcase.

A couple of years later and across the water in Austria, the Austrian Rothschilds faced their own complications. At Wallis Simpson's suggestion, the recently abdicated Edward VII, now the Duke of Windsor, took refuge in Eugene von Rothschild's beautiful castle, Schloss Enzesfeld, near Vienna. Until Wallis's divorce was finalized, Edward and Wallis were forced to separate. Edward had planned to stay in a small hotel in Switzerland, but Wallis thought this would be too humbling and miserable and so called upon the services of the Baron and Baroness Rothschild. Baroness Rothschild was very glamorous. She was the European, aristocratic rein-carnation of one Kitty Wolff, the daughter of a dentist and formerly from Philadel-phia, and, as a fellow American, Kitty seemed a natural ally for Wallis.

Edward threw in the crown on December 11, 1936, and within a few days arrived on the Rothschilds' doorstep. Kitty had not set foot in the castle for a few years, so she rapidly put a call through to her estate manager to get it shipshape. The gloomy, rather cold but beautiful baroque Schloss Enzesfeld stood near a small village, but the majority of the servants Kitty hired were speedily recruited from Vienna. The stables were swept out and filled with white carriage horses and hunting horses.

Eugene von Rothschild found Edward in a state of disarray in his bedroom, his things all over the floor, bewildered by the complexities of unpacking his own case without a valet to do so. "I'm not very good at this," he confessed. "You see I've never done it by myself." A German valet was arranged. Edward felt gloomy with-out Wallis and was still reconciling himself to the seismic shock of his abdication. He slept with sixteen pictures of Wallis around him while hugging a little pillow embroidered "WS." Meanwhile, the baron told the *New York Times* on December 16, 1936, "The Duke is not especially ill. . . . He cannot be entirely well, under the circumstances." Edward's ears hurt. The weather was rotten. Putting on the golf course was a damned bore, and when Kitty challenged Edward to a game of bowls, he lost. Sometimes he just sulked alone. Nothing pleased him very much, even though the locals brought him fresh trout. Parcels and gifts from loyal well-wishers stacked up in the castle: hundreds of turkeys died in his honor, and these feathered or plucked fowl were sent to the castle. Cakes and barking dogs arrived, wrapped in bows, as did no less than eighty fountain pens. Sullen and bad tempered, the duke seemed to appreciate little about his surroundings. He wanted half-price skiing lessons because he felt hard up now that he was no longer king of Britain. Kitty's patience was wearing thin, but Edward's charm worked for longer on Eugene, who was jubilant when Edward told him he was going to write a book in defense of the Jews. Edward spent hours in Enzesfeld's library but was mostly preoccupied with designing the cover of his book. Finally, he settled on royal blue Morocco leather; the book, however, remained unwritten.

Edward watched Mickey Mouse films (the ever-patient Rothschilds ordered these especially for him), drank regular doses of warmed and spiced Austrian red wine for his cold, and sang (sadly and croakily, no doubt) in the bathtub. Most of all, he rang Wallis in Cannes, France, for long, pining, romantic conversations at least three times a day. He found such calls very soothing and so kept the phone busy for hours, leaving the Rothschilds with the phone bill (incidentally, Edward also put many calls through to his ranch in Canada, to London, and to several far-flung acquaintances).

Austrian Glühwein

INGREDIENTS

2 bottles of good red wine
½ cup brandy
¼ cup cherry brandy
1 cup water
Juice of 1 orange and 1 lemon

½ cup granulated sugar
6 cloves
2 cinnamon sticks
1 vanilla bean, split down the belly
1 orange, quartered and sliced

METHOD

Place all the ingredients except the wine and brandies in a large pan and bring to a simmer. Let this simmer for about 1 hour; it will reduce, so after half an hour add 1 glass of wine. When the hour is up, add the wine and brandies and heat to a gentle simmer for 10 minutes. Serve warm.

The Rothschilds tried to cheer Edward up with dinner parties. Dining with Eugene and Kitty and the sophisticated, wealthy elite who convened about their table, Edward was responsible for two innovations: First, his evening costume pioneered a switch in posh European gentlemen's fashion to wearing soft as opposed to starched collars for dinner. Next, because he always got up late for breakfast, he made brunch fashionable. Kitty worried that Edward would feel especially down on Christmas Day and packed the castle with glitter, Christmas trees, and Parisian performers. She got a very special Christmas present for him: some Cartier sapphire studs, which she placed on his breakfast tray. Mollified, Edward reciprocated with a signed photo of himself. How clever of him to realize that this must have been just what she wanted.

The kindhearted villagers of Enzesfeld tramped up to the castle. The village choir, accompanied by jolly, rosy-cheeked schoolchildren, and a booming brass band were all ready to sing and play their hearts out in Edward's honor. But he wasn't in the mood, and they were turned away, perhaps by the scores of detectives, gendarmes with bayonets fixed to their guns, and pugilistic gamekeepers who guarded the castle. Photographers kept popping out of rabbit holes, appearing down chimney pots, and hanging onto tree tops; anything for a photograph of the disgraced monarch. Yelping police dogs followed on the heels of some frostbitten photographers in the woods.

Reportedly, Kitty, exasperated and exhausted, finally blurted out to a friend in London, "As far as I'm concerned, anyone can have him anytime." The Rothchilds had footed all the bills, which came in a steady, depressing stream. They dropped the odd hint or two that Edward might consider paying rent. But after legal consultation, the Rothschilds got those good townspeople of Enzesfeld to honor the duke with the title "master of Castle Enzesfeld," and suddenly bills now arrived addressed to the master. Churlishly, Edward took his own legal advice and decided he didn't want to stay with the Rothschilds anymore—he had stayed for *three* months. Reluctantly, too, he left them £900 for the phone bill.

By 1937, Eugene von Rothschild had decamped completely to his Paris residence; Austria was no easy place to be Jewish. The German army clustered about the German-Austrian border. Baron Louis von Rothschild, however, stayed put. Louis was a silkily cool and calm individual and a brilliantly successful banker, destined to be the last at the helm of the family's Austrian banking interests. As a powerful, moneyed, capitalist Jew, Louis was high up on Hitler's hate list. As the Germans moved over the border, Louis turned up at the airport. When questioned, he said he was on his way to join his polo team in Italy. The SS retained his passport; Louis had no choice but to return home. When two SS officers turned up that night at Louis's home, swastika armbands tight about their biceps, inquiring whether Herr Baron was there, the butler replied in the negative. Baffled, the SS left. Next, six soldiers came with drawn handguns and steel helmets. They demanded that Louis accompany them to the local Nazi headquarters. Louis said he would condescend to come but not until after lunch. Louis was going down with style. Butlers passed by the guards, carrying pungent and delicious plates of food. Slowly and deliberately, Louis savored each course, wiping his lips after elegant mouthfuls. Louis cleaned his hands in his fingerbowl after dinner, lit a cigarette, and scanned and approved the menu for the next day. Finally, he nodded his readiness to the SS, and they marched him off to his incarceration. The Nazi who was interrogating Louis said, "Well, so you're a Rothschild. Just exactly how rich are you?"

Louis replied that he'd have to consult his accountants.

"All right, all right. How much is your palace worth?" asked the Nazi.

"How much is the Vienna Cathedral worth?" Louis suggested.

The Nazi spat out, "*Impertinence!*"

As arranged, when it became clear that his master was not returning, Louis's faithful valet appeared at SS quarters with a beautiful, crested pigskin case full of fresh linen, toiletries, several learned books, and tailored, stylish gentleman's clothing. The SS snorted with laughter and sent him packing. Louis, meanwhile, was sharing some lumpy sand sacks with a couple of grizzled Communists who were fellow prisoners in the cells below. "We got on rather well," Louis reminisced later. "We agreed that this was the world's most classless cellar." Later, class did come into it, and Louis was removed to the Gestapo headquarters in Vienna, with the ousted Austrian chancellor as his neighbor. Louis's insouciant stylishness shone through again; bored, he gave his guards lessons in botany and geology. (His cousin Phillippe, when escaping over the Pyrenees with smugglers, gave them, effectively, a tip list on how to improve their smuggling operations, and when imprisoned in Morocco, Phillippe set up gymnastic sessions for the inmates.) When Herr Himmler tried to smarten up Louis's cell by sending in vases and Louis XIV clocks and had his prison cot draped with a velvet curtain (in orange, no less), Louis scorned them as fit only for a "Cracow bordello." Finally, having extracted enormous sums from the Rothschilds' coffers, the SS magnanimously announced Louis's freedom late one night. "But it is far too late for my servants to come," averred Louis, insisting they put him up for the night.

When they weren't setting up adult education classes, the Rothschilds were trying to hide their glorious art collections. Although thousands of pieces were secreted away in embassies, most were eventually stolen by the Nazis. The Rothschilds' mansions were shaken out like rich men's pockets. Robert de Rothschild's beautiful palace at 23 Avenue de Marigny-by-Seine held a secret chamber behind a bookcase, crammed with art treasures, which Göring used to stomp past, thinking hard about where on earth the hidden Rothschild art could be. What was taken by the Germans was collected in Bavaria in King Ludwig's castle, Neuschwanstein— Rubens's *Three Graces* was behind the stove. Partially burned ciphers in the castle's coal stove offered the key to where other glorious artworks were kept: in salt mines, monasteries . . .

But let us end with Maurice de Rothschild, the son of the Zionist Baron Edmond de Rothschild, who helped finance the creation of the State of Israel. Maurice, a brilliant French parliamentarian, was bald, witty, and very characterful, despite his ugly, expressionless face and bug-like eyes. And the ring of the name Rothschild made Maurice a magnet for beautiful adventuresses. Poor guy. With one luckless banking dynasty marriage under his belt, Maurice took refuge from the majority of the females of the species by employing "Milly"—purportedly a freelance nurse—who followed forever in his wake, apparently, Maurice claimed, because she had the same blood type, and who knew when he might need a transfusion? Indeed, it was alleged that Milly gave him some of her blood on a weekly basis, as it also pepped up Maurice's virility. Maurice took up permanent residence in a number of hotels on the French Riviera. First, he stayed for a long time in a hotel in Nice, which he left in the wake of a minor scandal. The scandal goes like this: Year in, year out, Maurice had his breakfast tea made for him by the same devoted room waiter, and Maurice always smacked his lips at the prospect of a cup of his specially brewed, steaming tea. Then the time came when the waiter passed away, much to Maurice's inconvenience. The first time Maurice drank tea made by the replacement waiter, he made a terrific fuss: What was this crap the hotel was giving him? It tasted nothing like the delicious tea he used to get. A full-scale investigation was launched only to uncover the terrible truth. It turned out that Maurice was a miser and always refused to give a tip to the room waiter. So what did the waiter do? In revenge, he pissed in Maurice's tea every morning and then served Maurice a cup of hot piss and tea. Clearly, an unforgettably delicious concoction. Needless to say, Maurice's stay at the hotel was at an end.

He ended up in the Hôtel de Paris in Monte Carlo, and it was there that the novelist Michael Korda caught sight of Maurice and his nurse dining together. Milly, a busty matron in her midthirties, wheeled the desiccated creature that Maurice had become into the hotel dining room, an evening suit pinned onto him. Milly wore a décolleté dress. Maurice, mummified in a plaid rug that was placed over his knees, sat opposite Milly and her snowy, mountainous cleavage. Korda noticed, "He ate sparsely, with a feeble hand, taking a spoonful or two of soup, a bit of minced veal, a piece of bread rolled and kneaded until it was soft, while his companion cheerfully made her way through a mighty dinner." Korda, his friend Freddy Lonsdale, and a couple of other chums watched from behind their napkins as Maurice grew very excited when dessert time came. What delicious dessert, they wondered, got him so worked up? Finally, the maître d'hôtel materialized with a single orange on a plate. He speared it and held it up for Maurice to inspect. Maurice nodded approval. The maître d'hôtel then peeled the orange. Segment by segment, Maurice ate his way through the orange, working the pips out of each segment with his ancient tongue. Then, before their eyes, Maurice took aim and spat a pip clear across the table and down Milly's cleavage. Every time he gave a snuffle of pleasure. Milly, meanwhile, sat expressionless over her magnificent breasts. The whole set of pips worked their way down. All over, Maurice sank back into a sort of post-coital senility. Milly tucked the blanket about his spindly legs and, without batting an eyelid, sailed forth from the dining room. Then one of Korda's friends said, "They say he also likes to go down to the kitchens and shape all the ice cream and parfaits into perfect little spirals by licking them." Freddy Lonsdale had also heard this rumor: "I've never been able to eat a parfait since," he shuddered.

Parfait

INGREDIENTS

¾ cup hazelnuts, crushed

2 eggs

½ cup granulated sugar

¾ cup heavy cream

METHOD

Preheat the oven to 200°C. Brush a mold with oil, dust with granulated sugar, and pop into the freezer. Put the crushed hazelnuts on a small baking sheet and toast in the oven until golden brown. Cool. Separate the egg yolks from the whites. Whisk the egg yolks and granulated sugar until they are fluffy. Take a clean whisk and in a second bowl, whisk the egg whites into a glossy mass. Next, whisk the heavy cream up until it is thick but not choppy.

Add the chopped, roasted hazelnuts to the sugar and egg yolk mix. Using a metal spoon, gradually fold in the cream, followed by the egg white. Fill the mold with the parfait, and freeze for approximately one hour. Serve alone or with hot caramelized banana . . . but whatever you do, make sure it hasn't been licked.

WINDY TIMES WITH CONRAD HILTON
(PLUS A SIDE ORDER OF ZSA ZSA GABOR)

Conrad Hilton, the founder of Hilton Hotels, was the son of Gus Hilton, a Norwegian immigrant with big hands and a handlebar moustache, and a God-fearing
Iowan German Catholic, Mary Laufersweiler. Conrad was born large-footed and
always hoped he'd grow into his feet. Mary believed prayer was the answer to everything except your shoe size. And Gus had a general store, "A. H. Hilton," in San
Antonio, New Mexico, a primitive adobe structure that also incorporated the Hilton
home, where most of the couple's children were born. They had Mexican help in
the form of handyman Gregorio, who would clean and wash dishes but refused to
eat with the family, cooking his own frijoles in a room off the barn.

Keeping their many mouths full required a communal effort from the Hilton
clan: Gus was a natural haggler and paid his children to work in the store, hoping
this would infuse them with entrepreneurial zeal. It worked. They sold everything
"from flour to coffins." Conrad planted his father's land and sold the vegetables
he'd grown. An entrepreneur from the start, he was driven by reading *Optimism*,
the biography of his heroine, Helen Keller. Gus decided to invest cash in coal
mines and made a killing in 1904, only to lose it all again in a financial squall
three years later. Desperate times called for desperate measures and they held
a family conference, coming, as Conrad recalled, to the following conclusion:
"We had, we decided, four assets. The stock on the shelves. . . . Carl and I were
distinctly of working size. We had the biggest, ramblingest adobe house in New
Mexico directly facing a railroad station on a main line. And we had my mother's
cooking. This added up to only one thing—a Hilton Hotel." Tired, flinty miners,
salesmen with bulky suitcases, and traveling businessmen would be their clients.
"If they get a taste of Mary's cooking," Gus predicted, "we'll have more business
than we can handle. Every travelling man in New Mexico will try to break his trip
at San Antonio."

While Mary slept with a gun under her pillow to ward off any stray salesmen,
Conrad made sure he was there at the local railway station to meet every train that
showed up, whether at 3 a.m. or high noon, to hustle for trade and make promises
about Mary's cooking. Soon the news spread (what better client than a traveling
salesman to advertise your hotel): "If you want to break up your sales trip, break it
at San Antonio and get a room at Hilton's. They serve the best meals in the West
and they have a boy there who is crackerjack at making things comfortable for
you." Conrad worked out that they could charge a daily rate of $2.50 and provide
three meals a day. He told his biographer Whitney Bolton of those days: "Everyone
got something out of our hotel. Travelers got cleanliness, comfort and a good table
for their $2.50 a day, even though we served three bountiful meals. We all worked

hard, and no one harder than my mother. I wouldn't take a million dollars for what those days taught me . . . and I'd give a million dollars for one of the suppers she served." Sadly, San Antonio is now a ghost town, as the entire modern town was moved a few miles away. Perhaps the tumbleweed still remembers that first Hilton hotel.

His mother's blessing followed him when, several years later and after Gus's death, Conrad headed off to oil-rich Texas, hoping to profit from black gold himself by setting up a bank. Instead, Conrad discovered a different kind of gold in the creaky, rundown flophouse, the Mobley, where he boarded. The owner was trying so hard to keep up with demand that he had to let out rooms in three shifts. Fortunately, the lure of imagining that he might make even more money in oil persuaded him to sell the Mobley to Conrad.

Now Conrad had a hotel of his own of sorts. Immediately, he refurbished. Upselling, he determined, was the way to make cash. In the Mobley, he set up a newsstand and a small retail shop. He scrapped the dining room and turned it into even more bedrooms. On his way now, he picked up small hotels, seeding oil-rich, industrious Texas with rooms for roughnecks. Eventually, though, he made his name when he bought the much bigger, city-based, famous hotels in Los Angeles, New York, and Chicago. These required lavish openings with their own moments of disaster, as biographer Randy Taraborrelli recounts: the death of Pope John XXIII meant the cancellation of the opening of the Hilton in Rome, leaving the chef with an over-order of some twelve hundred desserts of battered peaches, peppered with almonds and stuffed with ice cream. When the Nile Hilton opened in Cairo, a heavy gust of hot Saharan sand suddenly swept through the Bedouin tent they'd erected, dusting platters of succulent roast lamb with a film of grit.

Struck with wonder at the glory of his fate, Hilton went to pray in St. Patrick's Cathedral on the weekend of the Waldorf Hilton Hotel's silver anniversary. He prayed in thanks for the American dream, which allowed a big-footed boy from San Antonio to dance with the finest ladies and wine and dine 350 of New York's finest. Indeed, as he sat at a top table, amid all the finery of the Waldorf Hilton, he had a quiet, reflective chuckle about the vagaries of life: "There I was, amongst the gourmets, being served Fumet of Gumbo Chervil with Lucullus Crusts, loving every minute of it, and as nimble amid the vast array of knives, forks, and spoons as a Chinaman born to his chopsticks. I could not help chuckling inside, remembering how my mother always refused to be impressed by the trimmings. Under her breath she would have been saying, 'It's only fancy fish soup, Connie. And don't you forget it.'"

What Conrad hadn't counted on, though, was meeting Hungarian firecracker Zsa Zsa Gabor. Zsa Zsa seems the least likely person Conrad would fall in love with, but the lure of the flesh is strong. With her poodle-ish charms and husky squeak,

Zsa Zsa wasn't holy or God-fearing. But she was an arch manipulator (only eighteen, she had already been married to a Turkish businessman and served as the love interest of Kamal Ataturk, whom she drank lots of raki with in Ankara while staring into his "terrible, colourless eyes"). At sixty-one years old, Conrad was a naive pushover. Zsa Zsa saw him first in Ciro's and spotted that he had a tie with images of hotels on it. It should have been a warning sign. But she didn't take much notice; she simply vowed to take control of his wardrobe once she had married him. He was tall, with terrific posture, his hair whitening at the temples, contrasting with his tan. She liked the way he surveyed the room with his "upturned greenish eyes." Conrad reminded her of Ataturk, who had mesmerized Zsa Zsa, no doubt prey to the fatal aphrodisiacal mix of beheader and womanizer. Clearly, the patriarch in Conrad suited her. He was "like Father, like a wild Indian, like a cowboy, like Uncle Sam." Conrad's fancy was caught, but very prosaically he decided, on meeting her, that he couldn't pronounce "Zsa Zsa," so he'd call her Georgia. Hardly an auspicious note and not, one would think, in keeping with the romantic potential of a wild Indian, cowboy, or even Uncle Sam (plus, when they were dating, Zsa Zsa had to soak her feet every night as they danced for so long).

Keen to catch her fish, Zsa Zsa knew firstly that she must resist sleeping with Conrad until they were married. It worked. He was entranced by her, feverish for her touch, blinded by her goodhearted innocence and—get this—lack of materialism. Zsa Zsa, a complete hedonist, had managed—undercover, as it were—to ensnare the Catholic Hiltons. Even Conrad's mother, now living in El Paso, Texas, adored her.

But the romantic tables turned almost as soon as the wedding was consummated. Conrad had been in the process of buying the Blackstone Hotel. On their wedding night, a night of virility and sensuality, Zsa Zsa turned to him among the rumpled sheets, gazed into his mesmerizing green eyes, and asked softly, "Conrad, what are you thinking of?"

"By golly, I'm thinking of that Blackstone deal," he chirruped.

Still, this didn't quell Zsa Zsa's romantic ardor. When she joined him for breakfast in his rooms the next morning, she found him seated at breakfast, clad in a red velvet robe: "Remote and austere—like a king, like a potentate. . . . This is not my man, this is not my husband, I thought, this is a high priest sitting opposite me eating soft-boiled eggs."

Unfortunately for Zsa Zsa, there was a little too much of the priest about Conrad. His religiosity bewildered her; she tried to put it down to a fondness for nuns. He was always praying on his knees and usually about the Hilton hotel chain, as if God had a divine interest in hospitality. Keen to live up to her new name of Georgia, Zsa Zsa was set on becoming "a one-hundred-per-cent American," which she seemed to think could be achieved via golf and tennis lessons—plus English lessons, as she struggled over her *w*'s, which came out as *v*'s. Her teacher's solution was to make her endlessly recite "I walk westward, watching the wintry wind whip over the wide sidewalk."

Soon, Zsa Zsa was surprised by Conrad's thrift and stinginess. In her memoirs, she uses one story to illustrate this. Conrad was trying to rustle up the money to buy the Plaza Hotel and sought the support of a financier, whom he was going to treat to a special meal at the Plaza. Conrad had been out shooting and came home proudly with a brace of wild ducks. He'd bagged them himself in Texas. For dinner, he asked the chef at the Plaza to prepare the birds; he wanted to impress his guest. Zsa Zsa recollected, "When the duck was brought in, arranged artistically on glittering silver platters, Conrad went scarlet and boomed, 'Where's the duck's back? And where the hell are the legs?'" The maître d'hôtel looked terrified but then rallied, drew himself up to his full height, and, summoning every bit of hauteur he possessed, said, "Mr. Hilton, here in the Plaza we serve only the very best segments of duck to our guests." In a fury, Conrad roared back, "I shot this duck and by golly I want my guests to eat all of it—legs and back included." The financier was so taken with Conrad's thrifty ways that he backed him. When it came time for Zsa Zsa to get a car, she wanted a copper Cadillac. Conrad picked up a secondhand blue Chrysler for her. "I hated that blue car. . . . The colour reminded me of a kitchen stove. I wailed to Eva [her sister], 'Every time I drive it I smell potatoes cooking!'" The Cadillac had matched her hair color, *and* Connie drove a Cadillac.

She tried to keep up with Connie, stumbling out of her bed at dawn, a whirl of flouncy curls and little pearly colored feathers, and sat opposite him at breakfast, wondering how on earth anyone could find boiled eggs and French fried potatoes digestible at dawn. Connie, meanwhile, flicked through the morning papers, called New York, and gave her a peck on the cheek when he left. Zsa Zsa tumbled back to bed, her feathers a little more limp. As an antidote to all that parsimony, daily at 5 p.m., Zsa Zsa visited her sister Eva. What a delight: Eva's house was full of Hungarian chatter and truly delicious things to tuck into like green peppers and salami.

Conrad gradually slid into deep, immovable disillusion about his young bride. In bed with the flu, he watched one day with amazement as Zsa Zsa spent hours pouting in front of the mirror, jingling bangles, trying on scarves in all sorts of sporting and provocative angles, sweeping powder puffs about her person. His sons reacted very differently; they were in awe of her beauty. Barron asked, "Oh, Zsa Zsa, may I sit here and look at you while you make up?" Not so Conrad. He estimated it took her four long hours to make up.

Conrad was always off to bed early, closing the door to his bedroom rather firmly. To be desired by so many men but not Conrad broke Zsa Zsa's heart. She tried to win him back. She walked in on him when he was praying, pert and winsome in a sheer black nightgown. He said, "Dammit, go to your room and wait for me." Then one evening, finally, seductively, she knocked on Conrad's door. "Conrad?" she whispered. The silence inside the room was profound. She tried the door. It was locked. Cowardly Conrad had locked her out of his bedroom. Zsa Zsa was left with their rescue dog, Ranger, for company. He was the only one who understood.

Upon their divorce, Zsa Zsa consoled herself with an affair with Conrad's son Nicky and an evening with the king of Saudi Arabia. Zsa Zsa and the king tried to gain entry to the Stork Club and were refused because of a shameful color ban. They treated themselves to ice-cream sundaes with hot fudge and butterscotch. The king ended up tipping the waitresses $1,000 each—now that's *not* stingy.

Postdivorce Hot Fudge and Butterscotch Sundaes

FOR THE VANILLA ICE CREAM . . .

A generous cup organic full-fat milk	¾ cup granulated sugar
½ tsp. Maldon salt flakes	2 cups heavy cream
6 egg yolks	1 vanilla bean, split lengthwise

FOR THE CARAMELIZED PECANS . . .

½ cup granulated sugar	12 pecan halves
2 tbsp. water	A pinch of sea salt

FOR THE HOT FUDGE . . .

¾ cup heavy cream	1½ generous cups bittersweet
¼ cup dark muscovado sugar	chocolate, roughly grated
¼ cup unsweetened cocoa powder	1 tbsp. butter
½ cup maple syrup	A pinch of sea salt
½ tsp. vanilla extract	

FOR THE BUTTERSCOTCH . . .

4 tbsp. butter	1 vanilla pod, split down the side
¾ cup demerara sugar	A good pinch of sea salt
½ cup heavy cream	

METHOD

A few hours in advance of assembling the sundaes, you need to make vanilla ice cream.

In a medium-size saucepan, gently warm the milk, *half* of the cream, salt flakes, and sugar. Plop in a split-down-the-middle vanilla bean. When the milky mix is warm and the sugar has dissolved, remove the pan from the heat, cover it, and allow it to rest for about half an hour.

Postdivorce Hot Fudge and Butterscotch Sundaes (*continued*)

When the 30 minutes is up, place the egg yolks in a largish bowl and whisk them up. Gently and carefully add the warm, milky cream to the egg yolks—keep whisking—and then pour all of this back into the pan. Over a medium-to-low heat, begin to warm this mixture; it will be ready when it coats the wood of the spatula or spoon. When it has thickened, it is time to use the remaining half of the cream. Pool the cold cream into a largish bowl and pour the custard over the cream, stirring it in. Now you must cool this for about an hour.

When it is cooled, remove the vanilla bean and start to churn the ice cream, following the ice-cream maker's directions.

Make the caramelized pecans now. Line a baking sheet with wax paper. Pour the granulated sugar into a heavy-based saucepan. Add the water, and over a very gentle heat, dissolve the sugar. When it has completely dissolved, turn up the heat and bring to a boil. Boil until the sugar syrup turns a lovely caramel color. As soon as it does, add the pecan halves and the pinch of salt. Stir through, and then turn onto the baking tray, using a wooden spoon to spread out the pecans. They should form a single "floor" of pecan and candy. Cool in the fridge, and when thoroughly chilled, break the mixture up, keeping the pecans whole.

Now for the butterscotch. In a heavy-based saucepan over a medium heat, melt the butter. Now add the demerara sugar, cream, vanilla pod, and sea salt. Stir thoroughly until the sugar has dissolved. Slowly bring to a boil and cook for about 5 minutes, stirring occasionally. To serve, remove the vanilla pod. You want the butterscotch to have just the faintest warmth about it in order to melt your vanilla ice cream.

Time now to turn your attentions to the hot fudge sauce. In a medium-size heavy-based saucepan, mix together the cream, muscovado sugar, cocoa powder, and maple syrup. Stirring frequently, bring this to a boil—but only for about 30 seconds. Remove from the heat and stir in the vanilla, chocolate, and butter until the fudge sauce is smooth.

Assemble your sundaes, alternating blobs of vanilla ice cream with layers of warm butterscotch. Top with hot fudge and some caramelized pecans.

Cold-fish Conrad tried to bring his sons up right. He penned written contracts with them about behavior, which they had to cosign like a pair of little financiers. They were the future of Hilton Corporations. At the same time, it could be argued that he lived vicariously through his wilder, younger son, Nicky, who was more interested in girls than Barron. Barron went from a passion for aeronautics to hotels. After a first date in a Mexican restaurant with Elizabeth Taylor (Nicky had been collecting newspaper clippings about her), Nicky and Elizabeth flung themselves into a doomed marriage—they spent the short time they had together quarreling on beaches through a mist of Johnnie Walker Black. Nicky also dated Joan Collins and Natalie Wood and scanned young ladies at his father's Bel Air Hotel, his drink pepped up with a dash of Seconal. Very proud of his penis, Nicky liked to say that between Conrad, Barron, and himself there was a yard of cock. But this wasn't what made Joan Collins a bit jumpy with him; he got his kicks from discharging his handgun into the ceiling when he felt a little bored—just who you want to take home to meet the parents.

Nicky was grouchy with the staff in Conrad's massive home in Bel Air, Casa Encantada, sneering at their arthritic, elderly maid, Maria, for being too frail to hold a brimming coffeepot. "Why are you still working here," he whined, "if you can't lift a coffee pot?" What a sourpuss. Nicky liked his coffee sloppy with brandy. He was still nursing his wounds two years after the failure of his marriage to Liz Taylor when he got serious about the actress Mamie Van Doren. They dined at Romanoff's, where they'd see Humphrey Bogart, looking all crinkly and world-weary in a booth, hands cupped about his drink. Or there were evenings in Chasen's, with its Hollywood columnists and stars. Once, Mamie recalled in her memoirs, "I caught the eye of then president of the Screen Actors Guild, Ronald Reagan. His glance followed me across the room before his attention was diverted by a sharp nudge from Nancy."

Mamie was just biting into a very pleasant slice of Hawaiian pineapple cheese-cake when Nicky's friend, the actor John Carroll, told her that Nicky might even pop the question. He went on to say, "So, play your cards right, sweetheart, and you can have it all. All this? It could be yours." Mamie was pretty disgusted.

But if anything was guaranteed to make her turn down Nicky, it was dinner with Conrad at Casa Encantada. They entered a vast room and right in the middle, like an island of chair legs, gold plate, and wood, stood the vast twenty-five-foot dinner table with Conrad, all shined and polished, at the far end. With a faint version of his commanding stare, he said weakly, "Welcome to my home, my dear." Mamie was led to a seat at the middle of the table, and Nicky took the chair opposite his father. They were all so far apart Mamie probably considered sending smoke signals. Then it got very weird. Having fixed his gaze permanently on Nicky, Conrad asked Mamie, "So, my dear, how do you like the motion picture business?" The maid served the lobster pâté appetizer.

Mamie squeaked, "It's interesting. You meet so many people, you know?" Conrad may have known, but he wasn't going to look at her, apparently mesmerized by Nicky.

Nicky, a lump in his throat, echoed Mamie's answer, as if translating it further. "It's interesting for her, Pop. She meets so many people, you know?"

Still entranced by Nicky's forehead, Conrad fired off another question across the vast space between them. "Indeed," said Conrad. "And how, may I ask, did you happen upon the motion picture business, my dear?"

"Well, Howard Hughes helped me a great deal," she replied.

Then Nicky translated again: "Howard Hughes sort of discovered her, Pop."

"Indeed. I'm sure he did," Conrad smirked. The whole meal went on this way, broken only by a feverish row Nicky and Conrad had on the subject of ballpoint pens in hotel rooms. Then Mamie began to notice a noise erupting every so often from Conrad's end of the table. Whenever he made a comment—to Nicky, of course—a concentrated look came on his face and then *"Burrp!"* Conrad popped out a gassy burp by way of punctuation. He extolled Barron's marriage to his good Catholic wife, Marilyn, and their ability to produce children. "It's what you need . . . a family—*Burrp!*" Then came the port at the end of the meal. Conrad shifted in his chair, tilting it back. A penetrating fart made the beautiful upholstery shake. Neither Conrad nor Nicky paid the slightest heed, and Nicky puffed on a cigar.

Lobster Pâté

INGREDIENTS

1 ½ cups lobster meat
Juice of half a lemon
½ cup cream cheese

½ tbsp. brandy
½ tsp. cayenne pepper

METHOD

In a bowl, combine the lobster meat with the lemon juice. After 15 minutes, add the cream cheese, brandy, and cayenne pepper. Serve on hot, thin, buttered toast.

With Mamie seen off by Conrad's farts, Patricia "Trish" McClintock was to be the second Mrs. Nicky Hilton. She planned her first official dinner as a Hilton and called on Zsa Zsa Gabor for help. They debated the issue over cups of coffee and streusel cake while Zsa Zsa copied down their ideas into a ridiculous notebook. Zsa Zsa asked, "So, what would you like to serve?"

"Um . . . spaghetti?" suggested Trish, to Zsa Zsa's laughter.

"Spaghetti!" roared Zsa Zsa. "Oh, no, no, no! You do not serve spaghetti to the Hiltons!"

Steak, Zsa Zsa suggested, was the cornerstone of the Hilton appetite. They liked only "hearty American foods. Potatoes! Corn! Vegetables! All of the typical American foods. Just no hot dogs." Then, busily adding to her notebook, she scribbled, "French bread, red wine, salad, and cheesecake with strawberries for desert." Plus pink champagne. She smiled delightedly at Trish, exclaiming, "You and I will do this together, my dear. It'll be fun! I've been a part of this family for a long time, and I know just what we all like." Secretly, Zsa Zsa lent her staff to Trish for her inauguration. Conrad looked up from his plate and said, "Say, don't I know these people from somewhere?" Zsa Zsa's life remained entwined with the Hiltons (she had a daughter, Francesca, whose paternity was unclear). Even though 1976 saw Conrad marry his third and last wife, sixty-one-year-old and religious Frances Kelly, Conrad hired Zsa Zsa's former live-in personal secretary, Phyllis Davis Bradley. But as Phyllis recalled, "That didn't last long. One day we had a huge disagreement about something ridiculous and, much to my horror and astonishment, she [Zsa Zsa] hurled a plate of food at me. I was outraged and told her I would not tolerate that kind of behavior from her." Never one to stay cross, Zsa Zsa apologized by inviting Frances to her house for dinner. "'I will cook my famous Hungarian goulash,' she promised. 'But get there before eight, because the maid is always drunk after eight.'"

2

The Upper Crust

Royal Roastings and Stately Snacks

Where on the food chain do aristocrats eat? Royal watchers and history twitchers will love the fond irreverence of the tales within. Find out the effect of too many fairy feasts on Ludwig of Bavaria; how Hirohito and Ibn Saud tasted East-Meets-West diplomacy. Would you try a bit of the cake that killed Rasputin or suck on a suicide sweet with Antony and Cleopatra? Was it sex or raspberry soufflé that won Mrs. Simpson a king's heart? It's all here: abdications, executions, revolutions, coronations, tales of toothache, and posh picnics spiced with the odd military coup or two. Mind your manners now. . . .

THE TSARS (PLUS A LAST SUPPER WITH RASPUTIN)

The moribund, enclosed world of Nicholas II, tsar of all the Russias, and his wife, Tsarina Alexandra, allowed the couple to hide behind the walls of Tsarskoye Selo in an artificial, doomed, and fatally remote domesticity. To further compound their unpopularity, the close-minded Romanovs believed they had a divine right to rule and were autocrats far removed from their people, plunging into World War I with little thought for the immense loss of Russian lives. They did nothing in the way of buttering up their subjects and could have done with helpful pieces of public relations advice, such as "Smile more often!" Nicholas's own father, the large and bearish Alexander III, didn't hold out much hope for his son; with Nicholas's narrow shoulders and piping voice, he was a *devouchka*—a bit girly. When he reached manhood, all of this was unhappily combined with Nicholas's limited ideas and empathy, pale convictions, dullness, and generally gentle stupidity. Nicholas was fairly wishy-washy, and that could probably have been tolerated, but his empress, Alexandra, was deeply unpopular, mostly due to her pigheaded snobbishness and spooky goings on with Rasputin. She was, of course, desperately worried about the health of the future tsar, her desperately ill, hemophiliac son, Alexei. One thing the Romanovs didn't want the world knowing was how blighted Alexei's health was. The patrilineal Romanov dynasty would be in question. Enter mystic peasant Rasputin, lamppost tall with too much eye makeup and hair badly in need of a wash. He, Alexandra believed, could control Alexei's bleeding. Alexandra was already pretty difficult to like pre-Rasputin; she was a sickly, highly strung princess when Nicholas met her and cast a baleful light over the throne. One of their future prison wardens believed that Nicholas "feared his wife more than the Devil himself." She was always swooning, pinch-cheeked with insomnia, migraines, palpitations, and pins and needles. Her diet was a special one, mostly vegetarian, prescribed by doctors, and she was very keen on fasting whenever the church gave her the chance.

Then there was the 1905 revolution triggered by a massacre. On Bloody Sunday, the snow of Palace Square, St. Petersburg, turned red as imperial troops fired on the citizens. They had wanted to present a petition for reforms to the tsar—hardly an insurgency, really, as all were unarmed and, ironically, the tsar wasn't even in on the day. The separation of the people from the tsar had begun. In the name of "Nicholas the Bloody," dissidents were crushed mercilessly; exile and execution swept the land, while Nicholas wandered around Tsarskoye Selo, smoking Benson and Hedges, with a faintly distracted air. It took some considerable time before he was even informed about Bloody Sunday. Alexandra, "saturated" with doses of cocaine, morphine, and Veronal, looked on censoriously.

The glory of the tsar's court was unsurpassed. Young princesses wore flowers in their hair, the bright blossoms contrasting with the thick white and silver fox furs of the court matriarchs. Noble heads were frosted with diadems; rubies and emeralds ogled from their settings; white stockings and bare shoulders revealed peach-skinned beauty as ladies swept down the marble stairs of the palace. One fine lady had a pearl necklace that was so long it could rattle against her knees. The court's might was displayed in the footmen's uniforms, stitched with the imperial eagle of the tsars; the Cossacks in scarlet; and the black Christian Abyssinian servants magnificently turbaned. All was not pride and glory though—the Russian imperial habit of allowing the oldest servants to become the most august meant that one of Nicholas's chief waiters was a servant dating from his father's time. Shortsighted and trembling, the waiter would pour the tsar's wine while Nicholas held and guided his arm. Noblemen wore the softest of moccasins and open robes insulated with fleecy beaver fur. Large blocks of ice shimmered, too—hand-carved glaciers to chill the champagne. Waltz music rippled through the air. Though the children of the tsar loved to throw bread bullets at each other, statelier eating was the order of the day. Servants moved between the noblemen, offering cool ices and sweet morsels on trays before guests were invited to partake of the buffet, clustered with the most delicate, carefully wrought petits fours, laid out among sheaves of green, sculpted palms. Colonels—called "Cutlet Colonels"—masterminded the supper and worked for Count Benckendorff, the marshal of the court, whose role it was to manage all meals, such as ensuring they lasted only for their mandatory fifty minutes. The great and distinguished ate on a slightly raised platform, although Nicholas had an extra chair positioned at each twelve-person table to allow him to briefly join each table of guests.

With Count Benckendorff in charge of your every meal, what could go wrong? He made sure the Romanovs had the wonderful Muscovite kalatch bread they loved for special occasion breakfasts (reputedly, the dough's fineness depended on being mixed with the waters of the wide Moscow River). To accommodate the Romanovs, barrels of the miraculous water were transported to St. Petersburg in order to make the braided, ring-shaped white bread. The ring shape is because the kalatch used to be hung in batches on a wooden pole for transportation. Being given a kalatch was, symbolically, like being given a mouthful of good luck, served very hot and wrapped in a warm, linen napkin.

Kalatch

INGREDIENTS

1 lb. of the finest white flour
1½ tbsp. fresh yeast
⅔ cup milk
1 tbsp. water from the Moscow River
  (good luck with that!)

3 tbsp. granulated sugar
3 tbsp. melted butter
2 eggs, plus the yolks of another 2
1 tbsp. butter
Sea salt

METHOD

Warm the milk and Moscow River water. Mix the milk with the yeast and leave it in a warm place for 15 minutes in order to activate it. Sift half of the flour into a large mixing bowl; add the warm, milky yeast. Knead thoroughly, cover with a towel, and leave to rise in a warm place for an hour.

Now knead into the dough the remaining flour, sea salt, sugar, melted butter, and 1 egg plus 1 yolk. Knead for 15–20 minutes (if you get fed up, remind yourself that you are a Russian serf cooking for a tsar!). Cover the bowl with a towel and return it to that warm spot to rise for another 90 minutes.

Now take the dough and press it down a little; use your open palms to make about four gentle and light movements, ridding the bread of its gases. Leave it

Kalatch (*continued*)

to rise for another 90 minutes. Repeat. Leave it to rise for another 90 minutes. Repeat. Leave it to rise for another 90 minutes. Night may be falling by now. You may be feeling a bit revolutionary. Never mind. Repeat. Leave to rise for another 90 minutes. By now, you will have contemplated your existence thoroughly. . . .

Have a baking tray lightly buttered and ready to go. Flour a work surface. Divide the dough into 4 sections. Using a floured rolling pin, gently roll each section of dough into a 1-centimeter-thick oval. Now think of the shape of a handbag. You need to cut the shape of the handle of a handbag into the side of the oval. Let your handle be 2 centimeters in width. You now have this arc-shaped incision in your dough, so pull the "tongue" beneath the handle forward (as if you are making a tongue for your handbag). When you look at your kalatch, it looks like a handbag with a handle and a tongue. Now repeat with the other sections of dough. Brush all the kalatch with the remaining egg and egg yolk. Cover and leave to prove for 30 minutes (this will give you time to storm the tsar's palace). Preheat the oven to 200°C.

At last! It is time to bake the kalatch in the oven for 20–30 minutes. Eat nice and hot—it tastes slightly sweet and buttery—but keep your fingers from burning by wrapping the kalatch in a clean, warm napkin (I also like to slather butter on the warm, puffy kalatch as I eat it).

Midday was time for luncheon. In the tsar's summer retreat of Livadia Palace, everyone had lunch with the tsar, first quaffing glasses of vodka and the bounty of the zakusky (hors d'oeuvre) table. Hot and cold delicacies were there: plump pickled herrings bobbed about in rich vinegars, smoked fish lay on plates, and caviar gleamed; there were also small, golden squares of fried bread to accompany the fish. The hot section sported hot knuckles of ham and sausages in tomato sauce. Alexandra, cheerful as ever, disapproved of the zakusky table. Surely it couldn't be healthy to eat standing up, and she abstained from its pleasures. The zakusky table was also the result of the very special ceremony of "the present," dating back to the eighteenth century. Every spring, the Ural Cossacks brought to the tsar the finest fish caught in the first haul of the year along with barrels of fresh caviar, ranging in color from pearl gray to amber. The ritual of the present was taken very seriously. The Cossacks cut and drove holes into the deep ice of the Ural River. A Te Deum, or Ambrosian hymn, was sung, the opening Latin words rising in the frozen air. Priests sprinkled holy water on the holes while the governor general supervised. Then the Cossacks lowered nets into the Ural. The fish were slaughtered there on the ice and their caviar collected; immediately, a deputation of Cossacks set off for the palace to share a glass of vodka with the tsar and receive monogrammed watches in thanks. The present was symbolically a spontaneous act of devotion to the tsar, but it also had a very legal precedent. Exclusive rights to fish the Ural River were given to the Cossacks in exchange for the first catch, the tsar's imperial haul.

Dinner was always at eight, beginning with soup, clear or thick, like cream of barley, served with a crisped turret of vol-au-vent alongside. Baked little golden buns of pirozhky and cheese on hot rusks were starters, too. This was followed by fish, roast veal, chicken with cucumber salad or game, vegetables, fresh strawberry jellies, compotes, and tangerine ices. Dessert might even be iced cherries and fruit. The beer and Madeira that often accompanied lunch were replaced by fine wines during the meal, with liqueurs served with coffee at the end. All had to materialize seamlessly, one after another: Nicholas was not one for pausing between courses. Count Benckendorff had enormous heaters, filled with boiling water, installed in the dining room to keep dishes hot. The empress, though, had her special diet prepared on oil heaters in the pantry. The fifty-minute time limit became more important than the overcooking of delicate fish and fowl.

Another court official, Count Freedericksz, lamented long and loud about the massacring of the tsar's dinner. Finally, in Livadia Palace, he determined to follow his food principles and had engineers construct an electric railway and a lift. The railway would rattle along at top speed from the kitchens to the pantry, and from there the lift would shoot up to the dining room. Dishes would arrive fresh, succulent, and perfectly cooked. Not everyone was happy about Count Freedericksz's solution. Ironically, the cooks were very much put out. After all, what would all the young novices have left to do now? They had been brilliantly occupied in carrying the food from the kitchen to the pantry. The electric train was too jumpy and desserts might get jumbled up. The chicken croquets and sauces were paying the price for the shaking journey. In protest, the cooks sent Count Freedericksz's electric train along at the slowest rate possible, and it trundled too slowly to the pantry to be of much use. The heaters of boiling water were staging a comeback. All of this effort, though, was rather lost on the tsar. When he (ineffectually) became commander in chief of the Russian armies, he decided to eat the simplest of meals and declared, "Thanks to the war, I have learnt that simple dishes are infinitely nicer and healthier than all the Marshall's spiced cookery." Fortunately, his great French chef, Cubat, was not privy to Nicholas's sentiments. As soon as the tsar left the table, everything was removed. It was then redistributed to the kitchen staff, who could sell it for profit. Crowds would gather at the palace kitchens—but not crowds of the poor—lining up to buy the leftovers of the tsar's table and also representing the most aristocratic of houses. The wonderful cavernous wine cellars of the palace contained real jewels for the bibulous: Count Benckendorff, aware of such temptations, clung to the keys and made sure all wine was signed for. The other courtiers scoured the calendar looking for saints' days, always ready to put forward their case for opening a special bottle or two. Count Freedericksz was particularly partial to a drop of Chateau d'Yquem, nicknamed "Nectar." But, as ever, spoilsport Alexandra got in the way; there was never any chance of a glassful of Nectar if the

hawk-eyed empress was at dinner. In contrast, whenever the tsar saw a bottle coming out of the cellar, he smiled vaguely and said, "Have you another niece coming
of age today?" Incidentally, when the revolutionaries broke into the cellars of the
Winter Palace, the wine was relished by all; revolutionaries lay hopelessly about in
Palace Square, slain by mouthfuls of Nectar.

Pirozhky

FOR THE PIROZHKY DOUGH . . .

2 cups all-purpose flour   4 tbsp. chilled lard, cut into little pieces
A generous pinch of salt   4–6 tbsp. ice-cold water
¼ lb. chilled butter, cut into little pieces

FOR THE STUFFING . . .

2 tbsp. butter   4 tbsp. fresh dill, finely chopped
1½ cups onion, very finely chopped   1 tsp. salt
¾ lb. lean ground beef   Freshly ground black pepper
1 small boiled egg, finely chopped

METHOD

In a large mixing bowl, combine the flour, salt, butter, and lard. Using your fingertips, rub the lard and butter through the flour until a breadcrumb-like texture is
achieved. Now add the iced water in one go, and press the dough together into
a ball. If it's too crumbly, then add a little more iced water (and so on) until the
dough adheres well together. Wrap the dough in plastic wrap, and chill in the
fridge for an hour.

Flour a work surface. Shape the pirozhky dough into a rectangle. Now roll it
into a strip that is about 21 inches in length and 6 inches in width. Fold the dough
lengthwise in thirds so that it is reduced from 21 inches to 7 inches in length. Turn
it around and then roll out so that it reaches 21 inches in length again. Repeat
this process another three times until you end up with a 7-by-6-inch packet. Now
wrap in plastic wrap and leave in the fridge for an hour and a half.

Now to make the filling. In a skillet, melt the butter. Add the onions and sauté
them until they are soft. Add the beef and brown it. In a bowl, combine the minced
meat with the eggs, dill, salt, and pepper.

Preheat the oven to 200°C. Butter a baking sheet. Flour a work surface, and
reshape the dough into a circle; roll it out to a thickness of an eighth of an inch.
Using a 3- to 3½-inch round cutter, press out all the circles you can from the
dough. Use all the dough scraps, too. Now place 1½–2 tablespoons of filling
into the center of each circle and flatten slightly. Fold the top of your pirozhky
disk toward you and over the filling. This should still leave about an inch of clean
dough at the bottom of the disk. Then fold in each side of the disk. Finally, fold the
last bottom section of dough inward, over the top of the other folds. You should
be left with a rectangular parcel. Place each pirozhky, one after another, seam
side down on the buttered baking sheet. Bake for 30 minutes, until the pirozhky
are golden brown.

One of the most splendid meals to be held in Tsarskoye Selo was for one of the daughters of Nicholas, the Grand Duchess Tatiana Nikolayevna. She was eight years old. There were cake treats at ten o'clock in the morning with slices of "King's Cake" Baumkuchen—delicious, filigree-thin layers of pastry infused with rum, lemon, and almonds, glazed with apricot jam and dusted with powdered sugar. After a visit to church, Tatiana must have gazed in wonder at the imperial luncheon set out at the family's special table with its yellow-gold chairs, their feet pressing into the red carpet, in the semicircle of the Portrait Hall. Set out were goblets of crystal, and the blue-edged china was embossed with the black eagle of the tsars. Often there was a carafe or two of cloudy kvass and another of Madeira. Kvass is an incredible alcoholic concoction made by fermenting bread—sourdough, black, or rye—with honey, caraway seeds, yeast, and berries; aromatics like violets, mint, and blackberry leaves could be added for more exotic flavors. Food and drink on the imperial table was an interesting amalgam of the nineteenth-century passion for French food (courtesy of chef Cubat) and items like kvass, which harkened back to the table of Catherine the Great.

Sixty guests were expected, and extra seats had been drawn about the guests' tables so that the tsar could exchange more intimate pleasantries with each group; he would often eat a course at each table. The luncheon began with soup: botvinia, served just to the royal family—a delicious cold soup made variously of beetroot leaves, beetroot, radishes, cucumber, sorrel, nettle, and dill, cooled with crushed ice and served with cold steamed sturgeon—while the guests had buttery leek and potato Soup Bonne Femme. Next came pies: generously proportioned, ornate kulebyaka (pastry stuffed with salmon, rice, crumbled eggs, mushrooms, and herbs) and warm kurniks (chicken potpies). Then mutton cutlets and chicken. Next, bowls of heavy red strawberries and a mysterious dessert.

Botvinia

INGREDIENTS

6 pints water
3 cups fresh stemless sorrel
3 cups fresh stemless spinach
½ cup freshly grated horseradish
Juice of 3 lemons
1 tbsp. salt
1 tsp. granulated sugar

6 cups kvass
1 cucumber, peeled, seeded, and diced
10 scallions, finely chopped
1 cup fresh crabmeat
1½ lb. cold poached salmon or sturgeon, divided into 8 pieces

Botvinia (*continued*)

METHOD

In a large saucepan, bring the water to a boil. Add the sorrel and spinach, and cook uncovered for 4 minutes. Drain the leaves and immediately douse them in cold water. Now puree them in a blender.

In a large bowl, combine the horseradish, lemon juice, salt, and sugar. Add the spinach-sorrel blend and then, more slowly, the kvass, about a fourth of a cup at a time. Finally, add the cucumber, scallions, crab, and fish. Leave the botvinia to chill for 2 hours before serving.

Kvass (dare you make your own?)

INGREDIENTS

1 lb. slightly stale black bread (you can use pumpernickel instead)	¼ cup lukewarm water
6 quarts water	1 cup granulated sugar
2 tbsp. active dry yeast	2 tbsp. fresh mint leaves
	2 tbsp. raisins

METHOD

Begin by preheating the oven to 200°C. Dry the bread out in the oven—this will take about an hour. Chop it coarsely. In a large pot, bring 6 quarts of water to a boil. Add the bread. Now remove this from the heat; cover and leave to do its murky business for 8 hours.

After this, strain the bread fluid through a finely textured sieve, catching the strained water in a large bowl. Keep pressing the bread to extract all its goodness.

Now dissolve the yeast in a fourth of a cup of lukewarm water. Put it in a warm place for 15 minutes, until it froths and doubles in volume. Combine this with the bread liquid, sugar, and mint leaves. Stir well, and leave to ferment for 10 hours.

Sterilize 2 or 3 quart-size bottles. Strain the kvass through a sieve, and get ready to bottle it. Using a funnel, pour the kvass into the bottles, filling them by two-thirds. Add raisins to each bottle. Shove a plug of kitchen roll into the top of each bottle, and leave them in a moderate spot (cool but not cold) for about 4 days (by this time, the sediment will have fallen to the bottom). Now rebottle the kvass, leaving the sediment behind. It will be a deliciously amber color and should be kept it the fridge until you are ready to drink it.

One of the oddest figures in the downfall of the house of Romanov was Rasputin. He seems, at least to me, the most unlikely person to put any sort of faith in. First, his role of savior to hemophiliac Alexei and his future job as spiritual advisor to the empress were secured through a telegraph. His reputation as a miracle worker was confirmed when Alexei lay ill, apparently dying, his will drawn up, until, lo and behold, Rasputin's telegraph arrived from Siberia. Alexei made a miraculous recovery. Perhaps the success of Father Grigori (as Rasputin came to be known) came down to two things: his great stare—his eyes glowed with a near-phosphorescent light—and a disarming physical tic, which, as we know, every self-respecting mystic needs. His eyes he used for hypnosis on Alexei; scientific discovery has confirmed that hemophiliac bleeding can be exacerbated by stress and slowed down when a calm, peaceful state is induced—hence hypnosis. Other than his stare and tic, Rasputin was also very good, at home in the Siberian village of Pokrovskoye, at denouncing horse thieves. Beyond this, he was an utter rake in his village, trying to unbutton peasant girls' dresses and slaking his thirst for vodka. When he raped his female followers, he would mutter the assurance "Now, Mother, everything is in order."

Even on the day of his death he knocked back a dozen bottles of Madeira and found it impossible to resist temptation in the form of an invitation to meet Prince Youssoupov and his gorgeous wife at midnight. Youssoupov had determined, with his co-conspirators, to kill Rasputin—only this drastic action could save the Romanovs from the malign influence of Rasputin, who had soured public opinion so massively that it was rumored he was ruling Russia by proxy. He had even taken to calling Empress Alexandra "old girl." Rasputin arrived, grinning through his blackened teeth at Youssoupov, dressed in a game silk blouse embroidered with bright cornflowers. A heavy cord hung about his waist. Youssoupov took Rasputin down to rooms in the basement, where a samovar smoked and a log fire blazed. The would-be assassins had gone to the trouble of discovering what Rasputin's favorite cakes were: petits fours filled with rose-flavored cream. Two types, then, of petits fours were set on the table: one plate was filled with chocolate cream (which Youssoupov could eat), and another plate held six rose-cream petits fours packed full of cyanide (one Doctor Lazovert, wearing rubber gloves, had ground the potassium crystals to a powder and, lifting the top of each petit four, had inserted enough poison to kill several men). At first, Rasputin politely declined the offer of a cake, claiming they were too sweet. He quickly crumbled, though, and scoffed several of the rose-cream petits fours, their crumbs lodging in his beard. Youssoupov held his breath. Would Rasputin keel over, the last rose cream lodged in his throat? No. Bottles and glasses stood on the sideboard. Desperate to see some effect, Youssoupov offered Rasputin a glass of his favorite wine, Madeira and Marsala, laced with poison—this was more nerve-racking, as Youssoupov had to add cyanide to the wine on the spot, lest it evaporate. To assure Rasputin that Youssoupov's wife and jolly friends were indeed upstairs, on the brink of joining them, the conspirators played "Yankee Doodle Came to Town." The only effect this seemed to have was to electrify Rasputin's fun-loving side: he insisted that Youssoupov play him jaunty songs. Finally, feverish with exhaustion and at his wits' end, Youssoupov rounded on Rasputin with a pistol and shot him dead. Youssoupov fled the dreaded room but then had a premonition that he had to go back and see Rasputin's body.

He cracked open the door, knelt down beside Rasputin, and clutched his shoulder. Boo! A pair of green, devilish eyes opened! A couple more bullets and a dip in the river did the job in the end, though: Rasputin was finally dead.

Rasputin's Last Temptation

INGREDIENTS

1 cup all-purpose flour
2 tbsp. fine white sugar
4 eggs

1 tbsp. potato starch
4 tbsp. Cointreau

FOR THE FILLING . . .

¾ cup rose jelly
¾ cup marzipan
1 cup heavy cream

1 tbsp. powdered sugar
1 tsp. rose water

FOR THE ICING . . .

1½ cups powdered sugar
Juice of 1 lemon

½–1 tsp. cochineal
1 tsp. rose water

METHOD

Preheat the oven to 180°C. Prepare a square or rectangular baking sheet by lining it with parchment paper. Sieve the flour and potato starch together. In a large bowl, whisk the eggs with the sugar until they are fluffy. Now fold the flour into the egg-sugar fluff. Pour the mixture onto the baking sheet and try to even out the surface and make sure the mix fills the corners. Bake for 15 minutes. Meanwhile, lay out paper towels the same size as the baking tray and dust it lightly with confectioner's sugar.

Now make the rose-cream filling. Put the cream into a chilled glass bowl. Using an electric mixer, add the powdered sugar and rose water: whisk for about 1 minute, until the cream, although soft, dimples and can retain soft shapes. Keep to one side.

Remove the cake from the oven. Turn it out onto the kitchen roll and leave it to cool completely. Now, using a pastry brush, sweep Cointreau over the cake. Cut off a third of the cake and lay it—gently—to one side.

Smooth the rose jelly over the remaining ⅔ section of cake. Using greaseproof paper on each side, roll out the marzipan to fit the same size as the ⅔ section of cake—cut the shape out if necessary (and, yes, use a ruler). Carefully place it on top of the rose jelly (remove the greaseproof paper, of course). Now cut this section of the cake in two so that you now have 3 sections of cake. On both of the marzipan-covered sections, apply a thick layer of rose cream. Now put this in the fridge to cool for 1 hour.

It is time to make the rose-flavored icing. In a bowl, mix the powdered sugar with lemon juice, cochineal, and rose water. Depending on the shade of pink you want, adjust the amount of cochineal you use. If the icing seems too smooth, simply add a little warm water. Now cut the cake into a series of small perfect squares. Ice each of these, place a tiny iced rose on each, and then leave them to dry.

When the Romanovs were overthrown in the Revolution of 1917, and by the time the tsar abdicated, he had already been told that Alexei, his beloved son and heir to the throne, would not survive to his sixteenth birthday. The tsar and his family were placed under house arrest at the Alexander Palace. Empress Alexandra, bereft after the murder of Rasputin, sat in her rooms burning cases of letters while revolutionaries strolled about the hallowed royal quarters and hunted the tsar's favorite wild goats in the grounds. The children had their heads shaved—not as a postrevolutionary act but because they were ill with measles. Alexei was also confined to a wheelchair. Escape seemed impossible; exile was to be desired, either to Japan or to Scandinavia. All was in doubt, however, when the family were moved to the former governor's house in Tobolsk in Western Siberia (though there had been pressure to incarcerate the royal family in jail). The revolutionaries ordered the Romanovs into the circular hall of the palace at midnight—the tsar and empress, the four daughters, and Alexei—and kept them waiting until 6 a.m. before putting them on a train bound for Tobolsk, the shades closed whenever they stopped at a station. Commandant Yakovlev, shepherding the Romanovs, noted that only three things seemed to matter to the tsar: "his family, the weather, and food." Nicholas's diary, with bland understatement, recalls the journey: "It was very stuffy and dusty; 26 degrees in the [train] car. . . . [We] eat in the train restaurant, the kitchen feeds us very well, Eastern-Chinese food and etc." The Romanovs were still laden with precious possessions and a retinue of thirty servants. When they arrived in Tobolsk, Nicholas noted the "terrible kitchen garden" and, in between readings of *The Scarlet Pimpernel*, proceeded to dig up the greenhouse there, as well as the duck pond, and then went back to playing bezique. On December 6, he was given no less than three name day pies and generously gave one to his guard. Alexandra tut-tutted over such behavior, scolding Nicholas publicly for talking to their guards; she always maintained a haughty, bitter iciness. The tsar marked the days indifferently, recording the weather in his diary, now reading Arthur Conan Doyle's *A Study in Scarlet* and endlessly shoveling snow and cutting logs. Some enthusiast in the Revolutionary Guards thought they spotted signaling to collaborators from a window in the Grand Duchess Anastacia's room, but it turned out she kept nodding off while reading, her head causing the lamp to fade and bloom.

Cousin George V of Britain, having been less than eager to save the tsar, did send a boat, the *Marlborough*, to the Crimea to rescue about seventeen of his relatives, including Nicholas's mother, the dowager empress Marie; Youssoupov (our assassin); and the tsar's sister Xenia. The fleeing Romanovs were hurriedly packed bags with Tartar earth as soily mementoes of the motherland. They had been living on their estates in the Crimea on very frugal rations for the last few months—though they still had a cook who had managed to rustle up a clever Weinerschnitzel, which, instead of being breaded, pan-fried veal cutlet, was composed

of onions and cabbage. They made coffee from roasted acorns, and Youssoupov
held that they'd started to eat donkey meat. Prince Dimitri Romanov claimed that
"apart from the pea soup, there were two different dishes; fried potatoes with
onions and fried potatoes without." The revolutionary forces took great pleasure
in humbling the extended royal family through rationing, gleefully reporting that
weak, aristocratic requests for extra sugar were denied—they also kept an eye out
for any promonarchist peasants who might be smuggling the royals extra food (this
was indeed the case). In a sadly poignant moment, when what remained of the Romanovs finally turned up, bedraggled, at Victoria Station in London to be greeted
in person by Nicholas's look-a-like cousin, George V, one of their exhausted servants burst into tears of joy at the sight of George and fell at his feet, thinking that
George was Nicholas, saved and returned to them.

A second revolution shook Russia when the Bolsheviks grasped power, and
with it there was to be a far greater restriction on the Romanovs' privileges as well
as a new home, at No. 49 Voznesensky Prospekt—creepily called "the House of
Special Purpose" by the Bolsheviks—in Yekaterinburg, a large city deep in the
dreaded Urals, where there was great local hostility toward the Romanovs, probably because Yekaterinburg was the dismal transit center of the tsar's own penal
system, shuffling political prisoners on to places of death and dread. The writer
Chekov wrote a very colorful description of the inhabitants of Yekaterinburg when
he had the misfortune to spend a night or two there. Everyone, he said, had big
fists and little eyes with wall-busting foreheads—they were delivered not by mid-
wives but by mechanics. The climate of Yekaterinburg offered plenty of interesting weather for the tsar (now called "Citizen Nicholas") to record in his diary: it
froze all the year round, was lit up by the midnight sun for a month, and then froze
over again. The tsar took so many baths that the family regularly ran out of water.
Alexandra comforted herself with holy water, ointments, morphine, and tinctures
for her aches and pains; poor Alexei often lay moaning from recurrent, agonizing
hemorrhaging in his knee. The empress always spoke to her children in English, but
the revolutionaries decreed that for the Romanovs to communicate in any language
other than Russian was forbidden.

The windows of No. 49 were painted white and sealed; the house guarded by
dozens of soldiers. A palisade of wood encircled the house so that no one could see
in or out. Now the Romanov retinue was down to three servants: the middle-aged
cook, Ivan Kharitonov (who had left his wife and child behind to follow the tsar);
a skinny, egg-headed kitchen boy called Leonid; and Demidova, a large, blonde
parlor maid. All had come voluntarily to share the Romanovs' exile. Some cheer
was brought by the pet spaniel, Joy; a pet Pekinese called Jemmy; and a gift or
two from relatives—the last being of coffee and chocolate before this, too, was
stopped. Ration cards were in order, and the Romanovs ate unceremoniously with

their servants at the dining room table, the room filled with a whitened, foggy gloom from the sealed windows. Their food was prepared by Kharitonov in the cramped, smoky kitchen on a gasping oil stove. Or food like black bread and tea came from their chief guard, Commandant Avdeev. Lunches of thin soup speckled with meat or scrawny cutlets arrived from the revolutionary canteen. Kharitonov tried to tempt the empress's appetite with meat-free vermicelli. At first, the family had no samovar, so they had to ask the guards for tea. The daughters occupied some of their time learning what they could of cooking from Kharitonov. Nicholas recorded, "The daughters are learning to cook from him and are kneading dough in the evenings and bake bread in the morning! Not bad!" Demidova taught them how to launder their clothes. When Dr. Derevenko examined the family, he saw how malnourished they were and asked if the sisters of the Novo-Tikhvinsky Convent could bring the Romanovs milk, fresh eggs, and cream. Thank goodness that food could corrupt Avdeev; he permitted the nuns to supply food and allowed sausages and pies through the doors of No. 49, too—as long as this allowed him and his cohorts to take an ample share, pilfering cream and butter. Meanwhile, the family played cards, polished their icons, mended their clothes, and sang sacred songs; they even managed to celebrate the Resurrection at Easter with kisses, kulich (Easter bread), and red eggs, though they felt the absence of any pashka (Easter cake).

Unfortunately, Commandant Avdeev was removed from duty; he had been letting things slip. One of the tsar's daughters, Maria, had been discovered with a guard, young Ivan Skorokhodov, showing too affectionate thanks for a birthday cake he'd given her. Ivan was jailed and there was a clampdown on fraternization. The new commandant was Yakov Yurovsky with his dark-natured, sadistic assistant, Nikulin (Alexandra, showing typical misjudgment of character, thought him "decent" at first). Yurovsky also borrowed from the spoils offered by the nuns, savoring the cheeses they brought while sternly informing the Romanovs that there would be no more cream on their table—a smuggled letter was discovered tucked inside the cork stopper of a bottle of cream. Food wrappers were scrawled with messages, and secret missives were concealed inside bread loaves. The nuns had been up to no good, and Yurovsky took a very revolutionary satisfaction in drastically reducing the family's rations while ordering some fifty eggs from the nuns for his troops.

His thoughts had turned to regicide, and the many soldiers who would bury the Romanovs in Koptyaki Forest needed to be fed. On Wednesday, July 17, 1918, at 2:15 a.m., the Romanovs, their three faithful retainers, and their dogs (the smallest being carried in the arms of a princess, as its little legs couldn't manage the stairs) were taken down to the basement of No. 49.

"TUM TUM" BERTIE: EDWARD VII

Like many parents, Queen Victoria and Prince Albert tried to keep track of the pastimes of their exasperating eldest son, Edward (known as "Bertie"), in some attempt to moderate his behavior. Even his daily diary was up for scrutiny; a scrutiny Bertie must have disappointed with such brilliantly dunderheaded observations as this one on the emperor of France: "The Emperor is a short person." Or this entry: "Walked about the town of Leeds which is very dirty, and the inhabitants low people." Bertie also kept a notebook at the time, cutely called "Wit and Whoppers," full of jokes about Bertie and his chums eating eel pies. Ominously, though, the teenage Edward had written a boyish essay on the topic of "Friends and Flatterers" for his personal chaplain, Rev. Charles Tarver, in which he opined that friends will point out your faults helpfully, while flatterers will "lead you into any imaginable vice." Somehow, the flatterers sound like much more fun, don't they?

So great was his longing to escape Victoria's household that Bertie begged the empress of France to let him stay with her. She refused, saying his parents would miss him, to which he moaned beautifully in the royal plural, "Don't fancy that! They don't want us, and there are six more of us at home."

Fortunately for him, his fifteenth birthday on the ninth of November 1856 held new freedoms and delights. He was given the right to choose his own food (and hats!), and his ever-expanding girth in the years to come shows just how well Bertie handled that responsibility (as does his taste in hats). Queen Victoria tried to strike a middle ground: "We do not wish to control your tastes and fancies . . . but we do expect that you will never wear anything extravagant or slang." A prince could not slouch or have anything about him "of the groom or the gamekeeper," but Queen Vic didn't hold Bertie's chances high: he liked lying about in bed (at least it was on his own when he was a teenager) and was a "cunning lazybones." Victoria and Albert hired the renowned phrenologist Sir George Combe to study Bertie's skull for ominous bumps. The future Frederick III, emperor-to-be of Germany, chimed in to the general estimation of Bertie's character, concluding that Bertie could be witty and amusing—he liked to rap his valet on the nose—"but usually his intellect is of no more use than a pistol packed in the bottom of a trunk if one were attacked in the robber-infested Apennines."

Oxford University didn't allow Bertie free rein, either; he wasn't allowed to take part in any manner of debate, and he couldn't stay in Halls of Residence. He did, however, have a private chef, who dished up whatever took his fancy. In February 1860, Prince Albert wrote, scolding him for his rich, excessive diet, which "an experienced and prudent liver will carefully avoid." Bertie was duly sent off to the army (though Queen Victoria opposed a military career for him), and fellow officers smuggled one Millie Clifton, an actress, into his "sleeping quarters" in the barracks. Bertie's personal diary on September 6, 1861, records the loss of his virginity as he cutely refers to his "first time," and then on September 9 a "second time" (September 10 was his "third time"). Somehow, Prince Albert found out about Millie and decided Bertie was depraved. Queen Victoria blamed Albert's death from typhoid on Bertie's wickedness.

Things never got much better for Bertie, and his relationship with the widowed Victoria was troubled and resentful. Victoria always refused to power share—but then who can blame her? According to one biographer, Bertie had a habit of getting his hands on state dispatches and passing them around at dinner tables, asking people what they thought. Indeed, deep, deep down, beneath his colorful waistcoat, Bertie himself harbored doubts about his fitness for the throne. Fortunately for him, marriage to Princess Alexandra offered just the sort of steadying influence he needed. Marriage was a "desperate remedy" to the "Bertie problem": a wife and stability were an excellent means of avoiding scandal. The Windsors hunted through the royal houses of Europe to find a wife for Bertie, finally happening on a "winner," the beautiful, kind, jolly, and penniless Alexandra of Denmark. She had to have such good qualities in excessive measure in order to survive marriage to a faithless husband, and her desperate kindheartedness meant she was adored by her children and grandchildren. The couple were soon setting the trend in London fashion: when the Princess of Wales developed a limp after a bout of rheumatic fever, several fashionable ladies took to aping her limp. Bertie's unusual tastes meant that he was a trendsetter but also difficult to copy with equanimity. Highly unpopular was Bertie's passion for knee breeches, but Tyrolean hats, felt hats, and Norfolk jackets were successes. His avid hatred of Panama hats killed those for a decade or two. Meanwhile, Bertie was very alert to what he deemed appropriate dress for meals. He once asked an unfortunate who appeared dressed in tweed at a Windsor picnic, "Goin' ratting today, Harris?"

One of the first things that must have struck Alexandra about her new husband was how intensely he enjoyed his food. A habitual bolter, Bertie told doctors he could hardly bear to chew food. In the early years of his marriage, his waistline ballooned, earning him the nickname "Tum Tum." Indeed, when he tried to get young Sir Freddy Johnson to calm down during some late-night fun in Sandringham, saying, "Freddy, Freddy, you're very drunk," Freddie poked him in the tummy and slurred, "Tum Tum, you're very fat!" The next morning the harshest of penalties was meted out to Freddy: he was to leave Sandringham *without* his breakfast. Breakfasts were followed by midmorning meals, then lunches, then the ritual of tea. There might be savory snacks like a Sandwich Palais Royal (hot Parmesan-and-butter baked crackers filled with haddock puree) or Croutes de Princesse, with their yummy piscine topping of kipper puree.

Sandwich Palais Royal

FOR THE PARMESAN BISCUITS . . .

3 tbsp. butter, softened
¾ cup all-purpose flour
½ cup Parmesan, finely grated

2 tsp. olive oil
2 tsp. fresh thyme leaves
1 tsp. cayenne pepper

FOR THE HADDOCK PUREE . . .

1 smoked, undyed fillet of haddock
½ tbsp. butter
⅓ cup milk
The grated zest of 1 lemon

½ cup cream cheese
Freshly ground black pepper
1 tbsp. freshly chopped chives

METHOD

In a bowl, cream the butter. Sieve the flour and add it, followed by the Parmesan, olive oil, thyme, and cayenne. Use your hands to thoroughly combine the biscuit mix. Now form it into a squared sausage shape about 10 inches long; wrap this in plastic wrap and chill in the freezer for 40 minutes.

Preheat the oven to 180°C. Lightly flour a work surface; unwrap the biscuit mix and slice it into 20 squares. Place these on a baking tray (or even two baking trays), leaving sufficient room for each Parmesan biscuit to expand. Bake for 20 minutes; they will become golden. Remove from the oven. You will find they are quite pliable, but they firm up when cooled. Leave them on the baking tray to do so.

Now make the haddock puree. Melt the butter in a medium-hot skillet. Add the haddock fillet, skin side down. Let it fry for 1 minute and then add the milk. Cover the skillet and leave the haddock to steam in the milk for 5 minutes or until the haddock becomes opaque. Remove the haddock from the skillet, and drain off what remains of the buttery milk. When the haddock has cooled sufficiently, peel off the skin and flake the haddock, taking care to remove any bones. Put the haddock in a bowl and shred it further. Now add the lemon zest, cream cheese, 1 tablespoon of the buttery haddock milk, black pepper, and the chives. Mix together thoroughly.

Now assemble the Sandwich Palais Royal just as you would a sandwich—you should end up with about 10 of these small, delicious, and delicate morsels. Before serving, though, warm them in the oven for 10 minutes—Tum Tum liked them hot!

Then, before you could do so much as fart, along came dinner, with its twelve courses, plus a sandwich at bedtime never did anyone any harm. Pigeon pie should be taken when watching the Ascot horse races—attendance at a lively horse race required a breakfast of woodcock or bacon, some poached eggs, or even a haddock. Derby dinners at the Jockey Club would only work if there was whitebait and turtle soup on the table. Hunting and shooting meant food; deer pudding was a favorite savory in the heathery wilds of Balmoral. The posh, rich, and titled "Marlborough House Set," which revolved around Bertie and Alexandra, had huge shooting parties; one of 1890 had them bagging 2,600 rabbits and 408 pheasants. Bertie's weekend visits to stately homes meant that the pantries also had to be kept bulging with tidbits. He adored ptarmigan pie, and those who knew him kept this in stock. Even staff benefited from Bertie's food rituals; employees at the Sandringham Christmas party always drank the special palace recipe for spiced old ale, with small pieces of toast bobbing in it. Then it was heated in a great flourish when a red-hot poker was plunged into the ale.

Ptarmigan Pie

Ptarmigan are hard to come by and are relatives of the grouse, so you can use grouse! If not grouse, then look no further than the humble pheasant.

FOR THE PIE CRUST . . .

2½ cups all-purpose flour
¾ cup pork back fat, minced
1½ tbsp. iced water

Nutmeg
Sea salt
Freshly ground black pepper

FOR THE FILLING . . .

2 ptarmigan (complete with giblets)
4 tbsp. butter
8 shallots, finely chopped
2 cloves of garlic, crushed
2½ cups brown mushrooms, finely chopped
½ cup Madeira wine
½ pint game stock
½ cup finely chopped carrots, celery, and shallots

2 tbsp. leeks, finely chopped
6 quails' eggs, boiled and shelled
Generous ½ cup foie gras
Sea salt
Freshly ground black pepper
3 tbsp. olive oil
3 egg yolks, whisked
1 pat of butter

METHOD

Preheat the oven to 200°C. Using a very sharp knife, cut the ptarmigan breasts off the bone and remove the legs. Keep the meat, and legs, together with the livers and hearts, to one side. Oil a baking tray, put the ptarmigan carcasses on it, and roast in the oven for 10 minutes.

In a skillet, melt 3 tablespoons of butter until it is bubbling. Seal the ptarmigan breasts in the butter, allowing 1 minute per side. Remove from the heat and cool.

Now fry the shallots in the butter for 2 minutes, then add the garlic and mushrooms. Cook for a further 3 minutes, stirring regularly. Now add 50 milliliters of the Madeira and cook until the wine has evaporated. Keep to one side.

Ptarmigan Pie (*continued*)

Using a sharp knife again, chop up the small, frail ptarmigan bones. Add olive oil to a skillet and, over a medium heat, sauté the bones along with the carrots, celery, shallots, and leeks. Add the next 50 milliliters of Madeira and the game stock. Cover and simmer for 1 hour.

When the hour is up, sieve the mixture into a new saucepan. Place the ptarmigan legs in this strained sauce. Turn down the heat to low and braise for a further hour and a half. This will eventually become the braising sauce you pour over the pie.

Now make the pastry. In a mixing bowl, combine the flour, pork back fat, iced water, pinch of nutmeg, sea salt, and black pepper. Mix thoroughly with your hands; form into a ball, wrap this in plastic wrap, and put it in the fridge to chill for 1 hour.

Next, finely chop the ptarmigan livers and hearts. Add these to the shallot-garlic-mushroom mixture. Cut the foie gras into 2 slices. Heat 1 tablespoon of butter in a skillet, and then fry the foie gras for about a minute and a half on each side or until it colors. Remove and drain any foie gras–butter leftovers into the shallot-garlic-mushroom mixture.

Heat the oven to 230°C.

Take the pastry out of the fridge, flour the work surface, and remove the plastic wrap from the pastry. Butter a pie dish. Roll the pastry out to fit the pie dish; trim, and leave enough pastry for the pie's lid.

Now begin to assemble the ptarmigan pie. Fill the pie using this pattern: shallot-garlic-mushroom mixture followed by grouse breast followed by foie gras. Then place the quails' eggs on top of this, and, finally, add another layer of mushroom. Now brush the edge of the pie with egg wash. Carefully place the pie lid on top, crimp the edges with a fork, and make 2 slits 1 inch across the top of the pie. Bake the pie in the oven for 20 minutes.

It is time to prepare the braising sauce. Remove the ptarmigan legs from it and turn the heat up to reduce the sauce by half. While it reduces, strip the meat from the legs, chop it up, and return it to the reduced braising sauce with a pat of butter. Taste and season.

The prince, who loved shooting pheasant and partridge, was rumored to be a bad shot, but apologists claimed he simply found it tough to concentrate. Or perhaps it was the thought of one of his extramarital paramours that occupied his mind. The good looks of Frances Warwick, known as Daisy, slayed the prince (in photographs, her heavily curled fringe actually made her look as if she had a tea cozy on her head). Edward was forty, and Daisy was half his age. She was part of the Marlborough House Set and was willingly, wildly eccentric and fabulously rich— she had her own railway line constructed to bring guests conveniently to her home. According to her biographer, Sushila Anand, Daisy had a soft spot for animals: she bought a baby elephant from a door-to-door circus salesman (you could in those days) and decided it might be a good idea to set up a zoo at her home, Warwick Castle. This was a lively affair and culminated in two emus chasing a bishop—in his gaiters—through the shrubbery. Ask no more! The meals the Marlborough House Set scoffed were different from the formal and grand state dinners (though Alfred de Rothschild kept his own orchestra at his country seat). The meals were smaller and more intimate, full of ribald practical jokes, horseplay, and boisterous fun, fun that became much more pronounced when Princess Alexandra was left behind at home. Slapstick food games were the rage: soap served up as a fine rare cheese, froths of whipped cream replaced with soap suds, and outlandish combinations of pharmaceutical tonic switched for wine in some victim's glass. Rooms in various country houses were conveniently allocated to allow for much sneaking about after dark, Daisy's hair perhaps still damp from one of their soda-siphon fights. Adultery was fun. Thank goodness news of these dinners did not often reach Victoria's ears, which is amazing given that Daisy was so indiscreet as to be nicknamed "the Babbling Brook."

Edwardian nightlife meant food, too. Bertie would sally out to the billiard tables, some of them decorated with pornographic sketches; the Marlborough Club (he founded this in a huff so that he could smoke the adored Coronas and Henry Clay cigars he kept in a leather pouch); or the libertine cockpits of the music hall and nibble his top midnight snack of cold roast chicken, the grease on his fingers, his pinkie ring twinkling. Although he was very partial to cuisses de nymphes Aurore (thighs of the dawn nymphs or, for the more pedestrian, frogs' legs in champagne jelly), it was the thighs and aspic that appealed to Bertie rather than the champagne. He wasn't much of a drinker and was content with a glass of brandy after dinner, always keen to join the ladies. His frequent excursions to Scotland as a young lad had left him with a love of herrings fried in oatmeal and shortbread.

An elaborate entourage followed Bertie wherever he went: when he went skating in his curly brimmed bowler hat and knickerbockers; when he went yachting, his little beard trimmed to a naval precision. His Austrian valet, Meidinger, presented him with a biscuit and a glass of warmed milk at 7 a.m. every morning. Hawkins, an English valet, made his bed. Romantically, when he traveled, a small Arab boy would make his coffee. Like many of the European rich and royal, Bertie casually acquired things on his travels, such as other humans and dangerous beasts, all of whom must have been bewildered to find themselves in the rainier counties of Britain. After traveling through India, he fetched back with him a surprised Madras curry cook, plus assorted leopards and bears. When Bertie expressed a desire to move incognito through crowds of his subjects in order to discover the "common man," his entourage would panic. The prince wasn't *really* at all sure who the common man was or how to be incognito but decided the best place to mingle with the common man might be a restaurant. To really blend in, he often used the modest pseudonym of the Duke of Lancaster, or once he even ventured to book a table in the name of a humble courtier. He blew his cover almost immediately by being too impatient to wait for a table, and then a band materialized and began to screech out "God Save the King." When he did remember to wait in line, he'd slip up in other ways, as when a lift arrived and Bertie forgot he was meant to be pretending to be humble and steamrollered forward, upending a surprised American.

Scandal was always just a letter away. His many mistresses floated by: Lady Harriet Mordaunt (he almost came unstuck with this one), Daisy, Lily Langtree, Jenny Churchill (Winston's mother), and Alice Keppel. Francis Knollys, his private secretary, was procurer of women for him—married women were preferred. Bertie was ever canoodling, his adulterous hand doing plenty of bosom pressing. When hunting for ladies in the more dismal, less reputable parts of London, he became the Duke of Lancaster and Baron Renfrew. The Continent was at a safer distance from London, though. In Paris, he kept permanent rooms in the Hotel Bristol and would invite ladies up for supper after the opera. One Parisian brothel reputedly had a chair specially designed for him so that he could have the most fun with the least effort. "Kinky," as he was known by some, also liked to bathe in champagne with his lady friends after a sole soufflé or two.

Finally, Victoria died. It was Bertie's moment. He had had to hang around for an inordinately long time before succeeding to the throne—an apprentice prince until 1901 when, aged sixty, Bertie puffed his way up to the throne. Even at his coronation, though, there was a box set aside for his dalliances and a special box for his favored mistress, Alice Keppel. The reign of Edward the Caresser (a play on Edward the Confessor) had begun.

At first, social commentators regarded him with some dismay. Was Bertie struggling with the weight of his new responsibilities as King Edward VII? He began to eat even more, in an anxious, bulimic fashion, doing even less chewing and more inhalation of food. It was difficult for him coping with "the sepulcher," as he called Buckingham Palace—modernization was the name of the game, beginning with suave suppers at the palace following an evening at the theater. Grilled oysters were a tip-top seasonal hit, followed by quails à la Grecque. In a manner that was to typify the future behavior of royals and their pets, Queen Alexandra's favorite Russian borzoi dogs supped on bowls of milk set out for them and trotted silkily about Buckingham Palace, their long, slender faces making them look like canine aristocrats, in company with a pack of tiny, yapping Pekinese from the emperor of Japan. The staff was exasperated—a team had to brush and powder the canine horde every day, and the Pekinese were often mistaken for slippers. Every evening a tray of sandwiches, soup, and cold game was brought to Queen Alexandra's chamber. Her Majesty seemed miraculously able to eat it all.

Grilled Oysters

INGREDIENTS
20 oysters
2 tbsp. butter, melted

FOR THE GREMOLATA . . .

2 cups breadcrumbs, browned in a little butter	1 tbsp. finely chopped flat-leaf parsley
½ tbsp. grated lemon zest	Freshly ground black pepper
1 tbsp. freshly grated Parmesan cheese	Sea salt

METHOD
Preheat your grill until it is nice and hot. Shuck the oysters, separating them from the abductor muscles. Mix together the breadcrumbs, zest, Parmesan, parsley, pepper, and salt. Put the oysters on a grill tray, pour a little melted butter into each shell, top with the lid, and put under the grill for 3 minutes. They are ready as soon as the edges tighten and begin to curl. Remove from the heat, sprinkle with gremolata, and serve.

Bertie and Alexandra set themselves up as the consummate hosts but weren't very flexible when it came to "foreign food" or table numbers. The king steadfastly refused to eat at a table whose diners numbered thirteen—he only once did so because he was reassured that one of the women there was pregnant. Then there was foreign food—French was the accepted predominant style, but all else was viewed with caution. Bertie didn't like starchy, carbohydrate-heavy Italian pasta but would allow macaroni on the royal table if some Italian dignitary was to be appeased. Another slim concession made to one's nationhood might be the naming of a dish after a dignitary or offering some tenuous connection to an aspect of one's homeland—for instance, Mandarines à la Mikado (mandarin with sugar) was bestowed on one Japanese visitor. One Indian guest was offered a vast selection of dishes to ensure he could avoid meat at all costs. Asparagus with butter sauce was on the table, and the serving staff were spellbound when the guest ate the tender branch of asparagus and then threw the woodier base over his shoulder. It flew through the air and landed moistly on the state carpet. Bertie, straight-faced, had the aplomb to follow suit, as if this were the only reasonable thing one could do with leftover asparagus. The king, when dining in a grand manner, adored small-boned, tender-fleshed ortolans sweetened with aromatic brandy. Game birds stuffed with further game birds and truffles, served with a rich, luscious sauce, had him licking his lips. Or such morsels as the savory Cotelettes de bécassines à la Souvaroff (boned and split snipe, packed with forcemeat and foie gras, shaped into dinky cutlets, bundled up in pig's caul, and grilled) accompanied by a deep Madeira sauce and slices of truffle.

After this diet, the royal couple decided that every Sunday evening would be spent over a simple and modest supper of roast beef and Yorkshire pudding. There would be roast potatoes and horseradish sauce—a break from all the heavy, rich food they had eaten during the week. Hmmm.

Yorkshire Pudding

INGREDIENTS

3 tbsp. beef dripping
2 cups all-purpose flour
5 eggs

2 cups milk
Freshly ground black pepper
Sea salt

METHOD

Preheat the oven to 230°C. Heat the beef dripping in a baking tray in the oven. You need it to be very hot. In a large mixing bowl, beat together the flour and eggs until they are completely blended. Now add the milk, a little at a time, whisking it in. Pepper and salt. Now, open the oven, pour the batter into the very hot dripping (you should see it bubble and hiss), close the oven door tightly, and let the pudding bake for 25 minutes. Serve with gravy and roast beef.

Sweetie Queen Alexandra was always late for supper and would rush in at the last moment. Bertie, enraged by this, decided to teach her a lesson. Custom has it that a bell is rung to indicate the king has finished one course. The plates of all and sundry are then removed. Furious with Alexandra, Bertie decided to race through each course. Consommé, ortolans, lamb in champagne, duck, chicken, all were whisked away in a tasty blur every few minutes as the bell clanged. You were left merely with the chance to lift a flake of salmon to your lips. Not that this was necessarily much of a hardship for Alexandra; her appetite was much more modest and delicate than the king's. Game and venison were too rich for her; she liked crayfish poached in Chablis, gentler chicken dishes like Poulet Danoise followed by the fruity, claret-infused Danish rødgrød dessert (the male diners refused this dish, as it was thought too effeminate a sweet).

Poulet Danoise

This would be served most often on a bed of buttered noodles.

INGREDIENTS

1 large chicken	1 bay leaf
¼ lb. butter	Freshly ground black pepper
Juice of half a lemon	Sea salt
1 tbsp. parsley, finely chopped	1½ cups chicken stock
1 onion, sliced	1 cup heavy cream
1 carrot, sliced	1 tsp. lemon juice

METHOD

Preheat the oven to 160°C. Insert into the chicken's cavity the butter, lemon juice, and parsley. Place the chicken in a casserole dish and add the onion, carrot, and bay leaf. Add a quarter of a pint of chicken stock. Salt and pepper. Cover and cook in the oven for an hour and a half, checking to make sure it does not burn; the oil from the butter and the juices from the chicken keep the dish moist. When the chicken juices run clear, remove the chicken and keep warm to the side. Drain most of the buttery chicken grease off. Place the casserole dish on the stove top over a medium-high heat. Add the remaining half pint of chicken stock and the cream and reduce by half. Now season with the lemon juice and a little more black pepper. Serve the chicken as you would a roast chicken, and pour the sauce over each portion.

Rødgrød

INGREDIENTS

6 cups blackcurrants	⅓ cup potato starch or cornstarch
3 cups raspberries	⅓ cup arrowroot
1½ quarts water	¼ bottle of claret
2 cups granulated sugar	

METHOD

Put the blackcurrants, raspberries, and sugar into a large pan. Add the 1½ quarts of water, bring to a boil, then allow to cool a little before straining the fruit mess through muslin or cheesecloth. Mix the potato starch and arrowroot with half a pint of cold water, adding the water a little at a time to keep the mixture smooth. Now return the fruit juices to the heat. Add the potato starch and arrowroot, whisking the rødgrød. Now add the claret. Keep whisking until the rødgrød is thoroughly warmed and thickened. Serve with heavy cream and little sweet biscuits.

Beyond the formal dinners, Bertie's fondness for dining in a familiar way in the homes of his subjects was a departure from the norm. Queen Victoria rarely dined out and never lost her veneer of formality. It was at one of these little dinners that Lillie Langtry met Bertie—she was so nervous she claimed she would have gladly climbed up the chimney to escape but relaxed when dinner gave her a chance to observe Bertie closely and admiringly. He often visited Mrs. Alice Keppel for a bite or two at her house in Portman Square (they were lovers for twelve years until his death, their affair beginning when Alice Keppel was twenty-nine to Bertie's fifty-six). He'd arrive at her house circumspectly, his brougham parked farther up the street. Tea would be brought in, plus Bertie's favorite cakes. The butler kept watch over the door. Alice learned quickly about the best sorts of food, realizing that her own cook, Mrs. Wright, might be a very fine cook but not capable of reaching the dizzying heights of gourmet dining the king was used to. Bertie's increasing girth meant that sex required a supple partner, unless of course the lovers were in Bertie's own rooms, where he'd had constructed a hanging harness plus handy footholds for sex.

But none of this was to last: Bertie was increasingly impotent, overweight (at sixteen stone, he was more prone to a tumble), had chronic emphysema, and by 1910 had endured a series of heart attacks. Alice Keppel and Queen Alexandra were present at his death; Alexandra resisted releasing his body for eight days, saying she couldn't "bear to part with him." He is best remembered, though, for a meal when he was nearing the end of his reign: he settled down into his seat for dinner at the Hotel du Palais in Biarritz. He wasn't very hungry but would do his best, he informed the other guests. Eventually, boggle-eyed with food after many courses, fruit was passed weakly around the table, at which point Bertie, bursting beneath his collar, asked sadly, "Is there no cheese?"

THREE IN A BED: CAESAR, ANTONY, AND CLEOPATRA

Cleopatra, the doomed and brilliant queen of Egypt, lover to both Julius Caesar and Mark Antony, had not a drop of Egyptian blood in her. Many of her predecessors, including her chubby father, were a boring, dull-witted set of kings of Egypt and, as the line of Ptolemy, originally Macedonian. The Ptolemys in general were very keen on murdering each other; there was nothing they liked better than some fraternal knifing or poisoning. When they weren't chopping up their children and delivering them to each other, they busily ruled Egypt from 300 BC onward. They only spoke Macedonian. According to Plutarch, they never bothered to equip themselves with any other language, perhaps only a word or two of Egyptian—and even that was a struggle. In contrast, Cleopatra was much more curious about language. She learned, Plutarch says, the languages of the "Ethiopians, the Arabs, the Troglodytes, the Hebrews, the Syrians, the Medes, and the Parthians," *among* others. She was also the first-ever pharaoh to take the trouble of learning Egyptian. Promising times—and just some fifty years before the birth of Christ. Female rulers tended to be strong characters in Egypt. Herodotus said some of them wore false beards, and Nefertiti was such an adept cross-dresser that her underlings sometimes referred to her as "he."

The great-great-great(etc.)-granddaughter of Ptolemy, Alexander the Great's general, Cleopatra had inherited the remains of Alexander (considered a god), Cleopatra kept the mummified corpse of Alexander-the-God in a crystal tomb; she could still make out his features and have chats with him about Egypt. Egypt had a healthy trade in animal mummification on the go—a bit like today's London tea towels. If cats or rats were what you liked to worship, then the ancient Egyptians could see their way to popping a mummified bundle in your hospitality bag, a bit like those chocolate rectangles Indian restaurants are fond of putting on your tips saucer. There were plenty of corpses of every conceivable species—stockpiled, wrapped, and ready to go—cramming warehouses in downtown Memphis. Not only that, but women in Egypt were employed in trades while the men stayed at home and spun wool. Women stood up to pee, and men sat down—all of this so scrambled the brains of the Greeks (who liked their women kept in the home) that they called the Egyptians "crocodiles" and thought there must be something funny in the papyrus they ate. Whether or not they actually ate papyrus, the Alexandrians did use its leaves as vegetal plateware to dine from, and papyrus leaves could be used as drinking vessels when the Alexandrians navigated through the swaying papyrus plantations of Lake Mareotus, which lies pooled near Alexandria. In Alexandria itself, the Mediterranean metropolis Cleopatra called home, the consumption of the grain emmet was vast, as the city represented the largest emmet market in the world—indeed, Caesar commended his soldier's endurance in eating emmet when in Egypt.

The Alexandrians, then, were sophisticates beyond measure, racers of horses, and famed eaters. Not that any of this would particularly impress Cleopatra's first amatory conquest, Julius Caesar. Although he was unstintingly generous with food, realizing that feasting makes you friends (as was the way in ancient Rome, Julius held huge public feasts, and at one point some twenty-two thousand dined at his expense), Julius himself wasn't one for fine dining. He had too much on his mind. Nor was he a drinker. Indeed, one wisecracker, Marcus Cato, said that Julius was about the only man to "overthrow the state when sober." Cleopatra was bound to fall for him—he was magnetizing and an excellent strategic ally—when he arrived in Egypt hot on the tails of his archenemy and son-in-law, Pompey. Julius was, after all, descended from Venus and wore an armed image of Venus on his ring. Remember, these were such early days that the zodiac had just appeared on the scene, courtesy of Babylon, and was heralded as the best new gadget for working out your future. So some Venus credentials really helped.

When fifty-two-year-old Julius Caesar sailed in, Cleopatra (in her early twenties) was supposedly co-ruling Egypt with her vicious brother Ptolemy XIII, whose idea of ingratiating himself with Julius was to send him the sticky head of his enemy Pompey as a welcome gift to Alexandria. Then, when Caesar requested the return of a loan of 6,000 talents from Ptolemy, his servants were ordered to serve up Caesar's meals on crappy plates rather than the customary "best service" of gold and silver— a bitter little food quip to suggest someone had stolen all their cash. Nor was any of this helped by the fact that, as much as Pompey was an enemy, he had been married to Caesar's doomed daughter, Julia (she died in childbirth). To circumvent her brother's immense stupidity, and to meet Caesar without facing the hostility of her brother's forces, Cleopatra devised the cunning plan of being rolled up inside a carpet. What a move. Cleopatra proved deliciously attractive to Caesar; he was in her thrall. Both had a rich flamboyance to their characters, revealed as they conversed in Greek. It helped, of course, that Julius was very keen on women; he was known as the "bald whoremonger" by his troops on their return from Gaul and had a chief of staff who went by the nickname "Penis"—no prizes for guessing why. Classical sources quiver with the sexual prowess of both Caesar and Cleopatra. Caesar, called "every woman's husband and every man's wife," hardly sounds difficult to get into bed. Cleopatra's promiscuity was supposedly leonine, but then the detractors of female rulers often try to discredit them this way. For Julius to be hot in bed simply made him manly; for Cleopatra to be the same or, indeed, to exhibit any kind of self-directed sexual appetite was to be whorish, fuel for anti-Cleo propaganda among the miserable Roman scandalmongers. This "prostitute queen" wore out slaves with her demands. Purse-lipped Aurelius Victor claimed that she "became so debauched that she often sold herself as a prostitute; but she was so beautiful that many men bought a night with her at the price of their own death."

Cleopatra bedded Caesar and became pregnant by him; then the two embarked on an impressive jaunt through Egypt, Cleopatra having considerable pull as the living Isis. At her first banquet for Caesar, Cleopatra was covered in constellations of gold jewelry, her body glimpsed through see-through diaphanous linen robes. Flowers were so thick upon the floor that it resembled a living meadow beneath the heavy incense of burning cardamom curling through the air. The Romans had to tiptoe along in their hobnailed footwear, careful not to slip on the roseate alabaster and marble floors. Crowned with roses, Cleopatra would have initiated Caesar into the Cult of Isis before dinner in the temple. Cult? Initiation! Before you gulp and begin to worry about Caesar and snakes, this simply involved what in our world is receiving a dinner invitation from "Lord Serapis," eating lots of grub at the banquet, and having plenty of fun. Cleopatra's table manners were beautifully measured and sophisticated. In order to avoid seeing two Caesars or two Cleopatras, the lovers-to-be would have laced their drinks with perfume, believed to counteract some of the more addling effects of alcohol.

Service for the night was provided by white-skinned, blushing, red-haired Celts; Nubians and Libyans; and a smattering of Greeks. All enslaved, of course, and hovering at your elbow to offer agate cups of vintage wine and delicious, rare delicacies on Memphis silver plates. Was this lost on Caesar? Well, certainly not Cleopatra's wares but probably the food. Famed for his indifference to food—and alcohol—Caesar's eating habits are the source of various apocryphal tales. Caesar once ate asparagus floating in rancid oil or ointment, noticing nothing until his fellow diners pointed out the dish's shortcomings. In fact, he even thought their quibbles feeble and urged them to try a mouthful. And this was a world in which food poisoners loitered around every turn. Alexander himself died after a mouthful of poisoned wine, and Caesar once nervously put a baker in irons for giving him bread that was different from everyone else's. Death could grip you by the tonsils. The high and mighty preferred the services of a food taster. But what Caesar really loved above any stew or sauce was clever conversation at the table, and he shared many such evenings with Cleopatra; "he often feasted with her until dawn" between the walls painted cinnabar red, detailed with iridescent tortoiseshell and gold-painted columns.

After the birth of their child, Caesarion, and an "Egyptian marriage" (which Rome snubbed), the lovers were not the luckiest of pairs: Rome demanded Caesar's return. Rumors drifted through the senate that Caesar intended to shift the empire to Alexandria. The knives were drawn, and several blades made their mark on the Ides of March. Cleopatra, left alive, would do anything for Caesarion, anything to secure Rome for her son. And it was at this juncture that the opportunity for an alliance with Mark Antony presented itself: he guaranteed her political power. He was to be Cleopatra's key ally, which was a good thing *and* a bad thing.

Mark Antony was both a bit louche and a bit of a lush. The Cult of Dionysus, to which Antony was a confirmed member, was always bad news for your liver in ancient Rome. Membership often meant drinking buckets of wine, dangling little images of penises all over your back garden, and possibly finding yourself a cave that you could drape with faun skins. When in Athens, Antony liked to host his fun from the top of the Acropolis, and as a pagan mover and shaker, Antony knew how to play the pre-Christian power game. If you wanted to get ahead in pagan circles, there was no better thing than to be hailed as a god; hence Antony was dropping pretty heavy hints with the faun skins in the cave and was keen to march about in faun-style outfits whenever the chance arose. And it worked a treat: women in Ephesus dressed up as Maenads (followers of Dionysus), wriggled about suggestively with snakes, and Mark Antony was hailed as the new Dionysus in the East.

Antony was bloodthirsty, ambitious, and, reputedly, not too bright. He did, however, command the respect of his men when they struggled, starving, to cross the Alps, leading by example in drinking puddle water, chewing tree bark, and dining on such beasts as "never man tasted of their flesh before." And this was someone who *really* liked his food; he gave one man's house to a cook on the grounds that he cooked an excellent supper. Antony also had a very fierce wife, Fulvia (one of the very few Roman women to have her profile stamped on coins). Plutarch says of her that she was "somewhat sour and crooked of condition." When Antony had Cicero's head and hand cut off, the terrible Fulvia reputedly wrenched his tongue from his head and used her hairpins to jab Cicero's tongue in revenge for all the things he'd said in the past. This also gave Antony "great joy."

Cleopatra was undeterred in her pursuit of Antony—she needed to make some quick alliances following the murder of Julius Caesar. When she heard Antony was in her vicinity (give or take the odd landmass), she hopped on her golden ship with silver oars, which was steered by a helmsman in its stern sheltered by a shining gold, massive elephant's head, its trunk raised. Musicians playing flutes and viols kept time with the beat of the oars; pretty boys dressed as little Cupids, fans in their hands, cooled Cleopatra as they sailed past Sicily, the birthplace of Aphrodite, and on to the lake beside Tarsus (beneath the wooded slopes of the Taurus Mountains in modern-day Turkey).

Antony was sitting, alone, on his imperial throne in the marketplace, waiting to greet her. Coyly, she refused to join him for supper there but sent word that he should drop in on her gilded boat (which, incidentally, even had alluring sails—they were soaked in rose water). The boat's censers billowed out fragrant smoke, and Cleopatra lay—dressed as Venus, of course—beneath an awning of golden tissue, its spangled gold patterning her skin. Again, Cleopatra pulled out all the stops in her game with Rome. Infinite lights and torches lit Antony's way.

The people whispered that Venus had come to meet Bacchus.

Dinner was served on golden dishes set with bright, precious stones; the Egyptian wine and Cleopatra turned Antony's wits (this may well have been the case: Egypt was famous for the "Egyptian drugs" that could be added to its wine). Cleopatra had the right clothes on to get Antony's attention: a see-through sea-green chiton made of linen (the same cheeky number, perhaps, that allowed Julius Caesar a glimpse of her breasts). She wore earrings of pearl and a pearl necklace, their opalescent luster symbolic of the riches of Egypt. She held not one but several banquets for forty-year-old Antony, and she captivated him. Completely. She was witty, packed with character, attractive, and of her voice Plutarch says, "It was a pleasure merely to hear the sound of her voice, with which, like an instrument of many strings, she could pass from one language to another." And then there was the sheer sensory excess her wealth, imagination, and power made possible. Cleopatra knew that food was one way to Antony's heart, making the wooing of him a very different prospect from Caesar, whose appetites were sharply sexual.

So what do we know about this banquet? There may have been game and fowl, some birds the like of which we would never see on any modern table: weirdly angular cranes and spectacular peacocks from the islands of the Aegean, often arranged after cooking in brilliant visual tricks and theatrical poses. Preserved fish from the Black Sea; fat scallops and shellfish; rock-tight, briny oysters perhaps from as far afield as Britain; fish, smoked and unsmoked, that were netted from the many seas; tuna; sturgeon; or clams and cockles dredged from the sanded blue waters about Alexandria. Apparently, those clams drawn from the waters near to the palace had the flavor of acorns.

And all to excess.

Enchanted, Cleopatra drew Antony toward Alexandria, all the while continuing with "one feasting the other by turns, and in cost exceeding all measure and reason." According to Plutarch's grandfather, one visitor to Cleopatra's kitchen was amazed to see a lineup of eight boars, skewered and roasting, their fat dripping onto the hot coals. These must, he decided, be to feed a huge number of guests about to fall upon the palace. Instead, he was told there were only twelve for dinner but that perfection was demanded: each boar must have been cooked at a different rate for, said the chef, "maybe Antony will sup just now . . . maybe he will call for wine, or begin to talk, and will put it off. So that it is not one but many suppers must be had in readiness, as it is impossible to guess at his hour." Those kitchens held much more than wild boar: there were winged creatures, hares, lavish pastries, sea nettles, sea hedgehogs, peacocks, cranes, oysters, sow's udder, field fares, sturgeons, acorns and nuts, and vegetables galore (but no potatoes, of course). Food was eaten with the fingers, and each feast might swell out into a drinking party; a master of revels was appointed with a cast of the dice, and it was his job to mix the wine.

In an act that typifies the culinary indulgence a Roman general and an Egyptian queen are capable of when thrown together, she and Antony founded a sort of club, which they called the "Inimitable Livers" club, whose members should be dedicated to the entertainment of each other in the most lavish way possible. At one feast, Antony challenged Cleopatra to one of the most excessive food wagers of the ancient world: he bet that she couldn't personally spend ten million sesterces in one single go at a dinner party. Cleopatra called for a slave and a cup with a little vinegar. She slipped a large, pearl earring from her ear and dropped it in the vinegar. Then she drained the cup. Skeptics held that the pearl must have been crushed by Cleopatra before she poured the powder into her glass; others that she must have swallowed it whole, only to retrieve it later. What Cleopatra knew, however, was that vinegar was capable of dissolving pearls. Needless to say, she had won the bet, and Antony's forfeit—a death blow to his street cred in Rome—was to perform on Cleopatra the traditional female or slave's homage at Roman and Greek banquets: to massage men's feet. In a brilliant, feminist about-face, Cleopatra had demanded the same. In front of the assembled guests, Antony rose from the banquet. He knelt before her and took her feet in his hands, being a "woman" to the "man" that was Cleopatra. Not a spectacle Rome could forgive. Antony "became her captive as though he were a young man, although he was forty years of age."

Sobersides Rome watched, scandalized, as Antony and Cleopatra romanced each other: through pranks, dice playing, drinking, and hunting, Cleopatra had made Antony forget his nation, his toga (only a true Roman citizen could wear one), and his name. He was like a cheap "cymbal player from Canopus," playing to her tune. Rolling into the city disguised, respectively, as a slave and a chambermaid, Antony and Cleopatra tried to look into the windows of poor men's homes and shops, set out to brawl with them. They loved the theater and financially supported some rascal called Chelidon, a "performer of improper dances." They persuaded Antony's sidekick Planus, governor of Syria, to undress, paint himself blue from top to toe, and attach a fish tail to his bottom. He then crawled about on his knees before a select audience, pretending to be a sea god.

One day, fishing in front of Cleopatra, Antony crowed about his success as a fisherman (while secretly with each throw having a fisherman dive underwater to attach a fish to his line). Apparently falling for the trick, Cleopatra clapped and applauded but ordered one of her servants to creep down and tie a *salted* fish from the Black Sea to Antony's rod. When the salted fish was landed and Antony realized Cleopatra had not been fooled, she said, "Leave the fishing-rod, general, to us poor sovereigns . . . *your* game is cities, provinces and kingdoms."

In the struggle for power in Rome between Antony and his archenemy Octavian (who was a past master at shirking battles, claiming to have scraped his knee or stubbed his toe, but who still managed to earn for himself the cheering nickname of "the Executioner"), Antony and Cleopatra were the losers. Octavian was furious on many counts: that they had Caesar's son, Caesarion; that they had declared

Caesarion Julius Caesar's natural heir (Octavian was Julius's adopted son); that Antony had married Octavian's sister (imaginatively named Octavia—Fulvia had died) and then ran off; and, most of all, that Antony was too popular and powerful. Octavian was a brilliantly vindictive enemy and set the spin doctors of Rome to work on destroying Antony's reputation. Because the Romans were a sexist bunch, their best plan was to come up with a line of attack that focused on the idea that Antony trotted along in Cleopatra's skirts—and it proved pretty devastating. Antony had really gone downhill, they whispered, running behind Cleopatra's litter in newfangled "Eastern dress," keeping company with a bunch of eunuchs. And— get this—he'd even taken to doing all his "business" in a giant gold chamber pot.

In the last days of their pomp, fifty-four-year-old Antony and thirty-nine-year-old Cleopatra shook off the blues and began to hold . . . more feasts! Feasts at which they gave such lavish presents that guests who had arrived hard up went home wealthy, their pockets jingling. They established a sort of invitation-only "Suicide Club"—yes, that was its name—who had great ghoulish fun wearing crowns of poisonous greenery (edible poisoned hats, essentially), which you were supposed to grab and nibble when Rome came calling, and the price of membership was your willingness to die with Antony and Cleopatra, an end many found preferable to being mocked in Rome. The Suicide Club held a final banquet on the evening of July 31, 30 BC. In what she must have intended as a deadly remake of her stunt with the pearls, Cleopatra suggested that they all take the poisoned flowers from their crowns, douse them in wine, and drain their glasses. No one took Cleopatra up on the suggestion, which wasn't a bad one, given what was to come.

Strange pipes and music were heard departing from the city. Surely this, they reasoned, was Dionysus, Antony's god, taking leave of him?

And we all know about what was to come, don't we? Octavian (a.k.a. Emperor Augustus) entered Alexandria on August 1 and found Antony dead by his own hand (Cleopatra had refused to kill him). Swiftly making Cleopatra captive, Octavian hotfooted his way to the mummified remains of the great Alexander, placing a crown of gold on the mummy's head and managing, through stroking, to break off a part of its nose. Then he hurried on to give orders for the beheading of Antony and Cleopatra's fourteen-year-old son and, that done, bustled back to address Cleopatra; dying was not allowed. Octavian insisted that she, like her sister Arsinoe, would be taken to Rome to be paraded in front of its citizens and mocked.

Wily as ever, Cleopatra promised to be true and on August 10 had a good bath, dressed up, and prepared to eat a delicious lunch, topped off with juicy figs and wine. Cleopatra and her two attendants all killed themselves and, contrary to popular myth (which would require three cobras, all squashed into a bowl of figs), their poison probably came bottled, hidden in an ointment concealed in a vial in Cleopatra's hair that could then be wiped onto a pin (it's no coincidence that one of Cleopatra's fellow suicides was her hairdresser, Eiras). Furious, the Romans burst in—too late.

P.S. Octavian went on to use Cleopatra's gold to buy himself the island of Capri.

Roasted Wild Boar

Given that most of us have neither the means nor the appetite for Antony's 8-boar lineup, let's stick to a smaller section of the beast.

INGREDIENTS

2.2 lb. wild boar

Sea salt (though our ancient Egyptian friends were pretty suspicious of sea salt because of its associations with the dark god Seth—aaarrghh— and would have consumed salt from the Siwa Oasis)

1 tbsp. cumin seed

3 cloves garlic

3 tbsp. butter

Marjoram

Thyme

1 tbsp. cilantro

Freshly ground black pepper

1 tbsp. all-purpose flour

1 glass dry white wine

2 tsp. honey

2 tsp. mustard

1 tsp. sesame seeds

METHOD

In a large mortar and pestle, grind the cumin seed with a little salt (to add "grist"). You should be left with whole seeds, partially crushed seeds, and a fine aromatic dust of raw cumin. Next, add the garlic and pulverize it, mixing it with the cumin seed. Now add the butter, using the pestle to knead the cumin and garlic through the butter. (By the way, Egyptians did use other oils, a whole range, including the very popular horseradish oil.)

Place the boar on a flat surface. Using a fine-tipped sharp knife, pierce deep into the boar's flesh (try not to think of *Lord of the Flies*), and, taking fronds of thyme and marjoram, slide and stuff these into the deep, narrow incisions. Try to create and stuff about 15 of these incisions. Rub the boar all over with the tablespoon of cilantro. Season with black pepper. Having done this, slather the boar in the cumin butter, massaging the butter into every crevice.

Cover and leave it in the fridge, encased in this aromatic butter, for 2–3 days.

Now it's easy: Preheat the oven to 200°C (well, we're *not* using a spit this time, OK!). Wrap the boar in aluminum foil and place in a roasting pan. Place in the oven. Leave on 200°C for 5 minutes and then reduce the heat to 180°C. Cook for 2 hours.

When the 2 hours are up, remove the foil and allow the boar to brown. Then take it out, carefully retaining the spiced, buttery juices from the foil-wrapped boar in the roasting pan. Allow the boar to rest for 15 minutes before serving.

While the boar is resting, place the roasting pan on a burner on the stove, add a tablespoon of all-purpose flour, and stir quickly, combining the juices with the flour. Next, pour in—slowly—the glass of wine, stirring to meld it with the flour-butter paste. Add to this the honey, mustard, and sesame seeds. If it looks too thick, add some water; if too thin, allow it to reduce a little on the stove. You should end up with a thin, runny gravy of honey and sesame.

Serve the boar with the sauce drizzled over—and no knives or forks!

Suicide Club Sweets

INGREDIENTS

1½ cups plump, moist dates
1 tsp. powdered cinnamon
1 tsp. fennel seed
½ tsp. cardamom seeds
¼ cup walnuts, broken and
  some crushed

¼ cup almonds, broken and
  some crushed
A small bowl of runny honey
½ cup almonds, ground

METHOD

Place the dates in a food processor and whiz into a thick paste, adding a little water if necessary. Remove and place the date paste in a bowl. Using your hands, work in the cardamom and fennel seeds and the cinnamon. Add the broken walnuts and almonds, and then form this stiff paste into small balls, between a ½ inch and 1 inch in size.

Dip each ball in the runny honey and then roll in the ground almond dust. Serve with a platter of purple figs, oblong toffees of dates, halved pomegranates, and bunched grapes. Whatever you do, don't nibble your garland.

TAKING TEA WITH HRH QUEEN ELIZABETH II

They seem an odd couple: She prefers a bath; he a shower. He is handsome and dynamic; she has a dowdy, patient prettiness. She has Twinings Special Blend Tea with milk and no sugar; he has his coffee black, blended for him by the Savoy Hotel's coffee department. Yet Prince Philip and Queen Elizabeth have been together since childhood.

The Windsors—King George VI; his wife, Elizabeth; Princess Elizabeth; and her sister, Margaret—had berthed the royal yacht, the *Victoria and Albert*, in Dartmouth, near the Dartmouth Royal Naval College. It was a Sunday. Elizabeth (or Lilibet, as she was known) was thirteen, and she and Margaret had been sent off to play with the Dalrymple-Hamiltons' children. The main attraction was a clockwork railway on the Dalrymple-Hamiltons' nursery floor. The children were all clustered around it when a boy with Viking-like bright blonde hair and fierce blue eyes strolled in. He knelt down beside Elizabeth, said, "How do you do?" and played with the trains. He couldn't conceal his restlessness, though, and after a snack of lemonade and ginger crackers, he proposed, "Let's go to the tennis courts and have some real fun jumping the nets." The children trooped after their carefree leader, who showed off leaping over tennis nets before an audience of admiring little girls. Elizabeth told her nanny, Marion Crawford (known as "Crawfie"), "How good he is, Crawfie. How high he can jump." He shrugged off her admiration and poked fun at little chubby Margaret.

The boy's identity was revealed when he came to see them the next day: he was Prince Philip of Greece. When it was time for tea, teenage Elizabeth asked by way of invitation, "Would you like to eat?" Marion Crawford recalled in her memoirs, "The Queen said, 'You must make a really good meal, for I suppose it is your last for the day.' Philip had several platefuls of shrimps, and a banana split, among other trifles. To the little girls, a boy of any kind was always a strange creature out of another world. Lilibet sat, pink-faced, enjoying it all very much. To Margaret, anyone who could eat so many shrimps was a hero."

The hero continued to prove himself as such when the royal yacht left Dartmouth. The teeming boys at the naval college all set out on little boats to bid farewell to the royals. But one boy proved persistent, following the *Victoria and Albert* in his own boat, rowing vigorously, and staying a course in the wake of the boat long after all the other boys had returned to shore. It was Philip. It is not surprising that Philip was so independent: his parents had to flee Greece when his father's brother, King Constantine, was deposed in 1922; the infant Philip was bundled into a fruit crate. His mother, the lovely, deaf Alice Battenburg, great-granddaughter to Queen Victoria, began to hear divine voices. Freud was consulted. He decided that Alice's libido needed to be controlled by exposing her ovaries to X-rays (Alice wasn't keen on this and kept trying to escape the sanatorium that she was forcibly kept in for two years). On release, she became a nun. She sheltered Greek Jews in Athens during World War II, gave away all her possessions, and is buried on the Mount of Olives. Philip's playboy father, Prince Andrew of Greece, meanwhile, yachted in the Riviera with his mistress, the Countess Andrée de la Bigne, until he died of heart failure in Monte Carlo. Philip, though, was given no warning of his mother's incarceration. His grandmother took him out for a picnic, and when he returned Alice had been taken away. Fortunately, Philip had his Mountbatten relatives in Britain to keep a kindly eye on him (including one who demanded a champagne footbath after dancing the Charleston too vigorously). Poignantly, when Philip signed the Mountbatten's guestbook, he wrote, "No fixed abode."

Banana Split

INGREDIENTS

1 banana
1 scoop each of vanilla, chocolate, and strawberry ice cream

2 tsp. pineapple sauce
2 tsp. strawberry sauce
2 tsp. chocolate sauce

TO DECORATE . . .

Kibbled, toasted almonds
3 tbsp. whipped cream

Maraschino glacé cherries

METHOD

Split the banana in two and lay it in an oblong dish. Along the middle, lay a scoop each of vanilla, chocolate, and strawberry ice cream. In whichever order appeals to you, drizzle pineapple, strawberry, and chocolate sauce on each scoop. Decorate with kibbled almonds, whipped cream, and maraschino glacé cherries.

Austerity Britain curtailed Elizabeth and Philip's wedding breakfast in 1947; King George wanted his loyal British public to know that their king would stick to the postwar food regulations. None of Philip's German relatives were invited, either—all three of his sisters were married to German princes. Dispossessed and deposed European royalty descended on Buckingham Palace. There was a party so riotous that King George danced the conga (a favorite with the Windsors), and an Indian raja got so drunk that he tried to smack the Duke of Devonshire in the face. On the day, though, there was a feast to be had, made in the venerable kitchens of Buckingham Palace, where there are working jelly molds going back to the eighteenth century and the table of George III. Winston Churchill thought the celebratory wedding feast could bring color and joy back to Britain. The meal opened with Filet of Sole Mountbatten. Partridges were unrationed, so these were casseroled and served to guests. The vegetables had all been grown in the royal gardens and hothouses. Finally, there was a scrumptious, victorious cannonball of Bombe Glacée.

Marriage between Elizabeth and Philip had its ups and downs. Philip was untamed and had already had to give up his red sports car. The British monarchy were hard up after the war (for Elizabeth's coronation, they had to scoop up lots of footmen from the other aristocrats' homes, disguise them in royal livery, and pretend they worked for the queen). Philip thought they should tighten their belts and decided to conduct his own survey. The old guard at Buckingham Palace found him excessively bossy: he went about with a clipboard or notepad and asked servants, "So what do you do?" Lots of people who had been just marching about in uniforms looking stuffy and busy for a couple of decades turned out to be doing the same jobs as other stuffy, busy people or not doing very much at all. Philip struggled to be simply consort to the queen and, in the 1950s, started having lunches of champagne, whitebait, and oysters with the seamy, risqué, all-male Thursday Club above Wheeler's seafood restaurant in London's Soho (Maria Callas was reportedly the only woman ever invited for lunch—by Aristotle Onassis, who broke the men-only rule). Fellow cronies, voluptuaries, and raconteurs were Arthur Koestler, jazz guru Larry Adler, Stephen Ward, the Soviet spy Kim Philby (predenunciation, *and* he was considered so boring they never asked him back again), Peter Ustinov, and David Niven. Lunch continued into the night and into private parties with female companions. Philip once returned home so late he had to climb the locked palace gates. They had a nomination for "Cunt of the Month," given to whichever member had screwed up the most. During the Cold War, a Soviet spy, Yevgeny Ivanov, penetrated the club, took compromising photographs of Philip, and sent them back to his fur-hatted spymasters in Moscow (though it was stressed that Philip remained fully clothed in these). The Soviets decided not to release them in a Communist exposé of the royals called "Operation Royal House," and so they have never been seen.

There is a self-absorption to the dining habits of the British royal family that defies all incomers to either accept its eating rituals or go away. Brilliantly crusty and selfish, there is not one member of the royal inner circle who isn't used to having their food preferences pandered to. Princess Anne, for one, is a plain eater (one *could* even hazard that she is an ignorant eater) whose no-nonsense approach to grub resembles the brusque speaking on which she—and her father, Prince Philip—prides herself. On skiing holidays, she doesn't muck about with fondues but tucks into chips and ketchup. She downs numerous cokes when abroad, as it "kills all known germs." Like Prince Philip, she doesn't suffer fools gladly—clearly not counting herself as one of this benighted number. There is, of course, the apocryphal tale of the Blairs staying with the Windsors briefly, which goes something like this: Cherie Blair, on finding Anne breakfasting with her, struck up a conversation. Warming to Anne, Cherie said companionably, "You can call me Cherie if you like." Anne's reply was a pinched "I'd rather not."

The royal kitchens are full of surprises. An old student friend of mine managed to get a summer job washing dishes in the kitchens of Buckingham Palace. There she was one Tuesday morning, up to the elbows in suds, whistling, farting discreetly. Then, very gently, a voice behind her said, "May I have a banana sandwich?"

Then there was the time when another innocent—a chef this time—turned up in the kitchens. He had to learn the ropes, first by watching a demonstration of how Queen Elizabeth liked her carrots. Split clean down the middle, the carrots were sliced into large chunks and then bundled into a paper bag, which was then to be placed discretely in her pocket. He worried about how she'd manage to swallow these and wondered if he'd stumbled onto an immense state secret, but—ho ho—it turned out the carrots were treats for her horses! Hiding things in pockets is quite the royal in-thing, as is the sandwich-crazy culture: there is a custom in the royal household of smuggling tiny sardine sandwiches up sleeves, down socks, and deep in pockets to keep court officials' tummies from grumbling during long, hungry, and arduous ceremonies. So next time you watch a coronation, consider the number of sardine sandwiches that must be tucked away there.

State dinners have witnessed all sorts of royal gaffes. Queen Mary, fondly wishing to reward one of her dogs, handed a dog biscuit to a guest who, hard of hearing, thought it was some monarchial amuse-bouche and popped it into his mouth instead. Royal eccentricities abound as well. When the queen of Sweden comes to stay at Buckingham Palace, she likes to meander around London on her own, but just in case anything untoward ever happens to her, she carries a card saying "I am the Queen of Sweden" in her handbag.

The queen has a notebook in which she can leave helpful messages for the royal cooks—if the sultan of Brunei is partial to Brie, she quickly jots this down so that her chefs can accommodate his tastes in the future; plus she likes to record Prince Philip's favorite wines. She once left a dead slug in the notebook with a message for the chef asking, "I found this in the salad—could you eat it?" Another great servant-to-the-royals gaffe recounted by biographer Brian Hoey was when a policeman on a bicycle stopped the queen's car in the early days of her reign. The bodyguard leaned across the passenger seat and said, "Do you realize we've got the Queen and Prince Philip in the back?" To which the policeman, referring to the famous cowboy, scoffed, "Yes, and I'm Roy Rogers and this," he said, slapping his bicycle with his hand, "is my horse Trigger." Imagine his consternation when the queen's permed head popped out of the back window and she barked, "Well, you and Trigger had better let us get on our way."

The queen's eating schedule holds no surprises, however; her habits are beautifully punctual (unlike the Queen Mum, who, by all accounts, often skidded in late for meals) and have a Genesis-like certainty to them. Breakfast at 9 a.m., lunch at 1:15 p.m., tea at 5 p.m., and dinner at 8:15 p.m.—like clockwork. At breakfast time, Elizabeth drinks tea, not coffee, and it is best served in a silver teapot. Like James Bond, she knows a brown boiled egg tastes superior to a white one. If poached, the egg should be served with croutons (are these a rich man's toast soldiers?). She may dally with a sausage or a fillet of smoked haddock, as she's partial to these, but they come a poor second to her admiration for kippers. When Elizabeth and Margaret were little girls, they paused one day in their play when the rich aroma of something very delicious wended its way down the corridors of Windsor Castle. The girls followed their noses all the way to the private kitchens of Alice Bruce, the housekeeper, who was cooking kippers. There the sisters tasted their earliest flavorsome mouthfuls of this humble fish. Eternally true to this memory, every week the queen has a supply of Manx kippers delivered to her, which seem to get everywhere; Prince Philip was once startled to find a box of kippers packed into his clothes. And, always, the queen's breakfast is laid out on an "aircraft carrier," a tray that holds hot water inside it to keep her breakfast warm while she listens to her trusty Roberts radio, tuned to the BBC's Radio 2. She never, *ever* eats between meals. To a certain British mind-set, snacks between meals are just the beginnings of the sort of loose, uncontrolled behavior that will lead irrevocably to you waking up one day smelling of cherry brandy, an enema up your bottom, among an orgiastic tangle of limbs. This behavior stands alongside other immoralities such as not standing in line or sleeping in stuffy rooms (fresh air keeps body and soul clean).

Like her namesake, good Queen Bess, Elizabeth often eats lunch alone, modestly apportioned, but she more than makes up for this a few hours later with a rather piggy afternoon tea. The tea itself will be Earl Grey—the pot will be warmed and, following in Queen Mary's footsteps, the teapot is given three minutes to brew—and is made according to the following formula: one teaspoon for each person and one teaspoon for the pot. Prince Philip is a stickler for coffee; he might also branch out and have an oatcake with honey. To accompany the tea, the table will be laden with potted shrimp, deeply warm homemade fruit scones— often fed to the corgis, who will apparently roll over at the prospect of a bite of scone—and sticky slices of Dundee fruitcake (also an old favorite of Churchill's). There might be one of Elizabeth's favorite tea cakes, chocolate biscuit cake or lemon sponge, and a plate of crustless cucumber or ham and tongue sandwiches (for a time—about fifty years—salmon sandwiches were banned, as the Queen

Mum detested these). The sandwiches are always cut round-edged, as sharp edges and pointed corners are supposed to indicate that the sandwich maker has a treacherous urge to overthrow the royal family.

Each of the Windsors' castles or palaces offers a different food experience. Foraging from their extensive lands offers rich pickings (Charles has been known to pad along behind the Italian gourmand Antonio Carluccio on fungal forays). Charles uses his damsons at Highgrove to make damson gin, and the old mulberry trees on the Windsor estate hang heavy with clustered fruit for mulberry gin. He also makes a mean orange gin. Both mulberry gin and orange gin are deeply delicious, but you must be prepared to wait months (or even a few years, in the case of the orange gin) for them to mature, so plan this well in advance.

Chocolate Biscuit Cake

INGREDIENTS
½ tbsp. butter for greasing cake tin
½ cup butter
3 tbsp. golden syrup
1 cup bittersweet chocolate, finely chopped
1 tsp. vanilla extract
1 egg, beaten

2 cups oatmeal cookies, broken into 1 in. chunks
¾ cup broken walnuts
½ cup sultanas
½ cup dried apricots, roughly chopped
½ cup dried figs, roughly chopped

TO DECORATE . . .
⅓ cup maraschino glacé cherries

METHOD
Grease a medium-size square cake tin with butter, then line it with baking parchment. In a saucepan, melt the ounces of butter, add the golden syrup, and then bring to a boil. Add the chocolate, turn the heat right down, and whisk the chocolate in until it is thoroughly melted. Add the vanilla extract. Slowly add the beaten egg—keep the heat low—and stir until the lush, chocolatey mixture thickens further and takes on a sheen. Never let it boil, or you will have chocolate scrambled eggs in your pan.

Remove the chocolate mixture from the heat. Put the cookies, walnuts, sultanas, apricots, and figs into a bowl and pour the chocolate mixture over them. Now mix it all together before pouring it into the square cake tin. Press the mix down so that it fills the corners. Decorate with the cherries. Cool in the fridge for 3 hours. Slice up this figgy, chocolately heaven and try not to eat it all in one go. The queen never does that.

Mulberry Gin

INGREDIENTS

6 cups ripe, fresh mulberries   2 cups granulated sugar
1½ liters good-quality gin

METHOD

Pop the mulberries into a demijohn, add the sugar, and top with the gin. Seal
and shake the demijohn. Leave the gin to infuse for 2–3 months. If you don't want
to keep the mulberries in the gin, then strain it, removing the mulberries. They
are now delicious, fruity, gin-infused bullets. Gorge on them, warmed, with cold
vanilla ice cream.

Mulberry gin, kept in a hip flask, makes for a lovely warming snifter when out at
shooting lunches in the Scottish Highlands or at Sandringham. Prince Philip plucks
and cleans the snipe he shoots at Sandringham and the capercaillie, ptarmigan, and
grouse he shoots at Balmoral, selling the excess to the local butcher there. Shooting
lunches offer a bloodier kind of foray and begin with a gruff, tasty, macho early
breakfast of deviled kidneys (why is it that offal eating, like barbecue cooking,
tends to be a masculine affair?); a scrumptiousness called eggs en croute, which
involves baking eggs into hollowed-out buttery French bread; and curried salmon
kedgeree. Lunches are transported in red leather boxes fitted with lidded silver
trays or "hot boxes."

Shooting-Party Curried Salmon Kedgeree

INGREDIENTS

2 onions, finely chopped   1 tbsp. heavy cream
2 tbsp. olive oil   Sea salt
1 cup basmati rice   Freshly ground black pepper
1 tbsp. curry powder   4 hard-boiled eggs, peeled and halved
2 tbsp. sultanas   but still warm
2 cups boiling water   2 scallions, finely chopped
2 hot smoked salmon fillets   2 tbsp. parsley, finely chopped

METHOD

Heat the olive oil in a deep frying pan. Sauté the onions until they are soft. Add the
basmati rice and coat this in oil, frying gently. Add the curry powder and sultanas.
Add the boiling water and simmer, covered, until the rice is cooked. Flake the
salmon fillet, and add to the rice for the last 5 minutes. Add the cream, stirring it in
very gently so as not to further break up the salmon pieces. Salt and pepper to taste.
Serve in a warm dish, decorated with boiled egg halves, scallions, and parsley.

The women of the party, if not also shooting, often spend their time collecting felled birds and tagging them. All of this immensely irritated Lady Di, who shuddered at the shooting, moaning to one confidante, "Why does everyone in this family like killing things?" On such excursions, when everyone tumbles into jeeps and heads for the hills, Prince Charles moves like a goat over wild, tumbledown rocky outcrops, his gun man (or loader, as he is called) panting behind him, sweating under plus fours of tweed and jackets of Balmoral tartan. Prince Philip likes to whip out his special outdoor pan and rustle up his signature dishes. He can make a mean scrambled egg and smoked haddock in his beloved pan and likes to wow his guests at summer barbecues far off up in the lavender and dun hills by cooking up, all on his own, Gaelic steaks—beef tenderloin sautéed with whiskey, cream, and mushrooms (only the leanest of meat for Philip). All the family is supposed to pitch in and help with the food and clearing up afterward, but yet again Lady Di was not keen on cooking, and you could catch sight of her after dinner, disgruntled, in a pair of yellow rubber gloves, washing pots in a little plastic bucket alongside the queen.

Gaelic Steaks

The Gaelic steaks have sweet undertones of mushroom and West Coast Scottish whiskey that perfectly evoke the slightly saline smell of earth and bell heather. Well can I imagine the Duke of Edinburgh in years past, crouched in a manly way in the heather, basting his steaks (though I doubt he chops up his own shallots).

INGREDIENTS
4 beef tenderloin steaks
½ cup butter
4 shallots, minced
8 chestnut mushrooms: 4 finely chopped, 4 sliced
2 cups heavy cream

2 tbsp. Laphroaig or Lagavulin whiskey
1 tbsp. mushroom ketchup
2 tbsp. flat-leaf parsley, chopped
Sea salt
Freshly ground black pepper

METHOD
Melt the butter quickly in a very special, very hot frying pan—the butter will brown and froth. Add the steaks and cook them quickly for about 3 minutes on each side; keep spooning the butter over. Remove the steaks from the heat and keep them warm. Quickly add the shallots and mushrooms to the pan—plus some more butter (if necessary). Keep stirring. Sprinkle with flakes of sea salt and black pepper. Pour the whiskey over this. Add the mushroom ketchup, douse with cream, and mix it with the meaty, mushroomy juices. Let this bubble away for a minute or two—you'll see that it reduces really quickly and turns a deeper golden color. Drizzle the sauce over the steaks, sprinkle with parsley, and serve.

Dating back to the reign of Queen Victoria, royal picnics in the heathery distances of the Scottish countryside around Balmoral have been very jolly, and the Queen Mum used to love these, lugging with her the choicest samples of Christmas or plum pudding on every picnic. They are taken in all weathers; whistling winds, a light sleet, nothing deters the Windsors from a picnic. And why not? The Windsor picnic basket holds the tastiest of morsels: round-breasted chicken and ham buns, venison pâté, and a zippy consommé called Bull's Blood that has a slick of vodka in it.

Any misconceptions about Queen Elizabeth quaffing champagne should be dispelled—both she and Philip hate it (unlike the Queen Mum, whose relentlessly high spirits on her 1989 visit to Canada were attributed to her bone china cup being topped up with champagne rather than tea). When times are particularly tough, frugal Liz has been known to buy store-brand champagne for banquets and bundle it up in lots of white cloth, claiming that no one will know the difference. State banquets tend to be limited to four courses rather than the elephantine, groaning banquets of the Victorian and Edwardian eras. Indeed, the queen makes no attempt to add any artificial glamour to the occasion, fishing a meat hook out of her handbag at dinner in order to hang her bag from the table.

If the queen has any pre-dinner tipple, it would be something like a gin martini or pink vermouth with soda. Philip, of course, remains loyal to his favorite beer, Double Diamond (brewed especially for him to this day). Footmen at Buckingham Palace are trained in how to pour a Double Diamond so as to get the perfect head. The mythology is that the royals don't like the grating sound of ice cubes in a glass, so they insist on round ice balls.

Philip's bluster and bluntness has left him inured to personal boundaries; he can sometimes be startlingly intimate. Once, as the royal yacht *Britannia* was trailing along the Ivory Coast, submerged in heat, all who sailed on the *Britannia* were driven to sunbathe, but with the usual master-servant distinctions: the duke was sunbathing on the royal deck, and his staff were on the upper deck. One footman woke from a deep, sweaty slumber and was startled to find the duke lying fast asleep beside him. He had dragged his sunbed onto their deck. The footman lay still, reasoning to himself that the duke must have wanted human company. When he finally woke, Philip said brightly, "I'll have to down a drink with you later."

The "Yotties," as yachtsmen are known on board the royal yacht, love to pester the royal staff with cheeky demands. On one occasion, the royal staff was holed up in the royal mess, supping on gin and tonics, when there was a sharp knock at the door. "It's one of those Yotties," someone muttered, and a footman yelled out, "Piss off!" "I won't piss off," came back the muffled voice of the duke, "I want a drink." And the offending footman had to buy the duke a Double Diamond by way of apology.

In contrast, the queen has in the past bemoaned the fact that she is too often offered alcohol, while she secretly hankers for a good cup of tea (even the queen's nightcap is tea, placed by her bedside). Traditionally, on board the *Britannia*, the

Windsors love a drink called lemon refresher made with Epsom salts—it has laxative properties so must be measured out and consumed with care.

On sea or land, starters don't suit this pair, either. Though the queen does sometimes begin with a salad, they prefer to go straight to the main course for dinner. And that main course is ring-fenced by personal foibles: odd, weird tomato sauces have been struck off the royal menu, as have funny Italian messes with pasta and sauces. Shellfish seems un-British, and wet, jellified oysters are a real no-no, while smellies like onions and garlic raise a shudder. Even pepper is viewed with suspicion (though with the younger royals, gnocchi and risottos and even noodles have made their way onto the table, and the reign of the mashed potato has passed). When in 1986 a fish bone stuck in the Queen Mum's throat, a stink was raised, particularly since someone clearly had slipped up—all game, fish, and chicken are supposed to be deboned before they are served to a royal. Beware the seeded fruit such as the blackcurrant or the raspberry, since they are banned from the table for their propensity to wedge themselves between the monarch's teeth.

With all outlandishness chased away, on the private Windsor dinner table would be the queen's favored staples of duck a l'orange, Irish stew, or her favorite game bird, pheasant. Broad beans might be served, too—she loves these. Or there might be lamb cutlets with mint sauce (Philip and Elizabeth take their own bottles of mint sauce with them when they go on foreign trips), poached salmon, fish and chips, and roast beef. But Elizabeth's all-time favorite is unsmoked haddock dipped in breadcrumbs, fried, and accompanied by a tidy stack of slim French fries and Béarnaise sauce alongside. The queen is also a stickler for eating yesterday's leftovers.

All of the Windsors like the edible patriotism of traditional puddings. Prince Andrew, the Duke of York, has been noted for liking steamed sponge syrup pudding a little too much (a genetic tendency inherited from his grandmother, the Queen Mum, whose weakness for the steamed pudding is well documented), leading to the unhappy nickname the "Duke of Pork." When he isn't working as a roving business ambassador for Britain, I like to imagine Prince Andrew of an evening, hair parted on the left, slippers on, and a bowl of this syrup sponge on his lap, far from the madding crowd.

As befits a royal pudding, syrup sponge is of the lightest, airiest quality, with kindly aromas of vanilla and egg, and is topped with a seam of caramelized toffee syrup. The main points to beware when making syrup sponge are the business of mixing it by hand and how weirdly anyone you feed it to will behave ever afterward: their eyes will shine like an addict's, and they'll say, voice husky with lust, "Are you going to make *it* again tonight?"

You will have to get away fast.

Ideally, in order to make the sponge base by hand, you should have either (a) arms like hams or (b) a servant (Prince Andrew has lots) for the amount of businesslike stirring you have to do, slapping about the sponge mix with a wooden spoon. It's like being trapped in too long of a kitchen scene from *Downton Abbey*.

You hope someone might come in and say, "Ooooh, Mrs. Humbleby, has your Sidney seen his lordship this morning?" so that you can hand them your spoon and shoot off after Sidney. If a servant is unavailable to do the all the stirring, some slightly dim but willing relative would do; just say something like "Do you mind stirring this for a moment? I think I hear the phone ringing. . . ." and then hole yourself up in the bathroom for fifteen minutes with a bit of light reading.

Eventually though, after much slapping and creaming and dropping and adding about three tablespoons of milk, you'll end up with a creamy, pale buttercup sponge mix, like the color of a good childhood.

Duke of Pork's Syrup Sponge Pudding

INGREDIENTS

1 generous cup self-raising flour
2 tsp. baking powder
Pinch of sea salt
Scant ½ cup butter, cut into
   little cubes, plus a little
   extra for buttering the
   pudding bowl

2 tbsp. golden syrup, plus a little
   extra for dripping over the
   pudding at serving time
2 eggs
½ cup vanilla caster sugar (granulated
   will do too)
A little milk (about 3 tbsp.)

METHOD

Sift the flour and baking powder into a large bowl. Add a pinch of sea salt. Add the cubed butter and rub it into the flour until the mixture is crumbly. Stir in the vanilla sugar. Whisk the eggs. Using a wooden spoon, stir the eggs into the mixture. Keep stirring, working toward a smooth consistency, adding milk if necessary, a tablespoon at a time. Eventually, the mixture should have a dropping consistency.

Butter a Pyrex heatproof basin. Chill for 5 minutes in the fridge. Pour the golden syrup into the bottom of the basin. Pour the sponge mixture in and cover in the following way: butter a square, 1-foot piece of greaseproof paper. Fold two 1-inch pleats into the center of it. Repeat this process with aluminum foil of the same size (but unbuttered!). Place these greaseproof paper first, with foil as the outer layer, over the top of the pudding basin. Make sure they are at right angles to each other (this will allow the pudding to rise and "grow"). Secure these homemade "lids" with string, tightly knotted around the rim of the bowl. Steam for 1½ hours. To do this, simply fill a third of a large saucepan with boiling water, lower the pudding in, cover the pan, and cook for about an hour and a half. After this time, remove the string, foil, and greaseproof paper and tip the pudding out onto a plate (best done by covering the pudding basin with a plate and then turning the whole lot over, holding the plate tightly against the bowl and not allowing slippage).

Serve the pudding and, if you wish, dribble a little more syrup over it; have a pool of custard or cool vanilla ice cream alongside. It will be difficult to leave the table for a number of reasons. I almost took this pudding to bed with me.

Long have I dreamed about making Prince Philip's favorite dessert, Andrassy Pudding. It just sounds swanky, doesn't it? And it is. Andrassy Pudding tastes aristocratic: it is rich, intense, with ebony, sassy, expensive chocolate tones. In truth, though, Andrassy Pudding is named after a bleak-looking Austro-Hungarian count, Julius Andrassy, a relative of the Windsors, who had a brief and relatively undistinguished career in the lead-up to World War I (he managed to be Hungary's foreign minister for only nine days before he threw in the towel).

Second-cousin-twice-removed Julius turned up for dinner one evening at the start of the twentieth century, and far from his table, in the commoner underworlds of Buckingham Palace, some unnamed chef had been instructed to make a simple, puffy little bundle of chocolate soufflé. This was to be Andrassy Soufflé. But it sank. Our pâtissier must have cursed as he looked at his limp, punctured soufflé. All he had left was more soufflé mix (without the whipped egg whites added yet) but no time to bake it. Quickly—perhaps even furtively—he decided to slice the soufflé up like a cake and disguise it behind an artificial wig and beard of frosting (the second soufflé mix), finally throwing chocolate curls all over it. That's just the ticket, he thought: Andrassy Pudding.

So how to make Andrassy Pudding? Follow the recipe below and it is really easy. The soufflé does as it is told. Eighteen minutes baking is long enough at 200°C, but—a word of warning—make sure it's ready. I know it seems counter-intuitive to stab a soufflé; however, given that this soufflé is destined to become a pudding, you are allowed to test whether it's ready by skewering it. A quick, clean blow will put it out of its misery. Do this before you commit to taking it out of the oven. If it is set inside, the blade will come out clean. If it is chocolate coated, it's too soon, and you should keep the soufflé in for another few minutes.

Andrassy Pudding ends up having a frangible, delicate soufflé core, and there is a clear distinction between the sweetness of the soufflé and the taste of the frosting, even though the only real difference between them is six egg whites. The frosting has a bittersweet, sulky edge that contrasts with the milder, more homely chocolati-ness of the soufflé.

Andrassy Pudding

FOR THE SOUFFLÉ . . .

4 tbsp. butter, plus extra butter for buttering the soufflé dish

½ cup all-purpose flour (sifted)

⅓ cup caster or granulated sugar

Generous ½ cup unsweetened cocoa powder

1 cup milk

6 large eggs, separated

Andrassy Pudding (*continued*)

FOR THE FROSTING . . .

4 tbsp. butter

⅓ cup vanilla caster or
   granulated sugar

½ cup all-purpose flour

Generous ½ cup unsweetened
   cocoa powder

1 cup milk

6 egg yolks (keep the whites for
   making meringues another time)

1½ cups grated milk chocolate

METHOD

Heat oven to 200°C. Butter a soufflé dish. Place 6 egg yolks in a large glass bowl and whisk them. Reserve the whites for a later stage. Melt the butter in a saucepan, and once melted, whisk in the flour, sugar, and cocoa powder. Whisk quickly and add the milk, beginning very cautiously with a gentle dribble. Gradually incorporate the milk with your whisk. Next, remove the pan from the heat. Again whisking, add this smooth, chocolaty milk to the egg yolks. Let this mixture cool for about a quarter of an hour.

Now whisk the egg whites in a separate bowl until they form lovely, glossy, glacial peaks. Using a metal spoon, fold the egg white into the egg-chocolate mixture. Heap this mixture into the buttered soufflé dish and bake in the oven for about 20 minutes or until risen. Test the soufflé with a skewer.

Take the soufflé out of the oven and let it cool. It will gradually deflate, but while it still retains some warmth, turn it out. Leave to cool.

Now busy yourself with the frosting. Melt the butter in a saucepan, and once melted, whisk in the flour, sugar, and cocoa powder. Whisk quickly and add the milk, beginning very cautiously with a gentle dribble. Gradually incorporate the milk with your whisk. Next, remove the pan from the heat. Again whisking, add this smooth, chocolaty milk to the egg yolks. Sound familiar? Allow this to cool.

When all is ready and cooled, slice the soufflé in half like a cake, fill with frosting, then cover the whole cake with the rest of the frosting. Finish by sprinkling with grated chocolate.

Oh, to be a corgi. Queen Elizabeth's favored dogs get the best deal all around and don't have to bother with forks and knives. These lucky dogs get freshly baked fruit scones, broken up by the fair hands of their mistress while she sucks on a Bendick's Bittermint (chocolate and mint combinations do it for the queen, she's also partial to Elizabeth Shaw peppermint creams, Terry's Twilight, and mint chocolate chip ice cream). The corgis compete for these fragrant morsels through performing rolling, spinning, and wriggling tricks for their mistress. There's pheasant, mixed with Pedigree Chum, and rabbits, and all out of their own named little bowls. The corgis never have common tinned dog food, always woofing down fresh food, lamb, beef, or rabbit with gravy and mashed potatoes and cabbage . . . mmm . . . hungry? This, then, is transported from the kitchens to the dogs but passes through the hands of the queen, who likes to personally mix this with dog biscuits and more gravy. *But beware*: if you ever happen to be passing the time of day with the queen, don't pet her corgis—she gets jealous and thinks you are trying to suck up (which you wouldn't be, of course, would you?). One of the royal butler's onerous duties was to check that the corgis were all in bed at night. Bless.

THE AGA KHAN'S ICE CREAM

In many ways, Sir Sultan Muhammed Shah, the third Aga Khan, descendant of the Prophet Mohammed and leader since the age of eight of the widespread, numerous Ismaili branch of Islam, was the very incarnation of everything a member of the colonial English aristocracy should be. Aged eleven, he could think of no greater treat than eating slabs of seedcake (only Jane Eyre had this much fun with seedcake before him) and loved the regalia of a British gentleman, the meticulous tucks and folds of morning dress, the crispness of starched collars (though, in later life, he got his trousers caught in his socks and often forgot to button his fly). The Aga Khan was spellbound by Europe, hopelessly drawn to it, cherishing its gilded casinos; the muscled, sweat-lathered racehorses thundering over the green courses at the Derby, Ascot, and Epsom; and the delicate, perfectly sauced dishes of Paris. And he had the vast wealth to savor its glories. His diminutive mother, the punchy Lady Ali Shah, had held together her son's imamate; a shrewd investor, she vastly increased her son's fortune through her financial acumen. There were mining investments, nine palaces in India, jewels, a stable of horses, land that stretched for kingdoms, and multitudes of servants.

Although the Aga Khan often looked as though he were in theatrical disguise, with comic bottle-end glasses, a woolly waistcoat stretched over his tummy, he had the presence of a great man. And it was as a great man—albeit a very young one (indeed, when Mark Twain dined with the eighteen-year-old aga, he thought him a man in his late thirties)—that he set out in a flourish on his European tour in 1897, determined to meet that great, skirted representative of the British Empire he so adored: Queen Victoria.

He tracked Victoria down first in the Riviera, where she was passing a few pleasant weeks in the watery spring sunshine. To his great delight, he managed to elbow his way into the same hotel as her—the newly built Hotel Excelsior Regina in Ciminez—and listened daily to reports about Her Majesty's movements (Victoria's other stalker in Nice was a resourceful one-legged beggar who would race behind her carriage in his careering cart, drawn by two dogs). Finally, the Aga Khan was invited for dinner but found himself marooned at the other end of the table from Victoria, only able to gaze wistfully at her distant, mountainous profile across the napkins, crystal, and flower arrangements. Tantalized, he wanted much, much more from Victoria. A real audience. Slowly, his grand tour followed Victoria's progress back to Britain. In her wake, the Aga Khan had his first, heady taste of Monte Carlo, tried out spats and a straw hat, and watched the monarchs of Europe and Russia with their pets and mistresses. Next, he went on to the theaters of Paris and mingled with its beautiful sophisticates. He already regretted his marriage to his cousin, Shazadi Begum ("begum" is the title of the Aga Khan's wife), a year earlier; the marriage was arid, sexless, and childless. Here he could have Europe's vivacious, dark-eyed, witty women on his arm. He took rooms in the Hotel Bristol in Paris, who were much put out by the prostrate forms of Ismaili followers of the Aga Khan turning up at his suite, clustering outside his hotel room door with only their socks on, faces down. Paris was the place to eat, and the aga hunted out the best restaurants in cobbled streets of Paris, no matter how humble they were, on the lookout for the next gourmandizing thrill. Soon, though, he couldn't resist the lure of the wind-hugged shores of Britain and Buckingham Palace, carrying in his luggage a solid-gold elephant for his beloved queen.

Fin de siècle London was a powerhouse of commerce, the gray epicenter of the empire, and it was here, with his leather brogues squeaking and best tailored frock coat on, that the Aga Khan arrived, an invitation to Windsor Castle in his pocket. And yet, even in his best clothes, some dinner companions found him wanting. While burping in approval of a dish was good form in Karachi, it was considered very poor taste in Kensington. Nor is it good form to wipe one's mouth on the corner of the tablecloth—especially if you have been placed next to Florence Nightingale, who sourly observed that the Aga Khan was "a most interesting man, but one is never likely to teach him sanitation."

Undeterred, the Aga Khan donned his silk top hat and descended joyfully on Windsor. The old castle was damp and glacial in parts; chilly air trickled down corridors. There were wheezing fireplaces, drab decorations, greasy-haired maids, and, in the midst of it all, seventy-nine-year-old Victoria, shrouded in her dark, crow-black widow's weeds. Although he couldn't quite work out her height or figure, she was clearly stout, stubby fingered, a ring on one hand with the image of Albert fixed there forever and a little napkin of lace on her silver hair, but her gaze, thought the khan, was magnificent and fierce. Despite Windsor's miserable interior décor, his hostess also seemed determined to impress him. He was whisked in to be knighted by Queen Victoria but didn't have to kneel before her in the timeworn fashion, as he was kingly himself. Instead, he stood transfixed before her and may have been there to this day had not Lloyd George tapped him on the shoulder to remind him his knighting was over.

Dinner was wonderful: the Aga Khan was perched between Victoria and Princess Beatrice, marveling (jubilantly and uncritically, of course) at the gargantuan appetites of the British upper crust. Lord Salisbury, with great purple pouches of fat hanging beneath his eyes, demolished, over the course of two hours, salmon cutlets, clear soups, thick soups, roast pigeons, chickens, ham mousse, asparagus (a favorite of both the Aga Khan and Victoria) dressed in white sauce, and even a dessert in flames. Sorbets sporadically appeared to "cool" the tummy between the twelve courses. Not only that, but Salisbury, who seemed to have the ability to consume dishes in one gulp, was so paunchy in his overcoat of fat that he had to be winched

in and out of his dining chair, as his legs could no longer support him (Lord Salisbury was also "a keen amateur scientist who was among the first to have electric
wiring in his house"—it took a while for Victorians to get used to electricity, and
it was not uncommon to find a Victorian, lit match in hand, bent over a socket).
The queen's diamond jubilee was under discussion; the Aga Khan found the queen
was sharp and shrewd, speaking in what he thought was a peculiar mixture of a
Scottish and German accent. Indian servants attended her. And, despite his gentle
disappointment in the lack of color and opulence of Windsor Castle, the Aga Khan
noted with approval the many diamonds twinkling on the queen's person.

Ham Mousse in Truffled Aspic (but would the Aga Khan have had a slice?)

FOR THE ASPIC . . .

2 cups chicken stock

2 shallots, sliced

The white of 1 egg—retain the
egg shell and crush it

Blade of mace

1 tbsp. gelatin

¼ cup dry sherry

TO GARNISH THE ASPIC . . .

4 bay leaves

2 black truffles, finely sliced

FOR THE MOUSSE . . .

2 tbsp. gelatin

¼ cup dry sherry

3 cups smoked ham, minced and
then passed through a sieve

1 handful of parsley, finely chopped

4 scallions, very finely chopped

2 tbsp. butter

2 tbsp. tomato puree

2 cups chicken stock

1 cup heavy cream

A pinch of ground nutmeg

Freshly ground black pepper

METHOD

First make the ham mousse. Plan to make it a day in advance of serving. Mix the
finely chopped parsley with the smoked ground ham. Pepper and lay to the side.
Place the gelatin to soften and meld with the sherry in a Pyrex bowl. After about
5 minutes, place the bowl over a pan of simmering water. Stir the gelatin-infused
sherry until the gelatin granules have dissolved. Remove from the heat and immediately combine with the chicken stock and tomato puree. Melt the butter in a
saucepan, and then add the scallions. Put a disk of buttered greaseproof paper
over this and let the scallions soften. Add the scallions to the sherry-chicken-tomato
liquid and stir through. Now add the ham and combine thoroughly. Add the black
pepper and nutmeg. Cool. In a separate bowl, whisk the cream until it is thick
and billowy. Fold in the savory liquid. Chill this in the fridge for up to 10 hours,
stirring regularly.

Ham Mousse in Truffled Aspic (*continued*)

Now for the aspic. In a saucepan, mix together the chicken stock, shallots, egg white, crushed shell, and blade of mace. Simmer for 12 minutes. Remove from the heat and let the mixture infuse for a further 30 minutes. Next, strain the mixture into a bowl through a fine muslin cloth. Combine the sherry and gelatin in a Pyrex bowl. Let them rest together for 5 minutes. Now place the Pyrex bowl over a pan of simmering water and stir until the gelatin granules dissolve. Add this to the strained stock-shallot liquid and whisk together. You now have the makings of aspic. Let it cool but not set. Get a pretty, 2-pint cut-glass mold, rinse it with cold water, and pour in a layer of the aspic. Lay the truffle slices and bay leaves onto the liquid aspic in an arrangement of your own devising. Chill this for at least 3 hours or until such time as it is firm. Whatever aspic remains, pour into a shallow tray and chill this also.

When the aspic has set, pour the chilled ham mousse into the glass mold and chill, covered, for a further 3 hours. Finally, when your guests have arrived, tell the cook to remove the mousse gently from its mold and garnish it with the leftover aspic, chopped up, plus whatever greenery (liked chopped parsley) comes to hand.

Tantalizingly, the queen was absent from breakfast the next day, but again her table was groaning with woodcock and brassy kippers, hefts of bacon, sweetbreads, regiments of cutlets, sausages, steaks and kidneys—every mouthful and every abandoned, uneaten leg of woodcock emblematic of the vast power and wealth of the controlling aristocracy.

More of a soul mate, though, was Victoria's son and successor, King Edward VII. He invited the aga to join his gentleman's club, the Marlborough Club, full of wealthy, liverish rakes who liked to dress up for dinner. Edward often dropped in there, garters on tight, for his favorite late-night tipple of gin, lemon, and hot water. Their shared passion for horses made the two men ideal companions when they visited Ascot on a Friday in 1909. The aga recalled in his memoirs that luncheon was served in the royal box. He was seated (to his delight) at King Edward's table, but looking up expectantly for his luncheon, he watched as the waiters sailed past him until, eventually, a couple of cutlets were placed before him. Finally, noticing the aga's perplexity, the king boomed, "I thought you wouldn't like the thing on the menu, so I ordered those cutlets for you." The aga spotted the ham on his neighbor's plate and realized that the king, tactfully, had taken matters into his own hands, understanding that the khan would have felt compelled out of politeness to eat the offending pork. His heart filled with gratitude.

Over the course of his long eating life (he even turns up having tea with Queen Elizabeth II half a century or so later in 1953), the Aga Khan witnessed many such cross-cultural food faux pas. There was the state banquet given by Lord Curzon in honor of an Afghan prince. Sitting opposite, the aga watched hesitantly as the Muslim prince lifted a spoonful of soup laced with sherry to his lips—his political agent squeaked, "Your Highness, there is sherry in this soup." Hastily, he laid down his spoon. They were on safer ground with the next course of fish. Next, though, arrived an entrée flagrantly draped with slices of ham. Then there were bacon bits smuggled into the vegetables, tiny porcine assailants; finally came the ice cream, but just as the prince was moistening his lips, the political agent piped, "Your Highness, it's got chartreuse in it." Or there was the travail of the Hindu maharajas the aga invited to dinner at the Willingdon Club in Bombay (the Willingdon was founded expressly to allow wealthy male Indians and Europeans to mix). The aga firmly instructed the Parsi head steward that cow (which has the good fortune to be considered a sacred beast by Hindus) was strictly off the menu, only for the dinner party to be presented with a large plate of puckered ox tongue. The Hindus took a dim view of it, and, when berated, it turned out that the steward swore by the fact that ox tongue bore no relation whatsoever to beef: it was from an ox, wasn't it? Another Hindu friend almost fell prostrate into a nervous collapse when a calf's head was put on his table in Europe; he likened it to being served the head of a human baby. Then there was the aga's visit to China in 1906. Dining in Shanghai with influential Chinese businessmen was culinary torture. The Muslim guests were lulled into a false sense of security with run-of-the-mill chicken dishes. Then appeared an anonymous flesh titled "Tartar grilled meat." The Muslim guests, murmuring, debated the issue until everyone agreed that it was probably kebab. Inquiry was made as to the identity of the chef: he was a Chinese Muslim. All's well, then. Buried eggs and bamboo shoots followed and, finally, a dish that they all decided was eel. "We know this very well," ventured one of the aga's companions. "It is eel." How the Chinese businessmen laughed and shook their heads: "Oh no," their Chinese host interjected, "this is snake!" That really whetted their appetite. Soon the snake pieces slid under the table and into napkins. Lucky they did so, as the aga recalled in his memoirs: "Long years later I remember reading a newspaper account of the effect of a similar dish on some foreigners at a Chinese official dinner. All were very ill and some died." Curiously, another oddity the aga spotted in China was "Welcome Houses," forbidden to Chinese and packed full of fair, blue-eyed prostitutes from Minnesota, rumored to be saving up for their dowries to take back home with them. Americans were an odd lot, as the aga found in the devastation that was San Francisco after the 1906 earthquake. Everything was closed; yet the aga still managed to find one shop open: a drugstore where he could lick a delicious ice cream. It was very odd, he concluded, "amid all the devastation—to be served ice cream and cold drinks in what, elsewhere in the world, we call a chemist's shop."

Earthquake or not, there would be no roughing it for the Aga Khan. Even when he took himself off on safari in Africa (taken in 1948 at the point of the Partition of India and Gandhi's assassination), fourteen food trucks trundled alongside him, rattling with jars of caviar, foie gras, and tins of asparagus—not to mention the porcelain bath in which the aga luxuriated at each camp stop. Despite all this finesse, dinner alone with the Aga Khan didn't sound like a barrel of laughs. In his villa Yakymour in Antibes, the dining table was a long, refectory-style expanse, and the aga had the menu embellished on a very unglamorous plastic memo card. According to biographer Anne Edwards, if you so much as hesitated with your fork and knife over your dinner, he'd inquire solicitously, "Perhaps you don't like squab. Would you prefer fish or veal?" And, irrespective of your reply, the squab would be whisked away and the alternative dish presented to you (all served by a maid distractedly clad in a short skirt and silk stockings). If at a buffet-style meal he noticed you were helping yourself to a less than superb portion of lobster, he'd whip it off your plate and replace it with a more succulent crustacean, a style of hosting that runs counter to more apocryphal stories of dinner out with the aga when he apparently always snatched the best wine for himself, saying, "This is for me." Meals always ended with the aga's adored ice cream, made fresh every day with thick, rich cream and fruit and served in chilly silver bowls.

The Aga Khan's wild-living son and supposed heir, Aly Khan, was not brought up in India but tutored in France—a sadly solitary boyhood, far from the wise ministrations of his grandmother but still with all his father's passion for European women and horses (plus fast cars). Wife number one was Joan Guinness. He met her at a dinner party; at the time, she was married to the British conservative MP for Bath, Thomas Loel Guinness. Suddenly, Aly turned to her and said, "Darling, will you marry me?" Everyone laughed—little did they know. Aly seems to have treated marriage as blithely as he did the declaration of war between Britain and Germany three years later in 1939. With his chauffeur, Emrys Williams (nicknamed "Daffy"), Aly sped to his mother's old villa in Antibes. He was under orders to remove family treasures there from a strong room full to the brim with valuables. Aly tried his key in the lock, rattled it; tried again. The strong room was impenetrable. Desperate, he paid a blacksmith to break down its door. There before them were arching ivory tusks mounted in gold, saris heavy with rubies and diamonds, seed beds of opalescent pearls, ornate tapestries. They dragged the treasures to the car and loaded it up. Finally, they started the engine and, laden with priceless jewels, headed north for Deauville. Aly then had a bright idea, as Emrys Williams relates in his memoirs:

"Let's go to Rumpelmeyer's in Paris," he suddenly said. "It won't take us long."
"With this loot on board! Whatever for?"

"I fancy an ice-cream, Daffy."

I roared with laughter. "At a time like this you're prepared to go miles out of your way to buy an ice-cream!"

"It may be the last one, Daffy. Who knows what may happen to either of us in the near future."

So off they went, adding several hundred miles to their flight, the family loot risked for the sake of an ice cream. In truth, Aly was in some ways a vapid imitation of his father's appetites, aping his passion for food by hiring the best chefs and stocking his table with delicacies but without the keen interest of the epicure in what he was eating. Even in a favorite restaurant like the Pré-Catalan in the Bois de Bologne, Paris, the food was rather lost on him. He wanted to talk, not eat. Only ice cream could really command his attention.

Daffy and Aly had further adventures together in the years to follow. There were some low points, as when once, postwar, Aly was on his way to visit India as his father's emissary (there had been great violence and discord with partition). Their air passage was fraught with difficulties, but they managed to work out they could fly in a Dutch army plane. The first stop of their journey was Amsterdam, but when they got there they had no money and only managed to change £2 for some Dutch guilder using the black market. Prince Aly found it hard to cope without money and grew very gloomy. The lowest point of this brief experience of poverty being that they were reduced to going to the cinema to watch *Fanny by Gaslight*. They managed to make it to Rome, where Aly was able to access family investments, and with his newly acquired wealth they headed off to an ice-cream parlor to eat at least a dozen ice creams each. A luxurious dinner of scallops and spaghetti in a black-market restaurant was followed—at the prince's insistence—by a second orgiastic visit to the ice-cream parlor. Best of all, Aly loved rich, bittersweet orange ice cream, packed into the tight drum of the orange's skin. This repast prepared them for the journey to come, which included a parched crossing of the desert in Sindh only to be met by an Indian brass band blasting out tunes while dressed in the boots and clanking helmets that had originally belonged to the London Fire Brigade.

Famous socialite and party fixer, the stentorian, grandmotherly Elsa Maxwell (whom Cole Porter lyrically and comically made reference to in the lines "I'm dining with Elsa [and her ninety-nine most intimate friends]") introduced thirty-eight-year-old Prince Aly to wife number two, the actress Rita Hayworth. Rita was in Cannes, wounded from the end of her marriage to Orson Welles, when Elsa phoned to tempt her out of hiding with the promise of a lovely soirée in honor of a Texan millionaire at the Palm Beach Casino on July 3, 1948. Rita turned her down: "Don't speak to me about a dinner or anything else; my heart is broken." But, like Rita's very own heavyweight fairy godmother, Elsa suggested, "Go and buy a dress. Make it white. Come in late. I want you to meet a Persian Prince." Elsa recalled

Orange Ice Cream

INGREDIENTS

4 oranges
1 cup full-fat milk
2 cups heavy cream
A pinch of sea salt

¾ cup granulated sugar
The zest of 2 oranges (if you'd like a
  bitter orange, use Seville oranges)
6 egg yolks

METHOD
Cut the top off of each of the oranges and remove the flesh down to the white pith. Cut a very thin slice off the base of each orange so that they can stand upright. In a saucepan, warm the milk and half of the cream, sea salt, and sugar. When the sugar has dissolved, add the orange zest; take the pan off the heat and cool for 30 minutes. After this, put the egg yolks in a largish bowl, whisk them, and then gradually add the warmish milk to the eggs, whisking all the time. Now return the mixture to a saucepan and, over a medium-to-low heat, warm the mixture, stirring constantly. A custard is forming, and when it is ready the custard will coat the back of your spoon. When the custard has formed, remove the pan from the heat and transfer into a bowl. Add the rest of the cream and stir it through. Allow to cool thoroughly—you can speed this up by putting the bowl in the freezer for half an hour. Now empty the chilled mix into an ice-cream maker and churn for about an hour. When the ice cream is made, use an ice-cream scoop to fill the oranges with it. Now share it with your chauffeur!

the moment of Rita's alluringly late entrance: "I'll never forget. We were playing a game. Rita came in the door; everybody gasped. Aly said: 'My God! Who is that?' I said, 'She's sitting next to you at dinner.'" Aly was already renowned among the ladies for his abilities as a lover and had developed a crush on the on-screen Rita. No more *Fanny by Gaslight* for him; he had watched her film *Gilda* repeatedly throughout the summer of 1948. Gilded in white, with the sheen of Hollywood magic about her, Aly danced with Rita until midnight. If only Rita had known about Aly's summer activities, she might have seen her doom advance upon her, as she was to announce gloomily, "Every man I had married had fallen in love with Gilda and awakened with me." At that first moment, though, all the power was Rita's. Aly shot back to his house, the green-shuttered Chateau Horizon, and was so delighted that he jumped up and down on his bed. He'd invited Rita for tea and she'd accepted; he had to get his palace ready for her arrival. The three-storied house was memorably beautiful (it was also full of stashes of money in every conceivable currency, so Aly could just shoot off on a whim on his airplane, *Avenger*), but for Rita it had to be perfection. Rita, meanwhile, had told Elsa that she thought him "a nice little fellow." Hmmm—would any of us be satisfied with this description?

Aly had other princes to do battle with for her company: the shah of Iran was lurking about the Côte d'Azur, trying to catch Rita's eye, inviting her for champagne lunches at the Eden Roc restaurant (she stood him up to make her second date with Aly). Aly—in a Mr. Rochester–style move—decided to tamper with fate. It just so happened that a gypsy fortune-teller turned up at Rita's hotel suite with—how very fortunate—a *translator* in tow to read Rita's fortune. While for most of us the translator's presence would have made us a tad suspicious about this prediction racket, Rita drank in the gypsy's words. Strike me down, it turned out that Rita was about to have the love affair of a lifetime with someone she already knew, whom she must "give in to totally."

While we leave Rita puzzling about whom her new romance would involve, behind the scenes, Aly was in overdrive. He sped to Paris to grab a chef (there was dawdling over ice creams at Rumpelmeyer's this time); chef secured, he was rushed across to one of Aly's Parisian houses, the Maison Lafiette, and ordered the finest crockery and cutlery to be sent to his kitchen in Cannes. Aly even went so far as to dig out extra, impressive reams of table linen.

With such frenzy, what romance? The lovers spent days together, but always tracked by a pack of pressmen; they went from place to place, trying to shake them off. One female acquaintance explained the impossibility of the couple ever escaping the press: "You're not exactly John Doe," she reasoned. Aly flushed, shot Rita a jealous glance, and spat, "*Who* is John Doe?" Biarritz, Cuba, Seville, Madrid flashed past. Daffy was their only servant, washing out Rita's underwear in the place of untrustworthy maids, cooking for them, and driving them everywhere.

Calling in on America at Christmastime during these early stages of their relationship afforded Aly more anonymity. The American press had little idea of what he looked like, and he could meander about Hollywood, trying on outfits and sampling ice-cream parlors. Rita, meanwhile, had no idea Aly intended to surprise her and was feeling a little melancholic; the gossip columns didn't help her mood. Aly had vanished on a ski trip and had been sighted on the piste with a toothsome blonde. When she wasn't aching for her lost marriage to Orson Welles or feeling put out by Aly, Christmas made Rita think of iced vodka and caviar. A world of elegance she had first glimpsed when working as a child dancer—with her allegedly incestuous father, Eduardo Cansino, as her dance and bed partner—on Christmas Eve in Caliente, Mexico. The stylish, remote thrill of toasts and white coattails left the juvenile, vulnerable Rita breathless with its loveliness. She was hot and tired, thirteen years old, and decided it was as good a time as any to toast her own lonely, half-childish Christmas with the leftover iced vodka she found abandoned on the tinseled tables, lipstick prints still on the glasses, accompanied by a salty soupcon of someone else's caviar. Ever after, for Rita, vodka and caviar had an extra glitter of nostalgia to them.

Fast forward some fifteen years, and, in Aly's supposed absence, Hollywood junior writer James Hill was making a play for Rita. Hill had a friend who was a neighbor to Rita, and a series of minor mishaps meant that Hill landed on her doorstep that Christmas Eve. To his triumph and confusion, on knocking on Rita's door he was immediately misidentified as a cleaner sent by an agency. Hill decided on the spot to carry on the facade, waxing floors for Rita and answering the door with autographed pictures of her. Then he overheard Rita recount her poignant story about being a lonesome teenage performer and eating Christmas leftovers. Half in love with her already, Hill decided to somehow get his hands on caviar and Stolichnaya and give Rita back her childhood. And if he added a little mistletoe, this might just win him a kiss. Out into the chilly night he went and bartered and wheedled caviar and champagne out of the local stores. He returned, chuckling a little to himself, and set about boiling eggs and toasting bread.

Soon he was all set to go: he had managed to arrange Rita, the vodka, the caviar (which he had lovingly prepared with sides of chopped boiled egg—the whites separated from the yolks—and wedges of toast), and the mistletoe in front of the Christmas tree. Suddenly, the doorbell jangled. "Just don't move," James told Rita. When he answered the door, guess who was there, arms festooned with gifts? Aly Khan! "Candles and caviar!" cried the prince joyfully, sweeping past Jimmy. "You *knew* I'd be here! You darling!" James could only close the door quietly behind him and limp away. (N.B. All hope was not lost for James Hill; he became husband number five, but it didn't work out.)

Caviar with Eggs and Toast

INGREDIENTS

2 oz. jar of caviar

2 hard-boiled eggs

1 lemon, cut into slices

2 tbsp. finely chopped chives

¼ cup sour cream

1 small red onion, very finely chopped

1 loaf of sliced white bread

4 tbsp. melted butter

METHOD

Preheat the oven to 180°C. Empty the caviar into a glass bowl. Take the shell off the eggs, separate the orb of yolk from the white, mince both, and place in separate glass bowls. Put the lemon, chives, sour cream, and red onion all into bowls. Make sure each bowl has a tiny spoon. Now make the toast. Trim the crusts off each slice and then cut each slice into 4 triangles. Brush each of these on both sides with melted butter. Lay the triangles of bread flat on a baking tray and bake in the oven for between 2 and 5 minutes. Remove when golden.

Pour each of your guests a small glass of chilled vodka. Lay out your toast and all the scrumptious little dishes. Don't answer if the doorbell rings.

Despite the passionate attraction between Rita and Aly, the gypsy fortune-teller should have warned both not to tie the knot. Daffy watched Aly's antics two nights before the wedding. Aly and his friend Ellroy were holed up at the Chateau Horizon, and Aly invited Ellroy to gamble at the casino in Cannes. In the casino, Aly inquired thoughtfully of Ellroy, "You've been here a week or so now, haven't you?" He then vanished, only to return with two lovelies. "Take your pick," he said. Ellroy refused the offer, so Aly shrugged obligingly and vanished with the blonde one. Meanwhile, in another corner of the Riviera, Rita had begged Orson Welles to come and see her. Orson, concerned for her well-being, turned up, only to be greeted by Rita in a negligee, her room aglow with candles and champagne. She whispered, "Here I am. Marry me." He declined, but he seemed to understand Rita's inner demons better than most, saying once of her, "If this was happiness, imagine what the rest of her life has been."

Rita spent days being measured for her wedding dress, with bales of gossamer materials arriving with the master couturier Jacques Fath; meanwhile, Aly's tailors bustled over from London. Aly loved visitors—Rita didn't—and these poured into Chateau Horizon from every corner of the world. A spaniel puppy—sent by Orson Welles and dubbed Poogles—joined the melee, and no doubt Poogles had a grand time among the scraps falling from the running buffet of busty gateaux, legions of petits fours, and tangles of pink crayfish and lobsters. It was enough, Daffy bemoaned, to make him long for his mother's bread pudding. If guests wished to see Rita's latest film, *The Loves of Carmen*, Aly had rented the Theatre Alexandre III in Cannes to screen it. On the night before the wedding, Rita and a modest sixty guests were taken to the tiny village of Mougins, set in the Valmasque forest, for a special Rita-inspired menu Aly had designed himself—a menu arguably for the Gilda of his dreams rather than for Rita herself. It reads like a filmography, including Coupe "Cover Girl" and Bombe "Gilda." Meanwhile, the prince's last bachelor dinner was to be with the Duke and Duchess of Windsor, but he couldn't find a taxi (the guests were all using them) and had to hitchhike his way to dinner.

Finally, the couple were married in the small French town of Vallauris. Holed up in a tiny hotel in Cannes had been a cabal of Mahometan priests, who arrived at the chateau "very conspicuously dressed in long white robes" and performed a second secret wedding ceremony. At the wedding reception, the swimming pool was topped up with eau de cologne, and fifteen-foot flower arrangements twisted into *A* and *M* (for Margarita, Rita's full name) floated there. Yves Montand throatily serenaded the guests. The likes of Pablo Picasso picked at some hors d'oeuvre and perhaps, feeling bold, tried a Ritaly cocktail, invented by Jules, the bar manager at the Carlton Hotel in London, who had been flown in to mastermind drinking arrangements. Ritaly was a mixture of two parts of Canadian Club whiskey to one part of Italian vermouth, with a dash of bitters and a cherry—the press downed more of these than the guests.

The Aga Khan, having given his approval to the whole affair, swapped his "horrid champagne" for something else: all he really wanted was a cup of tea. Moodily, he sat, mechanically conveying spoonful after spoonful of caviar into his mouth, his current begum sitting morosely by his side, doling out wooden smiles. Impatient, his tummy rumbling, he decided to start on his meal. The chef, Gondolfo, had been reminded not to serve ham. Caviar and salmon was accompanied by the lobster à la Parisienne, the lobster gently poached in bouillon, cut into tender slices, coated in aspic, accompanied by stuffed tomatoes, and dressed with aspic, mayonnaise, and shards of pungent truffles. There was roasted fowl from Grasse and a splendid pineapple ice cream.

Pineapple Ice Cream

INGREDIENTS

2 cups ripe and juicy chopped
  pineapple
¼ cup granulated vanilla sugar

1½ cup heavy cream
½ cup milk
½ cup granulated vanilla sugar

METHOD

You have to begin by cooking the pineapple; raw pineapple puree will curdle your ice cream. In a medium saucepan, heat the pineapple with a quarter cup of sugar. Cook this gently for about half an hour; stir regularly to ensure there is no sticking. Allow to cool and then blend the pineapple in a food processor.

Warm the heavy cream and the milk in a saucepan. Add the sugar and stir until the sugar dissolves. Cool in the freezer for half an hour and then stir the pineapple puree through it. Process this in an ice-cream maker for about an hour and then serve.

While Rita's popularity soared in Ismaili communities (they stoutly and devotedly went to see her films in Bombay), Aly's faithfulness, always questionable, rapidly declined. He had an octopus-like ability to keep eight arms around eight different girlfriends, and Rita was soon exhausted by his wandering eye. Meanwhile, having wooed Gilda, Aly found himself married to the more pedestrian homebody Rita. She laid in bed until the early afternoon, supping late on breakfasts brought to her by Domingo, a handsome, muscled Hawaiian bodyguard Rita had brought over from America. Bacon and eggs every day, the plate decorated with flowers. Downstairs, Aly would have gathered his bright-eyed guests to go out for lunch; secretly fuming with his sloppy, casual wife. The number of guests downstairs seemed to double miraculously: international racing hucksters, beautiful women, a light sugaring of the jet set. Not only were there many of them, but they also sported many names. When the Duchess of Devonshire joined Aly's entourage for the Carnival in Rio de Janeiro in 1955, she was delayed by a suspicious immigration official. He scrutinized her passport, which read, "Her Grace Deborah Vivian Cavendish Duchess of Devonshire." "Yes, that's me!" she affirmed cheerfully. "But where are the others?" he squinted, no doubt expecting Grace, Vivian, Devonshire, and Cavendish to be kicking their heels farther down the line. Rita found socializing with wits like Debo Devonshire petrifying; they left her tongue-tied. Not all celebrities, though, offered much of a verbal challenge. Elsa Maxwell claimed that one of the worst dinner conversationalists around was Greta Garbo. When Elsa asked her if she was happy to be in Europe, she responded hollowly, "What is happiness? I never have known it."

Too soon, Chateau Horizon was ever busy with hangers-on; solitary Rita would often be found sitting alone, dancing by herself in her locked room after one too many highballs. Alcohol soothed Rita's troubled heart as it had when she was thirteen, paving the way for the alcohol-induced dementia that destroyed her later years. Even when they tried to patch things up on an African safari, Aly managed to slip four Muslim millionaires into his luggage, with whom he could play bridge, as well as a batch of secretaries, a couple of aides, and the odd pilot.

Rita's final despairing statement to the press was "I love Aly very much. He is very nice. But he doesn't understand family life. He thinks only of gambling, horse racing, and big-game hunting. . . . When I come to Paris, it is not to live in a house where there are eighty friends of all kinds coming and going, and it is not to dine at Maxim's. What's more, Aly spends too much, while I have to work for both of us."

Exit Rita.

The Aga Khan gloomily watched his son's indiscreet philandering—where was Queen Victoria's table now, he must have wondered, when he sat at the New Year's Eve party Aly has thrown in a Cannes nightclub, his arms raised to avoid being pelted in the latest "game" of throwing champagne-sodden green wads of cotton at other guests. Now Gene Tierney was the lady of the moment instead of Rita. The Aga Khan was increasingly dissatisfied with his philandering, un-Islamic son. There was, as always reported in the news, one champagne cocktail too many in the life of Aly.

The succession was in question.

With his wrecked reputation, womanizing, and gambling debts, Aly could never become the Aga Khan. Aly waited, hoping that his father would announce his succession; he expected an announcement at the grand spectacle that was held at the Aga Khan's jubilees. The aga was weighed against a precious metal and the accumulated metal was given to the aga's coffers—you could imagine how great that was on his gold jubilee! His platinum jubilee hit his seventy-seventh year, and it was at this ceremony that he was expected to name his successor. Ominously, the Aga Khan was silent. Heart attacks came and went, and still the aga did not name his successor, living out his final years in one of his homes in Aswan, Egypt.

Food-wise, things became depressingly dull for the old gourmand. He was placed on a diet of yogurt for weeks and, according to an article in *Paris Match*, one day the ancient, decrepit Aga Khan decided to break loose, have a taste of the old days in Paris. Evading his nurses, he shambled off and came across a delicious dinner set for six (apparently intended for those attending him). Slowly, bite by delicious bite, he made his way through portion after portion of plump little roast quail, rice pilaf, and—glory of glories—Poires Belle Hélenè. What a shame there was no ice cream.

Roast Quail

INGREDIENTS

6 quail
The juice of 1 lemon
2 tbsp. olive oil
1 clove of garlic, crushed
4 tsp. ground cumin

2 tsp. cinnamon
1 tbsp. honey
4 tbsp. butter
1 cup homemade chicken stock

METHOD

In a bowl, mix together the lemon juice, olive oil, garlic, cumin, cinnamon, and honey. Now add the quails and massage the marinade into them. Cover and leave to marinate in the fridge overnight.

The next day, preheat the oven to 180°C. Get a baking dish and line the quails up, breast side down. Slip a piece of butter into each quail. Pour the chicken stock around them and roast in the oven for 25 minutes or their juices run clear.

Rice Pilaf

INGREDIENTS

1½ cups basmati rice
1 tbsp. butter
Sea salt
2 tbsp. butter
A pinch of saffron threads

A 2 in. stick of cinnamon
3 cardamom pods, split
½ tsp. grated lemon zest
2 tbsp. chicken stock

METHOD

Rinse the rice in cold water. In a saucepan, melt a tablespoon of butter. Add the washed rice and stir through the butter for 3 minutes, toasting it. Pour boiling water into the pan and salt it. Bring the water back to a boil; stir it and cook for 7 minutes. Now drain the rice.

In a pan, melt the 2 tablespoons of butter. Add the saffron, cinnamon, cardamom, and lemon zest. Warm for a minute, then add 2 tablespoons of chicken stock and pour this spicy, buttered stock over the top of the rice. Using the end of a knife, push 6 holes into the surface of the rice. Place a square of muslin or cheesecloth over the pan. Place the lid on top and cook on a very gentle heat for half an hour.

Poires Belle Hélenè

INGREDIENTS

4 ripe pears
1 cup caster or granulated sugar
1 vanilla pod, split

2 lemons, zested and then juiced
3½ cups water

FOR THE CHANTILLY CREAM . . .

1 cup heavy cream
1 tbsp. powdered sugar

1 tsp. vanilla extract

FOR THE CHOCOLATE SAUCE . . .

1½ cups dark chocolate, broken
   into small pieces

¾ cup heavy cream
3 tbsp. brandy

TO SERVE . . .

Sliced, toasted almonds
Vanilla ice cream (we don't have to
   repeat the disappointments of
   the Aga Khan)

METHOD

Peel the outer skin carefully from the pears, leaving the stem intact and retaining the distinctive shape of the pears. Cut a small disk of pear from the base of each—this will allow your pears to stand upright. In a deep pan, combine the water and sugar, lemon juice, and lemon zest and, stirring constantly, bring to a boil, until the sugar has dissolved. Now add the pears and the vanilla pod to the lemony sugar water. To ensure the pears remain submerged, cut out a disk of greaseproof paper and place this over the surface of the pan—it will weigh just enough to stop the pears from bobbing up. Simmer for about 20–25 minutes, until cooked—a toothpick should run easily through each pear. Turn off the heat and allow the pears and syrup to cool.

Now make the Chantilly cream. Put the cream into a chilled glass bowl. Using an electric mixer, add the powdered sugar and vanilla extract; whisk for about 1 minute, until the cream, although soft, dimples and can retain soft shapes.

Heat water in a small saucepan and place a heatproof Pyrex bowl over it; the base of the bowl must not touch the boiling water. Now add the broken chocolate, brandy, and cream. Stir constantly until this has melded into a glossy dark chocolate sauce.

It is time to assemble the Poires Belle Hélenè. To make one: in the base of a glass bowl, place a dollop of vanilla ice cream. Top with a drained pear; allow a spoonful of dark chocolate sauce to tumble over the pear, sprinkle with toasted almonds, and put alongside a buttery dollop of Chantilly cream. Scatter an almond or two over the cream.

Aly was not to inherit his father's role as the aga khan; too much of a playboy, he was bypassed in favor of his own son, the Aga Khan's first grandson, Karim. Karim, the present Aga Khan, had the sort of oddly remote solitary schooling to which the children of the super-rich and royal are so often subjected. Karim was educated at Le Rosey in Switzerland, a super-posh school that hosted such luminaries as the shah of Iran; the last king of Egypt, Fuad; Dodi Al-Fayed (of Lady Di fame); King Juan Carlos (General Franco chose his school); the heir to Heinz; and the heir to Nestle and all things chocolate—all once lonely little boys at boarding school with combed hair and satchels. At dinner, Karim and his schoolmates were served by Swedish waitresses and wore pressed tailored suits and ties. Karim and his brother, Amyn, were visited occasionally by their grandfather; these peculiar visits were witnessed by other boys as the Aga Khan's vast, ship-like Rolls Royce swept up the graveled drive of Le Rosey. The window would be rolled down, and the pudgy hand of the Aga Khan would appear, clutching five Swiss franc pieces. In order to receive the francs, the boys had to fall to their knees onto the gravel before the car.

Chapter 2

THE DRAGON EMPEROR, COMRADE PU YI

The empress Tzu-hsi lay dying among her robes of longevity. She had taken her last supper of crab apples and clotted cream. Magnificent and terrible, she had held China in her grip for fifty years, and now it was time to name her heir. She had already discarded her venereal-ridden, ineffectual son and was a demonic, fierce woman; she flogged one of her servants so fiercely that he was left with a permanent facial tic. Now she knew who she would choose as her heir: her infant nephew Pu Yi.

When the imperial cavalry and a stuffy chamberlain arrived at his chambers, little Pu Yi decided his best bet was to hide in the cupboard. Already, all the adults around him were behaving oddly: someone had fainted, the eunuchs had been preparing vast amounts of ginger tea and calling for doctors, and Pu Yi had had enough. But cupboards offered no escape from his imperial destiny, and the chamberlain and eunuchs plucked him out. His adored nanny, Wan Chao, looked sorrowfully at him, and his mother bade him farewell—he was not to see her for another six years. Through snowy Peking, Pu Yi was led to the Forbidden City and the bedside of Tzu-hsi.

When he got to her bed chamber in the Forbidden City, the first thing he saw was her skinny, ghoulish face staring at him through drab curtains. As any three-year-old would, Pu Yi started to cry. "Give him sweets!" barked Tzu-hsi. Some-one handed him a string of candied haws, which he immediately dropped on the ground, roaring, "I want nanny. I want nanny."

Tzu-hsi, enraged and enfeebled, ordered, "What a naughty child. Take him away."

Not the most auspicious of beginnings.

Candied Haws

Haws are wild hawthorn berries.

INGREDIENTS

1 cup granulated sugar	½ lb. haws, freshly picked and cleaned
Scant ½ cup water	Bamboo skewers

METHOD

Skewer the haws onto the bamboo stick—about 10 per stick will be fine; make sure they are clustered near the top of the bamboo skewer. In a small saucepan, combine the sugar and water. Heat them over a medium-low heat for 5 minutes—do not stir. When 5 minutes have passed, increase the heat; the syrup should now boil, and you should continue to cook it until it takes on a light gold color and begins to bubble. Turn down the heat to low again and dip the haws in the syrup; a light layer should form. Keep redipping them to create a hard candy carapace.

Pu Yi wailed again in the Hall of Supreme Harmony during his "Ceremony of Enthronement" when he became emperor. The eunuchs whispered that this was a bad omen; was the Ching dynasty doomed? He was now a tiny, living god who fidgeted on his throne. Pu Yi only felt safe with his nanny, Wan Chao, and liked to suckle her breast in the cold rooms in the Palace of Heavenly Purity, doing so until he was seven years old. Wan Chao's life was a cruel one. After her husband died of tuberculosis, she needed to support her daughter and parents. The richness of her milk and warm, comely appearance made her the perfect wet nurse, but she was no longer allowed to see her daughter or return home. Daily, she had to eat a bowl of unsalted meat fat to enrich her milk. Unbeknownst to her, her little daughter died of malnutrition after she had been suckling Pu Yi for three years, but Wan Chao was not told in case her grief affected the quality of her milk. It was not until the high consorts expelled Wan Chao in her ninth year of service that she discovered her own child was dead. Such was the inhumanity of the imperial court.

Everything around the little emperor was colored an auspicious yellow; indeed, his childhood seemed to be yellow tinted, cast in a yellow mist, from the cushions to tiles to the girdle around his waist. The bowls that he drank from and the dishes on which his food was served were yellow, right down to the padded lid of the saucepan for making rice gruel. Yellow was the color of the imperial household, symbolizing the uniquely "heavenly nature" of the little emperor.

The thousand or so eunuchs at the court of Pu Yi performed a multitude of tasks: carrying the emperor about on his palanquin—one eunuch made a chirring sound to warn people to clear the way for the presence of the emperor—and there were even eunuchs of the Imperial Tea Bureau, who carted about delicacies and cakes in boxes. Some eunuchs were corrupt and involved in dark, internecine scams, pilfering treasures from the imperial palace. But they were untouchable: they would make formidable enemies. And they clustered around the diminutive Dragon Emperor. Pu Yi recalled in his memoirs the enormous fuss surrounding getting a bite to eat: extravagance, solemnity, ceremony, and ritual were the keys to Pu Yi's eating. First, it came with its own language, a set of terms used to refer to the emperor's eating. Food could not possibly be called *food*—it had to be referred to as *viands*. Reference to merely "eating" wasn't heavenly enough; the emperor had to be "consuming the viands." There was no serving of meals, only "transmitting the viands," and the kitchen was obliquely named the "imperial viands room." There were no set times for meals, they had to appear whenever the divine tummy rumbled. Pu Yi had to call out "Transmit the viands" at such times, a call echoed along a relay team of young eunuchs until the order reached the eunuchs standing in the hall. They then called out to the eunuchs in the "imperial viands room," which lay on the Western Avenue of the Forbidden City. While the cries were still echoing, an ant-like, pompous progression would march forth from the "viands room." Dozens of immaculately dressed eunuchs, in a column, carried seven tables and multitudes of red lacquered boxes, all painted with golden dragons, into the "Mind Nurture Palace." Their load would be handed to white-sleeved eunuchs who then set out the "viands" in the palace's designated room. All dreadful, of course, if you were just after a piece of toast. Set up in the eastern room would be tables with dishes and bowls of yellow for serving, with dragons again and the inscription "Ten thousand long lives without limit." On these tables were the *thirty* main dishes; in the winter, an extra table held warm chafing dishes, and the little emperor dined from silver dishes that were placed on top of hot water, held in porcelain bowls. The next tables were set with porridge, rice, and cakes, and the fourth table with salted vegetables. To hinder any sneaky poisoner, every dish was tasted by a eunuch (except it wasn't called tasting; it was "appraising the viands"). Perhaps, at last, there might be a chance of a bite to eat? Ironically, no. As Pu Yi recalled, "These dishes which were brought in with such ceremonial [*sic*] were only for show. The reason why the food could be served almost as soon as I gave word was that it had been prepared several hours or even a whole day in advance and was being kept warm over the kitchen stoves. The cooks knew that at least since the time of Kuang Hsu the emperor had not eaten this food."

The food the emperor did get to eat was sent over by his mother, the Empress Dowager Youlan, and, after his mother's death, by the high consorts (a petrifying clique of imperial concubines and wives). All of these ladies had their own kitchens with excellent cooks who made scrumptious food. The high consorts would then send a eunuch to solicitously inquire about how well the emperor had enjoyed his meal, again a matter purely of form. Irrespective of what the emperor had actually eaten, the eunuch, kneeling, gave the same report to the consorts: "Your slave reports to his masters: the Lord of Ten Thousand Years consumed one bowl of old rice viands (or white rice viands), one steamed breadroll (or a griddle cake) and a bowl of congee. He consumed it with relish." Strangely, though, the household accounts for his reign when he was four years old record that he managed in one month to consume 240 ducks. Either Pu Yi was an infant with a prestigious appetite or embezzlement was afoot.

This terrible, formal, and false concern led to the real neglect of the little emperor; he was often desperately hungry due to the vagaries of his mother and the high consorts. When, aged five, he ate too many chestnuts, his mother insisted that he have nothing but brown rice porridge for a month. Though he wept with hunger, no one paid any heed—eventually, sent with some old steamed bread rolls to feed the imperial fish, he crammed one into his mouth. Every time his mother imposed greater strictures on his diet, he became more determined to filch food. When he found some tribute food of cold pork had been left in the Western Avenue of the palace, Pu Yi grabbed it and sank his teeth into it while a horrified eunuch tried to wrest it from his small fist. Another eunuch noticed one day that Pu Yi had eaten six pancakes in rapid succession and worried he'd be unable to digest these. He and two other eunuchs picked up the emperor by his arms, lifted him, and repeatedly slammed him feet first into the floor, feeling very pleased with themselves at having saved him from the pancakes.

Chinese Pancakes

FOR THE RED BEAN PASTE . . .

1 cup adzuki beans, soaked overnight and cooked
⅓ cup palm sugar

¼ tsp. sea salt
½ tsp. vanilla essence
Finely grated zest of 1 orange

FOR THE BATTER . . .

2½ cups all-purpose flour
Pinch of sea salt
2 large eggs

½ tsp. vanilla essence
¾ cup cold water

FOR GARNISHING . . .

1 cup red bean paste (as prepared before)
Groundnut oil; about 5 cups for deep frying, plus about 5 tbsp. for skillet frying

1 tbsp. confectioner's sugar, for dusting pancakes
2 tbsp. sesame seeds, dry toasted in a skillet

METHOD

Begin by making the delicious red bean paste, which you will smear on the pancakes. Take the cup of cooked, drained, and soft adzuki beans. In either a mortar and pestle or a blender, puree the adzuki, mashing in the palm sugar and salt. Warm a skillet and dry cook the puree for a couple of minutes. Add the vanilla essence and zested orange. Mix thoroughly, and lay to the side.

Now make the pancake batter. Sieve the flour and salt into a large mixing bowl. Beat the 2 eggs with the vanilla essence. Make a well in the mound of flour, add the egg mixture, and, using a whisk, incorporate the egg. Add the water a little at a time until you have a smooth batter. Allow this to sit for about half an hour.

In a deep saucepan, heat the groundnut oil until it crackles and then falls silent. While this is heating, pour a tablespoon of groundnut oil into a skillet. Make sure it is hot, and then add enough batter to coat the pan. As this cooks, wipe a strip of red bean paste across its surface. Then fold the pancake over the paste on either side (creating a rectangle). Next, fold in the top and bottom. When the envelope folds appear, add a little more batter to seal it. Flip, and then fry until the pancake is light gold. Remove from the heat and pop into the saucepan of hot groundnut oil; it should rise to the surface with a fizz of bubbling oil around it. When it looks crisp and golden, remove from the heat, dust with confectioner's sugar, and sprinkle with sesame seeds. Repeat.

Being divine didn't last long: Pu Yi had to abdicate at the age of six on February 12, 1912, when China became a republic. Nevertheless, he still "enjoyed" the life of an emperor within the Forbidden City; in short, he remained a prisoner of his role. The dowager consorts determined the emperor had to choose a bride. Innocently, he had no idea that this would have any influence on his life, and he hadn't a clue about husbands and wives. He was given blurry pictures of girls' faces and had to ring whoever he thought looked all right. Diligently, he put a circle around one face in a small photograph; it wasn't an acceptable choice (the girl of his choice, Wenxiu, was twelve years old but did become his secondary wife), so he was urged to put a pencil circle around another face, that of his future empress and fellow captive, Wanrong.

All was not somber all the time; there were moments in the young emperor's life that held both hilarity and adventure. In 1918, Scottish gentleman Reginald Fleming Johnston was approached to tutor the fledgling emperor in order to prepare him for his role in a constitutional monarchy. Elements of Western education, it was thought, might be just the ticket. Pu Yi was less sure: he found foreigners unattractive and weirdly multicolored, with their pink, marked skin, ludicrous hair colors, and odd eye colors. The eunuchs had whispered to him that foreign people had very rigid legs and liked to carry around sticks with which to whack people. These, the eunuchs confided, were called "civilization sticks." On meeting Johnston, however, Pu Yi was delighted to note that his legs did bend and that a stick was nowhere to be seen. Even better, Johnston introduced him to Western sweets: iridescent pastilles, uniform in size, wrapped in silver and rattling inside a tin box. Johnston explained—possibly to quell his charge's appetite for them—that they were made by machines and the wizardry of chemical techniques. The emperor immediately experimented by feeding a colony of ants the sweets to "let them try the flavour of chemistry and machinery." Lessons also included visits to "Johnston's Lodge," Johnston's two-storied grand house in Peking, and there, chaperoned by her governess, Miss Isabel Ingram, also came the emperor's bride-to-be, Wanrong, in order to be gentrified in the ways of Western eating. Ironically, Johnston loved all things Chinese and liked to use chopsticks at his own table. British table etiquette, with all its knives and forks of "civilisation," was on the curriculum. Table settings were explored and explained, as were the complications of cutlery. Small talk and table deportment were revised, and the geography of afternoon tea traced, where it was soon stressed that this repast was intended to refresh the spirits rather than glut the appetite. Belching was poor taste rather than a compliment to the host, and one drank tea noiselessly, without any smacking of lips or sucking in of fluids. Pu Yi confessed, "I forgot much of Johnston's careful instruction and threw the caution with which I ate the first cake to the winds by the time I came to the second." Johnston, nevertheless, "became the major part of my soul." Aged sixteen, Pu Yi wanted nothing more than to shrug off his imperial title, adopt permanently Johnston's chosen name for him of Henry, escape his arranged marriage, and travel to Oxford University. He secretly stashed imperial treasures to fund his escape. It was not to be.

Pu Yi pored over Johnston's Western magazines and pictures. He ached for a peaked tweed cap like Edward, the Prince of Wales, so much so that on his wedding day to Wanrong, he quickly changed afterward from ceremonial dragon robes into a cherished Western outfit of Western trousers and a peaked cap. A foreign lady spotted Pu Yi's remarkable appearance and asked Johnston, "Who is that young man?" Johnston blushed feverishly and, enraged, demanded furiously, "What do you mean by it, Your Majesty? For the Emperor of China to wear a hunting cap! Good lord!"

The moment, though, when the consummation of the marriage was supposed to occur was, without a doubt, the most painful moment for the innocent couple. They had drunk deep of the nuptial cup, which are twin cups bound together, and each had eaten longevity noodles and the ceremonial sons-and-grandsons dumplings—these are dumplings stuffed with many smaller dumplings, believed to bring *male* children to the couple. Then they entered the bridal chamber in the Palace of Earthly Peace. Inside the red room was nothing other than a bed raised on a platform. Red-faced Wanrong sat on the edge of the bed, wilting. Everything seemed cloyingly red to Pu Yi, like a huge, melted candle. He didn't know whether to stand or to sit next to her. The room was stifling him, so he simply turned around and left for his rooms in the Mind Nurture Palace, leaving Wanrong alone and humiliated.

Once back in his chamber, he wondered to himself, "I have an empress and . . . I'm grown up, but how are things any different from before?"

Longevity Noodles

To have real luck with these, you have to try and get them to slither down your throat without biting down on then—an act that could also guarantee a shorter life as you choke on the noodles.

INGREDIENTS

2 cups fresh yi mein noodles
1 tsp. sesame oil
½ tbsp. fresh ginger, finely shredded
1 tbsp. Chinese rice wine
½ tsp. cornstarch

½ tbsp. soy sauce
1 tbsp. peanut oil
½ cup scallions, finely shredded
A generous pinch of red chili
   pepper flakes

METHOD

Bring a saucepan of water to a boil. Plunge the yi mein noodles into the boiling water for 3 minutes. Drain and rinse in very cold water. Drain again. Toss through with the sesame oil. In a bowl, combine the ginger, rice wine, cornstarch, soy sauce, and dried chili flakes. In a wok, heat the peanut oil, add the noodles, stir-fry quickly, and then add the ginger–rice wine sauce. Add the scallions and stir-fry for a minute.

In 1924, Pu Yi, having abdicated his imperial title, was banished from the Forbidden City; he became "Mr. Pu Yi," a free citizen of the republic. But he was far from free. Johnston mistakenly encouraged him to take refuge with the Japanese. Pu Yi trusted Johnston and did so, swapping one gilded prison for another: the Japanese were to use him as the puppet emperor of Manchuria for eleven long years. Poor, clever, and vulnerable Empress Wanrong smoked pipes of opium, ordered opium as an ointment to increase longevity, and became thrall to its addictive demands. She had a doomed affair with the chauffeur and gave birth to a daughter who, she was assured, would be adopted but whom, in truth, the Japanese slaughtered at birth. On the edge of a breakdown, Pu Yi drove his Buick round and round and round the Weihuang Palace and became very keen on lots of flogging (and beating with wooden paddles for infringements of some spurious rules he'd determined). Strangely, along with this new heartlessness, came a commitment to vegetarianism. He insisted all his retinue espouse vegetarianism and was inwardly troubled about the morality of eating eggs, so much so that he would bow before them and offer a prayer before eating them.

After the Japanese could no longer find a use for Pu Yi, he spent the next fifteen years in various states of captivity, being immersed, post-1949, in a Communist reeducation program. It was hard to get rid of bad old imperial habits; used to eunuchs waiting on him, he'd leave the toilet unflushed or the tap running after washing his hands. Any proper grasp of money evaded Comrade Pu Yi, and he couldn't tally up the cost of food he'd eaten to pay a bill in a public restaurant. One thing had been successful: he was utterly faithful to Chairman Mao's proclamation to "Serve the People." Waiting for a bus, he would insist on being the last to get on when it arrived; all other citizens were more worthy than he. Often he would be left behind, a slight, lone figure waiting for the next bus. Or in public restaurants, he would gently confess to the waitresses, "You should not be serving me, I should be serving you," and execute a humble bow.

DINING WITH QUEEN VICTORIA AND HER MANY MEN

Queen Victoria had a German accent, was boggle-eyed, and had a weak chin; her husband, Prince Albert, was shrill-voiced and loved coursing for hares (a sport that involves greyhounds chasing hares). Nevertheless, they remain iconic—slightly chipped, perhaps, like their statues and monuments in London, but still resolute and imperial. About the pair grew a vast, elephantine royal apparatus, with many tiers of power and influence, and their marriage lasted twenty-one years, until Albert's death in 1861. During this time, the couple were highly visible, as both great hosts and visitors. Michael De-la-Noy makes the point that Victoria and Albert were "immensely hospitable," putting up royals from across Europe such as Prince Napoleon, the queen of Holland, and even a shower of royal Prussians. When they visited the French royal family, Victoria and Albert ate very well at their hosts' expense. They not only enjoyed breakfasts of "soup and large strong sausage," according to Charlotte Canning, a lady of the bedchamber, but also had all the meals of a day in one go. Victoria was sociable, almost gregariously so, very unlike the reclusive, solemn little widow she was to become. She could roar with laughter. Once she mistook her fork for her fan and swept into the ballroom with it, which caused great hilarity. Entertaining, Victoria found, was much more difficult in widowhood. She never ceased, though, to have the most prodigious appetite and also brightened up considerably with staunch, and at times exotic, male companionship in the post-Albert years.

When not away on some grand adventure, Queen Victoria and her prince consort, Albert, liked nothing better than lunch tête à tête, companionably chewing on quiet slices of modestly apportioned boiled chicken or sirloin, complemented, perhaps, with a bowl of white soup. Breakfast was even plainer. Boiled eggs and toast, a stout little fillet of smoked haddock. Nothing outlandish. And always in the afternoon the familiar ritual of afternoon tea; since the early days, when their Highland servant, John Brown, or one of the other gillies (male outdoor servants) would crouch down in the purpling heather to boil the kettle on the moors of Scotland, cups of tea forever held the highest of places in Victoria's food tastes. Albert and Victoria's nine baby royals were fed unusual things early on in the nursery: some asses' milk, a dash or two of arrowroot, mutton cutlets, and, on a good day, chicken broth. Victoria was a firm believer in fresh air—hence her love of Scotland, as there is always plenty of gusty, cantankerous wind there.

In August 1848, Victoria and Albert set sail for Scotland on the *Royal George* yacht. The *Royal George* seems like a rather dangerous tub, but then so many of the things that Victorians did seem remarkably hazardous nowadays. In the galley of the yacht were coal stoves. Eeek! Some of the ship's inhabitants suffered seasickness, bobbing about on Britain's choppy waters and further nauseated by the odor of cooking pheasants that sweatily permeated the corridors of the *Royal George* for the whole trip, as Victoria and Albert supped on light pheasant consommé. When they hit the Scottish coastline, the couple were struck by how wild and beautiful it was compared to the tame English shoreline. Soon there were all sorts of cheery Scottish eccentricities popping up everywhere. Victoria and Albert were first greeted by a steamer of people all hopping about on deck and dancing a reel; the girls of Edinburgh had flame-red hair; the bagpipes were haunting and beautiful; you could even walk through Macbeth's Birnam Woods. And the queen, overdosing on the novels of Sir Walter Scott, watched the reserved quiet beauty of a woman, her skirts tucked up to her knees, washing potatoes in the river. Albert loved Perth—it was so like Basel! He also thought the Scots looked like Germans—a real compliment from homesick Albert.

Scottish food was novel, simple, and delicious. While they stayed near Edinburgh at Dalkeith House with the Duchess of Buccleuch, Queen Victoria recorded in her diary, "At breakfast I tasted the oatmeal porridge, which I think very good, and also some of the 'Finnan haddies [haddock].'" The queen had discovered oatmeal, one of the great commodities of Scotland. A future lay ahead of her of porridge, haggis, and even the drink Atholl Brose; she was not even averse to a little whiskey made near Balmoral for her by the small distillery of John Begg, and which, when she was not quaffing it in her Atholl Brose, she would have mixed with Apollinaris, soda, or Lithia water.

Finnan Haddie in Milk

INGREDIENTS

1 finnan haddock (this is a naturally smoked haddock, pale golden, and—crucially—only partially filleted, so it is still on the bone and has a backing of aluminum-silver skin: its taste is heavenly)

1 cup milk
2 tbsp. butter
Freshly ground black pepper
1 egg

METHOD

In a shallow frying pan, melt 1 tablespoon of butter until it bubbles. Place the finnan haddock, skin side down, in the butter, and watch it shrink slightly. Pour the milk into the pan, pepper, and raise the temperature until the milk bubbles and simmers. Now crack the egg into the milk, turn the temperature down to medium-low, cover the pan, and allow the egg to poach in the milk for 4 minutes (keep checking to make sure the egg yolk is still soft). After 4 minutes, dot the pan with fragments of the remaining tablespoon of butter and serve the finnan haddie on a warmed plate, the pool of buttered milk about it and milk-poached egg alongside.

Atholl Brose

Brose is the Scottish Doric word for a broth, be it savory or sweet.

INGREDIENTS

½ cup medium-cut oatmeal
1 cup water

2½ cups malt West Coast whiskey like Laphroaig or Lagavulin
2 tbsp. runny heather honey

METHOD

Put the oatmeal in a bowl, add the water, and leave for half an hour. Strain the oatmeal thoroughly; discard it and retain the cloudy liquid you have left. In a cocktail shaker or bottle, combine the oatmeal liquid with the whiskey and honey. Shake it up and enjoy. Watch yourself, though; Atholl Brose has been used to befuddle enemies in Scotland, so don't do anything rash, and look out for anyone shady in a kilt.

Generally, Victoria liked to adopt a cheeky come-hither approach to her male subjects and servants and their drinking. One morning on board the royal yacht, Victoria and Albert were plaiting straw for bonnets (a vivid image, yes?). They noticed a queer hubbub of restlessness among the sailors, and Victoria asked jokingly if mutiny was on the cards. Dramatically, the boat's commander, Lord Adolphus Fitz-Clarence, replied that all would be well if Victoria moved. "What harm am I doing?" she asked. To which he replied, "Well, ma'am, Your Majesty is unwittingly sitting in front of the door of the place where the grog is kept, and the men cannot get at their drink." Victoria found this great fun: "'I will move,' she stipulated, 'if I can try some of the grog.'" She tasted it and pronounced, "I fear I can only repeat the remark that I made once before. The grog would be much better if it were stronger."

Like some of their more adventurous or desperate royal predecessors, Victoria and Albert liked to travel incognito through the Scottish Highlands, boarding in small Scottish inns that varied from clean, tartan dignity to mutton-greasy bedspreads (they always smuggled in their own wine, though) with witless characters smiling at you through porridgey teeth. This could come fraught with the considerable risks faced by their normal citizens. Take the Inn of Dalwhinnie, for instance. Victoria and Albert arrived on a frozen, blasted night. In tow were Princess Alice and Prince Louis of Hesse, Lady Churchill, General Grey, two maids, and three gillies. But there was nothing to eat, only tea, and two very lean-looking Highland chickens, sunken beaked. Without any chance of so much as a potato along with the chickens or *even* pudding to follow, Victoria and Albert sat dripping in their damp things, unappreciative of the chickens' sacrifice. Things were even worse for the five royal servants, who had to dine in the "commercial rooms" downstairs on whatever bare wishbone was left of the two chickens after their removal from the royal table upstairs. Yes, Scotland taught the Windsors some harsh lessons (even Victoria's first impressions of Balmoral were unpromising, arriving at its gray exterior as she did on a wet and cheerless morning at 3 a.m.); yet Victoria loved it all the more. It was full of treats, like the bluff, rascalish company of her servant and gillie John Brown. John Brown led the queen's pony on Highland expeditions, and he was bright and well read enough to entertain Victoria while Albert hunted stags. Over the years, Victoria grew to dote on him; he was the best of servants.

Again, in September 1860, Albert and Victoria were journeying incognito (well, not exactly—they still remained aristocrats as "Lord and Lady Churchill and party") in Scotland. John Brown was with them, his kilt swishing about his strong, hairy Scottish knees. The couple tried to be inconspicuous and noted lots of things that were shabby and miserable. Finally, they eventually arrived in Grantown to discover the commoner's lot. John Brown and the head keeper, John Grant, were supposed to serve the royal couple their supper but appeared to be rather drunk. Someone with ringlets stepped in and served them mutton soup, which can be a deadly, greasy affair, and the queen politely confided in her journal, "I did not much relish [this]." Lamb and chicken in bridal-white sauce followed, plus some dishes Victoria did not identify, and that may be why she left them untasted. Her spirits lifted, though, when a "tarte of cranberries" materialized.

A Tarte of Cranberries

In her sixties, Victoria suffered from painful wind after eating a cranberry tart and cream; when she was told "Don't eat it again," she became most annoyed.

FOR THE PASTRY . . .

1 cup all-purpose flour	½ cup butter, cut into cubes
1⅓ cups powdered almonds	1–2 tbsp. cream

FOR THE TART CUSTARD FILLING . . .

1 egg, plus an extra yolk	The seeds and pulp from inside 1
3 tbsp. vanilla sugar	vanilla bean, plus the bean "shell"
2 tsp. cornstarch	1 scant cup full-fat milk
Pinch of sea salt	1 scant cup heavy cream
3 tsp. powdered gelatin	

FOR THE CRANBERRY GLAZE . . .

1¾ cups cranberries	½ cup granulated sugar
½ cup water	

A Tarte of Cranberries (*continued*)

TO DECORATE THE TART . . .
1 tbsp. milk

METHOD
Sieve the flour into a large, cold bowl; stir through the ground almonds. Now add the butter, rubbing it into the flour-almond mixture until a pastry forms. Work quickly, as you don't want your pastry to become warm. If it seems too dry, add a little of the cream. Form the paste into a ball; wrap this in plastic wrap and chill in the fridge for 3 hours.

In the meantime, set about making the custard and cranberry filling. Start with the custard. In a large bowl, whisk the egg, extra egg yolk, and sugar until the mixture become fluffy and pale yellow. Add the cornstarch and sea salt. Whisk well. Now add the gelatin. In a saucepan, heat the milk with the vanilla paste and pod. When it is hot, remove the vanilla pod and, still whisking, add the hot vanilla-infused milk in a slow trickle to the egg mixture. Return all of this to the saucepan and whisk over a moderate heat until the custard is thick. Never allow it to boil. Remove from the heat and keep whisking as it cools down. Once it is only warm, cool in the refrigerator.

Set the oven to 190°C. Butter an 8-to-10-inch tart dish. On a floured surface, roll out the pastry until it is a third of a centimeter thick, and, using the rolling pin to manipulate and lift the sheet of pastry, fit it over the tart dish. Trim the pastry. Cover the tart pastry with greaseproof paper and baking beans. Bake in the oven for 10 minutes or until the pastry has become opaque. Remove the greaseproof paper and baking beans. Return the pastry case to the oven for another 10 minutes to brown, and then let the case cool.

Make the cranberry sauce. Put the cranberries in a saucepan and add half a cup of water. Put the lid on firmly and heat for about 5 minutes; the cranberries should have started to pop. Now add the sugar and stir through until it dissolves. Allow to cool.

Whip the cream for the custard filling into soft, undulating peaks; fold this through the custard gently. Pour this thick custard into the pastry case. Pour the stewed cranberries on top. Serve in generous slices with cream.

Victoria and Albert began the grand Windsor tradition of picnicking in Scotland—Victoria loved eating outdoors. On top of Ben Macdhui—which is Britain's second-highest mountain and reportedly haunted by a loping, sinister shadow, the Big Grey Man of Ben Macdhui—in the thick swirling mist with a sharp wind leaning in from the side, Victoria couldn't have been happier, picnicking with Albert and her daughter Princess Alice. Her pony tethered to a tree stump, John Brown refreshed the queen with whiskey and water, his reasoning being that "pure water would be too chilling." When one polite soul asked Brown if he and the queen were going to take tea together on one of their drives, he replied wryly, "No, she don't much like tea, we tak out biscuits and sperrits." "Sperrits," or spirits, was a reference to whiskey, usquebaugh, the "water of life." John Brown always brewed Victoria's pot of tea: she found this very warming and invigorating and, on one outing in 1851, her admiration for Brown's brew led her to exclaim, "[This is the] best cup of tea I ever tasted." "Well, it should be, Ma'am," explained Brown. "I put a grand nip o' whisky in it." Whiskey went hand in hand with the queen's regard for Brown. She started to experiment with it. When, in October 1864, William Gladstone, destined to be prime minister in four years' time, ate with the queen at Fasque House in Scotland, he not only found Brown very agreeable but also wrote to his wife that he was shocked to witness Victoria's drinking style: "She drinks her claret strengthened, I should have thought spoiled, with whisky." It is not surprising that Gladstone didn't join Victoria, as he could get very nervous around her; once Gladstone was so nervous about being late for dinner with Victoria that he tore his trousers. There is even a hint of pre-Christian Celtic paganism (though Victoria would never have realized it as such) in her willingness to taste the communal whiskey handed around on Halloween after the completion of a cairn or at a christening.

The Scots had decided Victoria had a "lucky foot," and this must have saved her from many of the Scottish oddities to pass her lips: hotchpotch soup, which she found not to her taste (one can only imagine what was floating about in there); fowl with white sauce; and roast lamb and potatoes. On one bitterly cold October morning on the moors above Balmoral, she helped to boil up broth and potatoes, while another time she was surprised by the deep-gravy deliciousness of a hot venison pie the Duchess of Atholl had given her for a picnic in the woods beside Loch Ordie. Coincidentally, it was also the Duchess of Atholl who, when Victoria was a widow, introduced her to the consolations of good haggis, which Victoria found of great comfort to a broken heart.

Hot Venison Pie

INGREDIENTS

2 lb. venison, diced roughly into chunks
6 juniper berries, crushed
2 bay leaves
1 small bunch of thyme
½ bottle of red wine
2 onions, sliced
3 carrots, thickly sliced

1 tbsp. all-purpose flour
Sea salt
Freshly ground black pepper
2 tbsp. butter
1 tbsp. olive oil
2 tbsp. whiskey
1 tbsp. blackberry jelly

FOR THE ROUGH PUFF PASTRY . . .

2½ cups all-purpose flour
1 tsp. sea salt

1 cup butter, very cold
6½ tbsp. ice-cold water

Hot Venison Pie (*continued*)

FOR ASSEMBLY OF THE PIE . . .

1 beaten egg	2 shallots, minced

METHOD

Place the venison in a deep casserole dish and pour the wine over it. Add the juniper berries, sliced onions, carrots, bay leaves, and thyme sprigs. Stir the whole together and cover. Leave in the fridge for 24 hours.

The next day, remove the venison chunks from the casserole dish, reserving the marinade. Preheat the oven to 180°C. On a plate, combine the all-purpose flour, sea salt, and black pepper. Heat 2 tablespoons of butter in a skillet and add 1 tablespoon of olive oil to prevent the butter from browning. Dip the chunks of venison in the seasoned flour and then brown them—probably in 2 or 3 batches—in the skillet. As you remove the browned chunks, drain them on a paper towel.

Now deglaze the pan: over a medium-high heat, pour the whiskey into the skillet and, stirring vigorously, scrape the caramelized venison juices from the base of the skillet. Pour in the wine and vegetable marinade and turn the heat right up. Bring it to a boiling point. Return the venison to the original casserole dish and pour the marinade on top of it. Now cover and place in the oven for 1½ hours.

In the meantime, prepare the rough puff pastry. Sieve the flour and sea salt into a large mixing bowl. Chop the butter into little chunks; add these and loosely rub into the flour (you want to be left with rich little gobbets and freckles of butter lodged in the pastry). Now add about a scant half of the water, mixing by hand until you have a dough, adding a little extra flour or water if necessary.

Flour the board you intend to work the pastry on. Gently shape the pastry into a rectangle. Begin to roll, working in one direction until it is three times wider. Don't lose the clear straight lines of the rectangle. Take bottom third of the pastry and fold it up to the center. Then take the top third and fold it down over that. Turn the dough by a quarter; repeat as before, rolling out in one direction until the rectangle is three times wider. Once you have completed the folding this second time around, cover with plastic wrap again and let it rest and cool in the fridge for 20 minutes before rolling to form the pie crust.

Once the venison casserole is ready, add the tablespoon of blackberry jelly, stirring it through. Allow the casserole to cool.

Preheat the oven to 200°C. Now you can begin to assemble your pie. In a large pie dish, pour the venison casserole. Put a clay pipe funnel or an upturned china or wooden egg cup in the center of the casserole. Sprinkle with the raw, minced shallot. Roll out the pastry lid and cover the pie dish with this crust. Brush with a beaten egg.

Bake in the oven for 30–40 minutes.

Although they were married for two decades, it was in her forty or so years of widowhood that Victoria became the British monarch familiar to us all. The "Widow of Windsor" dressed in black satin and wore a white tulle cap and shiny little black boots with elasticated sides; her children were always trying to get her to smarten up. Hence the story of a newly appointed equerry who came across Queen Victoria, a simple, dumpy, silver-haired old lady tucked into a mushroom hat and black gown, and barked at her, "My good woman, you must get out of this! Strangers are not allowed here, especially when Her Majesty is in residence." Victoria wore a bracelet containing the portrait and hair of Prince Albert (the Victorians were much keener than us on hanging onto dead people's hair and doing arts and crafts with it). She was naturally frugal, a hoarder and creature of habit; Victoria only ever used wax candles to light her rooms but conceded to modern electricity in public rooms. She liked to check excess in the royal household and shirkers were not tolerated, as seen in the expulsion of a chimney sweep—"the boy Jones," as he was known—a lazy, lackluster youth who was found several times idling and hiding from his work in the queen's own apartments. Victoria was childishly fond of making tea (having been enchanted by a silver nursery tea set she played with as a child), but she didn't like bishops, coal fires, telephones, or anyone with a booming voice. When the inventor Alexander Graham Bell proudly demonstrated the use of the phone to Victoria in 1878, she simply held it to her ear and said the sound emitted was "rather faint." She also had no dealings with cats and strangers; she wanted no cat within her sight. Dogs and horses, in contrast, were adored, especially Skye terriers and retired turnspits (this remarkable and now sadly extinct breed of dog was also called the kitchen dog, cooking dog, or underdog, as it was used to turn the spit as meat cooked). She was very fond, too, of collies, especially one named Sharp, who had all his meals with her and slept by John Brown's door—more peculiar pets included two Scottish eagles and a pet fawn called Victoria, whom the queen saved from death by starvation in a gravel pit.

Various statesmen and ladies-in-waiting complained about Queen Vic's dinner parties being indescribably glum post-Albert. Nobody had anything to say to each other over the barley broth; some people were deaf and others were dull. Chaps like Lord Kitchener refused even to speak to the ladies, and a heavy listlessness drifted over the diners. Occasionally, excitement would flare, as when the queen and Princess Beatrice hotly debated where they'd rather be sent were they condemned to exile: Beatrice was all for the equator, while Queen Vic stuck by the North Pole. Why the North Pole, you may ask? Because there's plenty of fresh air there, of course! The cold is wholesome. Victoria liked to set a brisk eating pace by flinging the windows open at state banquets. You'd be shivering over your soup. Queen Vic gobbled her food so quickly that slow eaters had to choke down as many mouthfuls as possible before their plates were whisked away. Freida Arnold, who was in service to Queen Victoria as her dresser from 1854 onward (part of her duty was to prepare and dress the dead queen for burial, which she did eventually), recalled Buckingham Palace when she first arrived there in the winter months. It was an icy, magnificent mausoleum, surrounded by heavy, sooty London smoke for the most part; the pollution was so dense that the sun resembled a dark red ball in winter. When snow fell, it turned black. While the poor starved and froze to death outside, the rich within Buckingham Palace stood close to their fires, burning on one side, freezing on the other. When the sky cleared enough after several days, Freida saw the stars for the first time in London and thought, wistfully, "You poor people, you have not even the stars." On a lighter note, she also spotted that "the English never forget to eat."

How right she was. Victoria had a Swiss chef, but traditionally the royals favored French chefs; British chefs had a fierce sense of their own inferiority, with one observer noting that many trainee chefs would try to cultivate fancy moustaches to pretend they were French. The servants often relished the delicious leftovers from royal meals; a five-course breakfast meant there were always hard-boiled eggs left over, the servants slipping the warm eggs into their pockets. Unfortunately, the service of royal appetites also has a downside: you have to eat what the boss eats. At one point, the endless consumption of chicken at Windsor Castle left some of the kitchen staff unable to bear so much as another mouthful. Then, due to royal hunting, game came in all shapes and sizes. In an obliquely grisly observation, the chef Gabriel Tschumi recounted that "Prince Francis Joseph of Battenberg was particularly poor as a shot, and the cooks came to recognize only too clearly the birds which had eventually been brought down by his gun." Queen Victoria, who loved marrow toast, wanted it for dinner every day—her favorite recipe was that of Charles Elme Francatelli, who cooked for her and Albert in the early 1840s, and as she grew older she considered it a great aid to digestion and salve to tummy upsets. Francatelli uses "ox piths" in his recipe, which is the cow's spinal cord. Thus, he calls marrow toast "Croustades or Patties of Ox Piths." Here he is:

> In this case, the ox piths must be prepared according to the first part of the directions for dressing them a la ravigotte. They must then be cut into half inch lengths, and placed in a small stewpan, with about half their quantity of prepared mushrooms, and two artichoke bottoms, previously cut into small dice; to this may be added some finished Espagnole sauce, a little cayenne and lemon juice, warm the whole together on the stove fire, and garnish the croustades with it.

In order to dress the ox piths "a la ravigotte," he suggests the following:

> Procure about 1 lb ox piths, steep them in water for a couple of hours, wash them thoroughly and then carefully remove the membranous covering, and change the water.

Next slice up an onion and a small carrot very thin, and put these into a stewpan with a quart of water, mignonette pepper and a blade of mace, and half a gill of vinegar. Set these to boil on the fire. Drop in the ox piths and allow them to boil gently for ten minutes; then set them aside to cool.

The Espagnole sauce, he adds, is made as follows:

Let the stock Espagnole be turned out into a large stewpan, adding there to some essence of mushrooms, and sufficient *blond* of veal to enable the sauce to clarify itself. Stir it over a fire till it boils, and then set it down by the side to continue boiling gently. When the sauce has thoroughly cleared itself, by gentle ebullition, and assumes a bright velvety smoothness, reduce it over a brisk fire to the desired consistency, and then pass it through a tammy for use.

The stock he mentions is based on chickens, wild rabbit, and veal udders.

Francatelli also mentions Victoria's pleasure if offered a sorbet before the roast meat course to "cool the stomach" and assist digestion (in case the ox piths didn't do the trick) at long ten- or twelve-course royal dinners; the favorite of both Victoria and her son Edward, the Prince of Wales, was rum sorbet. Again, obligingly, Francatelli has left us his recipe.

Francatelli's Rum Sorbet

INGREDIENTS

1 lb. 6 oz. sugar	8 whipped egg whites
2 quarts water	Flavoring
Juice of 2 lemons	A little rum kirsch
Juice of 1 orange	

METHOD

"Boil sugar and water to a syrup. When cool, whip in the egg whites, fruit juice and flavoring. Freeze."

Victoria's favorite means of conveyance around the grounds of her various palaces (remember, she often liked to eat breakfast outdoors) and in the Scottish Highlands were all four-footed and relatively small: as a small child, Victoria drove a tiny pony carriage over the expensive cobbles of London's Kensington; in Scotland, she trotted about on ponies called Fyvie and Lochnagar and had a donkey called Jacko, whom she spotted looking very wretched in Nice and shipped back— though he went with her between Britain and France, decorated in bells and brass leather, which Victoria had made for him on the Riviera.

There was always a flurry of packing when Queen Victoria and her entourage decamped from one royal house to another. Victoria's lady companions had to be well prepared for treks to Balmoral from London. Frieda Arnold described trying real Scottish bread at Windsor, which she said "tasted like sawdust and chopped up straw." Marie Mallet laughingly wrote to her stepsister of the train journey from Balmoral to Windsor: "My dear, I can't tell you how much food we were provided with. . . . A baker's shop would have been adequately stocked with the biscuits and cakes that went with them; bottles of champagne and claret clinked against each other; there was tea ready to wash down the cakes with and hampers bulged with every kind of cold meat. . . . But this was evidently not deemed sufficient to support life, so we had a hearty tea at Aberdeen, where royal footmen rushed about wildly with tea kettles gazed at by a large crowd, and a huge dinner at Perth, with six courses . . . and at 11.30 p.m. on our arrival at Carlisle we partook of tea and juicy muffins." Well, well . . .

Malcontents compared life at Balmoral to a second-rate private school. Not for Victoria though; she found Windsor Castle prison-like in comparison to Balmoral and wished snow would stop her leaving Balmoral in 1858. Stuffed birds and stags' antlers decorated the corridors of the "lonely and quiet" castle. Victoria loved to venture out on expeditions into the hills. Wrapped in furs and coats with only their noses peeping out, she and her ladies set off in a carriage, or more often by pony, to pick their way through the ravines and gray crags that circled the dark bloom of the black lake, Loch Muick. Brown was very direct; when one of Victoria's ladies-in-waiting slipped as she descended from a crag, Brown picked her up and said, "Your Ladyship is not as heavy as Her Maa-dj-esty." "Am I grown heavier, do you think?" piped up the queen. "Well, I think you are," replied Brown candidly. As far as Victoria was concerned, her Highlanders could do no wrong. She ignored drunkenness, claiming they were confused or bashful. She had always adored the gillies' (servants) ball at Balmoral. At this entertainment, royals would mix with Highlanders; there were reels and hoots of joy, whiskey galore. Serving the queen dinner afterward was comic—the crash of crockery would be heard distantly and wine spilled by less than steady a judgment of the distance between bottle and crystal glass.

John Brown was as plain speaking as the Scottish weather: after one picnic lunch at the small (ten room!) house Victoria built on the grounds of Balmoral, Victoria wanted to draw and asked for a table to be brought out to her. One table after another was carted out and pronounced unsuitable until eventually Brown sighed, picked up one of the discarded tables, and plonked it at Victoria's feet. "It's na possible to mak' anither table for you up here," he said firmly. He sensibly put her right at times, even chastising her, as when one butter-fingered young footman let some silverware crash to the floor, alarming the queen. She had him demoted to kitchen duty until Brown said, "What are ye daein' tae that puir laddie? Hiv' ye never drappit onything yersel?" The boy got his job back the next day.

Empress Eugénie of France turned to Victoria and the Scottish Highlands in 1879. Her only child, Louis Napoleon, was killed by Zulus when he was serving in South Africa during the outbreak of the Anglo-Zulu War. Louis was only really there as an observer, and his death in a skirmish shook the European monarchies. Eugénie was destroyed by the death of her child. The two queens took refuge in the "Queen's Sheil" at the base of the mighty mountain Lochnagar; a *sheil* is a small hut or cottage, and Victoria's had two little rooms and a kitchen. While they walked and talked, the dogs at their heels, John Brown fished in the stream. They returned to the sheil through what Victoria describes as "a glorious evening—the hills pink, and the sky so clear" to be welcomed by a cup of tea and a dinner of fresh trout, which Brown had caught, rolled in oatmeal and fried. Whatever the condition of her heart, Empress Eugénie said she would very much like trout for dinner.

Trout in Oatmeal

INGREDIENTS

4 trout fillets   Sea salt
2 eggs, beaten   Freshly ground black pepper
4 tbsp. medium-cut oatmeal   3 tbsp. butter for frying

METHOD
Put the beaten egg on a plate and the oatmeal on another. Salt and pepper the oatmeal. Dip the trout fillets first in the egg and then in the oatmeal. Heat the butter in a wide skillet until it is bubbling. Add the trout fillets skin side up; they should immediately shrink in the heat. Cook for 2 minutes on each side; the skin side should be last in order to become crispy. Serve with a little lemon juice or a dash of vinegar.

John Brown was Victoria's honest, faithful servant; he buttoned her coat, adjusted her shawl, and was very paternal toward her, which was of great comfort to Victoria. He always packed every single one of her favorite things to eat in a hamper when they went on Highland expeditions and became the palace's expert at hunting down her favorite nut pralines, covered in a sweet carapace of brown sugar. Victoria wrote to her uncle Leopold, the king of the Belgians, "It is a real comfort for [Brown] is devoted to me—so simple, so intelligent, so unlike an ordinary servant." His gifts meant a great deal to her: he gave her a terrible set of eggcups, which she adored and used every Sunday at breakfast. But all was not well: the relationship between queen and servant was regarded very sourly by some of Victoria's children. The king-to-be, Edward, hated Brown with a slow-boiling, bitter rage. Princess Louise didn't like him, either, referring to him as "an absurd man in a kilt." He had risen from stable hand to be Victoria's personal attendant, and gossip fomented about the intense domesticity of their relationship; "Mrs. Brown" was a ribald synonym for the queen.

When John Brown died unexpectedly in 1883, Victoria found it unbearable, comparing his loss to that of Albert. To her daughter Vicky, she confided, "The shock—the blow, the blank, the constant missing at every turn of the one strong, powerful reliable arm and head stunned me and I am truly overwhelmed." When Victoria was laid to rest herself in 1901, nearly twenty years later, she had a photograph of Brown placed in her hand, carefully concealed from the eyes of her family beneath some flowers (and a lock of his hair tucked in somewhere). She even wore the ring he gave her.

June 1887 saw the queen's golden jubilee, which spanned several days. Amid the celebrants were some Indian princes—the Hindu royals visiting Victoria in London practiced eating meat in advance so as not to cause offense. Maharani Sunity Devee, an Indian princess, was seated next to Edward, the Prince of Wales, and recalled, "I saw a saucer which contained green chillies in front of him. 'Do you like chillies, sir?' I could not resist asking. And the Prince told me he liked nothing better than Indian dishes, a taste acquired, I feel sure, when he paid his memorable visit to our country." On the third day, Victoria, the empress of India, received a gift from India: two male servants who elected to stay with Queen Victoria, Abdul Karim and Mahomet Buksh. They were be-turbaned, with magnificent whiskers, and dressed in dramatic Oriental attire. The queen, ever in thrall to curiosity, was enchanted by them, particularly Abdul Karim, or, as he came to be known, the munshi. Abdul and Mahomet attended to Victoria, in magnificent gold-and-scarlet Indian livery, through the five courses of breakfast, gracefully placing her steaming-hot porridge or boiled egg (in a gold egg cup with a gold spoon) before her and then standing back, ever ready, behind her chair. These two Indian servants were referred to as her "Kitmutgars," waiting with her wheelchair.

The queen had never been to India and so wished to learn as much as she could about it. She began to learn Hindustani, and Abdul was her tutor, setting vocabulary tests for the queen. They had daily lessons, and the comic and amusing phrases Victoria learned appealed to her rather wicked sense of humor—for instance, "The tea is always bad at Osborne," a phrase that could be repeated in Hindustani while the tea-maker poured the tea in blissful ignorance at Osborne House on the Isle of Wight. Victoria and her servant were creating a private language for themselves, replete with private jokes. But Abdul decided there could be no better way of teaching his empress about her empire than through its food. With that intention, he prepared a surprise meal for her in the kitchens of Osborne House. When Abdul had been readying himself for Victoria's service, he had asked his wife to teach him how to cook prized North Indian family recipes from Agra. These were creamy, rich, and bold. Abdul's biographer, Shrabani Basu, writes:

> To the amazement of the cooks in the Royal kitchen, Karim was soon chopping, churning and grinding the masalas. The aroma of cloves, cinnamon, cardamom, cumin and nutmeg wafted through the room. Before long, Karim had prepared a fine Indian meal: chicken curry, daal and a fragrant pilau. More was to follow. Karim was soon stirring up exotic birianis and dum pukht, dishes from the Mughal kitchens, kormas simmered in the cast iron pots and ground almonds and cream laced the rich curries. For the first time in her life, Queen Victoria was introduced to the taste and smell of India. She described it as "excellent" and ordered the curies to be served regularly.

Again the queen was following the same pattern as with Brown; she showed her preference for her servant through embracing his habits of food and drink.

Chicken Curry

You will need a good spice grinder (or coffee grinder) for this.

INGREDIENTS
4 chicken supremes on the bone, skinned and chopped into thirds

FOR THE MARINADE . . .
Juice of 1 lime   1 tsp. chili powder

FOR THE SECOND MARINADE . . .
1 in. stick of cinnamon, split in   Generous pinch of sea salt
   2 lengthwise   4 pods of cardamom, cracked open
8 whole almonds   with seeds removed (discard
6 peppercorns   the shells)
2 tsp. cilantro seeds   ¼ tsp. grated nutmeg
¼ tsp. cloves   ½ cup plain yogurt (you can substitute
1 tsp. cumin seeds   this with coconut milk if you want
2 bay leaves   a sweeter curry)

FOR THE CURRY . . .
2 tbsp. butter   1 fresh chili, crushed
3 onions, finely chopped   6 ripe tomatoes, skinned and chopped
4 cloves of garlic, crushed   ½ cup heavy cream
1 in. ginger root, crushed   2 tbsp. finely chopped cilantro

Chicken Curry (*continued*)

METHOD

Put the skinned chicken pieces in a bowl with the lime juice, chili, and salt. Mix thoroughly and leave to marinate for 1 hour. Heat a dry skillet. When it is nice and hot, toast the cinnamon, almonds, peppercorns, cilantro seeds, cloves, cumin seeds, and bay leaves. Stir them frequently as they brown; they must not burn. This should take about 3 minutes; I tend to put the larger ingredients in first, allowing them the first minute and a half, followed by the cumin seeds and bay leaves. Next remove the spices from the skillet and pour them into a grinder, along with the sea salt, cardamom seeds, and nutmeg. Grind all together into a fine powder. Now add this to the chicken marinade, followed by the yogurt. Stir thoroughly and marinate the chicken overnight.

The next day, heat the butter in a large frying pan. Add the onions and cook very gently until they are a deep gold color. Spoon the dollops of garlic, ginger, and chili into the pan and sauté gently. Now add the chicken pieces and the marinade; allow the chicken to whiten. Now add the tomatoes. Stir thoroughly. Turn the heat down to medium-low and let the curry cook for about 40 minutes; let the sauce reduce by about a third. Finally, add the cream and cilantro just before serving.

Pilau Rice

INGREDIENTS

2 cups basmati rice
1 tbsp. ghee
4 cardamom pods
6 cloves

2 sticks of cinnamon
Pinch of saffron strands
Generous pinch of sea salt
4 cups boiling water

METHOD

Wash the rice in water three times, draining the water off each time. In a deep saucepan, melt the ghee. Add the washed rice and stir to coat each grain with oil. Now add the cardamom, cloves, cinnamon, saffron, and sea salt. Combine them thoroughly with the rice. Pour the boiling water over the rice. Seal the pot with a tight-fitting lid and cook over a low heat for about 12 minutes, until the rice has puffed and absorbed the water.

Naan

INGREDIENTS

2 cups all-purpose flour

1 tsp. sea salt

1 tsp. dried, activated yeast

1 tsp. sugar

1 tbsp. warm water

½–1 cup plain, natural yogurt

A little flour for rolling and dusting
the skillet

A couple of tablespoons of soft butter

METHOD

In a small bowl, combine the yeast and sugar with the warm water. Put this is a warm place to allow it to froth and bubble. Sieve the flour and salt into a large mixing bowl. Form a well in the center of the flour and incorporate the yeast mixture. Using your hands, combine the yeast and flour. Start adding the yogurt, a tablespoonful at a time, kneading it into the dough. You need to add enough yogurt to create elastic, pliable dough. Knead for at least 10 minutes. After this, divide the naan dough into four and, using a lightly floured surface and your hands, stretch these sections of dough out into elongated paddle shapes.

You now need to cook the naan breads; ideally, you would bake them in a tandoor oven—but I very much doubt that even Queen Victoria had one of these active and ready to use. I use an outside charcoal grill to cook naan bread, laying the bread on the hot griddle and turning after each side is baked, bubbling, and slightly blasted. If neither a tandoor nor an outside grill are handy, heat up your broiler. Then place a large, dry, lightly floured skillet on the stove. Heat the skillet and slap the first naan bread into it; give it 30 seconds and then, bread still in skillet, place the skillet under the hot broiler. The bread should rise and blister. Serve straightaway with a generous dollop of butter slipping about on the surface of the naan.

Victoria was hooked; she asked for curry daily—but only at lunchtime. French or British food was served in the evenings. Abdul and Mahomet dry-roasted spices in a pan, then ground them, dismissing ready-made curry powder. The chef, Gabriel Tschumi, watched in fascination:

For religious reasons, they could not use the meat which came to the kitchens in the ordinary way, so they killed their own sheep and poultry for the curries. Nor would they use any curry powder in stock in the kitchen, though it was of the best imported kind, so part of the Household had to be given to them for their special use and there they worked Indian style, grinding their own curry powder between two large stones and preparing all their own flavourings and spices.

Daal

FOR THE GARAM MASALA . . .

1 tbsp. green cardamom seeds (removed from the main husk of the cardamom)
1 tbsp. black cardamom seeds (removed from the main husk of the cardamom)

1 tbsp. black peppercorns
1 tbsp. freshly ground nutmeg
1 tbsp. whole cloves
3 sticks of cinnamon
3 bay leaves

FOR THE DAAL

1 cup red lentils
2 cups water
1 tsp. sea salt
1 stick of cinnamon
2 tbsp. ghee or butter
1 onion, finely chopped
3 cloves of garlic, chopped

1 in. fresh ginger, chopped
1 fresh red or green chili, finely chopped
1 tsp. garam masala (as prepared above)
1 tsp. turmeric
Sea salt

METHOD

Begin by making the garam masala. Put all of the spices in a grinder and whiz into a fragrant powder. Keep in a dry, sealed spice pot until you wish to use the garam masala.

Put the lentils in a saucepan with 2 cups of water, the salt, and the cinnamon. Bring to a boil and cook for 15 minutes; the lentils will absorb the water and become fluffy rather than disk-like. After this, drain the lentils. Heat the ghee up in a skillet. Add the onion and sauté until it is golden. Now add the garlic, ginger, and chili. Cook these, stirring, for 2 minutes. Pour the drained lentil mush into the frying pan. Add the garam masala, turmeric, and salt. Cook for another few minutes, and then serve.

Osborne House was lovely and balmy; some of its fireplaces were lined with mirrors, right into the hearth. There were also deep, richly colored carpets, and the sea wind had rounded off the trees beyond the house, stunting them. Queen Victoria had an iridescent, exotic Durbar room fashioned there, which she opened for banquets—often serving Indian food—and filled with Indian objects. What better way, she devised, to greet the young Aga Khan when he arrived to dine with her in 1897 than for Abdul, her tutor in Hindustani, to be part of her welcome to the Aga Khan? The Aga Khan's recollections of the occasion are telling enough; he makes no mention of Abdul in person:

I remember that three things struck me about Queen Victoria that night; one was how, despite her age, her mind worked clearly and she saw and heard everything. The second was her apparent dependence on the Indian servants who waited at table, though I didn't think myself that they were quite tip-top class—I had seen better at the Viceroy's house in India. And the third thing was her enormous appetite. In those days, you know, dinners were very long, with three or four main meat courses and two or three sweets—and the Queen ate everything that came along.

The Aga Khan was surprised to find that the elderly Queen Victoria spoke with a German accent, but he was dazzled by her. Of her Abdul and Mahomet, he continued, "They were distinctly second-class servants, of the kind you find around hotels and restaurants, the kind that the newly-arrived or transient European is apt to acquire in the first hotel in which he stays—very different from and very inferior to the admirable, trustworthy, and very high-grade men whom, throughout the years of British rule in India, you would encounter at a Viceregal Lodge or at Government House in any of the provinces."

The Aga Khan's perspective on Abdul and Mahomet is an interesting one; he understood far more than a European monarch what the ideal Indian servant should be like, and he found Abdul wanting. Furthermore, the Aga Khan would never dream of befriending his servants in this way. Again, the mistress-servant distance was broached, but now Victoria was older, more vulnerable, and Abdul was young and ambitious. Abdul was elevated to the position of Munshi Hafiz Abdul Karim by Victoria and had new secretarial duties (he had been a clerk in India) and was no longer to wait on her table. She was solicitous and maternal toward him, her pendulous face hovering over his sickbed; as the royal physician noted in March 1890, when Abdul was suffering from a painful carbuncle, "Queen visiting Abdul twice daily, in his room taking Hindustani lessons, signing her boxes, examining his neck, smoothing his pillows etc." None of this was liked by Victoria's court. Abdul was set above other servants and, unlike John Brown, became rather bigheaded about the sway he held over Victoria. Abdul complained if he found anything didn't suit him, if he were not honored enough. All photographs of himself serving the queen food were destroyed; he was her Indian secretary now. Not only did he get a cottage at Balmoral, but the queen also generously gifted him land in Agra. She fussed over Abdul and Mahomet's comfort on a trip to Balmoral in Scotland; did they have enough underclothes? She asked for tweed to be measured out to suit their Indian-style costumes.

And then the racism of Victoria's white entourage was at high dudgeon. Abdul dined with the white servants. This was beyond the pale—but, ironically, Abdul also considered himself too grand for them; he didn't want to associate with them. To top it, Victoria issued her British servants with Hindustani phrasebooks, misguidedly imagining that her narrow-minded staff would wish to exchange pleasantries with Abdul. He helped her work through her boxes of official correspondence with too great a degree of familiarity with both her signature and the box's contents. The stories he told her did not bear full scrutiny. Many about the queen believed the munshi was an impostor of the lowest class; he might even be a spy for Afghanistan, rifling through the queen's private papers. Abdul claimed his father was an Indian doctor, but on closer inquiry it was revealed that his father worked in a jail. Yes, he was a dispenser of medicines, but was that the same as a doctor, with all the nuances of respectability such a role carries? When Abdul's father came to visit, he shocked the staff at Windsor Castle by puffing away on a hookah. Ever faithful to the munshi and his father's reputation, Queen Victoria managed to sneak it into dinner conversation with the Aga Khan, asking him whether medical men were well thought of in his country. Lord Salisbury quickly changed the subject of conversation. At a later point, the queen (using the third person to refer to herself) wrote to Lord Salisbury, "To make out that the poor Munshi is so *low* is really *outrageous* and in a country like England quite out of place. . . . She has known 2 Archbishops . . . sons respectively of a Butcher & a Grocer." It was suspected that Abdul stole from her; he was accused of being complicit with "Muslim Patriotic League affairs" and considered venal and manipulative. Trouble brewed, but our staunch and loyal little queen would listen to no detractors, sweeping the contents off a desk in rage (including an airborne inkwell) when Abdul was slandered. Finally, she and her doctor, James Reid, met and had an "interesting talk" about Abdul having gonorrhea. Victoria did not send him away, but Abdul withdrew into the background at court.

Age and indigestion did nothing to tame Victoria's appetite. Her sweet tooth became even more demanding; fondant biscuits, cakes, and pralines arrived four times a week if she was in Balmoral. Afternoon tea was a highlight of her day. After wiping the remains of two scones, two slices of toast, and a plateful of biscuits from her lips with a napkin, the queen ruefully conceded to Lady Lytton, "I am afraid I must not have any more." Christmas Day of 1897 at Osborne House saw Victoria dine on woodcock pie and a roast of beef while a decorated boar's head looked sagely on from the sideboard. The summer saw her cool off with apricots and an enormous chocolate ice.

The end was nigh, though, as the tiny, fat queen tramped into her eighties. Her already poor eyesight deteriorated further, cataracts clouding her eyes. Rheumatism rendered her lame, and she stopped going downstairs for dinner; her food became an invalidish array of egg flips and broth. She lamented her lack of appetite in her journal. Her servants, too, deteriorated in manners and care. Abdul was heard shouting at her once, and her lady-in-waiting Marie Mallet raged that the cooks at Balmoral made no effort to tempt Victoria's appetite:

I could kill the cooks who take no pains whatever to prepare tempting little dishes and would be a disgrace to any kitchen. How I would like to work a sweeping reform, we are abominably served now. The footmen smell of whisky and are never prompt to answer the bell, and although they do not speak rudely, they stare in such a supercilious way. As for the Queen's dinner it is more like a badly arranged picnic.

Marie held the queen's small, soft hand as Victoria told her, "After [Albert's] death I wished to die, but *now* I wish to live and do what I can for my country and those I love." She had to leave her beloved Balmoral and the beloved ghost of loyal John Brown and travel to Windsor. On November 8, Marie, enraged again, wrote, "The servants here are too irritating. . . . The Queen ordered only one small dish—nouilles—for her dinner last night and it was entirely forgotten, so she had nothing." And so it went on, shamefully, until Victoria's death in January 1901.

Even before Victoria was laid to rest beside her darling Albert (his dressing gown was also in her coffin), the furious enmity that Edward, Prince of Wales and soon-to-be-king, had felt toward John Brown was unleashed. Even on the morning of Victoria's death, shepherds spotted that a cairn of stones Victoria had built in Brown's memory had been flattened and dispersed. Edward converted Brown's room at Windsor (kept in a shrine-like state by the queen) into a billiards room. He ordered busts of Brown to be smashed and photographs of him splintered and consigned to the flames. His jealous wrath went unchecked. Brown had smacked Edward's bottom when he was a boy; how could his mother have had this repellent love for her servant? The portrait of Brown that had hung in Windsor was torn from the wall and posted back to Brown's brother.

Then came a loud knocking on Abdul's door. He was to be subjected to a similar fate: all the letters, postcards, and notes Victoria had written to him were removed and destroyed, by order of the king. It was also commanded that he should, post-haste, return to India with his wife and nephew.

The queen was dead; long live the king.

HIROHITO BECOMES MORTAL

Hirohito was the 124th emperor of Japan and succeeded Emperor Taisho, who was himself mad from syphilis. Odd as it may sound—or perhaps very wise in this case—it was the norm for future Japanese emperors to be spirited away from their families and raised by outsiders. Purportedly, this would make such heirs more modest, humble, and tough. So it was that at three months old, Hirohito was taken from his teenage mother, given to wet nurses, and sent to the home of septuagenarian Count Kawamura. Kawamura also received advice on his charge from one Miss Ethel Howard of England, who claimed in her yellowing curriculum vitae to have a long experience of tutoring the kings and queens of England (she was also governess to the kaiser's son, whom she thought very stout-hearted and gallant) and whose first piece of advice was that the little prince's upbringing should be shaped by the fostering of abstract qualities, one of which was gratitude, another independence of spirit. Willfulness and soppiness were to be ironed out. A tall order if you are a toddler.

Count Kawamura, scratching his head, added one or two of his toddler tests for good measure. Aha! How about being able to withstand all hardships? Kawamura decided to start with food, so, when Prince Hirohito was served his dinner and, chucking his chopsticks into the air, was heard to wail "I won't eat it!" cunningly, the count replied, "If you don't like it, you don't have to eat it. But you will be served no more food." The little prince watched as all his dishes were removed from the table. It took about forty seconds of silent contemplation for him to submit: "I'll eat it! I'll eat it!" Count Kawamura wept—yes, wept—with elation (there is a great deal of manly weeping in Hirohito's life). A lesson learned, then, and many more came his way when, aged five, his father, Crown Prince Yoshohito (later Emperor Taisho), a debauched idler, forced Hirohito to take part in a series of toasts with him, knocking back thimblefuls of sake. Chubby little Hirohito was very ill. His grandfather, Emperor Meiji, was also partial to drunken exploits and open to carnal pleasures: he slept in a comfy, Western-style bed; drank vintage claret; and, if he wanted a concubine, used to drop a handkerchief at her feet to summon her to his chamber.

Freed from the clutches of Count Kawamura, Hirohito started at the Peers' School, overseen by one General Nogi. It was called the "Peers' School" because Hirohito's classmates were other carefully selected children of highly placed court officials and princes who were blood relatives. When his "peers" and constant companions wanted to notify the prince that he should not enter their chambers, they were instructed to hang a takuan (pickled radish) outside the door of their shared accommodation—so much did the prince loathe takuan that he would steer clear. General Nogi was a tough character. When Hirohito was twelve, Emperor Meiji died and Nogi ended his life dressed in a white kimono by committing seppuku—disemboweling himself—and then slitting his wife's throat (after they'd both had a quick mouthful of sake in front of Meiji's autographed photo).

Hirohito took after neither his father nor his grandfather. He was a teetotaler (thanks to Dad), myopic, round-shouldered, quiet, and mild, and he walked with a bit of a shuffle. Plain and simple living defined his style: he'd wear the same suits and slippers until people pointed out that they were threadbare and falling off. All he cared about was marine biology. When he was emperor, his summer palace in Hayama by Sagami Bay had a laboratory and a miniature aquarium; he liked to carry a magnifying glass about his neck. On holiday by the sea, the emperor would pop into his pockets "algae, starfish and sponges." He was excited by crustaceans, and, at the early age of seventeen, the prospect of becoming emperor was eclipsed by his most transcendent moment: having discovered a bright red prawn, eight centimeters long, he took it to Dr. Arata Terao, a marine species specialist, who declared it a new species. In 1919, it was given the name *Sympathiphae imperials*. This kind of dedication to small, unusual things is clearly genetic: Hirohito's son Prince Hitachi was to become an expert on Japanese bird lice.

Aged twenty-one, the insular Prince Hirohito embarked on a tour of Europe, the first *ever* Japanese royal to set foot on foreign soil, traveling by battleship, the *Katori*, from Yokohama harbor to England, complete with a fretful retinue of fifteen conservative counselors. The biggest worry that the retinue faced was the issue of etiquette in England. What, they wondered, would be expected of the crown prince's deportment? It was, after all, the home of the gentleman, and the British royal family would be watching his every move. Many tests would beset our nervous entourage. When the dashing Prince of Wales boarded the *Katori*, all handshaking went well. But it was when King George V met them at Victoria Station that comedy ensued. The Japanese entourage noted approvingly that Hirohito greeted King George in a natural and easy manner, but when the horse-drawn carriage arrived to take them to Buckingham Palace, things got complicated. First, the king invited the prince to get in; the prince insisted the king go first. The king invited the prince to go first. The prince asked the king to step on. The king invited . . . Eventually, King George had to resort to harrying the prince to get him into the carriage. Even the crowd applauded and . . . wait for it . . . one of the prince's entourage, Chief Attendant Chinda, "was so moved that his eyes clouded over." It absolutely amazed the Japanese that getting into a carriage could be so informal, with people simply inviting other people to hop in. How could they have prepared the prince for such a surprise!

Hirohito adored Britain and Europe and King George, who was full of bluff, cheery, and fatherly tips. Hirohito was amazed when King George strolled into his room at breakfast time in Buckingham Palace, wearing carpet slippers and an open shirt, without any formal announcement being made and without any courtiers. George clapped him on the shoulder and said, "I hope, me [*sic*] boy, that everyone is giving you everything you need. . . . I'll never forget how your grandfather treated me and me [*sic*] brother when we were in Yokohama. No geishas here, though, I'm afraid. Her Majesty wouldn't allow it." King George chortled knowingly. George thought it an excellent idea if Hirohito were fully kitted out in a British general's dress uniform for his visit to inspect troops at the "home of the British Army," Aldershot. To assemble the uniform, a bootmaker, hatter, and tailor came to Buckingham Palace, but the bootmaker, kneeling at Hirohito's feet, was unsure how to leave his presence with the due amount of obeisance; he solved this by leaving Hirohito's presence on his knees, without standing up.

On May 9, a banquet was held for Hirohito by the king and queen at Buckingham Palace, the dining tables decorated in the imperial colors of white and red. It involved much bowing with Lloyd George, while the prince's loving entourage doted on the pleasant smile playing on Hirohito's lips, the grace and ease with which he moved, and his conversation with Lord Asquith. He visited Manchester, Edinburgh, spent a magical day in Oxford, and had his first taste of golf with the Prince of Wales. In a hotel in Edinburgh, Admiral Togo worried when he found that he'd been given a double bed—this must mean that a geisha was going to join him. Whatever Admiral Togo imagined a Scottish geisha might look like, it wasn't pleasant, and the admiral requested a single bed pretty fast. Most of all, Hirohito loved Scotland and the three days he spent there in May 1921. He was first at Holyrood Palace and then traveled by train to meet the Duke of Atholl, or Lord Tullibardine, as he was known, at his ancestral seat, Blair Castle. The Japanese entourage noted approvingly that the duke and duchess treated the prince like a schoolboy son returning from boarding. The Japanese liked the duke, comparing him favorably to a feudal Japanese *daimyo*, with lands and hundreds of warriors at his command. The duke commanded eight hundred kilted Atholl Highlanders, the only legal private army in all of Europe. But what most impressed the Japanese entourage was the banquet laid on by the Atholls the night before the prince's departure. First, there was the unheard of social equality of masters mixing with servants or, as the Japanese perceived it, the Duke of Atholl meeting his shepherds. There was caber tossing, and bagpipes played Japanese airs and the Japanese national anthem, "Kimigayo." The prince rewarded one piper with a goblet of wine; the piper bowed elegantly and quaffed the wine. Next, everyone had to stand on their chairs—a *local* custom, were the Atholls pulling Hirohito's leg?—and sing "Auld Lang Syne," followed by more singing and lots of remarkable foot stamping. The Japanese entourage found the sight of an old farmer with a red beard swaying to the music particularly moving . . . hmm . . .

For the first time, Hirohito realized the breathtaking liberty of paying for things out of his own pocket. In France, he bought a metro ticket that he kept forever, as well as busts of Napoleon, Darwin, and Lincoln.

On his return to Japan, Hirohito's retinue watched, aghast, as he went to the Tokyo races and built a nine-hole golf course in the palace grounds (this later became overgrown and ruined after World War II), where he played golf religiously in tweed plus fours. This was life in the fast lane for Hirohito. He further horrified everyone by inviting his former schoolmates from Peers' School around for a party with a keg of Scotch whiskey (yes, given to him by those Atholl rascals in Scotland). What horrified Hirohito's chamberlains, those arbiters of courtly convention, the most was the dreaded informality with which the crown prince's former classmates began to address him as they became more muddled on the whiskey. Prince Saionji raced to Tokyo by train and took Hirohito in hand; the crown prince was dangerously close to shaking off those traditional values that had allowed the royal house to continue.

Finally, Hirohito became emperor in 1925. The imperial way demanded that Hirohito had a court physician who tasted his food, and there was a regular examination of the royal feces. He did away immediately with a series of what he considered outmoded traditions: It was no longer necessary to present him with a dead fish on special occasions; he preferred live ones. There was nothing festive, he concluded, about a dead fish. Fish were incredible creatures, like the catfish in Japanese legend that, by moving its whiskers, causes tsunamis and earthquakes. Two elegant and rare cranes were presented to him by a retired general; Hirohito refused to eat them, saying how sorry he was that they had been killed. He did not want to have any concubines; he would have one wife and one wife only. In this instance, Princess Nagako. She was almost struck off the list of potential wives by some jealous adversary suggesting there was color blindness in her family line—she turned out to be an excellent painter with a markedly keen sense of color. Even better, Nagako made her own doughnuts and sang lieder.

Having lost his heart to British ways, Hirohito insisted forever after on breakfasting on bacon or sausage, fried eggs, grilled tomato—or porridge—and coffee, which he didn't really like but drank out of faithfulness to his food memories of his trip to Britain. Traditionally, breakfast in Japan would be rice, pickled vegetables, and soybean soup. He took English tea in the afternoon. He also chose to sleep in a Western-style bed and wore a Mickey Mouse watch and Western clothes. In truth, though, there was still much that was typically Japanese about his diet. Eels and sea slugs were favorites, and he was desperate to taste the glories of fugu, or puffer fish, a delicious and dreadful morsel. The fugu has to be specially prepared by a chef (after he or she has completed three years of determined training) to remove its lethal poisons. Particularly appetizing is the fugu's liver, which, if not prepared properly, will strike you dead. Tempting, isn't it? Imperial household rules forbade Hirohito from eating it, whether it be raw, sashimi style, or tucked into a warming hot pot, but that didn't stop him from arguing his case with the imperial physician, Dr. Sugimura. Their argument became so involved that eventually the empress had to interject, "That's enough about 'fugu,'" she told both emperor and doctor. "Please stop arguing about it."

The Imperial Palace occupied 240 acres in the center of Tokyo and was surrounded by a moat. Within the moat, the emperor had grown and tended a rice paddy. He planted rice there every year and worked in the mud so that he could connect with the experiences of Japan's agrarian population. Rather more exotically, Empress Nagako kept silkworms, their rooms warmed by charcoal fires and attended to by half a dozen staff. At the beginning of the season, the empress would take a delicate feather brush and brush the first silkworm eggs onto a tray. The mature silkworms, one thousand to a tray, ate dried, shredded mulberry leaves so loudly that their eating could be heard in the room.

By 1937, Japan had invaded China and "was eating it, like an artichoke, leaf by leaf," warned Winston Churchill. While Japanese forces were busy raping Nanking and China in general, Hirohito faced severe criticism for being more interested in marine biology than warfare. During World War II, in an act of fidelity to the Japanese people, Hirohito abandoned his love of a British breakfast of bacon and eggs and supped on brown rice instead. He looked down-at-the-heels in his loose suits, his clothes a symbolic echo of his country's suffering. When asked by General MacArthur why he had not intervened to stop the war, the emperor replied, "I felt my heart was breaking," particularly as he had such fond memories of his time with the British royal family, "who treated me with great kindness when I visited them as Crown Prince. But the idea of gainsaying my advisers in those days never even occurred to me. Besides, it would have done no good. I would have been put in an insane asylum or even assassinated." Hirohito later renounced his godliness. By the end of the war, General MacArthur asked whether he could do anything for the emperor; this turned out to be providing a box of chocolates. In an effusion of gratitude, Hirohito came back with a gift of a huge sweet molded in the shape of a Japanese chrysanthemum.

The emperor refused to have the palace rebuilt after the war, when so many Japanese were homeless. The extended imperial family lived in different dwellings, but Hirohito and Nagako continued to live in Obunko, the former library that sat over the air-raid shelter. Starvation was widespread; one observer in Tokyo saw a woman picking spilled rice out of the gutter with a set of tweezers.

Elizabeth Vining was governess to Hirohito's son Crown Prince Akihito from 1946, when Akihito was twelve, onward. Her memoirs offer a unique window into postwar life with the imperial family. On her arrival and in her honor, the imperial family presented her with a dessert of some magnitude: an enormous eagle, chiseled out of ice, descending to feed an ice eaglet with some of the balls of vanilla ice cream that lay about the birds of prey. Miss Vining puzzled over the significance of the dessert, all eyes upon her. Akiyama San, the head chef who had so lovingly created the dessert, was disappointed when he had to explain its meaning to Miss Vining. The large eagle was clearly *her*, the American governess, bringing knowledge to the eaglet—Prince Akihito. Of course!

Vining's memoirs take us to an imperial picnic lunch in the countryside around Nasu, in the north of Japan, in the summer of 1947. A long line of the royal family and their retainers, sheltering from the rain under their black-and-yellow umbrellas, proceeded to the picnic spot. They reached Ōmeitei, the royal pavilion, with its views over the mountains and valley. Lunch was "delicious cold trout, potato salad, rice, sliced tomatoes, watermelon ice and sliced watermelon." Hirohito rode the traditional white horses of the emperor with his sons, while the empress hunted for wildflowers. At night, the governess sat on cushions at a low table and supped on a scrumptious dinner of trout and eggplant made by the royal princesses, though Miss Vining found eating a peach with a knife and fork confusing and poached eggs with chopsticks challenging. Japan, seasonally, offered mouthwatering fruity richnesses: peaches like white moons but with a pink blush, loquats in the spring, crisp apples and zesty and bittersweet mandarins in winter, fat figs at the summer's end.

Watermelon Ice

INGREDIENTS

½ cup water
½ cup granulated sugar
1 tbsp. fresh ginger, finely grated
   (discard any hairy clumps)

1 watermelon, skinned, chopped,
   and seeded
Generous handful of fresh mint leaves,
   finely chopped

METHOD

In a saucepan, warm the water and sugar; you are making a sugar syrup. Stir until the sugar dissolves, and then add the finely grated ginger. Bring to a boil and then simmer, uncovered, for 3 minutes. Allow to cool.

Puree the melon in a food processor, and then strain this gooey, pink pulp through a sieve. Combine the sugar syrup with the pureed melon. Add the mint leaves. Let the whole watermelon ice mix cool thoroughly, and then process in an ice-cream maker until it is thick and sludgy. Serve with paper-thin half-moons of watermelon on the side.

Miss Vining grew to love the food of the emperor's court: the salty senbei rice crackers and green tea, steaming in handleless cups. In the second year of her stay with the family, she was invited to share some of their New Year food. Trays assembled with rare delicacies appeared in the drawing room. Miss Vining usually found omochi (gluey balls of rice paste) in her Japanese soup, a watery, warm environment in which the omochi took on a gelatinous quality—she had found it difficult to swallow. But here was omochi formed into "two thin cakes, one pink and one white, folded over to make a sort of sandwich, with gobo, or slices of burdock root, in between." Instead of omochi, in the "delicious hot soup were quails eggs, hard-boiled"—again, hard to get hold of with chopsticks. Then there was tender, gamey pheasant cooked in wine (sake) and tai (sea bream), a fish often favored on such cheery occasions. Miss Vining caught sight of Empress Nagako in her ceremonial costume, a fan in her hand, her hair lacquered into wings of black but also falling to her waist, loosely bound at her shoulder blades with golden ribbon. Her scarlet-lined green-silk outer robe was clustered with white medallions of plum blossoms. Beneath, her slim, warm frame was encased in a stiff white kimono and a scarlet *hakama*. A pair of scarlet shoes peeked out from beneath the *hakama*.

Senbei Rice Crackers

INGREDIENTS

Generous ½ cup rice flour
4 tbsp. white rice, cooked
A generous pinch of sea salt
2 tbsp. groundnut oil

¼ cup water
1 tbsp. dried, crumbled seaweed
1 tbsp. soy sauce
1 tbsp. runny honey

METHOD

Preheat the oven to 200°C. In a bowl, combine the rice flour, cooked rice, salt, and oil. Now add the water, a little at a time. Next, using your hands, mix in the crumbled seaweed. On a work surface, lay a sheet of cellophane. Put the rice cake paste on this, cover with another sheet of cellophane, and smooth it out into a square about half a centimeter thick. Now peel off the top layer of cellophane. Line a baking tray with greaseproof paper. Cut the cracker paste into triangles, squares, or rectangles. Place these on the greaseproof paper and bake in the oven for 10 minutes, turning the crackers after 5 minutes. They should have begun to brown. When this happens, remove the crackers from the oven; combine the soy sauce with the runny honey and brush the surface of each cracker with this seasoning. Return the crackers to the oven and bake for another 2 minutes. Remove and allow the crackers to cool.

Soup with Quails' Eggs

INGREDIENTS

1 medium-size block of firm tofu,
  cut into cubes
½ cup sake
1 cup dashi
½ cup mirin (Japanese rice
  wine)

½ in. piece of fresh ginger,
  finely shredded
½ tbsp. shoyu sauce
Juice of 1 lime
4 quails' eggs
1 scallion, finely sliced

METHOD

Put a pan of water to boil, and when it has started to bubble, pop the quails' eggs in. Let them boil for 2½ minutes, then remove them, rinse in cold water, and shell. In a pan, heat the sake, dashi, mirin, ginger, and shoyu sauce. Add the tofu. Allow the soup to simmer for 4 minutes. Allow it to cool, and then when lukewarm, add the lime juice and scallion. Serve gently warm with the halved quails' eggs on top.

Pheasant in Wine

INGREDIENTS

½ lb. pheasant meat, cut into
  thin strips
¾ cup sake
1½ tbsp. shoyu sauce
1 tbsp. groundnut oil

2 tsp. sugar
1 tbsp. mirin
1 tbsp. shoyu
6 shitake mushrooms, sliced
4 scallions, chopped diagonally

METHOD

In a shallow dish, combine the pheasant with the sake and shoyu. Cover and leave to marinate in the fridge overnight. In a skillet, heat the groundnut oil and add the pheasant; sauté vigorously for 2 minutes. Add the remaining liquor from the pheasant marinade plus the sugar, mirin, and shoyu. Let this reduce slightly. Finally, add the shitake mushrooms and scallions. Sauté briskly for 1 minute, and then serve with rice and a cup of warm sake.

As part of the postwar rehabilitation of Japan, Hirohito visited America in 1975, and a pictorial history was published that informed the reader how utterly "normal" and Western the emperor really was: "He and Empress eat Western style breakfast—bread, oatmeal, eggs, vegetable salad and milk from the Imperial dairy farm."

For lunch, there is "sushi, sandwiches or noodles, often in his office, and dinner is early—at 6 p.m. His doctors insist on a low-fat diet, with plenty of green vegetables. All vegetables and fruit come from the Imperial Farm and are organically grown without any chemical additives. His French-trained chef prepares a mixture of Western and Japanese dishes, and menus are established two weeks in advance." In truth, it was less glamorous. Hirohito watched TV in his old slippers—ironically, learning from it many of the habits of ordinary Japanese life. Prewar, when Hirohito passed the houses of his commoners, ordinary Japanese were expected to go into their houses and close the shutters and windows. They should not be seen by the emperor. Now the emperor's life was all about tuning into sumo wrestling on TV and the delights of nature documentaries. Nagako and Hirohito liked to read *Stars and Stripes*, a newspaper for the U.S. military community, before turning in for bed at about ten.

IBN SAUD AND HIS SHEEP

The nomadic Ibn Saud tribal family was headed by the cunning and brave Bedouin Abdul Aziz bin Saud. A desert potentate and not an inch or two short of six foot five, he swooped down on Riyadh in a daring nighttime raid, taking it by force and reestablishing the rule of the Ibn Saud over the land of Najd. He had not yet clapped eyes on a European—until, that is, he met William Henry Irvine Shakespear, Britain's political agent in Kuwait. Shakespear had heard of Ibn Saud's prowess as a leader and warrior and had crossed the desert, tracking him. Unlike many British agents in the Middle East, Shakespear did not wear Arab dress (Wahhabism would later decree that no Westerners were allowed in the lands of Ibn Saud without adopting Arab dress), but Shakespear was skilled at the chosen sport of princes of the desert—falconry—and understood many of the ways of the Bedouin. He knew, for instance, that he had to exercise caution with the Bedouin, who would find his ways very foreign. Shakespear carried with him a bulky wooden box containing a camera, the act of photography or image taking, complete with the gaunt, many-legged tripod and black cloth, could easily persuade an innocent Bedouin that Shakespear possessed the evil eye. When it came to a tipple, Shakespear took a sort of traveling bar with him, rigging a camel with a crate of wine and several bottles of whiskey. These he kept concealed, knowing Ibn Saud's abhorrence of alcohol. He tended to avoid Bedouin until he reached Ibn Saud, protecting his privacy as he ate supper and sipped a glass of wine from behind the camouflage of his maps and compasses.

When he finally caught up with Ibn Saud, the two men took to each other; they were both bold and curious, fired up by convictions. They had a shared animosity toward the Ottomans and their leader, Ibn Rashid, and they dreamed of Arab freedom. Ibn Saud welcomed Shakespear in the traditional Bedouin manner: they feasted in a tent, Shakespear at Ibn Saud's right hand, part of a circle of the king's brothers, sons, and relatives. A whole sheep was served, with the choicest morsels offered to guests—it was dishonorable to refuse anything from the ears through to the feet, which, incidentally, have a gluey, gooey consistency. H. V. F. Winstone, Shakespear's biographer, describes the meal:

> As each man took his place he said, "Bismillah," In the name of God. The amir, in the way of the Arab host, tore off the tenderest parts of the lamb and laid them before Shakespear with lumps of fat from the animal's tail, and tongue and eyes, and Shakespear spoke in praise of his host's lavishness. And as each man finished his meal with dates picked from a sticky mound he belched with open satisfaction, uttering "Allah karim" God is bountiful, and wiped his mouth with his hand.

Shakespear would have dipped his dates in the yogurt drink laban and fresh goat's milk, served hot and steaming with ginger in small-handled, delicate glasses.

Determined to return the hospitality in a manly, British way, Shakespear coolly invited Ibn Saud and his men back to his place for a British "feast" of roast lamb, a mint sauce alongside, tinned asparagus, and roast potatoes in his private quarters in Kuwait. What the Bedouin made of it is unrecorded, but the friendship Shakespear and Ibn Saud struck up was a cordial one of kindred spirits. The British, however, were determined to use Shakespear's influence on Ibn Saud, and an opportunity presented itself when, at the outbreak of World War I, they sent Shakespear back to the desert to negotiate a pact with Ibn Saud against the damnable Turks. Touchingly, forever afterward, when Ibn Saud was asked to name the finest European he ever met, he never failed to reply "Captain Shakespear!" It is little wonder, as Shakespear gave his life for Ibn Saud's cause, fighting for him at the Battle of Jurab, when he was shot by one of Ibn Rashid's Turks. Ibn Saud had begged him to leave the battlefield, but Shakespear had refused point-blank. The Turks sawed off Shakespear's slightly balding head and hung his helmet on the gates of Medina to expose Arab collusion with the British.

Next, Ibn Saud took Mecca; then he subdued most of the central Arabian Peninsula. By September 1932, Ibn Saud declared himself king of his conquered lands, naming them the Kingdom of Saudi Arabia. Simultaneously, oil discoveries were being made, and by 1938 Ibn Saud was presiding over vast reserves of petroleum. Increasingly throughout the 1940s, Western powers took greater note of the incredible oil wealth of Ibn Saud's kingdom, and all sorts of "gifts" materialized; Winston Churchill sent Ibn Saud a bright-green Rolls Royce, complete with a throne-like back seat.

In 1945, the lackadaisical King Farouk of Egypt set sail on his yacht, the *Mahrousa*, to cross the Red Sea to Saudi Arabia and pay court to Ibn Saud. According to Farouk's biographer, William Stadiem, the two kings had a high time of it, gifting each other jeweled daggers and necklaces belonging to one of the Prophet Mohammed's wives. Each outdid the other, and by the time Farouk boarded the *Mahrousa* he had also acquired a stable of Arab pedigree horses and twelve po-faced camels: "Even if they had been made of gold," Ibn Saud boomed grandly, "they would have been a very small offering." Now *those* are the sorts of friends you need. Soon Farouk extended an invitation for Ibn Saud to join him in Cairo, where he could meet not only Haile Selassie, king of Ethiopia, but also Winston Churchill and Franklin Roosevelt, both heading back from the Black Sea, Stalin, and the Yalta Conference. Ibn Saud was game for it.

His aba billowing about him, Ibn Saud mounted the steps of the American destroyer USS *Murphy* in Jeddah, Saudi Arabia, sent courtesy of Roosevelt. Of course, like any monarch worth his salt, Ibn Saud had just under fifty relatives and servants with him, plus his royal coffeemaker, an enterprising gent who lit charcoal fires for brewing coffee on the deck of the *Murphy*, including one precariously close to the open storeroom for ammunition. Ibn Saud was flanked by ten bodyguards, swords at their waists. The Arabization of the *Murphy* had begun. Checkered rugs were thrown on the deck, and a tent of brown canvas was erected for shade. The Saudi retinue had never been on a ship that was motorized or ventured away from calm coastal waters and seasickness abounded (but not Ibn Saud, of course). They rejected the cabins they were offered on board the ship; their sleep would be under the stars, and Ibn Saud's silk tent was erected alongside the gun turret. Ibn Saud sat facing the bow but changed direction when it was time for prayer; his direction to pray was determined by the ship's navigators. A herd of ten sheep was also brought aboard, bleating worriedly, corralled in the fantail of the boat's deck, like so many woolly packed lunches—one awed observed noted it was "a spectacle out of the ancient past on a modern man-of-war." The sheep, Ibn Saud said, were to feed him and his men; they would not eat the frozen food from the *Murphy*'s supplies. But their Arab hospitality was never at bay; they requested that the *Murphy*'s crew eat with them (the king also made sure he knew the names of all the crew so that he could bestow presents on them). The American crew managed to sidestep the invitation to tuck into the bleating horde by claiming that naval law precluded them from eating anything other than their sailor's rations. Ibn Saud proved much more adventurous: he ate the first apple of his life and tasted his very first apple pie. He also saw his first motion picture—a lightsome reel about aircraft carriers, which he thoroughly appreciated, but he averred that the motion picture would not do for the populace of Saudi Arabia, as it might take them away from their religious duties (he was quite right—unbeknownst to him a number of his retinue were belowdecks watching Lucille Ball).

When they met up with Roosevelt on the Great Bitter Lake, Ibn Saud and his throne were hoisted off the *Murphy*; he had problems with his legs and feet and envied Roosevelt his wheelchair—Roosevelt gifted him his other spare "twin" wheelchair as a gesture of fraternity. His throne was then placed on Roosevelt's boat *Quincy* for talks. They carved out the future of the Middle East over a lunch, according to William Stadiem, of "grapefruit, curried lamb, rice and whatever they could scrounge up as condiments—eggs, coconut, chutney, almonds, raisins, green peppers, tomatoes, olives, and pickles." After eating, Ibn Saud asked if he might be so bold as to offer Roosevelt coffee. Ibn Saud had a magnificent wooden staff and Roosevelt, his hat on the table, a coat thrown over his shoulders, looked reverently at the splendid Arab king—they spoke in French. Our potential arsonist, the ceremonial coffee brewer, fell to his work, brewing aromatic, cardamom-rich coffee served in tiny cups. Roosevelt appeared to like it so much that he took a second cup—it was only later that he confided he thought it was "godawful."

"If you don't mind," Ibn Saud asked, "could I ask a small favour?" As one observer recalled, "He said the meal was the first he had eaten in a long time that was not followed by digestive disturbance and he would like, if the President would be so generous, to have the cook as a gift." Before consigning the mild-tempered ship's cook to a life among the Bedouin, Roosevelt diplomatically explained that the cook was under a contract to the marines that was unbreakable. Perhaps, though, he could offer some training or guidance to Ibn Saud's cooks? Phew.

After meeting with Roosevelt, Ibn Saud and the *Murphy* sailed up the Nile to Farouk's new hunting lodge, the purpose of which was to let Farouk kill as many ducks as possible. Sir Miles Lampson, British ambassador to Egypt, who had always been cross about Farouk's intellectual slovenliness and generally unkingly sloth, was delighted when he clapped eyes on Ibn Saud. This was more like it. As he recalled:

> I don't think anyone could help being immensely impressed by him. . . . He had with him an immense retinue and immediately behind him stood a bevy of slaves who ministered to his wants preparing his dishes for him, etc. He drank special water brought from Mecca which he insisted upon both Antony Eden and Winston sampling. The rest of us were supplied with whisky and sodas but served in coloured glasses and described (to spare Wahabi susceptibilities) as "medicine."

Ibn Saud was less than impressed by Churchill, considering him shifty and duplicitous, which is ironic, as Churchill's response to not smoking or drinking in front of Ibn Saud was "If it was the religion of His Majesty to deprive himself of smoking and alcohol I must point out that my rule of life prescribed as an absolutely sacred rite smoking cigars and also drinking alcohol before, after, and if need be during all meals and in the intervals between them."

Roosevelt's wheelchair may well have made a reappearance later in Ibn Saud's declining years. King Hussein of Jordan visited Ibn Saud just before his death; he could no longer walk, and his gaunt but still-massive frame was now confined to a wheelchair. When Hussein stepped out at the gates of the palace where he was staying to meet Ibn Saud, Ibn Saud was wheeled up, along with a second wheelchair. Ibn Saud casually gestured to the chair. Puzzled, Hussein asked, "I beg your pardon?" "It's for you, your Majesty," coughed a courtier. "Thank you very much," Hussein replied, "but I'm perfectly all right. I don't mind walking a bit." Then it dawned on him: for Hussein to walk while Ibn Saud sat in a chair would be damaging to Ibn Saud's dignity. There was nothing else for it; Hussein clambered into the second wheelchair, trying furiously not to make eye contact with any of his party for fear of laughing.

The power of Ibn Saud and the two sons, Saud and Feisal, who were chosen as princely understudies by him was maintained by a vast network of family connections (he had forty-five sons in total). The first to succeed Ibn Saud after he was felled by a heart attack in November 1953 was his older son, Saud, though everyone knew deep down that Feisal was considerably more capable. Saud managed to hang on to power for over a decade. An excessive spender, Saud constructed a huge wedding cake of a pink palace in Jeddah, with preposterous chandeliers and impossible fountains. Like his father before him, he sired a small population of children and had a weakness for the ladies (although he did worry about impotence, which may have been attributable to his passion for Cointreau). Disorganized, never in control of his finances, food vanished constantly from the palace kitchens—as did chunks of the palace fittings, which were then "recycled" in the Saudi black market. Meanwhile, Saud swanned about in a luxurious motorized desert caravan with a mirrored ceiling above his bed. His tummy was upset a lot of the time by what turned out to be internal bleeding, the result of too much consumption of what was euphemistically referred to as "irritating liquids." To top that, his wobbling gait could not support his wobbling girth. When he was hospitalized, more "irritating liquids" were hidden under his bed. But before he was carted off to the hospital, in a bid to confirm his virility, while being physically assisted by a troop of slave girls, he managed to have congress with his favorite wife, the portly Umm Hansour. Viewed with contempt, Saud's forced deposition was inevitable—his brother Feisal had been ruling through him all along anyway.

Cars instead of camels had become the most popular form of transport in Saudi Arabia. In a curious fusion of nomadism and modernity, the next king, Saud's wily and austere brother Feisal, roamed the kingdom in a motorcade of cars that also transported his radiant and grand white tents. Even so, Feisal got up to little good in privacy; when, in 1945, his father had sent him to London to represent Saudi Arabia at one of the inaugural sessions of the United Nations, Feisal failed to materialize and was tracked down by the police in a prostitute's bed in the London district of Bayswater. Lunches in Claridge's were also fun. Like his brother, Feisal had a fondness for alcohol and chain-smoking. When a nonmalignant tumor was cut out of his stomach in an operation in 1957, he kicked the habit and, furthermore, was condemned to a relentless diet of boiled foods, which is a great shame, since Saudi royal food consists of delicious dishes like kabbza made of goat meat, lamb, or chicken, traditionally barbecued in a mandi (this is an oven constructed by digging into the ground), served in fragrant rice spiced with cardamom, nutmeg, saffron, and bay leaves, and accompanied by the hot sauce shattah. If Ramadan is on, they might break their fast with savory sambusik pastries alongside shurba, a crushed-wheat, meat, and vegetable soup. Poor Feisal: only tea drinking remained—his last vice apart from the occasional scratch of his crotch in public.

Kabbza

INGREDIENTS

3 tbsp. butter

3 onions, finely chopped

3 lb. chicken, cut into pieces

6 cloves of garlic, minced

3 tbsp. tomato paste

12 tomatoes, chopped

4 carrots, skinned and grated

4 cloves

½ tsp. grated nutmeg

½ tsp. ground cumin

½ tsp. ground cilantro

½ tsp. saffron strands, ground

½ tsp. green cardamom, ground

½ tsp. ground cinnamon

½ tsp. ground allspice

¼ tsp. dried lime powder

Sea salt

Freshly ground black pepper

4 cups chicken stock

2 cups long-grain rice

⅓ cup raisins

⅓ cup slivered almonds, toasted

METHOD

In a large, deep saucepan, melt the butter. Add the chicken pieces and brown them in batches; as they brown, remove from the pot and lay to one side. Having browned all the chicken, add the onions to the sticky chicken-butter in the saucepan and cook gently until the onions are golden. Add the garlic and fry it for a minute or two. Add the tomato paste and fry it for a further 2 minutes. Return the chicken to the saucepan, along with the tomatoes, grated carrots, cloves, nutmeg, cumin, ground cilantro, saffron, cardamom, cinnamon, allspice, dried lime powder, sea salt, and freshly ground black pepper.

Cover and cook over a moderate heat for about 35 minutes. Remove the chicken pieces from the sauce.

To the sauce, add the chicken stock and rice. Stir thoroughly, cover again, and cook for another 20 minutes.

Heat the broiler and put the chicken pieces, skin side up, under the broiler to brown.

Add the raisins to the rice, remove the lid, and cook for a further 10 minutes. Serve with the broiled chicken pieces arranged on top of the rice, sprinkled with toasted almonds, and with some zippy shattah sauce on the side.

Shattah

INGREDIENTS

6 cloves of garlic, crushed
½ tbsp. vinegar
1 cup water
4 tbsp. tomato paste
2 tbsp. olive oil
2 tsp. cumin

1 red chili pepper, chopped
5 tbsp. flat-leaf parsley, finely chopped
5 tbsp. cilantro, finely chopped
Sea salt
Freshly ground black pepper

METHOD

Put all the ingredients in a blender and puree them. Next, place them in a saucepan, bring to a boil, and simmer for 10 minutes. Cool and then serve as a spicy condiment alongside the kabbza.

SUPPER WITH EDWARD AND MRS. SIMPSON

So much of romance depends on food. The right ambience, specially selected dishes—all part of the love wiles of Mrs. Wallis Simpson in her rise to power from navy housewife to Duchess of Windsor. Wallis began life with some pretty unusual notions about food and love in general—thanks to her grandmother. "Never," she warned the young Wallis, "allow a man to kiss your hand. If you do, he'll never marry you." Stern stuff. She even cautioned Wallis about coffee, which left Wallis laboring under the impression that she'd get a tan from a latte. "Don't drink that stuff," her grandmother warned. "It will turn your skin yellow!" Wallis's mother, Alice, was always a little short of cash but full of entrepreneurial zeal. When she and Wallis were tenants of the Preston Apartment House in Baltimore, not only did Alice let out their back rooms to cover costs, but she also discovered that all the other tenants went out for their supper. If there's one thing Alice could do, it was cook, so she concocted a business scheme where she (with the help of a hired cook) would dish up dinners for the other tenants—for a price, of course. Wallis, a bright-faced, talkative child, could serve the meals. Not only that, but little Wallis could try cooking herself, successfully mastering Lady Baltimore Cake before she'd seen out a decade of her life. Wallis watched her mother preparing terrapins (ouch . . . best cooked alive: you check that it's cooked by pressing one of its small feet between thumb and forefinger *and* you draw out its little toenails before serving). There was one fatal flaw in Alice's business plan: she loved giving her customers only the best—prime rib, Lobster Cardinal, soft shell crab, Terrapin à la Maryland—and her tenant customers loved sucking on flavorsome shells, supping delicate sauces. Who wouldn't? Not enough, though, to pay Alice sufficiently to balance her shopping bills, and so, in the words of Wallis, this was the demise of "the finest dining club in Baltimore history."

Lady Baltimore Cake

FOR THE SPONGE . . .

3½ cups cake flour
1 tbsp. baking powder
A pinch of sea salt
1 cup buttermilk
½ tsp. rose water

½ tsp. almond extract
1 cup butter, softened
2 cups granulated sugar
8 egg whites

FOR THE FRUIT AND NUT FILLING . . .

¾ cup sultanas
½ cup dried lingonberries
½ cup dried figs, finely chopped

¼ cup candied, chopped orange peel
2 tbsp. Cointreau
½ cup pecans, very roughly chopped

Lady Baltimore Cake (*continued*)

FOR THE MERINGUE FROSTING . . .

7 egg whites   ¼ cup water
1¾ cups granulated sugar   2 tbsp. light corn syrup
½ tsp. rose water

TO DECORATE . . .
A few tablespoons of pecan nuts and dried fruits

METHOD
Preheat the oven to 180°C. Get 3 cake tins (of the same size, about 8 inches),
butter them, and dust with a little flour. Combine the buttermilk, rose water, and
almond extract in a small bowl. Using an electric mixer, cream the butter and
sugar together until they are fluffy. Sieve the flour, baking powder, and salt into
a large mixing bowl. Alternately, add a quarter of the flour and then a quarter of
the buttermilk mix to the butter-sugar fluff; finish with the flour.

Now for the egg whites. In a very clean, large bowl, whisk the whites into a
stiff mass. Take a third and, using a metal spoon, fold them into the cake sponge
mix. Now fold in the remaining egg whites. Divide this mixture between the 3
cake tins. Bake for about 15 minutes, testing the cake is ready with a skewer.
Cool on a wire rack.

It is time to make the filling. Macerate the sultanas, lingonberries, and figs in
the Cointreau for half an hour. Add the orange peel and the pecans.

To make the meringue frosting, again in a large, very clean bowl beat the egg
whites until they are stiff. Next, in a small, heavy-bottomed saucepan combine
the sugar, rose water, water, and corn syrup. Cook over a medium heat until
the syrup is clear; then, without stirring, bring the syrup to a boil. Using a jam
thermometer to measure the heat, get the temperature to climb to 248°C. Remove
from the heat. Whisking the egg whites, add this hot syrup in a thin stream. Continue whisking as it cools—this will take about 10 minutes, but you'll eventually
be left with a lovely, glossy goo. Take about 2 cups of the meringue frosting and
combine this with the macerated fruit and pecan nuts. Spread this between the
cake layers. Now use the rest of the meringue to frost the cake and decorate with
dried fruit.

Wallis's culinary fate changed again in about 1916 when she received the book
she later referred to as her "bible"—Fannie Farmer's *Boston Cooking School Cook
Book*—as a wedding present after she tied the knot with her first husband, Lieuten-
ant Earl Winfield Spencer Jr. of the U.S. Navy. With this first marriage Wallis's
cooking aspirations were humble as she opened tins of Campbell's condensed—
little did she imagine that she would write her own cookbook, *Some Favourite
Southern Recipes of the Duchess of Windsor*, in 1941. "Win" was too partial to

martinis for their marriage to survive, although she picked up some good Chinese recipes trying to save her marriage when she followed "Win" to Hong Kong. How to fold a good won ton, however, may not have been the only skill Wallis acquired in Hong Kong; rumor has it that Wallis's skillful application of "oriental practices" (fellatio) won Prince Edward in St. James's Palace—though there have always been many dark allusions to her and Edward's sex life. How did she win him? Suggestions involved everything from foot fetishism to dressing the prince up in diapers.

It was, however, her second marriage to the redoubtable Mr. Ernest Simpson in 1928 that brought Wallis to London and her first encounters with the boyish Prince of Wales. Wallis's early days in London were confusing food-wise. In her attempts to negotiate the London smog and its strange food practices, she had to introduce her disgruntled butcher to diagrams of how to cut steak the American way, as laid out in the pages of Fannie Farmer's cookbook. A devoted wife, she would hunt out avocados at Fortnum and Mason's as a special treat for Ernest or scrape together the pennies for a jar of caviar or some brandied peaches.

Wallis and Ernest took every opportunity to tour the English countryside, and she expressed amazement at the quaint rituals of English inns: "After dinner the guests all repaired to the lounge for coffee, served by waitresses in stiff black alpaca dresses. Husband and wife, paired off like the species in Noah's Ark, would head purposely towards what were obviously their favourite chairs." Wallis found the food excellent—she relished delicious Yorkshire hams and delicate cheeses—but what delighted her most were the menu spellings of such things as "Sole O'Grattin" or "Cold Chicken in Aspect."

Old Ernest must have been a bit of a bore. Wallis forgivingly describes him as "methodical," but what would you think about a man who was found neatly packing his suitcase in the midst of a hotel fire while the women, Wallis and her ubiquitous and very cheerful aunt Bessie Merryman, rescued themselves? Aunt Bessie was later astounded to see Ernest descending the smoking stairway resplendent in a bowler hat and Guards' tie, with an umbrella sensibly tucked under one arm. Arguably, Ernest's attitude to burning buildings stood him in good stead for the months to come.

Number 5 Bryanston Court in London was where the Simpsons lived when they weren't out touring. It was pretty snazzy for its day: a spacious apartment in a rather grand, boxy, towering building close to Hyde Park. It was architectural testimony to Wallis's social ambitions. The couple shared a pink bed and had a fancy hot bar on which you could hang your damp towel in the bathroom. Wallis's maid, Kane, answered the door, leading visitors into the pale chartreuse living room, sleek with beige-and-cream furnishings. Or into the dining room, which was swamped by a giant mirrored table, decorated by elegant-necked vases holding

richly colored flowers or swooning arum lilies. The table was built to accommodate fourteen; Syrie, the wife of writer Somerset Maugham, had advised Wallis to
surround the table with white leather dining chairs (Syrie was to become famous
for her all-white rooms). Bryanston Court was part of a small, select American
colony in London. A party with the Simpsons was bound to be fun, with their zippy
vodkas, caviar, cocktails (with sausages on the side), and good food. You wouldn't
even realize it was 3 or 4 a.m. before people began to leave. Wallis, ever a hypo-
chondriac, believing she had developed an ulcer, was on a diet that excluded alcohol. Undeterred, she conjured up her own cocktail, an unappetizing union of club
soda and milk, and this repellent mix, seen in the hand of Wallis, was all the rage
(for a very limited time). When she wasn't across on a visit from Baltimore, Aunt
Bessie would send Wallis recipes from the States, and Wallis would hoard them
or get Mrs. Ralph, their cook, to try them out. Wallis had managed to scrape Mrs.
Ralph up from the leavings of the great, as she had previously worked under the
magnificent Lady Curzon's French chef. From her China days, Wallis had learned
the fine art of miniaturized eating and was very skilled at training Mrs. Ralph to
make the hot hors d'oeuvres, the novelty of which delighted her guests; the hot hors
d'oeuvres became the rage of London.

And no one had fun at those parties more than the future king, Prince Edward.
They all met through mutual friends, and Wallis took the time to watch Edward carefully. It was, in some ways, Wallis's attention to detail that guaranteed the longevity
of her relationship with the prince (although she was surprised by his shortness and
his passion for doing needlepoint—who wouldn't be?). Edward loved dropping in
on the Simpsons for cocktails or a homely cup of tea. It was often full of interesting
visitors whom Edward loved talking to. As he explained, "One met young British
and American men of affairs, foreign diplomats, and intelligent women, the talk was
witty and crackling with the new ideas that were bubbling up furiously in the world
of Hitler, Mussolini, Stalin, the New Deal, and Chiang Kai-shek."

Soon Edward was as thick as thieves with the couple; it was rumored that he
sponsored Ernest's entry into the Freemasons. Ernest, perhaps to dispel the vague
sense of threat he felt emanating from the prince, nicknamed him "Peter Pan." In
his memoirs, the prince recalled, "The Simpsons had a small but charming flat in
Bryanston Court, Bryanston Square. Everything in it was in exquisite taste and the
food, in my judgement, unrivalled in London. Having been raised in Baltimore,
where a fine dinner is considered one of the highest human accomplishments, Wallis had an expert knowledge of cooking. But beyond all that, she had a magnetic
attraction for gay, lively and informed company." Wallis was a perfectionist and
was very firm with local butchers and greengrocers about the quality and size of
everything she bought. Local fishmongers would groan when they saw the redoubtable Mrs. Simpson heading toward their shop fronts.

The prince, she noticed, "seemed to like to eat" but particularly good, uncomplicated food. Thus it was that clever Northerner Wallis first began to inch closer to Edward over a cunningly contrived supper. When she invited him around to her home for a first formal dinner party at Bryanston Court in celebration of Independence Day on Tuesday, July 4, 1933, she ensured the food was both tasty and plain. Ten guests came in total; the prince's companion was his dark-haired lover, Thelma Furness. The table was bedecked with a red, white, and blue color scheme. The prince sat at the head of the table, and Ernest perched at the foot. Wallis had cooked a typical American dinner. Black bean soup was followed by grilled lobster and fried chicken Maryland. The meal was concluded with cold raspberry soufflé and "as a concession to my English guests, a savoury of marrowbones." Wallis knew she had succeeded when the prince asked for her recipe for raspberry soufflé—would the Simpsons be so kind, he asked, as to spend next weekend with him at Fort Belvedere?

Fried Chicken Maryland

INGREDIENTS

4 breasts of chicken, skin still intact
2½ cups buttermilk
1 tsp. dried, crumbled rosemary
1 tsp. dried chili flakes
Freshly ground black pepper
Sea salt

2 eggs, beaten
1 cup all-purpose flour, plus 2 tbsp.
  for the gravy
2 tbsp. butter
1 tbsp. olive oil

METHOD

Preheat the oven to 180°C. In a bowl, combine the rosemary, chili flakes, flour, sea salt, and black pepper. Empty this mix into a plastic bag. Next combine half a cup of buttermilk and the beaten eggs. Take each individual chicken breast, dip it in the buttermilk-and-egg mix, drip dry quickly, and then drop it into the plastic bag containing the flour mixture. Now shake. The spiced flour should comfortably coat the outside of the fillet. Repeat. Heat the butter and olive oil in a shallow frying pan to a lively bubble. Add the chicken fillets and fry them for 10–15 minutes, until golden and crisp on both sides. Now place in the oven and bake for a further 10–15 minutes, until each fillet is cooked.

While the chicken fillets are finishing in the oven, prepare the gravy. Pour off most of the fat from the frying pan, but reserve 2 tablespoons. Return to the heat. Now stir in and blend the 2 tablespoons of flour with this. Stir constantly, scraping up the caramelized chicken splotches from the base of the pan. Gradually add the remaining 2 cups of buttermilk; continue stirring until the buttermilk gravy thickens and bubbles. Drizzle over the crunchy chicken breasts.

Serve with mashed potatoes or cornbread.

Raspberry Soufflé

FOR THE CRÈME PATISSIÈRE . . .

4 egg yolks
4 tbsp. vanilla caster or
  granulated sugar
2½ tbsp. cornstarch

3 tbsp. flour
Generous ½ cup milk
Scant ½ cup heavy cream

FOR THE SOUFFLÉS . . .

4 cups raspberries
6 egg whites
A few drops vanilla extract

6 tbsp. vanilla caster or granulated
  sugar, plus extra for dredging
Powdered sugar, to decorate

METHOD

First make the crème patissière. In a bowl, whisk the egg yolks and sugar together, then whisk in the sifted flour and cornstarch. Heat the cream and milk in a pan and bring to a boil. Remove from the heat. Very gradually add the scalding milk to the egg mixture, whisking constantly. Return this to a pan and heat, stirring with a wooden spoon until simmering. It will thicken—at this point it will coat the back of the wooden spoon. Remove from the heat; sprinkle with a little caster or granulated sugar to stop a skin from forming.

Blend the raspberries with half the vanilla caster or granulated sugar into a puree in a food processor. In a heavy-based pan, bring the raspberry puree to a boil and cook until reduced by half—you are making an intense paste. After this, allow to cool and then rub the raspberry paste through a sieve to remove the pips. Mix this with the cooled crème patissière and sprinkle with the vanilla extract.

Preheat the oven to 190°C and prepare the soufflé ramekins. Take 8 ramekins, butter them, and then dust with vanilla caster or granulated sugar.

In a large bowl, whisk the egg whites until they form delicate peaks and—slowly—whisk in the remaining vanilla sugar. Using a metal spoon, fold this egg-white cloud into the crème patissière.

Now spoon the soufflé into the ramekins, level the tops, and run your thumb around the edge of each soufflé; this helps them to rise. Place on a baking tray and bake for 10–15 minutes. On no account shout at the oven or open it.

Sprinkle some white pollen of powdered sugar on the soufflés, allow them to cool, and then serve.

Edward's habitual lover, Thelma Furness, was always about in his turreted bachelor home, Fort Belvedere. Their relationship seemed secure. Indeed, Thelma was in the top spot; she and the prince had tiny teddy bears that they would swap when they had to be torn apart. They had spent a lot of time cuddling on an African safari. Jealously, Wallis watched as Thelma and Edward embroidered together, and they

A Savory of Marrowbones

INGREDIENTS

3–4 lb. cylindrical beef marrowbones, cut into 3-inch sections and split in half (ask the butcher to do this)

1 tbsp. lemon juice

2 tbsp. olive oil

Sea salt

Freshly ground pepper

2 small shallots, finely sliced

2 tbsp. parsley, minced

2 tsp. capers

Toasted bread

METHOD

Heat the oven to 230°C. Place the bones on a baking tray and roast for about 20 minutes—but keep checking, the marrow jelly can evaporate, so you want to get it when it browns and just begins to pull away from the edges of the bone. In a bowl, mix the lemon juice, olive oil, shallots, parsley, and capers. Toast the bread. Remove the beef bones from the heat, scrape their marrow into a bowl, and mash. Serve on toast with sea salt and black pepper and top with a drizzle of the herb-and-caper mixture.

all applauded when the prince, who loved dressing up, played bagpipes dressed in his culottes. No mere sewing pattern would stand in Wallis's way; nor would Thelma, for that matter. Almost with perfect timing, in 1934 Thelma was called upon to visit her twin sister, Gloria, in the United States. She and Wallis went for an intimate lunch at the Ritz and exchanged confidences. Wallis sighed over her napkin, "Oh, Thelma, the little man [Edward] is going to be so lonely."

"Well dear," Thelma replied, "you look after him for me while I'm away. See that he does not get into any mischief." Little did she know! In hindsight, Thelma ruefully admitted, "It was later evident that Wallis took my advice all too literally."

Increasingly at ease in Wallis's company, the prince took to dropping by for "potluck" suppers with her and Ernest, staying after draining his cocktail while other guests eventually, reluctantly, went (it was custom not to leave before the royal personage did). One evening it just so happened that the prince, at a loose end without Thelma, asked if Wallis and Ernest could stretch their humble supper of beef stew to accommodate three. Mrs. Ralph was so excited; to look just right, she got out her "fancy apron." Her substantial frame was a-tremble with delight at the very prospect of cooking for "My Prince," as she called him. A strange trio they must have seemed (without Mrs. Ralph, who was trembling in some anteroom). It was the beginning of an oddly morganatic marriage between the prince, Ernest, and Wallis.

No sooner had Thelma returned from the United States than she turned up for dinner with Edward, Ernest, and Wallis at Fort Belvedere. She had a bad cold and probably a sore head, but Thelma was no slug and quickly guessed at Wallis's betrayal. First, Wallis and Edward seemed to be exchanging all sorts of little, irritating coquettish jokes. Then the prince picked up a piece of lettuce with his fingers and Wallis, playfully—but with a small, sexy, sadomasochistic under-tone—slapped Edward's hand. Thelma caught her eye and shook her head; the prince hated this sort of overfamiliarity. Edward giggled, and Wallis stared coldly back into Thelma's eyes, the brazen vixen. Openmouthed, Thelma realized Wallis had filched her prince. Not only was Wallis having a say over lettuce consump-tion, but she had also, to the despair of the staff at Fort Belvedere, laid siege to the kitchen, breaching the old, formal rules by materializing at the stove to make scrambled eggs for Edward. Then, to the cook's horror, came the apocalyptic mo-ment when the prince, perched at the common kitchen table, scoffed the scrambled eggs in front of the maids. Centuries of protocol creaked, groaned, and tumbled. The royal servants numbered among Wallis's first enemies. Thelma, meanwhile, packed her bags and left tearfully at dawn. Posterity is silent on the fate of the tiny teddy bears.

Wallis knew she had an established place in the prince's affections when he gifted her one of his beloved cairn terriers. She called the dog "Slipper." Ernest knew his homely star had been eclipsed. Scandal bubbled and steamed. Rumor had it that when Wallis was presented to Queen Mary, she looked imperiously out over the queen's adored flower beds and said, "Of course when I live here this will all be tennis courts." The cheek of it! One of Wallis's butlers, Ernest King, reflected on what life would have been like if Wallis really *had* moved into Buckingham Palace: "I shudder to think what a stir she would have caused among the servants, who have not the reputation of being unduly overworked."

Britain watched, spellbound with grief and outrage, as Edward, only just made King Edward VIII, announced his abdication a mere eleven months after taking the throne.

Naturally Auntie Bessie had sped across the Atlantic to be by Wallis's side to offer support during the abdication crisis, along with their cousin, Newbold Noyes. The erstwhile king returned to Fort Belvedere that night after announcing his ab-dication. Wallis curtsied to him, and then, being British, Edward spent the evening discussing the intricacies of jigsaw puzzles and game shooting. Perhaps Wallis and Edward conversed more privately in German; the couple spoke to each other in German when they didn't want the servants to understand (when Hitler heard of Edward's abdication, he said despairingly, "I've lost a friend to my cause!"). Wal-lis knocked out some stiff old-fashioneds with sugar and bourbon, and then they dined at the gleaming mahogany table on turtle soup, a delectable lobster mousse, golden roasted pheasant plus soufflé potatoes, and iced pineapple, rounding it all off with a toasted cheese savory.

Abdication Old-Fashioneds

INGREDIENTS

1 lump of sugar
3 dashes of Angostura bitters

A squirt of club soda
A jigger of bourbon whiskey

METHOD
Put the sugar cube in the base of a glass, add 3 dashes of bitters followed by a squirt of club soda. Crush the sugar with a muddler and smear the Angostura-soaked sugar around the glass; it should line the sides. Now add a single ice cube and pour in the jigger of bourbon. Drink in a desperate manner. You may find a sudden capacity to speak German after these.

It was decided that the couple maintain a respectful distance from each other for some time following the abdication until their wedding could take place. Wallis left for France, to which she made a trying journey, hounded by the press, picking on shrimp salad, tea and rolls, a smidgen of pâté de foie gras with a mouthful of white wine. The Duke of Windsor, as Edward was now to be, decided to hole up in the Rothschilds' Schoenbrunn Castle (he proved to be a difficult guest).

The couple's actual marriage ceremony was at Chateau de Candé near Tours, France, the home of their friend, the millionaire American-French Fascist Charles Bedaux. The day was a strain; they were snubbed by royal relatives, and Edward's "I will" came out in such ringing tones that it made the congregation jump. Cecil Beaton, the official photographer, was under instruction to only photograph Edward's left side. He noted of Wallis on the day, "She twisted and twirled her rugged hands. She laughed a square laugh, protruded her lower lip. Her eyes were excessively bright, slightly froglike, also wistful." Not to be beaten by public and private familial disapproval, a French plane dipped and wheeled above them, scattering rosebuds on the wedding (though nobody was actually aware of this). The couple served their sixteen guests Lawson 1921 champagne and a wedding breakfast of langoustines, chicken fricassee, coq en pâté (a plump rooster in shortcrust pastry, served with port and truffle sauce), a gateau, raspberries, and omelet. The duke, in homage to Wallis, unveiled his invention: the Wallis cocktail. Thank goodness Wallis had been doing the cooking all this time: Edward's contribution to food posterity was a stickily quaint combination of gin, peppermint, Cointreau, and lemon juice, with a burst of soda.

The Windsors' honeymoon (along with over two hundred suitcases) began on the Italian border. They climbed into a very swanky railway coach, reportedly sent by Mussolini, which then joined the Orient Express. Off they went, the duke popping up in Venice (where they gave a cheery Fascist salute to the crowds), Milan, and then Austria. Edward now in a straw hat, then in colored pajamas, then in a kilt, next in culottes, the duke and duchess hopped their way from one free accommodation to another. Finally, the *New York Times* spied them at the final destination of their honeymoon: Count Muster's Wasserleonburg Castle in Austria. "Attired in Tyrolean leather breeches, white hose and a short-sleeved shirt, [the Duke] watered flowers in the garden. In the morning he surveyed the tennis courts and looked for grass he might mow . . . the Duchess supervised preparation of an Austrian dinner." Mussolini's gift and the free honeymoon stay are prime examples of the way the Windsors were going to make their way through married life, always piggybacking on the wealth of friends who in turn basked vicariously in the glamour of their royal lost cause and love-against-the-odds romance, which cast its borrowed glory on the Windsors' associates. They were always parsimonious and pretty shifty at paying bills. This is beautifully illustrated by the remonstrations of the management of the Waldorf Astoria when they discovered that the Windsors had illegally been cooking their own food on a hot plate in their suite. The duke's friend Fruity Metcalfe noticed that the duke's cheeriness faded whenever a bill turned up, and servants within the Windsors' household were told to hang on to the used soap in guests' bedrooms for "other uses."

A fondness for all things German drew the Windsors to undertake an ill-conceived and unwise tour of Nazi Germany, eventually making their way to a fifty-minute private audience with Hitler at his "Eagle's Nest" in Berchtesgaden. Wallis disingenuously said she didn't understand a word of the German that passed between the men but that Hitler kept squeezing her hands at intervals. Then it was on to dinner with Ribbentrop in Berlin. The Windsors loved German beer; indeed, so moved was the duke after three pints of it that he leaped onto his chair in the Platzl, a *hofbräuhaus*, to make an impromptu speech about his love for Munich. This went down very well with anyone with chest hair and lederhosen. Wallis felt an abiding love for "those delightful little white sausages" she ate there, and a slice of apfelstruedel would always please the duke.

The Windsors went on to live in various rented houses until eventually buying their first house together in 1952, a former mill near Paris. One of their most memorable homes was Chateau La Croë. The prince inhabited the top floors, which he called "Belvedere" in memory of Fort Belvedere. Wallis had her own rooms, and if Edward decided to pop in, "she made him pop right out again," staff recalled. The tightfisted Windsors were dismayed to find their staff at La Croë was drinking bottled Evian water in order to avoid drinking risky French water. Edmund insisted, "Let them drink tap water." They threw a couple of dinner parties a week and dined out with friends the rest of the time. Wallis's butler, Hale, soon realized that the duchess intended to run the chateau less as a home and more as an "unending show." As he told Wallis's biographer Ralph Martin, "She was the producer; I was her stage manager." A phone had been installed in Hale's room so his employers could call him up on a whim. And in his bath. And in the lavatory. Hale was used to Fascist employers—Wallis had "borrowed" him from Charles Bedaux—but Wallis's pernickety standards were unsurpassed. Footmen, she thought, should run to the door, not dawdle. Before dinner, she whipped out a thermometer to check the temperature of the wine and would jot little precise notes on the menu about timings and the heat or otherwise of dishes. She always kept her gold "Grumble Book" handy, and when a guest professed a liking for some food, she'd scribble down the information. Actress Lilli Palmer's description of Wallis's appearance seems somehow apt: She had "voracious vitality. If she had happened to be hungry, she might have taken a bite out of you. Whenever I looked at her, I was reminded of the nutcracker we used for cracking walnuts when we were children. It was made of polished wood in the form of a woman's head, it would open its mouth very wide and—c-rr-ack! The nut disintegrated." A real nutcracker, one chef of hers obliquely told the London *Daily Mail* on February 27, 1957, "She knows precisely what she wants. . . . She is very critical. It is good to work with someone to whom only perfection is acceptable. Otherwise, one's standards would fall."

The Windsors adored their black pugs, one belonging specifically to each of them (remember Thelma's teddy bears!), and used a whip to separate the pugs when they fought. The pug dogs proved to be a liability at later Windsor dinners in France when guests would find their stockings gripped in the teeth of a pug dog roving beneath the dinner table and leaving a friendly trail of snot on their clothes. As the Duchess of Windsor, Wallis's attention to detail was given full vent—she would drill her chefs every morning and taught them how to make Mousse Glacée Aurore (a huge frozen tomato mousse) according to her specifications. Wallis had an abhorrence of tomato seeds; should she catch sight of an offending seed, she would return the entire dish. Elsa Maxwell, the society guru who went by the nickname "Plumpy," recalled eating with the Windsors in her memoirs:

> The Duchess . . . has perfect taste in food as well as furniture . . . for instance, the last time I lunched with them I noticed she had found the most enchanting little round porcelain pots with covers to contain butter and at the bottom of each there was ice to keep it firm. Because the Duke likes savouries, particularly crisp bacon cooked in molasses, savouries are always served at dinner parties. This completely mystified their French friends at first. Now, of course, they have taken them up with enthusiasm and savouries always appear whenever the Duke and Duchess dine. As a matter of fact, the Duchess eats very little at table. "I'm an ice-box raider," she always says.

In November 1949, Wallis shared her thoughts on entertaining with *Vogue*: "Any dinner of more than sixteen people I consider enormous. More than eight persons means no soufflé—always a melancholy omission. . . . Anyone who entertains a lot runs the risk of falling into a rut. . . . The hostess who relies on memory alone might find herself repeating . . . to friends precisely the same dinner, down to the *entremets*, that she provided six months before." Very stern stuff.

Bacon and Molasses Savory

INGREDIENTS

½ lb. smoked streaky bacon   Buttered toast, cut into little
4 tbsp. dark brown molasses sugar   triangles

METHOD

Preheat the oven to 180°C. Get a baking tray and line the bacon on it. Bake it in the oven until crisp. Now coat one side with molasses sugar and return to the oven until the molasses has dissolved. Turn and repeat. Serve curled on top of buttered toast triangles.

If there were any more than ten guests at your table, Wallis held, things might go awry. Ever cautious, though, if the Windsors were going to bring a new dish to the table, Wallis would do a taste test on a sample model of it days before. A delicious consommé might be on the table: jellied, it was pooled around a center of caviar and sour cream. Wallis was keen on doing innovative things with avocados; one dinner party had avocado halves filled with daiquiri. The same idea was replayed in Wallis's "Avocado Tahiti," where the halves held rum muddled with brown sugar. Perhaps this accounts for one guest hallucinating; he happened to glance out of the window only to see the duke, who had stepped outdoors for a minute, raise his kilt and pee on the grass. Hopefully, one of Wallis's fish soufflés served with a delicately spiced mild curry sauce and blob of warmed, gingery Major Grey chutney on the side brought him around. Then a Montego Bay ice would arrive. This was lime or lemon sherbet over which a hot rum sauce was poured. (Wallis could be very adventurous on the iced-dessert front—she liked to tease guests with her "Camembert glacé," which was Camembert-and-wine-flavored iced cheese.) Mahogany brown Viennese Sachertorte was often served (but never to the same guests), its fondant gleaming and its zip of apricot a mystery, perhaps in keeping with the duke's passion for Austrian and German cuisine.

Fish Soufflé

INGREDIENTS

¾ cup breadcrumbs

4 tbsp. Parmesan cheese

½ cup all-purpose flour

3 tbsp. butter, plus a pat of butter
for soufflé dish

Freshly ground black pepper

Generous cup milk

Freshly grated nutmeg

⅓ cup freshly grated Parmesan cheese

1 lb. uncooked lemon sole, diced

4 large eggs, at room temperature

METHOD

Preheat the oven to 220°C. Butter a large soufflé dish. Take the breadcrumbs and Parmesan, mix them together, and then line the soufflé dish with them—they will stick to the butter. Turn the dish to distribute the crumbs and cheese effectively. Keep a teaspoon or two extra to top the soufflé with.

Now it is time to make a collar for your soufflé. Cut out a strip of baking parchment, which will give you a collar of about 7½ centimeters extra, beyond the rim of the soufflé dish. Butter it on the inside. Tie this collar in place with string.

In a pan, melt the butter. Remove from the heat and stir in the flour. Little by little, add the milk, stirring the mixture smooth. Return to the heat and bring to a boil, then turn the heat down and cook gently for 5 minutes. Add the black pepper, nutmeg, Parmesan, and diced lemon sole. Remove from the heat and allow to cool (the sole will cook in the warmth).

Separate the egg yolks from the whites; add the yolks to the milky sauce. In a very clean, large bowl, whisk the egg whites until they are stiff and massy. Using a metal spoon, fold a couple of tablespoons of the whisked egg white into the milky sauce; this loosens it. Then, very gently, fold in the rest of the egg white. Transfer the soufflé mix into the soufflé dish and sprinkle the breadcrumbs/Parmesan crumbs on top. Bake in the center of the oven for about 30 minutes, until the soufflé is golden and well risen. On *no* account open the oven door while cooking or shout at the soufflé, as any such recklessness will cause it to fall.

When ready to serve, remove the collar from your soufflé and serve straightaway.

Montego Bay Ice

FOR THE LIME ICE . . .

Grated zest of 2 limes
1 cup granulated sugar
3 cups milk

Juice of 4 limes
½ cup water
A pinch of salt

FOR THE BUTTERED RUM SAUCE . . .

½ cup heavy cream
½ cup demerara sugar
½ cup dark rum

1 vanilla pod, split down the belly
2 oz. butter, diced

METHOD

Combine all the lime ice ingredients and chill. Process in an ice-cream maker for about 60 minutes. In the meantime, make the buttered rum sauce. Over a medium heat in a saucepan, combine the cream and sugar, stirring until the sugar is dissolved. Add the rum and the vanilla pod. Allow the sauce to reduce by about a third. Finally, whisk in the butter and serve drizzled over the lime ice.

Camembert Glacé

INGREDIENTS

¾ pint milk
1 tbsp. dry white wine
1 Camembert, peeled of its skin
   and finely diced
3 large eggs, the yolks separated
   from the whites

2 oz. granulated sugar
½ cup heavy cream
Freshly grated nutmeg

METHOD

In a saucepan, heat the milk and then, when hot, add the tablespoon of white wine and the diced Camembert. When the Camembert has melted through the milk, remove from the heat and set to the side. In a large mixing bowl, combine the egg yolks with the sugar. Whisk in the Camembert milk. Add a sprinkling of grated nutmeg. Return this mixture to the heat and slowly thicken, stirring constantly until a custard forms. Add the heavy cream. Now cool the Camembert mixture. Finally, process it until it becomes ice-cream-like in an ice-cream maker. Serve with other savory dishes, and if it doesn't turn out right, make a note in your Grumble Book.

The Windsors, always trading on their royalty, mixed with the celebrities and millionaires who lounged about the Italian Riviera and the Amalfi Coast. Lilli Palmer, the wife of Rex Harrison, found that the Duke of Windsor could be very obliging when the Windsors called on the Harrisons at their sun-dazzled villa, San Genesio, in Portofino, Italy. The duke took the hors d'oeuvres tray and handed it around, which Harrison found very off-putting, growling, "I just don't like seeing my former king passing the sandwiches." Lilli, meanwhile, pondered over how to amuse the duke—he told her not to worry. "You know," he told her, "I've got a low IQ."

"But sir, just think of your book, *A King's Story*. That's a fascinating tale and very well written," Lilli protested.

"Didn't write it myself," he chortled. "Anyway, that's all I know."

The Windsors also took up with Jimmy Donahue, an anarchic, amusing youth. Drifting about on a yacht in the waters of Portofino, Rex, Lilli, the Windsors, Jimmy, and a very boring American senator were having dinner. The senator was hell-bent on blaming the British for involving America in World War II. Rex was turning a furious puce color, and yet the American senator went on and on and on. Jimmy broke into his flow and asked if everyone would like to eat lobsters the next day. But this couldn't interrupt the senator's drone. Jimmy decided to take action. Dressed in beautifully polished dinner regalia, Jimmy stood up, walked to the boat rail, and threw himself overboard. The senator didn't pause. Ten minutes ticked by. Jimmy reappeared, dripping wet. The senator was still speaking. Jimmy muttered, "Oh hell, here we go again," went up to the rails, and flung himself overboard again. Even though there was a loud splash as Jimmy hit the water fifteen feet beneath the dining table, the senator never paused for breath.

Life became quieter as the Windsors grew older. Alone together, teatime was always at 5 p.m. It was the duke's favorite time of the day. A pot of China tea, piping-hot cheese-and-bacon morsels, petits fours, coral-pink shrimp before the fireplace. Edward loved his tea, with milk, in an oversize cup. Later in the evening, particularly if it were a Sunday night, the duke liked them to be alone. Wallis would rustle up dinner—no onions or garlic, which was "death to him." He was one, in the end, for simple food. Perhaps a modest haddock soufflé or a kedgeree made from shad roe and cooked with milk. No wine for Edward; left to his own devices, he didn't really like it. Nor did he like mutton broth, he and his brother George (the new king) having had a dreadful nanny in their childhood nursery who swore by mutton broth. Edward said "if he never saw or tasted mutton again he would be very pleased." Meanwhile, while Wallis cooked or bossed someone else about below stairs, Edward's job was to set out the card table—if this didn't happen, they'd eat on trays in front of the television. And this was the couple who had nearly destabilized the British monarchy. Edward explained to one interviewer, "Now we're just a very happy middle-aged couple." Both were weight conscious and dieted habitually. Wallis thought she had a roll of fat about her waist and used to make her masseuse work this area so hard that she worried she'd bruise Wallis. Not a chance!

ONE MONTE BIANCO TOO MANY: KING FAROUK OF EGYPT

How would you feel if your mother described you this way (pretend you're a "he")? "He was a monster, he was never destined to finish anything in his life—not his schooling, not his marriages, not his reign—not even his pre-natal development." Blimey. Now, although his mother was right in part—her son was born two weeks early—I'll leave it up you to decide whether King Farouk of Egypt was, indeed, as bad as his mother, the waspish, scheming Queen Nazli, claimed.

Granted, he never quite made the mark physically. His father, King Fuad, looked at him discontentedly: Farouk was on the chubby side (ironically, a little too much like Fuad himself). Farouk had to diet, the king decreed, and he ordered that gymnastics be part of Farouk's education. The boy learned to scale palm trees gracefully and leap, spin, and tumble with the best of them. His posse of nannies, a pair of staunch Edwardian gentlewomen whom Farouk suspected of working for the British intelligence services, followed the king's orders about diet; one Miss Naylor forbade sweets and drinks on demand. Farouk grew so hungry, though, that at one point he ate the cat's dinner. King Fuad was in a constant battle with Queen Nazli over Farouk's diet—and everything else. William Stadiem, Farouk's biographer, says, "A war of the larder broke out, with Nazli smuggling cream cakes . . . and Mrs Naylor seizing them and throwing them into the trash." A young Italian electrician from Naples who worked at the palace, Antonio Pulli, took pity on the young boy and cut him a set of counterfeit keys so that he could penetrate the palace's food stores. Despite her sternness, Miss Naylor (or "Ninzy," as Farouk called her) adored her charge. "He was the very essence of kindness and loyalty to servants," she wrote. Farouk was very happily in her thrall for fourteen years. When Sir Percy Lorraine of the British embassy urged some more cake on him at a tea party, Farouk refused steelily: "No thank you, Mrs Naylor said I was to leave some for the poor." Farouk had an official food taster (who was also the palace pharmacist) the Englishman Mr. Titterington (whom Farouk nicknamed "Titters"). Now, unlike Miss Naylor, Titters was *actually* a British spy, pumping Miss Naylor for gossip that he could report back to the British ambassador, Sir Miles Lampson, another figure who was forever in despair over Farouk.

What comes through most from Farouk's childhood is the preponderance of adults and servants about him, rather than other children. His royalty cast the shadow of a slightly forlorn isolation over his childhood. Pulli was firm friends with the prince. He used to tinker with and mend Farouk's toy trains in boyhood and remained his intimate, his confidante, and, later in life, his sexual "fixer" (by this time, Pulli had become the minister for personal affairs)—a relationship one British officer would snobbishly record as "very third class." When Oxford graduate Edward Ford turned up to tutor Farouk in British, gentlemanly ways, he found the staff dreadfully familiar: the Sudanese and Nubian servants were running to fat tucking into royal leftovers, and Farouk was "apt to interrupt any continued speech to interpose jokes of doubtful value." Ford was also startled when Queen Nazli confided that she was under pressure to acquire mistresses (yes, *plural*) for teenage Farouk. Ford's advice was deeply prim and deeply British: "I suggested to her that he would do better to take a lot of exercise now until he was a little older."

Farouk was never one to let April Fools' Day go wasted. Miss Naylor had given him a camera, and Farouk asked King Fuad if he could take his picture. The shutter clicked and a three-yard-long green joke snake sprang out at His Majesty, to Miss Naylor's blushes. She said, "Entering the room I was just in time to hear him say, 'Stand still, Papa, while I take your photograph.'" Such naïveté is glorious. A few corridors away in the palace, things were much more serious: Queen Nazli was trying to extend the reach of her power through magical, superstitious arts. Often, she would search for the future with a soothsayer, both pairs of eyes scouring the surface of a cauldron of boiling water. When trying for a male heir with King Fuad, she believed she could come to an arrangement with Allah and donated money to every single mosque on the birth of each of her children, despite being told firmly by Miss Naylor, "Majesty, you cannot bribe God."

Much to Nazli's delight, King Fuad died in 1936 and sixteen-year-old Farouk succeeded to the throne. Fuad had been an obstinate, argumentative husband (he also barked rather than spoke, as his first wife's brother shot him through the throat), and Nazli had ambitions to rule clandestinely through Farouk. Sir Miles Lampson, as the representative of Britain, had a miserable time at Fuad's funeral: he got blisters on the soles of his feet from the length of the funeral procession's march and had his top hat sprayed with blood from the throats of cattle sacrificed in Fuad's honor. Despite Nazli's hopes about solidifying her power, from the start Farouk managed to joke and chortle his way out of her attempts to make him a successful pawn.

Marriage was to come very soon. Aged seventeen, he was married to Nazli's handpicked choice for him—his seventeen-year-old bride, Farida. At this point, "Farouk the Pious," as the young king was called, was a more familiar figure in a mosque than in a brothel, and his lack of sexual confidence resulted in impotence. Stadiem tells us that, desperate to consummate his marriage, Farouk looked back to antiquity to see what sort of diet might add "vigour" to his performance in the bedchamber. The dietary habits of Alexander the Great seemed promising—in short, a continuous feast of mangoes, pigeons, and mutton, all washed down with very un-Alexanderish orangeade. This was tougher than it sounded for Farouk; mostly, he just wanted macaroni and cheese, and he used to skip breakfast and lunch. At six feet tall, beautiful, and strong, the Egyptian public cast rose petals before their king, and he was acclaimed by Boy Scouts across the land (he had been chief Boy Scout in Egypt). No indication of the excesses to come, then.

Charmingly, Farouk had an ability to shake off the miseries and responsibilities of life—perhaps not the best trait if you're king of Egypt, but certainly helpful if you're deposed. Ever the practical joker, he irritated Edward Ford with his slapstick practical jokes. Farouk picked pockets for fun and did so to Winston Churchill, filching the watch that Queen Anne had given to Winston's ancestor, the Duke of Marlborough, for his triumphs at the Battle of Blenheim. Farouk did return it later. When one Christian visitor asked him if, as a Muslim, he had heard of Palm Sunday, he replied irresistibly, "Have you heard of an ice cream sundae?" Disarmingly sweet, he kept toffees in his pocket and couldn't resist dipping in. He seemed to have the popular touch and, thanks to King Fuad's insistence, had learned to speak Arabic as a boy. When he turned up at someone's house in Burg el Arab and invited himself to dinner, he had a sheep killed for the local villagers and took great pleasure in listening to them singing around the roasting sheep that night; he stayed up until 3 a.m., puffing on big cigars and asking Pulli—sotto voce—to add a dash of whiskey to his coke. The next day, villagers sent him the sheep's kidneys and heart for his breakfast. The village also had to supply enough food to match Farouk's appetite, which was beginning to err on the wrong side of gargantuan. For breakfast, he had watermelon (they had stopped a train to get these), scrambled eggs, fish cakes, lamb chops, the sheep kidneys and, cutely, Rice Krispies. Ironically, he ate no bread whatsoever—he always avoided it, as he thought it fattening.

Pulli immediately benefited from Farouk's reign. Gone were his oily overalls, out came tuxedos. The British, also keen to manipulate Farouk, queried Pulli's fitness as a companion. Pulli and Farouk liked to roar through Cairo together in one of Farouk's fleet of two hundred cars; an insomniac, Farouk would roll out in his car at night to visit what he called "my pyramids." And Farouk himself wouldn't quite play by the British rules. When one guest at the Abdine Palace complained about the pesky Egyptian flies that kept bothering them, Farouk retorted, "Just like the British here since 1882."

Rumors abounded about Farouk's jokes and excesses. He was gossipy and idle but not stupid, just lacking in any real education (the tree climbing didn't teach him much about politics). The poor *fellaheen* (peasants) of Egypt were still plowing behind their water buffalo, while Farouk had nothing to trouble him but which particular shade of green he should order for his Mercedes. He had a private cinema into which you could fit four hundred people. Although he didn't eat bread, he loved rolling it into balls and pinging it at fellow diners. Could it have been true that the seat for guests, placed before the king's desk in Farouk's royal office, was a booby trap, rigged so that if he found you boring, with a flick of a concealed switch he could eject you through trapdoors into some murky room below?

Churchill's watch was just the beginning. Farouk was a kleptomaniac, happily appropriating anything that took his fancy. He borrowed someone's beautiful

shaving set and did not return it. If you lent him a stamp album, it would be returned—eventually—with your best stamps missing; even a sword of state that
sparkled too brightly would be admired and filched. He wooed ladies of the moment on the royal yacht, *Mahrousa*, though he also had a smaller, more intimate
vessel and liked to cruise around Cyprus or on the Turkish coast, entertaining
himself in shooting game. From this, according to biographer Stadiem:

> One of his favourite huntsman's suppers was to cook the partridge or quail that he had
> bagged, making a thick high-gusto gravy by mixing the animals' blood with egg and
> lemon, à la grecque. On the morning after, he would continue his high cholesterol orgy
> by topping off the Kellogg's Rice Krispies he loved for breakfast with a huge platter of
> eggs scrambled with the hearts and kidneys of the little game birds.

No surprise that he came to resemble a large dumpling—a dumpling who needed
a special chair built for him. Farouk tried to watch his waistline: he went on an
oyster diet (he also found them helpfully aphrodisiacal) and took vigorous massage
to help him shed inches. While twelve eggs for breakfast would still be the order
of the day, Farouk stipulated they should be poached, not fried. Vanity might just
redeem him, if not from obesity, then from baldness; he had special hair restoration
ointments rubbed into his scalp.

Dinner with Farouk was a joy. Starting at about 10 p.m., Farouk would never be
on time (much to the despair of the British) but was probably worth waiting for. He
loved to make a party of it. If anyone made what he considered too saucy a joke,
he struck a gong in mock horror. He'd offer you a light but would snap the lighter
closed on your cigarette, snatching it out of your mouth. The food was splendid, a
combination of traditional Egyptian fare and sophisticated French menus. If Egypt
was on the table, there would be lamb kebab, aromatic salads, pigeon stuffed with
green wheat, dolmades, honeyed cakes with cream, blood oranges and tangerines,
konafa (an oozy, nutty, buttery, sweet, hairy, cheesy glory with shredded filo
drenched in sugar syrup), mulakhiya (jute leaves, shredded and cooked with garlic,
chicken, rabbit, or lamb), and stuffed vegetables. The aroma of these would mingle
with that of classically French dishes such as galatine de faisan d'Écosse truffée
(truffled pheasant), pâté de gibiers à la Mirabeau (game pâté), asperges en branches
sauce divine (asparagus in a "divine" sauce), and langue de charolais à la gelée de
porto (tongue in port-wine jelly).

Farouk's gaming became legendary. There was baccarat in Cairo, roulette
wheels in Monaco, and chemin de fer in Paris. Farouk lost a fortune carelessly
and without conscience. In truth, throughout his late twenties and into his thirties, Farouk was in a slow decline. The steam ran out of his marriage to Farida
quickly; he suffered a terrible car crash in 1943; then there was the failure of Egypt
in the Arab-Israeli War after 1948 and, finally, all those summers in Europe, his

Mulakhiya

This Egyptian staple is also called Jew's mallow, nalta jute, and green mallow. It has an interestingly glutinous texture and can be used as a thickening agent in soups. I foraged a relative of it growing wild in the United Kingdom, but real mulakhiya grows in the Middle East. You can get it frozen in Arab food stores—do not venture near the dried version, as it tastes bitter and tea leafy.

FOR THE CHICKEN STOCK . . .

1 chicken, cut into eighths	Sea salt
2 sticks of cinnamon	Freshly ground black pepper
3 onions, quartered	6 pints water
3 bay leaves	

FOR FRYING THE CHICKEN . . .

1 tbsp. butter	1 tbsp. olive oil

FOR THE RICE . . .

2 cups basmati rice	Pinch of sea salt
3 tbsp. butter	4 cups water

FOR THE MULAKHIYA . . .

8 cloves of garlic, finely chopped	1 tbsp. butter
1 tbsp. coriander seed, ground finely in a mortar and pestle	2 lb. mulakhiya, shredded

METHOD

Begin by making a good chicken stock. Preheat the oven to 180°C. Place the chicken pieces in a baking tray and roast for an hour. Drain off the fat. Next, place the chicken in a large, deep saucepan. Add the cinnamon, onions, bay leaves, a pinch or two of sea salt, and freshly ground black pepper. Cover with water and bring to a boil. Once boiling, turn down the heat and let the stock simmer away, uncovered, for about 3 hours or until you have 2 cups of stock left. Drain the chicken pieces; strip the flesh off the bone. Melt 1 tablespoon of butter with 1 tablespoon of olive oil in a skillet, bring the temperature right up, and fry the chicken pieces until they are crispy. Arrange them on a plate and keep warm.

Next, wash the rice in warm water. Into a saucepan, put 3 teaspoons of butter, a pinch of sea salt, and pour over the 4 cups of water. Bring to a boil, and then add the rice. Give it a good stir; then cover and turn the heat down to low. The rice will be ready in about 12 minutes.

In a skillet, heat the butter. To this, add the crushed coriander seeds and half the garlic. Cook on a high heat until the garlic turns deep gold. Set to one side.

Pour 2 cups of chicken stock into a pan. Add the uncooked remaining half of the garlic and the chopped mulakhiya leaves. Bring the mulakhiya mixture up to a simmer, but do not boil. When it reaches this stage, add the coriander-garlic butter. The mulakhiya is now ready to serve on top of the rice, with the shards of fried chicken alongside.

coarseness encouraged by the gambling tables, nightclubs, women, and his own voracious, unseemly appetite. Even as his hold over Egypt crumbled, his wife grew to hate him, and his people lost faith in him, even while Nasser plotted his overthrow, Farouk continued to preside over a fiefdom of excesses, a palace built of vol-au-vents, with fountains of orangeade.

Many were his enemies, ready to blacken his reputation further. Farouk claimed his enemies in Israel put it about that he owned several whiskey distilleries in Jerusalem. In a plot to set him up, at least two dozen body doubles—some imbeciles, some fraudsters—had photos taken of themselves with beauty queens, pork chops, bacon sandwiches, and strong whiskeys.

Cairo in the early 1950s was glittering, cosmopolitan, Parisian. Farouk, in the clinquant, many-winged Abdine Palace, its rooms filled with lustrous gold, ringed by a scurf of slums, seemed blind to the social reform. In his memoirs, Adel Sabit, a cousin of Farouk's, describes the average tea party set out among the oleander on the shaded lawns of the Abdine Palace. *Suffragis* (table servants) from Sudan, liveried in blue and gold, poured drinks.

> An enormous table has been laid out, with cakes of every conceivable size and shape. A voluptuously inviting sacher torte rubs shoulders with lemon chiffon pie, strawberry shortcake, Black Forest gateau, mille feuilles en masse and an absolutely enormous crème Chantilly filled with meringues. There is, of course, the usual collection of batons sales, canapes, savoury pies and sandwiches a la Bourbon. There is tea, lemonade, orangeade, mango juice, sugar-cane juice and strawberry sundaes. Small tables are spread around the glade.

Farouk's vast feasts seemed increasingly grotesque. To celebrate the birth of his longed-for son with his second wife, Narriman, he treated six hundred luminaries to île flotant. His power was as nebulous as the meringue.

Farouk divorced Farida in 1948: he needed a wife who would give him a son. Then, in 1949, after a childhood of Nazli's boiling cauldrons, it is not surprising that Farouk put great faith in his royal fortune-teller, and when this individual saw through the mists that Farouk would meet the mother of his future son in a jewelry shop, lo and behold, he did just that (it turns out the jeweler bribed the fortune-teller).

The blonde, curvy teenager Narriman Sadek was busy choosing her engagement ring when Farouk "bumped into her" at the jewelry shop. She was with her fiancé, who didn't stand a chance against Farouk's kingly wiles and who was, besides, "quite small," in Narriman's words. She, meanwhile, was bewitched by Farouk's bank account and, as she told the *Ladies Home Journal* in February 1953, "his shoulders fascinated me, and his arms and his powerful wrists [were] covered with dark virile hair." Narriman was yet another teenage bride for Farouk, by which

Île Flotant

FOR THE MERINGUES . . .

6 room-temperature egg whites
1 tsp. lemon juice
Generous ½ cup vanilla sugar

2 pints milk
2 vanilla pods, split down the belly

FOR THE CUSTARD . . .

10 egg yolks
Scant ½ cup caster or granulated sugar

FOR THE CARAMEL . . .

½ cup granulated sugar

4 tbsp. water

METHOD

Begin by making the meringues. Get a large, very clean bowl and put the egg whites in there with the teaspoon of lemon juice. Whisk into soft peaks, adding 1 ounce of sugar at a time, until you have molded, massy meringue.

Pour the milk into a large, shallow pan. Add the 2 vanilla pods and, gently, bring to a boil, allowing the vanilla pods to infuse the milk. When the milk is simmering, using 2 warmed tablespoons, make quenelles of the raw meringue, and plop these gently into the milk. Cover and poach the meringues for around 8 minutes. When 4 minutes are up, roll each meringue quenelle over gently. After the allotted time, drain the meringue quenelles using a slotted spoon and place them on a fine mesh wire tray. Keep the delicious, vanilla-infused poaching milk; you will use it to make custard.

To make the custard, remove the vanilla pods from the milk, and then put the poaching milk into a saucepan and heat until it is close to boiling. Whisk together the egg yolks and granulated sugar. Gently pour the hot poaching milk into the egg yolks, incorporating it vigorously with a whisk. Return this mixture to the saucepan. Stirring continuously with a wooden spoon, heat this over a medium flame until the custard thickens and clings to the back of the wooden spoon. When it has "custardized" remove the mixture from the heat and allow the custard to cool, agitating it for the first 5 or 10 minutes to make sure it remains smooth and loose. When the custard has completely cooled, pool it onto a serving dish and arrange the white meringue quenelles over the surface of the custard so that they do, indeed, resemble floating, snowy islands on a custard sea. Chill this for a couple of hours.

Just before serving, you must make the caramel. In a heavy-bottomed, small saucepan, combine the water and sugar. Cook over a medium heat until the sugar dissolves and the sugar water caramelizes, deepening to a dark gold. Remove the meringues and custard from the fridge. Drizzle the caramel over the meringues and serve straightaway. Your île flotant will serve about 4 people rather than Farouk's 200.

point he was far from being a teenager at a burly thirty years old. He wasted no time in proposing and sent Narriman to Rome for etiquette lessons. Farouk even had the cheek to put her on a diet before marriage. Meanwhile, in the lead-up to their union, Farouk went to Deauville, France, arriving in a modest caravan of seven Cadillacs, as inconspicuous, one newspaper dryly observed, "as a brigade of fire engines," and taking a twenty-one-room suite on the fifteenth floor of the Hotel du Golfe, booked under the pseudonym Mr. Fouad al Masri Pasha. There he enjoyed, round-eyed, the gyrations of belly dancer Samia Gamel performing "The Virgin of the Nile." His Nubian food tasters made sure no assassin was on hand, but any assassin would have been more successful had they simply left Farouk to eat himself to death: "Farouk . . . ate enough cream sauces to warrant his own dairy as well as a coronary unit. One of his menus at the hotel featured sole a la crème, cote de veau a la crème, champignons a la crème, and framboises a la crème."

Off on a cruising honeymoon, Farouk and Narriman set out on the royal yacht, managing to embark on the eve of Ramadan—not a gesture that was going to endear Farouk to his Muslim subjects. And again an air of comedy clings to Farouk; there was something parodic about the newlyweds' appearance, dressed in identical navy sailor suits, each with a white yachting cap perched on his or her head.

The hot summer of 1952 blasted Egypt and witnessed the overthrow of Farouk. There had been raging anti-British civil unrest in January of that year: the opera house, Barclay's Bank, was looted, and the colonial Turf Club and its octogenarian members were laid to waste. Farouk declared martial law. The U.S. Central Intelligence Agency (CIA) backed Gamal Abdel Nasser to overthrow him (the CIA operation was called "Project FF"—"FF" standing for "Fat Fucker"). The wonderful colonial Shepheard's Hotel was torched—this was where the likes of General Gordon of Khartoum, the explorer Sir Richard Burton, and Lawrence of Arabia had sipped tea or cool gin slings (though at least one mid-Victorian travelers' handbook warned of the quality of its food)—its ashes leaving no sign of the European lovelies who had danced the Charleston there. And, of course, Farouk banqueted while Cairo burned.

His abdication was forced, and Farouk had to flee Egypt. Was he penniless? A faithful secretary had stuffed $600 in his pocket (it must have been empty of toffees), but that was all he had, claimed one newspaper. The Egyptian monarchs departed Alexandria, a trail of luggage in their wake into which was tucked gold ingots and jewels. Crates of whiskey and fizz among his possessions were testimony to Farouk's un-Islamic habits. The guards under orders to search his possessions tut-tutted; all those orange sodas had been too good to be true. Good Muslims themselves, the guards had no interest in pilfering the bottles or handling them. Brilliantly, Farouk had hidden away his fortune among the bottles; those were gold ingots rattling within the cases rather than booze. When his palace was reclaimed by revolutionaries, they found his stashes of hash and porn ranging from the fumbling, grubby sort through to mosaics of naked women in strenuous sexual poses. Mind you, Farouk's father, King Fuad, had been no angel: he had his female Circassian servant sleep at the foot of his bed. And Queen Nazli's taste in interior design in her private drawing room ran to saucy life-size images of sodomy and bestiality (Nazli, incidentally, was exiled by Farouk and ended up converting to Catholicism and living in Beverly Hills).

Abandoned by the British, forgotten by the Americans, Farouk left on his yacht, *Mahrousa*, on a cheerless journey, with the odd torpedo or two to dodge, to exile in Naples. The voyage seemed the gloomier due to a shortage of food on board; supplies were limited to oil, cheese, and bread, and the fallen royal family had only one daily meal of a grilled cheese sandwich. Food-wise things looked up by the time they'd settled in Anacapri in twenty rooms of the Eden Paradiso Hotel, perched on Capri in the Italian Riviera. Stadiem records, "Farouk laid out a first supper for his family of spaghetti marinara, cold lobster with mayonnaise, steak and French fries, green salad, chocolate ice cream, white peaches and a case of orangeade."

In exile, with his pomp and glory battered, Farouk's marriage to Narriman took a short time to flounder. She had flounced out by March 1953 and was whisked back to Egypt by Farouk's formidable mother-in-law, Mrs. Sadek, who, Farouk said, was "the most terrible woman in the world." Farouk was left to stagger around in small swimming trunks, his large paunch hanging over them, on the beaches of Capri and in Gracie Field's lush beach club, the Canzone del Mare.

Even though his appearance was a far cry from his boy-king polished good looks, right to the end a reputation for wealth clung to him, and his kingly status was a glamorous lure to women. He loved strip joints and had an affair with Swedish bombshell Brigitta Stenberg, a former lover of "Lucky" Luciano. Farouk fed her sugared Egyptian loukoum; she licked the sugar from his fingers while he chided her for her bad manners. In Naples, he spotted his last regular mistress, sixteen-year-old Neapolitan Irma Capece Minutolo, breasts spilling out of her bra, a would-be opera singer whom Farouk made eyes at over her spaghetti alla vongole veraci (spaghetti with clams). Habitually, when in Rome, he ordered gold compacts from a local jeweler to give to amorous young ladies. When money was short—which it increasingly was—Farouk sold chunks of jewelry.

By his forty-fifth year, Farouk's Rolls-Royce had been sold. He had been demoted to beetling about in a white Fiat, but, nevertheless, he knew how to woo. On the last night of his life, he persuaded twenty-something-year-old hairdresser Annamaria Gatti to accompany him to dinner. They drove to a little place he knew called Ile de France. It was midnight. In between mouthfuls of Coca-Cola and a bottle or two of soda water, Farouk swallowed raw oysters—possibly with a wink at Annamaria?—pepped up with a spike of tabasco, a rich lobster thermidor, a slice or ten of abbacchio al forno (roast lamb, sweet-scented with rosemary, with crunchy roast

Loukoum (Turkish Delight)

INGREDIENTS

1½ cups granulated sugar
1 tsp. lemon juice
¾ cup water
½ tsp. cream of tartar
1 cup cornstarch
1½ cups water
2 tsp. rose water or orange
   flower water

½ cup green pistachios, halved
   (optional)
Cochineal food coloring (to go with
   rose flavoring)
Orange food coloring (to go with
   orange flower water)

FOR THE LOUKOUM TIN . . .

1 tbsp. olive oil
1 tbsp. cornstarch combined with
   1 tbsp. confectioner's sugar

FOR COATING THE LOUKOUM . . .

5 tbsp. confectioner's sugar   1 tbsp. cornstarch

METHOD

In a heavy-bottomed saucepan, combine the granulated sugar and lemon juice with the water. Place over a medium heat. Stir at first, helping the sugar to dissolve. Then bring the sugar syrup to a boil. Once it has reached boiling point, reduce the heat to a simmer and cook—without stirring—for 35–40 minutes. I use a jam thermometer to check that the sugar syrup reaches a temperature of 240°C. Have a bowl of very cold water handy; a drop of the syrup should, at 240°C, form a pliable little ball when dropped into the cold water.

Into a large, heavy-bottomed saucepan, pour the cream of tartar and cornstarch and whisk in the water. Get this mixture smooth. Now heat moderately until the mixture becomes very thick. Slowly add the sugar syrup—whisking will become more and more of a struggle, but you have to persevere and not panic! Once it has combined, cook gently over a very low heat for between 30 minutes and 1 hour; the loukoum is ready when it is golden and very thick. Make sure you stir it often; as you can imagine, it can weld itself to the pan.

Now add the rose water or the orange flower water, depending on what flavor you wish your loukoum to be. Add cochineal coloring, too, drop by drop to get just the right shade of rose, or use orange coloring the same way if you are making orange flower water loukoum. Stir in the halved pistachios if you wish to use them.

Line a square tin with plastic wrap, oil lightly, and then dust with the combined tablespoons of cornstarch and confectioner's sugar. Empty the loukoum over this base. Allow it to cool overnight, covered.

The next day, dust a work surface with the confectioner's sugar and the cornstarch. Tip the block of loukoum out onto this, cut into 1-inch squares, and roll these in the sugar dust. Now enjoy the rich, sticky, and perfumed loukoum with someone who will lick your fingers.

potatoes soaking up the lamb juices), and green beans. Finally, he savored mouthfuls of Monte Bianco, spooning dollops into Annamaria's pretty mouth.

Sated at last, Farouk sat back, lit one of his big Havana cigars, and inhaled deeply. Suddenly, his eyes bulged, his mouth gaped, and Farouk clutched at his throat. His head fell back. Annamaria thought it was Farouk's pantomimic sense of humor, but then she started to scream.

One could say that Farouk was always only a belly dancer or a fried egg away from such a sticky end, but conspiracies abound. Had he been poisoned by the Egyptian secret service?

Could Ibrahim Baghdadi—who went by the cheerful nickname "the Undertaker" (because he smuggled and drugged Nasser dissidents back into Egypt in coffins)—be his poisoner? Baghdadi was in Rome at the same time and even purported to have worked as a waiter in the past at Ile de France.

Farouk was declared dead of a brain hemorrhage. But there was no autopsy. Rumor has it that it was the lobster what done it. Annamaria was never seen again.

A LAST SUPPER
Abbacchio al Forno

INGREDIENTS

½ leg of lamb, still on the bone
2 tbsp. olive oil
6 cloves of garlic, crushed
A handful of fresh rosemary, chopped
A handful of fresh sage, chopped

6 floury potatoes, peeled and split into halves
Sea salt
Freshly ground black pepper
1 glass good-quality dry white wine

METHOD
Preheat the oven to 180°C. In a bowl, combine the olive oil with the garlic, rosemary, and sage. Put the lamb in a roasting pan. Make deep scores and slashes in the lamb, and then, using your hands, massage the herby, garlicky oil into the meat, penetrating into the cuts. Arrange the potatoes around the lamb and drizzle the remaining flavored oil (plus a tablespoonful or two extra of plain olive oil) over the potatoes. Salt and pepper the whole lot. Cook for between 60 and 90 minutes, adding the white wine after 30 minutes and turning the potatoes. Serve when the lamb is no longer pink and the potatoes are crunchy and golden.

Monte Bianco

FOR THE CHESTNUT CREAM . . .

3½ cups precooked chestnuts
1 pint milk
3 tbsp. granulated sugar

2 tsp. unsweetened cocoa powder
3 tbsp. brandy or dark rum

Monte Bianco (*continued*)

FOR DUSTING THE MOUNTAIN . . .
2 tbsp. unsweetened cocoa powder

FOR THE CARAMEL . . .
½ cup granulated sugar   4 tbsp. water

FOR THE MOUNTAIN SNOW . . .
½ cup heavy cream, whipped   ½ cup confectioner's sugar
until light and fluffy

METHOD
In a large pan, combine the chestnuts and milk. Bring to a boil; simmer for 15 minutes and then allow to cool. Blend this mixture in a food processor, spooning in the granulated sugar and cocoa powder. Now gradually add the brandy or dark rum. Cool this mixture completely.

Equip yourself with a piping bag. It is time to build your mountain of chestnut puree. Pipe the chilled mixture onto a serving plate, building the puree into a stringy mountain. If you don't have a piping bag, press the chestnut puree through a mouli; it will come out as fat little worms, which you can build up into a mountain. Dust it by dredging the cocoa powder over it.

Now make the caramel. In a heavy-bottomed saucepan, mix together the water and sugar. Cook, without stirring, over a medium heat until the sugar water caramelizes. When it is dark gold, drizzle the caramel over the mountain. Leave this to cool and become brittle.

In a bowl, whip the heavy cream with the confectioner's sugar until you have a glossy pile to empty onto the top of the mountain. Now your Monte Bianco is ready. Take it easy, now!

THE DOOMED DINNERS OF CHARLES AND DI

Though there was little to suggest that the young, rosy-cheeked, and bright-lipped schoolgirl Diana Spencer would one day be Princess Diana, wife of Charles, the heir to the throne of Britain, there is plenty in her schooldays to suggest a fascination with food. At school in West Heath, the pantry was a treasured haunt of hers, and she loved binging in illegal cargoes of food treats to school when she returned after holidays at home. Baked beans, All-Bran cereal; as Diana remembered, "I ate and ate and ate. It was always a great joke—let's get Diana to have three kippers at breakfast and six pieces of bread, and I did all that." If only her application to schoolwork had matched her application to the plate. Leaving school with no qualifications, she was hustled off to finishing school—the posh but goofy Institut Alpin Videmanette in Switzerland—to learn dressmaking and skiing but she bombed out of that (although her thank-you letters were always exemplary). With no small amount of desperation, encouraged by Diana's supposed love of all things domestic, her parents sent her on a cookery course in Wimbledon, run by one Elizabeth Russell. Diana recalled, "I did a cookery course in Wimbledon. I quite liked it . . . I got terribly fat. I loved sauces, my fingers were always in the saucepans for which I got fined. It wasn't my idea of fun but my parents wanted me to do it. At the time it seemed a better alternative than being behind a typewriter—and I got a diploma!"

Meanwhile, Charles Windsor, the young heir to the British throne, was always interested in cooking, too. He was perhaps a bit of a prodigy: he loved making his own popsicles, even investing in a set of lollipop sticks and a plastic tray. Life at Buckingham Palace was heavenly to him, happy and cozy, with his favorite bread-and-butter puddings, but Prince Philip thought his son was a bit too much of a softie and wanted to toughen Charles up at Philip's old school, Gordonstoun, in the bleak northeast of Scotland. It was "Colditz in kilts." Charles's life wasn't always a happy one there; he wanted to run away and hide in the forest. He was bullied and wrote a plaintive letter home in 1963: "The people in my dormitory are foul. Goodness, they are horrid. I don't know how anybody could be so foul." He snored and the other boys threw slippers at him, and then he grew rather odd-looking in his teenage years, with sticky-out ears (these had always left him open to insults), a substantial Adam's apple, and a voice that was breaking. To top it all, the scandal of the cherry brandy affair broke. Fourteen-year-old Charles was with a party of schoolboys on Gordonstoun's training yacht, *Pinta*. They had berthed on the Hebridean island of Lewis—in the harbor of the town of Stornoway, no less. Seagulls and locals were all clustered around the windows of the Crown Hotel, murmuring to each other in Gaelic, spying on Charles trying to have a bite to eat. Shyness made him panic, and he decided to take refuge in the bar, although he didn't really know what to order there. Suddenly, he remembered the queen giving him a mouthful of cherry brandy on a royal shoot. Flustered and hunted, when the barmaid asked for his order, he blurted out, "Cherry brandy, please," took an uneasy sip, and the world exploded; a personal bodyguard hauled him out.

When Diana applied for work as a teacher's assistant at the Young England Kindergarten in London's posh Pimlico district, her job reference said that she was keen to help out, especially with washing up. She bought her luxury flat at Colherne Court, furnished it with wicker chairs and tables, and had great fun with her roommates there. She plastered a sign on her door saying "Chief Chick," and when the girls held dinner parties there, Diana often got up before everyone had finished eating in order to wash the dishes; dirty dishes always preyed on her mind. Prince Charles was getting closer and closer. He dated Diana's red-haired sister Sarah, an anorexic at the time, with the opening charmer "Do you have anorexia?" Not a great line, but something worked!

The prince was under considerable pressure to marry. He was increasingly seen as an oddball prince, taunted by the British press for his love of nut roast cutlets and for talking to his plants; he called it "instructing them." Charles's detective, Inspector Paul House, relished the fact that he was one of the best-fed policemen in the world, as he shared the prince's food. Hearing this, Princess Anne's detective grumbled about having to share her diet of scrambled eggs and Coca-Cola. Indeed, when Prince Charles and his valet first moved into his new home of Highgrove in 1980, the first thing they did was pick spinach from the gardens there for delicious, fresh eggs Florentine (later, Camilla Parker Bowles lent him her chef) cooked on the blue Aga stove.

Eggs Florentine

FOR THE SPINACH . . .
2 tbsp. butter
½ lb. spinach, cleaned
¼ cup heavy cream

Sea salt
Freshly ground black pepper

FOR THE HOLLANDAISE SAUCE . . .
3 egg yolks
Generous cup butter, diced
Sea salt

Freshly ground black pepper
A dash of freshly squeezed lemon

FOR THE POACHED EGGS . . .
4 eggs
Buttered toast

Eggs Florentine (*continued*)

METHOD

Begin by cooking the spinach. In a skillet, melt a tablespoon of butter. When this is bubbling, add the spinach; it will take about 4 minutes to wilt. Drain the spinach, pressing it to remove any excess water. Wash the skillet. Now melt the next tablespoon of butter in the skillet. Pour in the cream and, over a medium heat, reduce it for a few minutes. Next add the cooked spinach; stir it through, and then add sea salt and black pepper. Keep this all warm.

Put a saucepan of water on to boil; this will be for poaching your eggs, which you will do immediately after making the hollandaise sauce.

Now it is time to make the hollandaise sauce. Put the egg yolks into a Pyrex bowl and place this over a pan of simmering water—the water must not touch the bowl. Whisk instantaneously and vigorously, slowly adding the diced butter to the egg yolks. Make sure you incorporate the butter with the egg yolk thoroughly each time before adding the next lot of butter. Never race at this stage. Once the butter and egg have emulsified, switch from a whisk to a wooden spoon—keep stirring. The hollandaise will thicken enough to coat the back of the wooden spoon. Remove from the heat; add a dash of lemon juice and season with sea salt and black pepper.

Check that the saucepan of water you put on earlier is now at a gentle boil. Using a spurtle, agitate the water so that it forms a whirlpool. Crack the eggs and drop them into the whirlpool one by one; this will help them retain a good shape. Let them simmer for 3 minutes (this should produce a nice, runny yolk). When ready, remove the eggs with a slotted spoon and drain.

Finally, toast the bread and butter it. Put a generous scoop of creamy spinach on each slice of toast. Top with a poached egg, and then put a dollop of slippery, buttery hollandaise on top of that.

Nut Roast Cutlet

INGREDIENTS

1 tbsp. olive oil
1 onion, finely chopped
2 cloves of garlic, crushed
½ cup hazelnuts, toasted and then roughly ground
1 cup walnuts, toasted and roughly ground
1 cup Brazil nuts, roughly ground
2 cups whole wheat breadcrumbs
3 tsp. brown linseeds

1 tsp. poppy seeds
½ tsp. fresh thyme leaves
½ tsp. dried oregano
Sea salt
Freshly ground black pepper
½ tbsp. tomato puree
2 tsp. yeast extract, mixed into ½ pint vegetable stock
1 egg, beaten

Nut Roast Cutlet (*continued*)

TO COAT THE NUT CUTLETS . . .

1 egg beaten
2 cups brown breadcrumbs

3 tbsp. olive oil for frying cutlets

METHOD

Warm olive oil in a skillet and sauté the finely chopped onion and garlic until the onion is soft and pale gold. Now put the fried onion and garlic in a large mixing bowl and add the ground nuts, breadcrumbs, linseed, poppy seed, thyme, and oregano. Mix thoroughly. Salt and pepper. Now add the tomato puree, the yeast extract vegetable stock, and the beaten egg. Use your hands to mix thoroughly, shaping the nut paste into about 10 patties or cutlets. Into 2 shallow plates, respectively, put the beaten egg and the brown breadcrumbs. Dip each cutlet into the egg, then the breadcrumbs. Now put the cutlets in the fridge for 40 minutes to firm up. Heat olive oil in a skillet until it is nice and hot, and fry the cutlets in batches until they are brown and crispy, draining them on a paper towel. Serve with salad and coleslaw.

The public focus on Diana became intense during her relationship with, and subsequent engagement to, Charles from 1980 to 1981. She metamorphosed from a voracious eater into an obsessive weight-watcher. Diana became fixated on her image; she was incessantly being photographed and couldn't bear to look dumpy or puffy. She hardly stood still; she did exercises, attended ballet sessions, did tap and jazz dancing. But Charles's valet observed, "She loved eating sweets. She always got into the car with her Yorkie bars or bags of toffees." Vomiting increasingly offered the ideal combination of eating indulgent and delicious things while not paying the high-calorie price. Soon she was scoffing whole chocolate cakes (a sweet Prince Charles loathed), bowls of Frosties with fruit and heavy cream, and a leg of lamb, and then vomiting. Fiancé Charles, as ever sensitive to troubled women's needs, told her, "You're getting a bit chubby." For Diana, it was a death knell!

Of course, Charles had fallen in love forever with the unreachable, married Camilla Parker Bowles, but Diana was also disingenuous. Charles, a lover of the outdoors and a food forager who liked to eat the game he had shot, slices of gamey snipe from the Sandringham grounds, thought he was in luck when he met Diana. Here was a cheery, lively, and uncomplicated girl who adored the same things as him: hunting, fishing, fresh air, polo. But Diana had pulled the wool over his eyes; she'd really like to have been painting her nails, listening to pop music, and shopping. Keen to get her man, Diana went through all the various ordeals a bride-to-be does, including having lunch with her prospective mother-in-law. Diana had pretty red tights on and a pack of the queen's corgis careered toward her, barking; she suddenly realized they were fascinated by her red tights: "I thought, My God, what if they think my legs are steak? I had visions of the whole lot of them tearing into me and devouring my legs." It was difficult not to burst out laughing.

Diana moved into Buckingham Palace when her engagement to Charles was announced, and soon it was all pear gratins, borscht, watercress soup, souffléd exotic fruits, and goujons of sole dusted in panko breadcrumbs. Often Diana tried to curb her appetite by eating lots of fruit. She had grapefruit for breakfast and could work her way through a pound of lychees at a time—and always opted for low-calorie grilled trout or lobster, with a cup of ginger tea. But it became increasingly hard as bulimia took hold. To keep the common touch, she might get the servants to smuggle a Big Mac into the palace, or she would slum it with caviar piled onto a baked jacket potato.

When they became "Mr. and Mrs. Wales," as Diana liked them to call themselves, there were many, many unspoken complications hanging over them on their wedding day in 1981, tangled among the wedding bunting. Charles told his aide the night before, "I can't go through with it," and Diana had been encouraged to continue the engagement by her sisters, who said, "Once your face is on the tea towels, it's too late." Still, the mismatched couple managed to choke down quenelles of brill in lobster and brioche-crumbed chicken breasts stuffed with a lamb mousse, garnished with Norfolk samphire and mint sauce. On the honeymoon on the royal yacht, *Britannia*, around the Mediterranean, relations between the two went from bad to worse. Diana's heart sank when Prince Charles introduced her to his honeymoon stack of reading: chapters and pages from Laurens van der Post and Carl Jung. He thought they could work their way through and discuss them over lunch every day. Diana didn't read and had no intellectual inquisitiveness, so the shared mood of the couple was brackish. His conversation bored her, and she felt abandoned whenever he wanted to read or paint. She was inquisitive enough to discover his cuff links, however, engraved with an entwined "CC" for "Camilla and Charles." Soon bulimia was in charge, and Diana ate bowlfuls of jelly and custard from the fridge before applying her fake tan and then going off for a vomit. The *Britannia*'s staff was amazed at her ability to eat huge amounts and stay as thin as a rake. Charles kept his nose buried in the safer world offered by the pages of Carl Jung rather than deal with the smell of vomit souring the wedding bed.

The marriage teetered on, year by unrelenting year. Apart from the joy their children brought, there was little real connection between Charles, foraging for cèpes or cutting wild nettles for soup at his house in Highgrove, and "Disco Di." Charles was up promptly at 7:30 a.m., supping on Earl Grey tea sweetened with honey, and then, to the burble of BBC Radio 4, did his mandatory sit-ups in his boxer shorts while his valet (in flannels and blazer) sat on his ankles. Diana would swim instead and then sit down to a grapefruit breakfast—Charles had herb bread, though if a boiled egg passed his lips, it had to be cooked for three minutes exactly—and read the gossip columns. Bad commentary on her might mean Diana smashed some china or ran wailing down the corridor. Charles was spotted heading into his chicken shed to avoid Diana's fury. The war was fought over meals, too. Diana ordered dinner for herself and her sons in front of the TV in her bedroom at Highgrove, leaving Charles staring at the wall over dinner for one and a gin martini. Increasingly, Charles stayed behind at Highgrove, his friends clustering about him, while Diana withdrew to London. The first explosions of the "War of the Windsors" could be heard. Charles's love affair with Camilla renewed; staff at her house—Middlewick House, not far from Highgrove—nicknamed him "the Prince of Darkness," as he always turned up under the cover of darkness, and Camilla would black out the house, drawing every blind and curtain before the two took an intimate supper. They also noted that although Camilla never cooked, she always made Charles his breakfast. Diana called Camilla "the Rottweiler" or "the Presence," while Charles's set of friends named Diana the "Mad Cow," as she was always eavesdropping, looking for evidence against Charles, riffling through letters. Diana, in a way that characterized her isolation, began turning up increasingly in the kitchens of Buckingham Palace, hunting out a sweet snack or two from the chefs, who observed, "The prince hadn't been to the kitchens for years. They are right at the back of the palace and miles from anywhere. It seemed a long way to go for an apple." Diana liked to come into the kitchen, kick off her shoes, perch on the table, and say, "Right, let's have the gossip!" But let not this camaraderie deceive you—she could then, in a quick turn of temper, later pull rank on her servants, firing off the epithet "Stupid" when her needs were not met, jibing and taunting those in her power. One such occasion was witnessed by the Windsors' long-suffering housekeeper at Highgrove, Wendy Berry. Diana systematically bullied her personal dresser, Evelyn. When she took the princess's morning tray into her bedroom, Diana roared at her, "God, Evelyn . . . What on earth have you been eating? You absolutely stink of curry. Get out and wash your hair, will you. I can't stand that smell." Poor Evelyn was reduced to tears; fearful about having eaten a curry the night before, she'd been up since the early hours scrubbing her hair and body.

Charles, meanwhile, left to his own devices, was increasingly happy in Diana-free Highgrove, with his smart little Jack Russell terrier Tigger. Tigger, though, was less popular in the kitchen, and when Tigger sneaked into the kitchen for a snoop about the Aga stove, the chef popped him into the (gently) warm oven. The staff on duty giggled but jumped guiltily when the prince popped his head around the door: "Has anyone seen Tigger?" The culprit mutely shook his head, cursing Tigger for making scratching noises as he tried to dig his way out of the oven. "I think I saw him heading towards the garden," he managed to choke out. The prince immediately strode off in the direction of the dahlias, giving the chef a chance to let Tigger burst forth indignantly from the oven.

So much does Charles love the food he grows at Highgrove that he carts it around the world—he even turns up with it in Balmoral—and he likes as many as six different types of honey at breakfast; plus he's quite keen on Bran Flakes, lemon refresher drinks, and homemade Chocolate Oliver cookies (these are malty, plain cookies smothered in chocolate). This food fussiness can cause offense. Take, for instance, his visit to Chatsworth House and the Duchess of Devonshire. Charles wanted the "perfect" picnic sandwich, as the chef at Chatsworth recalled: "Charles wanted a homemade granary bap [roll] exactly eight centimetres in diameter, and cut in half. . . . I was told I had to cut it exactly to size if it were too big or small. I would butter the first half with mayonnaise, add pesto, shredded salad leaves and an egg, which had to be fried on both sides so that it was not runny. I would then have to season the eggs and add two thin slices of Gruyere cheese." Even this was not enough; the second half of the granary bap should be buttered and smeared with a dash of marmite. The two halves could then be united. Finally, Charles wished his roll to look "rustic," so the chef had to shake a little white flour over it.

Diana was far better at befriending "ordinary people" than Charles. Her large Chanel handbag flung over her shoulder, she insisted that people she met call her Diana. (Charles insisted on being called Charles in America, as Americans were prone to saying "Hi Prince!") Once she and Charles had separated, Diana moved into apartments in Kensington Palace, and among the eclectic friends she gathered about her was the spiritual healer Simone Simmons, who turned up to exorcise Kensington Palace of leftover bad energy from Diana's failed marriage. There were nineteen rooms in Diana's share of Kensington Palace, so Simmons had her work cut out (the palace also has all sorts of ancient creatures of royal kinship tucked into its many rooms; King Edward VIII used to call it the "Aunt Heap"). One evening, alarmed, Diana called Simmons: she had to get to Kensington Palace double-quick to cleanse it of a particularly bad and smelly marital spirit. Simmons went round, perhaps with holy water and a cross, but it turned out the evil-spirit smell was very similar to what is produced by British gas. Oh yes, Diana had blown out the pilot lights on her grill, believing "some idiot had left them on." Ho hum. In her book on Diana, Simmons offers amusing insights into Diana's practical understanding of food:

> Upstairs at Kensington Palace there was a well-equipped little kitchen, very clinical and stainless-steely, where the boys' meals would sometimes be prepared. Diana scarcely used it, however, preferring to use the huge, staffed one. She was so proud when she eventually learned how to heat a ready-made pasta meal or "cook" a baked potato in the microwave oven. Then, having torn the cellophane off a store's pre-prepared salad, she might proudly present an informal supper.

Note the phrase "eventually learned." Toasted cheese was within her grasp, but cooking pasta was as puzzling as the theory of relativity. When, food-wise, she was taking a trip down memory lane, she'd make guests her special bacon sandwich—it was special because she had learned to make it for herself in her old singleton flat. Generously, she also offered these bacon sandwiches to some Pakistani visitors to Kensington Palace.

Restlessly, Diana was searching for something more spiritual, beyond colonic irrigation and aromatherapy: a lover—though he would have to scramble over all the fluffy toys she kept on the bed (these included a felt frog, some koalas, penguins, and the odd wombat) to get to her. Enter James Hewitt, a staff captain in the Household Division, who first became close to Diana in 1986 during riding lessons at Windsor Castle on a horse called Gary. This, and all the lunches afterward in the Officers' Mess, led to increased rapport and mutual affection. James spent a lot of time mooning and dreaming about Diana over supper-for-one at the Suntory Japanese restaurant in St. James's, London. Perhaps he should have been looking up the word *treason* under T in the *Encyclopaedia Britannia*.

Finally, Diana invited him to her place for dinner. Over champagne, the paramours made small talk about traffic conditions on the M4. At the table, Diana reverted to mineral water, as she felt tipsy, but encouraged James to drink deeply of Chablis and claret. Having dismissed the staff, she demurely insisted on serving James from the hot plate on the sideboard herself, carefully laying out slices of roast beef, rare, on his plate, alongside nut-brown new potatoes and tiny, young carrots. When it came to dessert, she cut him a robust wedge of apple tart, reserving only a slim strip for herself. James drenched his in cream. Then she made her move, nestling into his lap, followed by an adjournment to the bedroom.

After lovemaking, Diana lay in his arms and wept for a long time. Of course. James, meanwhile, had all sorts of funny and not very pleasant thoughts about whether Prince Charles had ever slept where he was now.

The San Lorenzo trattoria in swanky Knightsbridge had already been a lovers' haunt for Diana when she was having an affair with car salesman James Gilbey. The restaurant's owner, Italian Mara Berni, always found a special corner in her restaurant for Diana, even acting as a "posting box" for illicit love letters. Diana favored Mara's astrological readings, delivered in hushed, confidential tones. Behind the rustle of paper menus and raffia, while Diana pretended to eat a lobster salad and James absorbed vast amounts of spaghetti alle vongole, Mara foresaw remarkable happiness ahead for them. Hopefully Mara's food was better than her clairvoyance.

Spaghetti alle Vongole

FOR THE SPAGHETTI . . .

6 oz. spaghetti

1 tbsp. butter

FOR THE VONGOLE . . .

1 tbsp. olive oil

1 tbsp. butter

2 cloves of garlic, chopped

Half a red chili, chopped

½ lb. small, raw clams

¼ cup good dry white wine

1 tbsp. flat-leaf parsley, chopped

2 tsp. finely grated lemon zest

A squeeze of lemon juice

Sea salt

Freshly ground black pepper

METHOD

Clean the clams thoroughly and then drain them. Put a large, roomy pot of water on and bring to a boil; add the spaghetti. Cook it until it is just about al dente, then drain and butter the spaghetti. In a skillet, heat the olive oil and butter. Add the garlic and red chili and sauté for a minute or two. Now add the clams and splash the wine on. Cover the skillet and let the clams cook and open in the aromatic wine cloud. After a couple of minutes, take off the lid and discard any unopened clams. Tweak half the clams out of their shells; add the spaghetti, chopped parsley, lemon zest, and juice. Combine thoroughly and then salt and pepper to taste.

Diana developed a brilliantly inane code of touching her nose whenever she was thinking of James, doing it, for instance, when she met his gaze. The couple also stole days together at Highgrove when Charles wasn't there. They wandered through his herb garden together (the cheek of it!), and there were summer puddings in the summer and steaming puddings with custard in the winter. On illicit evenings, Diana and James shared a high-octane romance with some very prosaic elements: together they'd eat pheasant, steak, duck, or cottage pie from lap trays as they watched videos. Diana loved the British soap *EastEnders*, purporting to envy the free lives of poor East End Londoners who drank in the Queen Vic pub. When they were happiest, Diana ate plentifully; when things were going badly, Diana would just pick at food, though it certainly never seemed to put James off his lunch.

Summer Pudding for Lovers

You will need a 3-pint pudding basin for this recipe.

INGREDIENTS

3 lb. fully ripened mixed raspberries, blackcurrants, blackberries, and redcurrants

10–12 slices of slightly stale, sliced bread, trimmed of its crusts

1⅓ cups white sugar

Lightly whipped heavy cream to serve

METHOD

Go through the fruit, discarding any that are moldy or unripe and picking out unwelcome stalks. Put the berries in a large mixing bowl and add the sugar. Stir and leave the sugar to dissolve in the fruit juices.

Now shape the bread. Cut the first slice into a circle that will exactly fit the base of a transparent glass pudding basin or bowl. Fit this in. Now cut the remaining slices into wedges about 4 inches wide at the top and 3 inches wide at the bottom. Line the sides of the pudding basin with these, snuggly overlapping them so that there are no gaps. Once you have built this bread carapace, pour the fruit into the pudding bowl; it should come nearly to the top. Cover the top completely with the remaining bread; there should be no glimpse of fruit.

Pop the basin onto a plate in case juices spill out, and then find a saucer or plate to put on top of the pudding's bread "lid." Weigh this down with something heavy. Put the summer pudding in the fridge overnight.

To serve, you are going to turn the pudding onto a serving plate. Begin by removing the weight and the saucer/plate. Using a palette knife, ease the pudding away from the edges of the pudding dish. Lay the serving plate over the top, and then, grasping the plate and the pudding bowl firmly, turn the pudding upside down in one quick, swift movement. It should now have turned out intact onto the plate, a purpling mountain of lusciousness.

Serve with softly whipped cream.

Diana tended to befriend the mothers of men she was interested in, and when James told his mum that Diana, the Princess of Wales, was coming to stay the night at Sheiling Cottage in Devon, Mrs. Hewitt asked tentatively, "Which room should I put her in?" James said, "Mine." The couple pushed the twin beds in there together, and before you knew it Diana was sampling James's homemade lemon vodka, laughing at his jokes at the Hewitt dinner table, and floating in the Hewitts' bathtub. She loved rolling up her sleeves and doing the dishes—smiling helpfully among the suds. Before this meeting, Diana had phoned Hewitt at his mum's house, calling herself "Julia" and adopting a Cockney accent.

A lover or two later and Diana began hankering after James Hoare, a forty-seven-year-old dealer in Islamic art who had eyes the color of "deep velvet brown." They shared one too many breakfasts together at the Chelsea Harbour Boat Club. Just as she had pretended to be intensely interested in fishing with Charles, now she discovered in herself a hankering for Islamic philosophy. Ever one for the phone—she spent £3,000 a month on her phone bill—Diana might call Hoare up to twenty times a day, which wasn't good news, as he was married. Diana called his family and was then silent when someone answered (incidentally, James Hewitt got silent calls, too, during his relationship with Diana).

In a way, James Hoare, or at least Diana's reading of Islamic philosophy, prepared the way for the arrival in her life of Hasnat Khan in September 1992 when she started to visit her friend Joseph Toffolo following an operation on his heart. One of the team who had operated on Joseph was thirty-six-year-old Hasnat, the brown-eyed, charismatic senior registrar.

Hasnat was tubby, smoked heavily, and had a tufty, black moustache and a dodgy car that backfired all the time—his exhaust was falling off. He loved lager and Southern fried chicken. He seemed the antithesis of what Diana would want, and yet she adored him. Until Diana came along, Hasnat led a very sheltered life. He worked hard as a heart surgeon at the Royal Brompton Hospital, and when he wasn't on duty, he was always happy to hold an informal meeting at the local pub or to share a fish-and-chip supper. Then he'd head off home to his one-bedroom bachelor pad in Chelsea. Hasnat—or "Natty," as his family called him—loved jazz, was intensely private and witty, and had all the authority of a true patriarch. Plus, he was always just beyond Diana's reach: he was a Pakistani Muslim and belonged to a world she could not even begin to comprehend. It was fatal for Diana. She thought he was "drop dead gorgeous" and started reading surgical reports, *Gray's Anatomy*, and books on Islam. Soon she was turning up at midnight to console dying patients at the Royal Brompton, hoping to impress Hasnat.

Then she invited him back to Kensington Palace to discuss heart surgery. Nights were stolen together at Kensington Palace, joss sticks burning, Diana looking lithe and glamorous in silky *shalwar kameez* or giggling in Hasnat's on-call rooms at the hospital. To accompany him into jazz clubs, she got herself a midlength light-brown wig and glasses with plain lenses (and, incidentally, discovered queuing for the first time). She took Hasnat's granny to Kensington Palace and showed her around. Diana even learned to work the microwave in the palace in order to make food for Hasnat, telling a friend, "Marks & Spencer have got these very clever little meals that you just put in the microwave and you put the timer on and press the button and it's done for you!" How she longed to be plain Mrs. Khan; she adored Hasnat and became increasingly possessive.

When Hasnat spent what she thought was too long talking to friends or relatives on the phone at Kensington Palace, Diana danced in front of him, trying to catch his eye. If he was in the operating theater when she called, she felt scorned. She tried to advance his career, win his gratitude. She directly approached his family in Lahore, Pakistan, following her usual tactic of befriending his mother. But this was no Mrs. Hewitt putting out the bubble bath; this was Mrs. Naheed Khan, a Pakistani matriarch who wanted a good Muslim bride for her son, drawn from her own Pathan clan. Without telling Hasnat, Diana, on a trip to Pakistan, popped in on Mrs. Khan for tea, patties, and pastries. Suddenly, there was a power outage and all the lights were extinguished. It was almost symbolic. When the power was restored, they watched cartoons, but something had not clicked. Diana, thought Mrs. Khan, lacked dignity.

Deeply hurt by Hasnat's unwillingness to marry her, Diana went about trying to make him jealous, propelled by the loss of him into a relationship with millionaire playboy Dodi Al-Fayed. Dodi was not ashamed to be seen in public with her, and the Al-Fayed wealth meant her every whim was met as they sailed around Corsica and Sardinia on the yacht *Jonikal*. With his fiancée Kelly Fisher abandoned in Paris, Dodi did all he could to win Diana at the behest of his father, Mohammed Al-Fayed. Diana loved *The English Patient*, so the theme music was played on a loop. Fresh carrot juice was supplied for Diana's breakfast, a platter of vegetables for lunch, followed by a sorbet. Fresh, lean fish was grilled in the evening and served with Loire white wine—chilled Baron de Ladoucette 1992. And, according to one chef on the boat, "There was always Mohammed Fayed in the background. It was obvious that strings were being pulled."

Little did she realize, but Diana, Princess of Wales, was to pay with her life for such revenge on Hasnat Khan.

DESERT DINING: KING HUSSEIN OF JORDAN

King Hussein of Jordan survived several assassination attempts in the course of his life. The first clue to one plot was the many furry cat corpses that began to appear in the palace grounds in various stages of rigor mortis and decay. At first, when he tripped over no less than three of them, the king thought the local cats were just suffering from some spectacularly feline bad luck. "Poor devils!" he exclaimed and ordered their burial. Then it turned out the gardeners had come across a staggering thirteen dead cats within a forty-eight-hour period. The hunt for a cat serial killer was mounted, and the palace's undercook was exposed as a Syrian assassin who, working out how to poison Hussein, had decided to do a feline test-drive first (though a total of sixteen cats might seem a tad excessive). Then *more* foreign spies caught wind of Hussein's sinus troubles and hatched a cunning plan: they would replace the fluid in his nasal inhaler with acid. This time it was a very close shave. Hussein recollected, "On the edge of the basin stood a half empty phial—the one I should have used. In the bottom of the basin were some of the drops. To my horror the liquid was bubbling. . . . I poured out more drops. The liquid looked as though it was alive; it twisted and bubbled and frothed . . . the chromium on the basin fittings had peeled off." Ouch. Imagine all that going on inside your nose.

Hussein was made of stern stuff, though. He was a direct descendant of the Prophet Muhammed and grandson to the brilliant King Abdullah I (who headed the Great Arab Revolt, his brother working conspiratorially with Lawrence of Arabia), with whom Hussein forged a close, inspirational relationship. Sadly, Hussein's father, Talal, was blighted by schizophrenia and, although Talal was king for a short time, Abdullah looked to his grandson to carry the burden of kingship. Grandfather Abdullah taught him how to get up early in the morning. Together they ate breakfast—but a modest one, as Abdullah believed a half-empty stomach energized a leader—they sat over glasses of deep brown, silty Bedouin coffee, aromatic with cardamom, or tea infused with fresh mint leaves and broke into warm, plain, flat cakes without any butter or jam. Abdullah was ever the Bedouin, and between the walls and pillars of the palace, in the gardens, he had tents erected, in which he held court. In the evening, Hussein would return, and the two would eat dinner together before evening prayers. Hussein recalled, "I would listen to him talking of the subtleties and pitfalls of being a king, or I would sit at meetings with notables, or watch him dictate or play chess, fascinated until, long after dark, he would say, looking at my drooping eyes: 'Go to your home, my son. Sleep and prepare for the morrow.'"

This intimate world was torn apart in 1951. Grandfather and grandson were visiting the Al-Aqsa Mosque in Jerusalem. Abdullah was willing to make peace with Israel; he had already negotiated often with Golda Meir. Young Hussein had dressed in a military uniform, and Abdullah had insisted he pin a medal on his chest. Security was tight, but a Palestinian assassin broke through and mowed down King Abdullah in a hail of bullets. He was fatally shot through the head, his turban darkening with blood. In horror, his grandson watched as politicians and hangers-on fled from Abdullah's body. Desperate, Hussein chased the killer but was hit in the chest. He survived simply because he was saved from the bullet's impact by the medal Abdullah had insisted he wear. Returning heartbroken and alone to Jordan, waiting on the airport tarmac to climb into the plane, Hussein was the loneliest he could ever be.

After the assassination, Hussein was plucked from the world of Bedouin kings and bundled off, with his cousin Feisal of Egypt, to the famous boys' boarding school, Harrow, in the muddy environs of London. Hussein polished and cleaned his room frequently in a way reminiscent of Queen Elizabeth II (as a child she would wake up several times in the night to check that her polished shoes were straight and parallel to the bed). Rationing was still severe, and each boy had an allowance of one egg a week. Sweets were issued if you had a coupon; Hussein never forgot the glory of tinned peaches when these were finally derationed. School teas and coffees were strange, insipid relatives of their Jordanian cousins, and Hussein ached for Arab food and drink. Feisal got nicknamed "Fuzz" and was confined to school grounds; Hussein smuggled him out and they zipped about together in cars. Wisely, Hussein kept a small store of tinned food in his bedroom to supplement school meals; however, strangely, he eventually found himself appreciating not so much the food content of the British schoolboy's diet, but rather the incredibly regularity with which food was stuffed into them. Then, during the school holidays in 1952, Hussein learned that his father had abdicated and he was now king. At seventeen, he knew that his youth was over.

Now it was time, he felt, to meet his people, the people of Jordan, face-to-face. He went on a three-week tour of the country but found himself being inspired more than inspiring others. The Bedouin welcomed him at their encampments. The fierce tribesmen sang and danced before him, firing their rifles into the hot, still air when his name was mentioned in song. Joyfully, the tribesmen pulled Hussein into their dancing. Then he paused: "As I stood there, the brown tents merging into the desert, I thought to myself: 'If there are men like these, Jordan will always be alright.'" The young king and other guests were seated on silken cushions at the head of the fifty-yard-long tent while the coffee was drunk, and poets materialized, giving impromptu recitations. Then one of the great glories of Bedouin feasts was served: a *mansef* (meaning "big dish") of lamb and rice, for which sometimes more than a dozen lambs would have been slaughtered. Not a single woman could be seen, and not a single grain of rice was eaten by the host tribe until the guests had wiped their lips. Later, walking past a tent in the cold desert night, Hussein heard some old Jordanian tribesmen speaking among themselves: "Abdullah would have been proud of his grandson," they agreed.

Hussein always wanted to mingle with his subjects in order to learn their thoughts and feelings, and what better way, he worked out, than to pretend to be a taxi driver. He dug out an old, beaten overcoat and swaddled his face and head in a red headdress. For two nights, at about 8 p.m., he ducked out of the palace, slipped his guards, drove about seventeen miles northeast of Amman, and waited for custom on the road to Zerka in an ancient green Ford, complete with battered taxi number plates. He was flagged down by a Bedouin vegetable seller lugging a massive sack of vegetables. After a bit of haggling, the vegetable seller hopped into the car.

Hussein asked, "How is the season? Have you had good crops?"

"Thanks to God and the King," replied the man, "everything is wonderful."

Then, tentatively, Hussein asked, "What do you think of this King Hussein?"

"He is our man after God, he is protecting us and giving all the help we need. We love him."

"I'm not sure about that," Hussein huffed.

The vegetable seller darkened with rage and yelled, "Don't you dare to say anything against my King. If you do, I'll beat you black and blue with my stick!"

Fortunately, just in the nick of time, Hussein's security guards, who had hunted him down, zoomed up to his car and put a stop to the impending beating.

Lisa, the future Queen Noor of Jordan and Hussein's fourth wife-to-be, first met Hussein when she took a photograph of him and her father, Najeeb Halaby, in the midst of an aviation deal. There was the dazzle of the planes about them and warm tarmac beneath their feet. Both men squinted through the light into the camera. But before this seems like a straightforwardly romantic moment, one of Hussein's daughters was behind them and he called his wife Queen Alia to join the photographed group. It wasn't until Queen Alia died in a helicopter crash that any romance kindled between Noor and the king.

Hussein had had a checkered marital career: his first wife, Queen Dina, was seven years older than him (he was on the cusp of adulthood at about nineteen years old). They had a daughter, Alia, but the arranged marriage barely lasted a year. His second marriage was to fresh, sporty, hockey-playing nineteen-year-old Englishwoman Toni Gardiner, whom he caught sight of on the set for *Lawrence of Arabia*. Her parents, Walter and Doris, invited him over for English tea and cakes, preparing themselves for their daughter's conversion to Islam and change of name to Princess Muna al-Hussein. Of the early days of his marriage, Hussein said, "We have a cook, but my wife is so busy in the kitchen that we hardly need help! Every other morning she cooks breakfast—eggs or sausages, coffee, toast and marmalade. The other mornings I do it myself! My wife had a long list of dishes she proposes to try out on me in the near future."

But were those dishes disastrous? After having four children in the space of eleven years, the couple divorced. Hussein's roving eye had got the better of him, and he went on to marry Palestinian Alia Toukan.

So it was that Lisa found herself the object of Hussein's attentions in 1977. Suddenly, the king began to appear at the airport, bumping into Lisa—she was working on architecture there temporarily. She began to avoid him, blushing and trying not to intrude on him. Then he asked Lisa to join meetings with her father and wanted to discuss "structural problems" back at the palace with her. Would her father allow her to come for lunch? Soon Hussein was calling her up, and she was taking a crash course in how to cook good Jordanian food, rustling up bamieh (stewed okra), cinnamon-rich string bean fasoulieh, and foul, a simple but delicious fava bean breakfast dish.

Bamieh

You need to select the smallest and tenderest of okra pods for this dish.

INGREDIENTS

3 tbsp. olive oil
2 onions, finely chopped
2 lb. lamb, diced into small chunks
2 tsp. sea salt, plus some to taste
1 tsp. freshly ground black pepper, plus some to taste
1 tsp. cumin
1 tsp. ground allspice
2 tsp. ground cinnamon
2 lb. okra

2 tbsp. olive oil
1 green bell pepper, finely chopped
1 chili, finely chopped
10 cloves of garlic, chopped
5 tomatoes, finely chopped
4 tbsp. tomato paste
2 tsp. sugar
1 tbsp. fresh cilantro, finely chopped
½ tsp. allspice

METHOD

In a large, heavy-bottomed pan, heat the olive oil. Add the onion and sauté until it is pale gold. Next, add the diced lamb and brown it. When browned, add the salt, pepper, cumin, allspice, and cinnamon. Top with enough water to cover the lamb. Bring to a boil and then simmer for an hour.

Clean the okra. Cut off most of the stem, leaving enough to keep the okra whole. Heat 2 tablespoons of olive oil in a skillet and fry the okra for about 20 minutes. When done, spread out the okra on a paper towel to absorb the fat. Now add it to the stewing lamb.

Meanwhile, in a large frying pan, heat 2 tablespoons of olive oil and fry the peppers, garlic, and chili for 2 minutes. Now add the tomatoes, tomato paste, and sugar. Cook for a further 4 minutes and then pour this into the lamb stew.

Cook, uncovered, for another 30 minutes (enough time to prepare some rice), and then add the cilantro and allspice. Salt and pepper to taste. Serve immediately.

Fasoulieh

INGREDIENTS

3 tbsp. olive oil
2 lb. green beans, sliced into thirds
6 scallions, finely chopped
6 cloves of garlic, finely chopped
2 tbsp. bharat
1 tsp. ground cilantro

1 tsp. ground cinnamon
5 tomatoes, peeled and chopped
Sea salt
Freshly ground black pepper
4 tbsp. flat-leaf parsley, finely chopped

METHOD

In a saucepan, heat the olive oil. Add the scallions and cook them very gently for 5 minutes. Add the garlic and cook this for a further 5 minutes—sweat the garlic rather than letting it brown. Now add the beans and spices. Cook, stirring, for 10 minutes; allow the olive oil to coat the vegetables. If necessary, add a little water to keep the dish moist. Now add the tomatoes; cover and cook gently for another 20–30 minutes, until the beans are soft. Season to taste, and finally stir through the chopped parsley. Eat with warm Arab flat bread.

Being wooed by the king was a whirlwind of his many children followed by dinner and movie evenings of John Wayne with a smidgen of Peter Sellers. He revealed his feelings for Lisa through imitating the speaking dolphins from *The Day of the Dolphins*, when Fa, the most brilliant of all the talking dolphins, gives George C. Scott's ear a watery nuzzle and confesses to loving his female dolphin counterpart, Be, piping in a high falsetto, "Fa loves Be." Such were the winsome ways of the king. When he wasn't being a dolphin, Hussein tried to cajole her into marriage with a lively rendition of ABBA's "Take a Chance on Me." The whole affair was exhausting and exhilarating. Lisa lost lots of weight, as Hussein bolted his whole meal during all those intimate dinners and she felt it was impolite to keep eating after he'd finished. And she had not a single moment to secretly stuff herself in her own little flat; if they weren't watching John Wayne until 1 or 2 a.m., they were helicoptering over the Dead Sea or riding a motorbike through Amman. A few weeks into their budding romance, Hussein declared he wanted to see her father. When Lisa finally gave the king the go-ahead to phone her father, Najeeb (who knew nothing about their relationship other than the lunch they shared) said, stunned, "I thought it was just for lunch."

Lisa became Noor al-Hussein on marriage and converted to Islam. Hopefully, she could at last have a decent, square meal, although, ironically, the couple shared a delight in the delicious Ramadan drink Qamar deen, cool, pine-nut-sprinkled apricot juice, which so refreshes after a long day of fasting.

Qamar Deen

This cooling, delicious drink depends on using sheets of dried apricot paste (available in Middle Eastern delicatessens).

INGREDIENTS

3 sheets dried apricot paste,   3 tbsp. sugar
   finely chopped   2 tsp. orange flower or rose water
3 cups hot water   ½ tbsp. pine nuts

METHOD

Soak the chopped apricot paste in hot water until it is dissolved. Strain this through muslin or fine mesh, and add the sugar and flower water. Stir to dissolve. Serve with a lump or two of ice and a sprinkling of pine nuts.

PHILADELPHIAN SCRAPPLE OF HOMESICKNESS:
GRACE AND RAINIER

Twenty-five-year-old Grace Kelly worried, Bridget Jones style, whether she'd *ever* meet Mr. Right. She'd have one of her favorite hamburgers for dinner and then head out to miserably sip vodka and soda in bars (this cocktail came to be known as "a Kelly"), with one eye on the door. Would Mr. Right walk in? She was quite keen on going to bed with plenty of Mr. Wrongs (think of most of the leading men she played opposite). Ever hopeful, in 1955 she threw late-night cocktail parties in her apartment off Fifth Avenue, playing hostess and handing out the nibble of peanut butter and bacon on saltines she'd invented to impress Mr. Right just in case he happened to darken the doorstep. "I seem to be the late bloomer," she sighed. "I love this apartment. But am I going to be living in it alone for the next twenty years going back and forth from Los Angeles and movie locations like a yo-yo on a string?" All her friends were married—some had even already racked up a couple of divorces. And, worst of all, would Mr. Right feel undermined by the fame of Grace Kelly herself? She recognized this, glumly: "I don't want to be married to someone who feels belittled by my success. . . . I couldn't bear walking into a restaurant and hearing the maître d' refer to my husband as Mr. Kelly."

And then, come April 1955, she went to Cannes and everything went crazy. First, because the French labor unions went on strike, there was no electricity. Silly old labor unions! The consequence of this was that Grace's hair dryer wouldn't work and her wet, straggly hair took on a life of its own, drying "naturally" into a wild, cave-womanish, uncoordinated frizz. Better still, *Paris Match* had organized a photo shoot for her at the Monaco palace, where the swanky thirty-one-year-old Prince Rainier was scheduled to give Grace a tour of the palace gardens—a photographed stroll, of course. Then her iron was kaput, so Grace couldn't iron the wrinkled rose-beige tea dress she had planned to wear. There was nothing for it but to drag out a black silk taffeta dress that her friend had already told her made her look like a pear. And not just any old pear: the dress was covered in lush green and red roses. The crew's Peugeot careered along the nauseating narrow coastal roads to Monaco (they were even caught in a minor accident), eventually screeching to a halt at the palace. Carsick, the ham sandwich she'd eaten earlier very much on her mind, Grace stepped out. Then Prince What's-His-Name wasn't even around. Darn! Three-quarters of an hour later, Prince Rainier skidded up, looking handsome-ish. Grace, despite being cross, was disarmed by the fact that Rainier had caught sight of her practicing her curtsey for him. Finally, he swept all her anger away by showing her around his private zoo, manfully thrusting his hand into his tiger's cage (it was a feline present from Emperor Bao Dai of Indochina) and fondling the large, playful tiger. Who wouldn't be impressed?

Rainier had been on the lookout for an eligible bride, using the services of a bridal talent scout, one Father Tucker, a sixty-two-year-old priest from Delaware who had been sent to Monaco to school the prince in matters of the spirit. He had arrived in Monaco with chewing gum for choir boys and rode a scooter. Father Tucker had written out a wish list of potential brides for the prince (who had spent far too long dallying with his French mistress, the sweet-faced Giséle Pascal). Grace was on the list—Father Tucker approved of her as a good American Catholic girl. When Rainier put a quick call through to Father Tucker, asking what his views were on Grace, Tucker said, "That's exactly the kind of young lady I'd like to see you married to." Aristotle Onassis, who had bought considerable stock in Monaco's casinos and hotels, becoming the principal stockholder in Société des Bains de Mer, had the bright idea that Monaco's fortunes would be boosted if Rainier married an American film star (Onassis approached Marilyn Monroe, who wasn't keen, believing Monaco to be in Africa). Top of the Tucker list, though, was Princess Margaret from the British royal family—though it was a long shot, as she'd have to convert to Catholicism. Interviewed for *Collier's* magazine, the prince totted up the qualities that made up the ideal princess and wife for him. One was her ability to cook: "How can she order dinner, or tell the cook what to make unless she herself knows how to cook." No mention of the future princess of Monaco actually wielding a rolling pin herself (though in later years in private family time with the children, Grace "would prepare experimental Chinese and Italian dishes, with varying success"). She should be very good-looking, Rainier continued: "I see her with long hair floating in the wind, the color of autumn leaves. Her eyes are blue or violet, with flecks of gold."

On Grace's return to the United States, the prince and the showgirl became pen pals and, slowly, fell in love by post. Then the prince hastened to America and called on the rambunctious Kelly clan in Philadelphia. Pa Kelly, Grace's gruff father, himself a multimillionaire, was childishly pleased that the prince was shorter than him. Grace never noticed: she was spellbound by her own fairy tale. Life in the South of France held great allure. Maurice Zolotow, the show-business biographer, recalled, "Once I was fortunate enough to have dinner at home with Grace in California before she was married. . . . Grace served a fine red Bordeaux, a Château Latour 1949 Grand Cru wine. Grace knows and loves French wines and can drink them without any inner torments. In fact, she has always been strongly drawn to French cuisine, French culture, and French literature. . . . I asked her once to name her favourite writers and she said, 'Balzac and Montaigne.'"

Grace may not have had hair the color of autumn leaves, nor was a wind blowing when she met Rainier, but come December 1955 the Kellys had parted with an eye-watering $2 million dowry, and Grace and Rainier were engaged to be married. The couple dined together to a string ensemble on airy puffs of salmon quenelles, poached in bouillon, followed by deeply aromatic roast lamb with mint sauce, haricot verts, and crunchy roast potatoes. A cheeky little salad caprese followed, after which a tower of baked Alaska arrived at the table, accompanied by 1949 brut champagne.

DINNER WITH MR. RIGHT
Salmon Quenelles

FOR THE QUENELLES . . .

1 lb. skinned salmon fillets, diced into small chunks
Sea salt
Freshly ground black pepper
2 shallots, minced
1 egg, beaten
1 tbsp. dill, finely chopped

1 tbsp. parsley, finely chopped
2 tsp. lime juice
1 tbsp. horseradish, finely grated
Pinch of cayenne pepper
1 tbsp. fresh breadcrumbs
1 cup dry white wine
1 cup fish bouillon

FOR THE CREAM SAUCE . . .

2 tbsp. butter
2 shallots, minced
½ cup dry white wine
Finely grated zest and juice of ½ a lemon

1 tbsp. chopped chervil
½ cup heavy cream
Sea salt
Freshly ground black pepper

METHOD

In a food processor, combine the salmon with a pinch of sea salt, black pepper, and the minced shallots. Now add the beaten egg, followed by the dill, parsley, lime, horseradish, cayenne pepper, and breadcrumbs. Chill in the fridge for several hours.

Pour the white wine and fish bouillon into a deep pan. Allow to simmer. Shape the quenelles using 2 wet spoons. Drop the quenelles gently, one at a time, into the simmering bouillon. Cover and cook for 5–7 minutes; remove with a slotted spoon. Repeat with the next few quenelles.

Now prepare the sauce. In a small saucepan, melt the butter and add the shallots. Salt and pepper. Cover the shallots with greaseproof paper and soften very gently over a low heat for about 10 minutes. Now add the white wine, turn the heat up, and allow the wine to reduce by half. Next add the zest and juice, followed by the chervil. Pour in the heavy cream.

Serve the warmed shallot-and-chervil cream with the quenelles.

Haricots Verts

INGREDIENTS

1 lb. long green beans
Sea salt
2½ tbsp. butter, softened
2 tbsp. chives, minced
2 tbsp. flat-leaf parsley, minced

2 tsp. tarragon, minced
2 tsp. freshly squeezed lemon juice
Freshly ground black pepper
2 tsp. mint, torn

Haricots Verts (*continued*)

METHOD
Fill a pan three-quarters full of cold water, salt, and bring to a boil. Plunge the green beans into the boiling water and cook, uncovered, for about 6 minutes. They should never become limp or dull: look for the point at which the green intensifies.

In a mortar and pestle, combine the butter, chives, parsley, tarragon, lemon juice, and black pepper.

Drain the beans and stir the herb butter through them. Serve immediately and sprinkle with the torn mint.

Mint Sauce

INGREDIENTS

1 small bunch of mint	4 tbsp. red wine vinegar
1 small red onion	1 tbsp. caster or granulated sugar
A pinch of salt	

METHOD
Strip the leaves of mint from the bunch and place in a blender with the onion. Put the blender on for 30 seconds to mince this finely. In a bowl, add the red wine vinegar, caster or granulated sugar, and a pinch of salt. Stir. Now add the minced mint to the vinegar solution. Chill.

Salad Caprese

INGREDIENTS

4 medium-size ripe tomatoes (look for tomatoes with a soft, dark-red "bloom" to their skin—they should also *smell* strongly like tomatoes)	Knot of Italian buffalo mozzarella
	Extra virgin olive oil
	Half a lemon
	Sea salt
Small bunch of basil leaves	Freshly ground black pepper

METHOD
After washing the tomatoes, remove the seeds and slice. Layer these with slices of mozzarella and torn basil leaves, building a small mound of red-white-green. Finally, drizzle with olive oil, squeeze a little lemon over it, and season with sea salt and black pepper.

Baked Alaska

INGREDIENTS

Vanilla ice cream
Really good sponge cake: fresh,
   moist, light, and eggy
4 egg whites
Pinch of sea salt

Scant ¼ cup vanilla caster or
   granulated sugar
½ glass of Cointreau
Powdered sugar

METHOD

Preheat the oven to 250°C. Place the egg whites in a bowl, add a pinch of salt, and, using a handheld electric mixer, begin to whisk the egg whites. As they build in bulk, gradually add the vanilla sugar. Eventually, you should be left with a solid white cloud of meringue. Take the ice cream out of the freezer to soften slightly.

Trim the sponge into an oval shape and place on an ovenproof dish. Drizzle with Cointreau. Now take the vanilla ice cream (about three-quarters of a pint of it) and mold it to sit on the sponge. Now use half of your cloud of meringue to entirely cover the sponge and the ice cream. Try to use a metal spoon or spatula. Use the remaining half of the meringue to create strange turrets on the top of the (un)baked Alaska. Dredge the top of your creation with powdered sugar and place in the 250°C oven until the meringue is colored.

Warm another tablespoon of Cointreau in a small saucepan, pour it over the baked Alaska, and light with a match.

Serve immediately!

Aristotle Onassis—his yacht, *Christina*, moored in the bay—watched with Olympian euphoria, a glass of milky, licorice-tasting ouzo in his hand, as Rainier and Grace sailed into Monaco's harbor on the prince's yacht, *Deo Juvante II*, Grace clutching a large white organza hat to her head, cannons booming, saluting the bride-to-be.

Grace was heading into no fairy-tale kingdom. All was not well in the land of the Grimaldis before her arrival. Prince Rainier had been cohabiting with Giséle Pascal and seemed incapable of marrying (the snobbish Grimaldis knew she was a grocer's daughter) or producing an heir. Alice Grimaldi, Rainier's sister and the black fairy in his life, lived next door to Rainier with her children and brooded over the injustices of her life—perhaps casting a sour eye over the fence or hedge or moat. Alice put it about that Giséle was infertile; a medical examination verified this (though Giséle went on to have a daughter later in life). Clearly, Alice was cunning, strong willed, and had her eye on Rainier's throne. She had, after all, been sidelined by her dipsy mother bequeathing the throne to her brother, and she was very popular with the Monégasques.

Alice plotted to have Rainier deposed, to have herself declared regent, and to set her own small son on the throne. Alice and Rainier's mother, Charlotte, was a neglectful and whimsical eccentric. Both Alice and Rainier had spent their childhoods competing for their mother's attention with a posse of overweight, wirehaired terriers. Charlotte adored her terriers so much that she left New York on the grounds that her dogs weren't welcome in restaurants. While Alice had to rot at home, Rainier was sent to school in Oxford and immediately was derided as "Fat Little Monaco" by the other boys. He was mystified by the British rain, the practice of caning boys and washing in icy water, and English steamed puddings and swimmy stews. Fat Little Monaco decided to run away from school and bought a ticket for London. Eventually, his school cap proved his undoing, as it identified him as a runaway schoolboy. He was marched back to school, but instead of punishing him, the headmaster wisely said he must be famished and, in Rainier's words, "welcomed me home with a gigantic high tea. . . . It was the first meal I'd had all day. I thought to myself, finally someone understands."

Rainier uncovered Alice's plot to depose him eventually; instead of exiling her, he just removed her temporarily from public obligations and duties. Alice's exclusion from the throne was punishment enough. Apart from being ambitious, Alice Grimaldi was herself an ogre-ish mother. After divorcing her husband, she kept her children's golden spaniel, Twinkle, locked up in a closet. Perhaps this was revenge on the terriers? Nanny Wanstall (a cousin of Churchill's and formerly Prince Rainier's nanny) offered sanity of a very British sort to Alice's young Grimaldi offspring. Nanny despised the French; they were, after all, always threatening to absorb Monaco into France, and she was convinced that the best way to instill "normality" into Grimaldi lives lay in a stodgy British diet. Nanny Wanstall kept a larder stuffed with British "health" drinks like Bovril and Ovaltine, milk of magnesia, and Marmite. In command of their menu, she dished out steak-and-kidney pudding and brown Windsor soup, all of which were very anomalous given the eight square miles of gourmet Monaco around them.

The fortunes of Monaco had been on the downturn, and Ari Onassis was determined to get a good return on his investment. The wedding of the Hollywood beauty and her Prince Charming did everything that Onassis could have hoped for, and more, to put Monaco back on the map as a glitterati destination. The bill for their wedding came to a tidy sum and was paid for by the Société des Bains de Mer; Ari Onassis was the main stockholder. A band piped up at the quayside with a rendition of "Love and Marriage," and jolly boats bobbing in the bay sent up cheerful jets of water. Onassis's own plane shook sacks of white and red carnations into the air.

The Kellys and the Grimaldis made an unusual wedding clan as they collided together to celebrate the marriage. Jack Kelly, a former bricklayer, made an art of plain speaking, while Rainier's mother, Charlotte, turned up with her rakish jewel-thief lover, René Gigier, who'd been released from prison into her custody. She informed the press solicitously, "His health is delicate after his years in prison." Interestingly enough, Charlotte voluntarily supported the prison in Pontoise in Paris and staffed her mansion in Paris with ex-jailbirds. When her grandson Christian de Massey visited her, he mused, "It was funny to think that I might have been receiving a glass of lemonade or soda from a former burglar, hitman or arsonist." Princess Charlotte was much more disdainful of Americans than jailbirds. When Margaret Kelly (Grace's mother) gave her a boisterous slap on the shoulder, shook her hand roughly, and said, "Hi, I'm Ma Kelly," she was less than pleased. Charlotte deplored the Kellys' table manners as they upended their glasses to turn down wine and Peggy Kelly, Grace's sister, glugged on a glass of milk while eating her escargots. Even more uncouth was the way that Jack Kelly decided to leg it down to the post office like a common tourist to buy sheaves of memorial wedding stamps, which he then handed out to his guests.

Meanwhile, Ma and Pa Kelly were alarmed by the sudden disappearance of Ma's jewels. Charlotte and René remained solemn-faced. Suspicious, Pa Kelly wasn't at ease with the servants and their stiff powdered wigs. They were around every corner; why were they always snooping about? Even worse, when he put a shirt down, it would be whisked off to the palace laundry and come back with its sleeves *pleated*. But that didn't stop him marching around topless among such spies after a stiff glass or three of rye whiskey. Onassis, the king-maker, eyed events from the distance of the *Christina*. The roulette tables of Monaco would whirl again; fortunes might be made or lost, but his investment in Monaco was assured. Rich pickings indeed.

Postmarriage Grace found the Grimaldi official residence, the Prince's Palace of Monaco, powdery with several centuries' worth of the dust of Monégasque rulers. Gusty chills blew through its two hundred rooms—it was a lonely place to be in tiny Monaco. She ached for the warmth and silly familiarity of things American, sending an SOS to the rest of the Kellys in Philadelphia. Where, she lamented, was she ever to find good old Philadelphian scrapple in Monaco? Soon regular, kindly Philadelphian parcels began to arrive, crates in which Betty Crocker angel food cake mix nestled among ridiculously cheering nylons, soft American toilet paper, and Prince Rainier's top tipple of Kentucky bourbon. There was even a shiny new set of American cooking utensils to be substituted for the cranky, rusty old palace ones. The palace chef huffily accepted the American utensils, seething, as he and his kitchen staff much preferred their timeworn, antique cooking utensils (no doubt they had been scraping the same pots for a few centuries).

Philadelphian Scrapple to Cure Homesickness

INGREDIENTS

2 lb. boned pork butt, chopped
   into large chunks
1 ham hock
2 tsp. cayenne pepper
1 tsp. dried thyme
3 bay leaves
1 tbsp. fresh sage leaves, chopped
10 black peppercorns
4 onions, quartered

1½ cups cornmeal
2 tsp. sea salt
2 tsp. freshly ground black pepper
½ tsp. ground nutmeg
1 Granny Smith apple, grated
2 eggs, beaten, plus 1 egg for topping
2 tbsp. olive oil
1 tbsp. butter, plus 1 tbsp. butter for
   greasing

METHOD

First you are going to make a stock using the pork butt and ham hock. In a deep, large pot, place the diced pork shoulder and hock. Add the cayenne, thyme, bay leaves, sage, black peppercorns, and onions. Cover this with water, bring to a boil, turn down to a simmer, and cook for about 3 hours. Remove and drain the meat, and then strain the stock; reserve both. When the meat has cooked, strip it down, removing any bone and chop finely.

Next take 5 cups of stock and put this in a saucepan. Warm to a simmer, then add the cornmeal, chopped meat, salt, pepper, and nutmeg. Keep stirring for up to half an hour, until the scrapple mixture is thick and smooth. Now add the grated apple and stir through the eggs.

Butter two loaf tins and pour the scrapple into them. Now cover and put in the refrigerator until thoroughly chilled. When you are ready to use your scrapple, slice it as you would a loaf. Fry up the scrapple slices in the remaining olive oil and butter in a skillet, making them crunchy and golden; don't turn too quickly—allow each slice to brown well before turning. In Philadelphia, you serve it with a fried egg on top, sunny side up and ready to run over the crisped scrapple. In Monaco, however you serve it, it reminds you of home.

Homesick and pregnant, Grace's hormones played havoc with her taste buds. The eclecticism of American urban food culture was what she longed to taste. She hankered for Chinese food; to satisfy this craving, she combed the streets of Paris for a Chinese restaurant. Next she discovered a hidden chemistry between her lips and spaghetti. If only spaghetti bolognaise was the antidote to pining for home. The doctor warned her to cut down on her portions. Only a visit home to Ma and Pa Kelly would help. Five months after the wedding, she and Rainier took off for Philadelphia, escaping from the internecine, European, brooding world of the Grimaldi family, with all its plots and feuds. Jack Kelly believed that he had paid dear for his daughter's marriage to minor European royalty with the $2 million dowry he had forked out, so he was less than impressed by having to foot the bill for a family lunch out in Philadelphia's Barclay's Restaurant. He grumbled bitterly at the bill of $95 (this was 1952, when very classy eating could be got for about $40) and Prince Rainier's posh tastes: "My son-in-law must have ordered every damned expensive dish on the menu. . . . And *he* had no money, so what they did is sign my name to the check." "What in God's name," he would wail occasionally at the memory in the months to come, "could four people have eaten for lunch that cost ninety-five dollars?"

Beneath the beautiful veneer of their marriage, the patina of royalty and romance, Grace and Rainier bickered and sniped and broke each other down. He was no Mr. Right; she was no Gisèle. She was resented by the palace staff; he had to sacrifice the room where he liked to keep his lion cubs for the zoo when it was made into a nursery. Grace was never to act in a film again. The royal image couldn't take it, Rainier insisted.

Monaco had become a gilded cage for Grace Kelly.

Happier times for Grace were spent in the more intimate surroundings of their house Roc Agel, high on the slopes of Mont Agel, where she, Rainier, and their children spent their summers. Grace was a dab hand at barbecues. She had installed an American kitchen inside Roc Agel, where she experimented with Provençal recipes. She loved cooking breakfast for the family, while Rainier made delicious crêpes Suzettes. True to her Philadelphian roots, though, Grace used Aunt Jemima mix for pancakes, with maple syrup on top.

Gradually, age crept up. Rainier was prey to snoring after dinner, or he could actually fall asleep *during* dull dinner conversation (the queen of Spain had this effect on him). Grace kicked him under the table. Joan Plowright and Laurence Olivier were invited by David Niven and his wife for dinner with the Grimaldis—plus an Arab sheikh who was staying with the Monacos. The atmosphere was constrained as the guests sought common conversational ground. The only thing they seemed to have in common was babies and Hollywood. Nor did Plowright and Olivier think they could very well call the couple "Grace" and "Rainier," so they fell back on "Sir" and "Ma'am." After wonderful food and wine, there was a further lull in the conversation over the coffee. From the sofa came a long, rattling snore: Rainier was asleep. The sheik, seated beside him on the sofa, pretended he heard nothing, while the other guests sat avoiding each other's eyes, holding on tightly to their saucers. Grace was paralyzed. Laurence Olivier, desperate to fill the silence, suddenly asked Grace, "Have you ever played Detroit, Ma'am?" A snore and whistle punctuated the air. David Niven fled the room. When he returned, Olivier was recounting a film he'd made with Marilyn Monroe. He was just getting to the title—*The Prince and the Showgirl*—when it dawned on him this might be a bit insensitive. He instead blurted out the film's original title, *The Sleeping Prince*. Niven bolted the room again, followed by Joan.

Marital rifts and sourness meant that Grace relied too much on alcohol, going the way of the lonely, the shy, the foolish, and the doomed. Ironically, there is little grace afforded to the lush. At times, this made for a quirky, heartwarming mix of royal duty with personal frailty. When in 1971 the Grimaldis went to the shah of Iran's magnificent banquet at Persepolis to mark several thousand years of the Persian Empire, Grace became a little drunk. The man next to her lit a cigar; the tobacco smoke made her sneeze, and all the buttons popped off the back of her shimmering, beautiful dress. It was the sort of behavior that could either make you like the hell out of her or want to shrug her off. Anthony Burgess liked her for her bold, uninhibited style. She could fix a drink that, according to him, "knocked your head off," while Ava Garner joked, "Give her a couple of dry martinis, and Her Serene Highness becomes just another one of the girls who likes to dish the dirt." By the mid-1970s, Grace cared less and less about being perceived as a drinker, about her weight, and about Rainier's brash infidelities. Gore Vidal bitched, "A friend of mine travelled with her for a time and they shared a bedroom at one point. My friend went into the bathroom and saw Grace's bra—it was, as this woman put it, the kind her grandmother had worn—made of *canvas*! Miles of it. And she'd rather wash these things out herself and hang these huge canvases. . . . But she got fat, so she had to strap herself in." Poor Grace; she deserved a better companion in her bedroom, be that her husband or Vidal's friend.

Gone were the Hollywood days for Grace, but she remained at her happiest laughing over dinner with David Niven or chatting to Frank Sinatra. They offered redemptive glimpses of her past and moments when she could be part of the crowd again; when she was that skinny, smart, sober(ish), talented actress who lived on Fifth Avenue independently, with her tray of peanut butter and bacon on saltines. One such time was on February 25, 1972. Rainier was not escorting her; he had gone back to his old girlfriends and yachts (he even asked David Niven to set him up with a flat in Monte Carlo so he could see his mistresses—or "Rainier's girls," as they became known in that small world). Grace was on her own, the mistress of her own loveliness, and Richard Burton was throwing a fortieth birthday party for Elizabeth Taylor at the Hotel Duna in Budapest.

Grace was flown by private charter along with Princess Elizabeth of Yugoslavia, Ringo Starr, and Guy de Rothschild. Richard Burton's brilliantly rough-and-ready Welsh brothers were there, too. Burton's brother-in-law, Dai, who worked on the roads in Wales, couldn't believe the assembled company. "I feel like a multi-millionaire who's just gone bust!" he laughed. Verdun, Richard's brother, a fifty-four-year-old steelworker, watched curiously as Richard ate caviar. "What's it like?" he asked. Richard had a good think: "It's a bit like laver bread." Laver bread was very familiar to Verdun—and was one of Richard's favorite dishes—and is a delicious, gelatinous paste made from boiled, minced Welsh seaweed. "Oh, that's all right, then," said Verdun, and, comforted, he got a slab of bread, slapped the caviar on it, and folded the whole into a sandwich.

Grace was the toast of the evening. All the Welsh relatives danced with her, and Burton elected her "Princess of Gwalia"—a real compliment from the Welsh cohort, as Gwalia was a medieval name for Wales.

Laver Bread for the Princess of Gwalia

INGREDIENTS

1 lb. freshly gathered and rinsed laver seaweed
Juice of half a lemon
3 tbsp. olive oil
Freshly ground black pepper
4 slices of brown bread
1 tbsp. butter, softened

METHOD

Put the cleaned laver seaweed in a pan, place over a low heat, cover, and simmer very gently for about 6 hours, by which time the laver will have been reduced to an ebony-green sludge. Now combine it with the lemon juice, olive oil, and black pepper. Toast the bread, butter it, and then splotch dark dollops of laver bread onto your toast.

Grace had never been happier, and all this fun was followed by an intimate, informal dinner on the Saturday night. Verdun couldn't believe his luck in sitting next to Grace, staring into her mesmerizing eyes while a band played Hungarian music. His shirt collar seemed to tighten round his neck. In fact, he felt as if he was being strangled. Grace said, "You must change. You can't sit there all evening looking as if you are about to have a seizure." It turned out that his physical reaction was less due to Grace's charm and more to him not having removed the cardboard stiffeners in the collar. Over the chat and laughter, they dined on delicious chicken Kiev, then chocolate and fruit. Grace matched Burton's family beer for beer, winning the deepest admiration from these gas fitters and coal miners. She invited them all to stay at the palace and then, full of beer, danced wildly to the Hungarian music in the arms of a handsome, dashing Englishman called Graham Binns. And that night, claims Wendy Leigh, Grace's biographer, Grace took a lover. I hope her revenge was sweet.

Chicken Kiev

INGREDIENTS

4 cloves of garlic	4 chicken breasts
Sea salt	4 eggs, beaten
4 tbsp. parsley, minced	4 tbsp. seasoned all-purpose flour
4 tbsp. butter, softened	8 tbsp. white breadcrumbs
Juice of half a lemon	A bottle of sunflower oil, for
Freshly ground black pepper	deep-frying

METHOD

Put a generous pinch of sea salt in a mortar and pestle; add the garlic cloves and, using the salt as grist, reduce the garlic to a gooey pulp. Now add the parsley and crush it through the garlic. Next add the butter, lemon juice, and a generous dusting of black pepper. If the butter isn't too soft, form it into 4 sausages, wrap in plastic wrap, and chill. If it's too soft to handle, give it 10 minutes in the fridge and then do the shaping and further chilling.

Using a sharp knife and a careful hand, butterfly each chicken breast; then place each between two sheets of plastic wrap. Bash them gently with a rolling pin until they are each about half a centimeter thick. Remove from the plastic wrap and season with sea salt and black pepper on both sides. Now work on each chicken breast one by one. Spread the chicken breast out and place near one edge of the chicken a roll or sausage of the garlic butter. Roll the chicken edge up over the butter and continue forward, wrapping more and more chicken around the butter. Tuck in the ends as you go along. Secure each Kiev tightly with plastic wrap. Put these 4 plastic-wrapped Kievs in the freezer until they are frozen.

After this, get 3 shallow plates. On one, put the seasoned flour; on the next, put the beaten eggs; and on the final plate, the breadcrumbs. One at a time, roll the Kievs in the flour-eggs-breadcrumbs. The roll again in the eggs and breadcrumbs. Put the Kievs in the fridge to thaw.

When they are thawed, put the oven on to warm at 150°C. Fill a deep pan with the sunflower oil and turn on the heat. The fat will crackle and then become silent; to test that it is ready for the Kievs, throw in a pinch of breadcrumbs—when they turn golden quickly, the fat is at its optimum temperature. Now deep-fry the Kievs one at a time, lowering each cautiously into the oil—they will each take about 9 minutes to be ready. Drain on a paper towel and keep warm in the oven until all four are ready. Eat immediately; the garlic butter will burst out and soak the tender chicken and crunchy breadcrumbs.

THE INVISIBLE GUESTS OF KING LUDWIG II OF BAVARIA

Holed up in nineteenth-century Bavaria and with a fortune at his disposal, Ludwig II of Bavaria, the "Fairy Tale King," created an immense fantasy world (think Neuschwanstein Castle in the Alps), part of which was propped up by food; the other props were the music of Wagner, architecture, and sublimated homosexual passions (presented as intense friendships). Everything about Ludwig was theatrical, mannered, and sensitive. He loved reading, hallucinating, and giving presents. In short, he was doomed. Ludwig came to a sticky end and his body was found floating in Lake Starnberg, near Munich. Was it suicide by drowning or was he murdered? There was certainly no water in his lungs, and although a strong swimmer, he had managed to drown in water that only went up to his waist. . . .

Even in childhood, his doctor watched in trepidation as Ludwig would drop his little pencil or paintbrush, look to the side, and converse with an invisible friend. He was also quite keen on dressing up as a nun. He was very sensitive to aesthetic matters; if he found you less than comely, he shuddered, closed his eyes, and hid behind the curtains. His father, Maximillian, was short on sympathy and a sharp disciplinarian. When he was told that his son dearly loved his pet tortoise, Maximillian made sure it was taken away from him. What a rat. Ludwig never lost his love of animals. When a wild chamois burst into the delicate mirror room at his Linderhof Palace, a servant rushed to trap the animal until Ludwig called out ambiguously, "Let him alone! At least he doesn't tell lies." Maximillian considered it a fine idea to restrict his sons' diet. Ludwig's brother, Otto, was another fey, misbegotten, willowy soul, who must also have seemed unfathomable to his stern, bullish father. Kindhearted servants took pity on the boys and smuggled a morsel or two into the boys' diets, taken from their own rations. Perhaps this is one reason why Ludwig himself could have real food empathy. He asked his father (big mistake) if he could give his evening supper to a hungry-eyed sentry guard at the ancestral home, Hohenschwangau Castle. Although he was only seven years old at the time, Ludwig had figured out the guard had not eaten since midday. Maximillian scorned Ludwig's suggestion, claiming no sentry on duty could eat; to do so was pure weakness. "Well, then," Ludwig persisted, "I shall put my supper in his ammunition pouch so he can eat it later." Another exhausted guard was given a chair on Ludwig's command, and as an adult, he was reputed to share cheese and ale with peasants in the forest, all sharing their love for Bavaria through its simplest food. Hohenschwangau Castle was a place of dreams for the dark-eyed, alabaster-pale little prince. The walls were alive with life-size images of Bavarian knights, calling Ludwig to another imagined world of valor and grace; sleepy-eyed Rhine maidens seemed to whisper to him that he was the Swan Knight of medieval legend. There was a dark side to Ludwig, too, though—it wasn't all swans and wild chamois. At age twelve, he bound and gagged foolish little Otto, tying a handkerchief around his neck and slowly tightening it by degrees. Otto, Ludwig claimed, was his "vassal" who had "resisted his will" and so must be executed.

Ludwig's obsession with German mythology and the music of Richard Wagner reached a crescendo in his teenage years. Aged fifteen, he went to see his first Wagner *Lohengrin* (starring none other than the Swan Knight) in 1861. After a spasm or two, Ludwig wept with rapture and the intensity of moment. This sort of passionate behavior went with other familiar manifestations of being a teenager. Bismarck dined alongside Ludwig, and he noticed Ludwig didn't answer any of his questions until he had swigged several glasses of champagne in rapid succession.

Finally, when he turned eighteen, Ludwig was given a place of his own. When he moved in on the first day, the servants offered him a dinner of meat and cheese. Ludwig, though, had a grander sense of his new independence and announced to his staff, "Now that I am my own master, I shall have chicken and pudding *every day*—every day, do you hear?"

King Maximillian died of "a catarrh of the nose, throat and trachea"—in short, untreated syphilis. Ludwig assumed the throne of Bavaria and immediately dealt with really important matters, like hunting down Wagner. Wagner had gone underground to escape his creditors—miraculously for him, King Ludwig would raise him from poverty. Wagner was an unlikely idol, being stumpy-legged with a very large head, but he knew how to set the torch to Ludwig's idolatry. He doused himself in the prince's favorite scent to disguise his unhygienic state and was presented to the tall, slender, and beautiful young king. Ludwig hugged him. And Wagner reciprocated his feelings, writing to a friend, "He understands me like my own soul." No doubt Ludwig did, having memorized swathes of Wagner's overwrought prose and the texts of his public works. Ludwig paid Wagner's debts, gave him a home, built him a theater, gave him a pension, and was the answer to Wagner's mendacity. When Wagner died, Ludwig was so overcome that he yelled, "Wagner's body belongs to me!" and had his corpse brought to Bayreuth. All the pianos in his palaces, he ordered, must be muffled in black cloth like four-legged mourners.

Ludwig's proposal of marriage to Duchess Sophie Charlotte, the daughter of a duke, was similarly dramatic. He immediately renamed her Elsa and had her bedchamber decorated with insignia and devices illustrative of the Holy Grail. Ludwig kept on stalling their marriage but at the same time would, at midnight, steal across to her palace (as quietly as you can in a carriage with six white horses) and place on the piano a heady bouquet of roses for her to find. Eventually, though, the engagement ran aground. Ludwig would have fled from any consummation and, sadly, was never at ease with his own homosexuality.

A passion for Naschwerk (delicious sweets) resulted in a problematic set of teeth, and poor Ludwig had to eat very soft meals that required a considerable amount of mincing. Naturally, he was a fan of soups; clear, gold-brown consommés were always welcome, with additions of rice, noodles, pieces of liver, and ham dumplings. He often ate fish, especially trout, seafood fillets in wine sauce or baked in herb butter or mayonnaise, followed by specially prepared beef. Most of the time it consisted of a fine piece of roast beef that had to be cooked into an utter tenderness for three to four hours, then served in four finger-thick pieces. Ludwig also had a liking for cooked lapwing and seagull eggs. He would only eat the yolks, discarding the whites. But none of that's really odd, is it?

Bregenzer Felchenfilets: Trout in Wine and Mushroom Sauce

INGREDIENTS

4 plump trout fillets
1 tbsp. freshly squeezed
  lemon juice
6 tbsp. butter
1 shallot, finely chopped
1 cup brown mushrooms, sliced

½ tbsp. capers, finely chopped
2 tbsp. good dry white wine
1 tbsp. flat-leaf parsley, finely chopped
Sea salt
Freshly ground black pepper
2 tbsp. heavy cream

METHOD

Sprinkle the trout fillets with lemon juice and chill in the fridge for 15 minutes. In a skillet, melt 1 ounce of butter, and then gently sauté the shallot until it has softened. Turn up the heat and add the sliced mushrooms; fry for a few minutes. Add the capers, white wine, and parsley; season with salt and pepper. Bring to a boil and then turn down the heat to very low.

In a second, large and roomy skillet, heat the remaining 2 ounces of butter. Let this bubble and, when it is nice and hot, add the trout fillets, one at a time; they should immediately shrink and curl in the heat of the butter. Fry them for 2 minutes on each side. Remove and drain on a paper towel.

Add the cream to the mushroom-and-wine reduction; bring rapidly up to a near boil.

Arrange the trout fillets on a plate and spoon the creamy mushroom-and-wine sauce over the fillets.

Fiercely shy, Ludwig was jettisoned into the public eye at many points but had several cunning ruses: He would order the music to be as loud as possible at state balls so that no one could hear what anyone else was saying and so courtiers just had to float about, benignly mute. He'd have to drink ten glasses of champagne before going to state dinners, which he called "Mounting the Scaffold," and at state balls and dinners he'd sit behind a top-heavy floral decoration so that people couldn't gawk at him. Ludwig drank more and more until alcohol had its grip on him; he loved to drink deep from a silver bowl, filled with champagne and Rhenish wine, with a layer of fresh, sweet-scented violets on the top, lending the wine its perfumed flavor. True to his romance of the Swan Knight, he donned medieval dress and went to his favorite spot in the wild, Hunding's Hut, built around a lovely tree, with stable boys dressed in Turkish costumes. They drained mead posset from a drinking horn. Even on the day of his death, he managed to knock back five glasses of wine, some beer, and two glasses of arrack.

Mead Posset (to be drunk from a horn shared with boys in Turkish costume)

A posset is made of alcohol combined with sweetened, warm milk and spices, while mead is a delicious and benevolently bucolic drink made with fermented honey.

INGREDIENTS

¾ pint full-fat milk
¼ pint heavy cream
1 tsp. ground cinnamon
4 eggs

6 tbsp. granulated sugar
2 tbsp. honey
1 pint mead
2 tsp. nutmeg, freshly grated

METHOD

In a saucepan, warm the milk, cream, and cinnamon until it is simmering. In a bowl, whisk together the eggs, sugar, and honey. Gradually add the mead. Next add the nutmeg. Put the egg-mead mixture into a pan and warm gently, stirring constantly. Now pour the hot milk into the egg-mead mixture from a height, whisking vigorously in order to create a foamy, rich posset. Remove the posset from the heat and drink from cups—or decant into a drinking horn.

Ludwig's Downfall—Needs a Silver Cup

INGREDIENTS

1 bottle of champagne
1 bottle of Rhenish wine

A handful of tiny edible violets

METHOD

In a large crystal bowl, combine the champagne and wine. Scatter with violets; inhale deeply and bless Wagner.

Ludwig's longing for male companionship and love is clear in the picnics he liked to hold, often at midnight in the crooked, magical mountains, for the king and his young grooms, where children's games were played—such as blindman's bluff—under a full moon. Later in his reign, Turkish parties were organized in the Oriental Pavilions around Linderhof, where young grooms and lackeys sat cross-legged and smoked hookahs. At these parties, the good-looking grooms stripped and danced naked together. Picnics, though, became distinctly less fun a few years down the line when the king would arrange mountain picnics during a blizzard and insist to anyone present that they were at the beach under a tropical sun. Even worse, Ludwig sometimes decided it was time for dinner at about two in the morning and then fancied a bite of supper at 7 a.m. And then, exasperatingly, Ludwig insisted he wanted to eat in the style of Louis XIV. Whenever Ludwig took it upon himself to go off on a jaunt, he still expected formal meals, and so the royal retinue of cooks and servants would have to trail after him, clanking along at all times and in all weathers with linen napkins, tablecloths, and a whole service of delicate China plates. He rode through the rushing night and the Bavarian Alps on a gold rococo sleigh behind white horses, ostrich feathers in their manes, and took refuge in peasants' cottages. As well as having his castles designed by theater designers rather than architects, he had many props to complete his closed, beautiful fantasy world: a skiff pulled by a clockwork swan drifted over the dark waters of a pond in the winter garden; he would row over the water in a suit of silver armor—he was the mysterious, enigmatic Swan Knight.

Ludwig lived by night instead of by day, rising at 6 p.m. for an aromatic bath, to perfume himself, and to take coffee and croissants. His hair had to be curled; as he said, "If I didn't have my hair curled every day, I couldn't enjoy my food!" He knew he was crumbling physically, many of his teeth were missing now. He avoided the court; rumors and dislike of this foolish, effete, mad king took root. Still, Ludwig drank deeply. And with drinking came corpulence; a bearskin of fat grew over the once-slender boy. Tormented by headaches, he suffered increasing pain in his teeth but refused the offices of a dentist, petrified, preferring instead to muffle his chin in scarves. Drinking helped, of course, but nothing was quite as good at setting him right as chloral hydrate mixed with rum and cloves. Chloral eased the pain, but what he and many of his subjects were unaware of is that a wicked side effect of potent chloral hydrate is hallucination. As if sealing the success of any conspiratorial, treasonable plot to kill him, Ludwig could be heard laughing loudly and chatting with invisible guests at dinner. He startled to the tap of footsteps others were deaf to. He sent a cordial invitation to his delectable gray mare, Cosa Rara, to sup with him on soup, fish, fine wines, and roast meat. In thanks, Cosa Rara trod over the beautiful china dinner set, crushing it beneath her hooves. On another evening, June 13, 1885, a year to the day before his death, the chefs were ordered to make haste in preparing dinners for Ludwig and three invisible French kings who were joining him. Conveniently, the kings all shared the same tooth troubles, and they all, in a kingly way, sucked their way through Ludwig's special soft-minced menu for that night in one of Ludwig's Tyrolese hunting cabins. "They" ate, among other things, a clear soup with liver dumplings, hechtenkraut (apparently adored by Bavarian royals), lemon sorbet, nice sloppy chicken fricassee, pâté, wine jelly, and vanilla ice cream (with sauce).

A MEAL FOR IMAGINARY FRIENDS
Leberknödelsuppe: Clear Soup with Liver Dumplings

FOR THE BEEF STOCK . . .

2 tbsp. olive oil
3 lb. beef shin and bones
3 onions, skin on, split
3 carrots, peeled and roughly chopped
3 leeks, quartered and split

4 cloves of garlic, split in half
4 ribs of celery, roughly chopped
3 bay leaves
1 small bunch of parsley
Pinch of sea salt
10 black peppercorns

FOR THE DUMPLINGS . . .

2 stale white bread rolls
2 cups full-fat milk
1 tbsp. butter
2 shallots, finely chopped
4 oz. calf liver
1 egg, beaten
1 clove of garlic, crushed

1 tbsp. flat-leaf parsley, finely chopped
1 tsp. fresh thyme leaves
Sea salt
Freshly ground black pepper
3 tbsp. fresh breadcrumbs
2 tbsp. chives, finely chopped

METHOD

Begin by making the stock several hours before you intend to serve the soup. In a deep stockpot, heat the olive oil until it is sizzling. Add the beef bones and brown them. When the bones are browned and sizzling, pour over enough boiling water to cover them; the stock will splutter, roar, and then die down. Next, add the onions, carrots, leeks, garlic, celery, bay leaves, parsley, sea salt, and peppercorns. Simmer, partially covered, for 3–4 hours, spooning off scum as it forms on the surface. Now strain the stock through a fine sieve, taste, and adjust seasoning. You want to have about 1 liter of stock for your soup. If you have too much, reserve for a later date; too little, and you need to top up the quantity with extra water.

Now begin to make the liver dumplings. Break the stale rolls up and soak them in the milk. Warm the butter in a skillet and sauté the shallots until they are pale gold. Leave to cool. Next, using a very sharp knife, mince the liver. Drain and squeeze the milk thoroughly out of the bread rolls. Mince the bread. In a bowl, combine the minced liver, bread, and shallot. Add the beaten egg, garlic,

Leberknödelsuppe: Clear Soup with Liver Dumplings (*continued*)

parsley, and thyme. Salt and pepper. Try to form a small ball from the dumpling mix. If it seems too wet, add the extra breadcrumbs. Put the mixture in the fridge for 15 minutes in order to firm it up.

Pour a pint or two of boiling water into a pan. Shape the dumpling mix into individual dumplings (you should have about 8). Plop them into the boiling water, turn down the heat to low, and simmer for about 10 minutes.

Now heat the beef stock. Put the dumplings in individual soup plates, ladle the stock on top, and top with chopped chives.

Hechtenkraut: Fish Pudding for Kings

Hechtenkraut is a pudding that is assembled in layers and then baked.

FOR THE SAUERKRAUT . . .

2 tbsp. butter	8 peppercorns
2 onions, finely chopped	2 tsp. sugar
6 slices of bacon, finely chopped	Sea salt
4 cups sauerkraut	¾ cup cider vinegar
1 tsp. caraway seeds	1 pint good fish stock
2 cloves of garlic, crushed	

FOR THE FISH . . .

2 tbsp. butter	1 tsp. fresh thyme leaves
2½ lb. pike, skinned and boned	1 tbsp. parsley
3 onions, finely chopped	3 cloves
1 carrot, thinly sliced	4 tbsp. dry white wine
3 bay leaves	

FOR THE NEXT LAYER . . .

2 tbsp. butter	1 large potato, diced
3 onions, finely chopped	Freshly ground black pepper
4 slices of bacon, finely chopped	Sea salt

FOR THE BAKING DISH . . .

1 tbsp. butter	3 tbsp. breadcrumbs

FOR THE SAUCE . . .

2 tbsp. butter	2 cups fish stock
2 tbsp. all-purpose flour	1 tsp. paprika
Remaining fish juices from baked pike, combined with ½ cup heavy cream	1 cup sour cream
	Freshly ground black pepper
	Sea salt

Hechtenkraut: Fish Pudding for Kings (*continued*)

TO GARNISH . . .

2 tbsp. butter   Freshly ground black pepper
3 tbsp. breadcrumbs   Sea salt

METHOD

Begin by assembling the sauerkraut-and-bacon layer. Melt the butter in a skillet and then sauté the onion and bacon gently until the onion is golden. Put the 4 cups of sauerkraut in a saucepan and add the onion, bacon, and scrapings from the skillet. Add the caraway seeds, garlic, peppercorns, sugar, and a pinch of salt. Pour over the cider vinegar and enough fish stock to come halfway up the sauerkraut (if you have any excess, reserve it for later). Bring to a boil, then turn down a simmer over a low heat for about an hour and a half. After this time, drain and cool.

Fifteen minutes before the sauerkraut is ready, heat the oven up to 160°C.

Butter a baking tray and place the pike fillets on the tray. Scatter with the onions and carrot. Dot all of this with butter; tuck the bay leaves, thyme, parsley, and cloves around the fish. Pour 4 tablespoons of wine over the fish; add black pepper and sea salt. Cover with buttered greaseproof paper and bake in the oven for 15–20 minutes.

Melt the butter in a skillet; add the diced potato, onion, and bacon. Season with black pepper and a little pinch of sea salt. Fry over a medium heat until the potato cubes are crisp and tender, the bacon beginning to crisp, and the onion to brown.

Butter a deep baking dish. Sprinkle this with breadcrumbs, shaking them around the dish to allow them to stick to the butter.

Remove the fish from the oven and drain off any liquid, reserving for later. Flake the fish.

Preheat the oven to 200°C.

Now make the hechtenkraut sauce. In a saucepan, melt the 2 tablespoons of butter. Remove from the heat and stir through the flour, making a roux. Gradually add the cream and fish stock, plus any of the liquid that remained from the pike, stirring thoroughly to make a smooth sauce. Return to the heat and, stirring constantly, bring to a boil; the hechtenkraut sauce will thicken and coat your spoon. Turn down the heat and simmer gently. Add the teaspoon of paprika. Stir through the sour cream. Season with pepper and salt.

In a skillet, melt the remaining 2 tablespoons of butter until it is bubbling and hot. Add the breadcrumbs and toast them in the butter until they are browned. Season with pepper and salt.

Now begin to layer the hechtenkraut. Into the baking dish, add a layer of sauerkraut. Top this with the potato-bacon-onion mixture. Now add a layer of fish; repeat, ending with a layer of sauerkraut. Pour the hechtenkraut sauce over the top and sprinkle the buttered breadcrumbs over the whole. Bake in the oven for 40 minutes, until the hechtenkraut is deliciously browned.

Wine Jelly

INGREDIENTS

1 bottle of rich dark-red wine
1 stick of cinnamon
Juice and zest of an orange

1 cup granulated sugar
6 leaves of gelatin

METHOD

In a saucepan, heat the wine, cinnamon, orange zest, and sugar until the sugar dissolves. Remove from the heat and leave the wine stock to infuse for 40 minutes. Then strain the liquid before adding the orange juice.

Soften the gelatin in a little cold water; this will take about 5 minutes.

Reheat the wine and, when it is almost boiling, remove from the heat. Drain the gelatin and add it to the hot wine, stirring until it dissolves. Pour the wine-jelly mix into individual glasses and leave to cool and set in the fridge for 3–4 hours.

Lemon Sorbet (perfect for dentures)

INGREDIENTS

4 unwaxed lemons
1 cup vanilla caster or
   granulated sugar
1 cup water

2 tbsp. grappa (you can use gin
   or vodka instead)
1 egg white

METHOD

Grate the lemon zest from 2 of the lemons, then juice all 4. In a Pyrex bowl, combine the lemon zest with the vanilla sugar. Pour 250 milliliters of boiling water over this. Stir and then leave to cool.

Once the lemony mixture is cool, add the lemon juice and grappa. Chill for a further hour in the fridge. Now beat the egg white until it is stiff and fold carefully into the chilled lemon mixture.

Churn the liquid in an ice-cream machine to a sorbet consistency. Serve to your invisible friends with a few strands of lemon zest on top.

FOOD TO DIE FOR: EMPERORS NERO AND VARIUS

One of the few good things to come out of nutty Emperor Nero's rule (about fifty-four years after the birth of Christ) was that roasted mini-whales of pigs were the order of the day and were constantly being wheeled out so that people could devour them.

So what was it about Nero that so shocked everyone? He seemed all right at first when he came to power at the tender age of sixteen. He held poetry competitions, disliked signing death sentences, and even gave slaves the right to complain against their masters. But vanity, greed, and insanity soon took hold of him. Carnage was commonplace to the Caesars, but the internecine struggles for power within families became all the more brutally clear with the more "unstable" of the Caesars. Nero killed a troublesome aunt and made many attempts to polish off his mother, the unpleasant Agrippina (she had a feral double canine tooth and is thought to have polished off Emperor Claudius with some mushrooms), by putting her in a boat with a specially designed collapsing ceiling. Undeterred, when that didn't work, he put her in another boat intended to sink, but she swam her way back! So he ordered a henchman to go around to her place and batter her to death. It seems that worked, but Nero felt guilty enough to honor her memory afterward *and* make her a pyre with her corpse on a dining couch. Nero also kicked his pregnant wife, Poppaea Sabina, to death; remorseful afterward, Nero stuffed her body with spices. Nero also liked roaming the streets—with a bodyguard to keep him safe, of course—and beating up strangers.

As if things couldn't get any worse, Nero also wanted to have sex, and, unfortunately, no one was safe from his roaming eye—he was bisexual. Imagine what fun his dinner parties must have been then! All right, you got to lie on rose-stuffed pillows, drink rose wine, eat rose pudding, and gaze upon fountains of rose water, but imagine the horror if he squeezed your knee and winked slowly at you. Brrrrrrr.

Patina de Rosis (or Rose Pudding, courtesy of Apicius)

METHOD
"Take roses fresh from the flower bed, strip off the leaves, remove the white [from the petals and] put them in the mortar; pour over some broth [and] rub fine. Add a glass of broth and strain the juice through the colander. Take four [cooked calf's] brains, skin them and remove the nerves; crush 8 scruples of pepper moistened with the juice and rub [with the brains]; thereupon break 8 eggs, add 1 glass of wine, 1 glass of raisin wine and a little oil. Meanwhile grease a pan, place it on the hot ashes [or in the hot bath] in which pour the above described material; when the mixture is cooked in the bain maris sprinkle it with pulverized pepper and serve."

At Nero's banquets, you had to keep going from noon to midnight and listen to him sing. Convinced he was an artist at heart, Nero liked nothing better than to give (long) exhibitions of his "celestial voice." People were known to feign death to escape these recitations. Despite being a reincarnation of Apollo, Nero grew fat—a waistline also to befall his relative and fellow-lunatic the former emperor (pre-Claudius) Caligula. Neither emperor was much fun to eat with. Caligula thought sawing people in half was fun; even a casual dismemberment could make him giggle. At a public banquet in Rome, he accused a slave of stealing a strip of silver from the couches. He ordered that the slave's hands be cut off and hung from his neck upon his breast. Then he was dragged about among the guests, preceded by a placard giving the reason for his punishment. At one of Caligula's more sumptuous banquets, he suddenly burst into a fit of laughter. The consuls, reclining next to him, politely inquired what so amused him. "What do you suppose," he chortled, "except that at a single nod of mine both of you could have your throats cut on the spot?" Petronius would have loved that. If you dared to reply, Caligula might set you on fire, cut out your tongue, or brand you on the face. After that, he might only allow you to be polished off when the odor of gangrene became offensive to him. On top of that, woe betide if you were hungry and Caligula was in one of his generous moods. While he drank (Cleopatra style) pearls dissolved in vinegar, he'd set before you loaves and meats of gold. Try chewing on that one.

The Romans, then, must have been hoping for better times with young Nero. But Nero's lunacy was no more apparent than in his "problem eating." The lunacy of Caesars was invariably revealed in their food excesses. In contrast, a sensible, stable soul like Emperor Augustus was partial to coarse bread, fish, cow's milk cheese, and green figs. Sometimes he barely remembered even to eat so much as a cookie.

The food dished up on Nero's table became increasingly elaborate and peculiar: teats of a sow's udder, wiry-legged flamingo, antelope. Guests reclined on three large couches (each of which accommodated three people) arranged along the three sides of each table. They barely moved; a slave wiped your hands between courses, another helped you to relieve yourself into a small chamber pot without even leaving the table. Belching and farting were de rigueur. Too full? Oh well, why not just vomit? Juvenal watched one female diner with disgust: "[She] souses the floor with the washings of her insides . . . she drinks and vomits like a big snake that has tumbled into a vat." Guests came with their own napkin (useful for carrying home any leftovers—some kept their pantries stocked this way).

Pleasure-loving epicurean Titus Petronius Arbiter was often in charge of Emperor Nero's delight department. And that was no small feat—imagine trying to keep up with all those fetishes! Petronius was more than up to the job, though.

Tacitus named him an "accomplished voluptuary"—not a bad description to leave to posterity. It may be that Petronius was, in fact, so keen on fixing fun for Nero because he was trying to contain the overspill of Nero's viciousness. Unofficially titled Nero's "judge of elegance"—hence his cognomen, "Arbiter"—Petronius left us with his fragmentary account, *Satyricon*, as an exposé of Roman excess, as criticized by our hedonistic Caesar, Nero.

Petronius was doomed. Not only did he work for a fiend, but he was also surrounded by fiends. What luck. Those jealous of his special relationship with Nero's dissipation produced trumped-up charges of treason against him. Nero ordered that Petronius commit suicide. Did he quake, tremble, weep, pass out, beg for his life? Probably, but then he decided to have a bit more style. Death was to be like life for Petronius: elegant, epigrammatic, and witty. Having opened his veins (the preferred Roman manner of self-murder), he drolly invited his closest friends to dine with him and spent his last remaining hours eating, drinking, controlling his blood loss through binding and unbinding his wrists, and winsomely cataloging Nero's debaucheries in the *Satyricon*. The last laugh belonged to Petronius. Even if Nero had ordered your death, you were expected to flatter him to the end and leave him your best and favorite things. Instead, Petronius took this opportunity for the ultimate revenge and sent the *Satyricon* to Nero. Petronius's description in *Satyricon* of the banquet of rich "Trimalchio" (a pseudonym for Nero) is the closest we can get to a blow-by-blow account of one of Nero's banquets.

Petronius gives a good idea of the flavor of the occasion when he details the banquet of Trimalchio (a.k.a. Nero). Petronius, of course, is a guest. After you had passed beneath the spotted magpie greeting you from its golden cage and sidestepped the slave dressed in green and cherry red, shelling peas into a silver bowl, you were invited to observe the gold casket in which Trimalchio's first beard was kept. Just as you entered the banquet hall, one of the slaves would suddenly bawl out, "Right foot first!" This left many guests stumbling with surprise. In the dining room, a trumpeter would regularly inform Trimalchio how long he had to live, not that such news distracted him from pissing in a silver bottle and then drying his hands on boys' heads.

Elegant hors d'oeuvres opened the banquet: white and black olives, hot sausages, and damsons on a bed of pomegranate seeds, bridge-shaped iron frames holding roasted dormice sprinkled with poppy seeds and honey. These were not the skinny, small-boned dormice of the common imagination; these babes were tubby treedwellers, about the size of a rat, with a good haunch on them. The famous food writer Apicius has them stuffed with pork forcemeat, spices, some mischievous leftover nuggets of dormice, and then roasted in the oven—though you can make a casserole for a tenderer finish. There were food illusions, and some illusions you wished were delusions: peahen's eggs (buried under straw to surprise guests) but which were, in reality, buried pastry cases. Guests were invited to crack theirs with a spoon and dig out "the plumpest little figpecker, all covered in yolk and seasoned with pepper."

Next came a deep, circular dish with the signs of the zodiac painted about its edge. In keeping with each of the twelve signs the chef had placed, a fitting food-stuff. Aries came with chickpeas; Taurus with beefsteak; Gemini with testicles and kidneys; over Cancer was a garland; Leo had a fig; Virgo, a sow's udder; Libra, scales with cheesecake in one pan and pastry in the other; by Scorpio nestled a sea scorpion; Sagittarius had a sea bream; lobster came with Capricorn and Aquarius with a goose; Pisces was wreathed with two mullets. How arch. While some luck-less slave wailed a popular song from *The Asafoetida Man*, the guests began to eat. No sooner had they raised so much as a dormouse to their lips than four dancers came hurtling in, removed the zodiac, and revealed, in a dish beneath, plump fowls, *more* sow's udders, fish in peppery sauce, and a hare, complete with artificial wings that supposedly resembled Pegasus. Petronius was feeling rather ill by now. But more lay ahead.

Servants entered and laid out hunting paraphernalia. Spartan dogs bounded in and behind them followed a preposterously enormous dish: a roasted wild boar sporting a freedman's cap on its head (a calf later appeared with a helmet on and was "fought" into pieces). A small basket dangled from each of its tusks: one con-taining Syrian dates, the other Theban dates. As if this weren't enough, arranged around the teats of the boar were little piglets made of cake. Sweet. To Petronius's surprise, a "huge bearded fellow" lunged forward and made a great stab at the boar's side. A flock of thrushes burst forth. But limed reeds were ready to catch the birds, one for each guest. What fun; each thrush was a take-home gift.

Just when Petronius had begun to cherish the hope that this was all over, an enor-mous cooked pig was carted in. "But you haven't gutted it!" Trimalchio roared at the chef. Trimalchio insisted he gut it there and then. Ho, ho, another joke—from the pig's belly poured blood puddings and sausages.

The meal was rounded off with a tray of cakes (which sent forth irritating clouds of saffron) arranged around a Priapus made of pastry, with apples and grapes in his lap. But no, it wasn't the last course—trays of snails, oysters, and scallops later ap-peared, followed by goose eggs in pastry hoods. Meanwhile, Trimalchio's "bleary-eyed," dirty-toothed "boy," Croesus, sat nearby, pushing bread down the throat of a puppy who never failed to vomit the bread back up. The guests plunged in and out of hot baths. Trimalchio went off for a good dump induced by pomegranate rind and resin in vinegar and generously suggested that his guests not hold back, either. Eventually, the fire brigade, laboring under the misconception that Trimalchio's house was on fire, broke down the door.

An opportunity had presented itself; Petronius could slip away, unnoticed.

Nero's Eggs in Pastry Hoods

Clearly, this is not one of Apicius's recipes, but it is a modern "take" on feasting fun.

INGREDIENTS

2 cups all-purpose flour   Cold water
1 cup butter   8–12 egg yolks; you can use chicken,
Pinch of saffron   duck, or goose
½ tsp. freshly squeezed   1 beaten egg
   lemon juice   2 tsp. ground ginger
½ tsp. salt   2 tsp. sugar

METHOD

Into a large mixing bowl, sift the flour and salt. Take a pinch of saffron and grind it in the mortar and pestle with a pat of the butter (about a large teaspoon's worth). Use this blob of saffron butter and rub it through the flour. Add the lemon juice and mix it through to form a rather rigid dough, adding a little of the cold water. Try to avoid getting hot, sweaty hands—get yours as cool as possible and begin, gently, to knead the pastry. Now flour the surface you will work the pastry on. Roll the dough out, shaping it into a rectangle. The rectangle should be twice as long as it is wide. Scatter the diced and cold remaining butter over the middle of the top half of the pastry. Now fold the bottom half over it. Using the rolling pin, press on top of the butter and roll the pastry out into a rectangular shape again, but now make the rectangle three times as long as it was before. Fold the pastry three times and leave it in the fridge to cool and rest for 15 minutes.

But . . . guess what . . . now you need to repeat the above 6 times (roll, fold, and rest) before placing it in the fridge again for a couple of hours.

Later, when you are ready to make Nero's eggs, preheat the oven to 200°C. Roll out the pastry. Cut out 8 rounds of pastry either with a knife or using a large cookie cutter. Butter 8 pastry shells (a tin with deep muffin cases will do) and lightly dust with flour. Place the pastry rounds in the cases and brush with beaten egg. Bake in the oven for 8–10 minutes.

Remove the pastry from the oven. Turn the oven down to 170°C. Into each round, carefully sprinkle ginger and sugar, and place on top 1 single large yolk or 2 smaller ones. Return these to the oven and bake until the yolks are just set. Serve immediately.

Food didn't fare much better during the later reign of Varius Heliogabalus. Varius's name had his enemies snorting with laughter. Was he called Varius because his mother had sex with so many men that he was made from all their semen? Clearly, the facts of life were different in those days. As a new emperor of Rome, Varius had seemed quite normal at first—even nice! He liked to free harlots and invited his mother, Symiamira, to attend the actual, male-only senate and set up a women's senate. But his supposed biographer, "Aelius Lampridius," moaned that all the female senate did was make rules about fashionable kissing, shoes, and how to furnish your litter. When Varius started shaving his body (he liked to sit with the ladies at the baths and use the same hair-removal ointment, even on his privates), dressing up as Venus with a gaudily painted face, and thrusting his buttocks in people's faces in a cheeky burlesque style, alarm bells started to ring. How the Roman Empire must have groaned.

Varius also liked large penises and to kiss favorite people (Lampridius calls them "parasites") in the groin. Doesn't sound too bad really, does it? Except that he also wanted to shave *your* groin with an open razor, lock you up overnight with ancient Ethiopian ladies, and if you were one of his less favored parasites, he might, in a fantastical play of the imagination, strap you to a water wheel, set it turning, and, every time you emerged, half-drowned, call you a "water-Ixion." (Ixion had the bad luck to be condemned to spend his time in Hades being perpetually attached to a feathered wheel and shouting out, "Repay your benefactor frequently with gentle favors in return," which was, perhaps, Varius's point.)

Come dinnertime, Varius deliberately modeled himself on Apicius. Varius's table might still have "ordinary fare," like the complicated polypus (the ancient name for the octopus), playfully draped, but Varius was very partial to food faddism, especially anti-plague foods such as camel heels, peacock tongues, or the combs of cockerels (which had to be sliced off the *living* bird). Avian brains might be on offer, like flamingo or thrush, plus high-nostrilled parrot heads and the barbs of mullets. Just for laughs, Varius might let loose his (tame) leopards into the dining room when you were just mulling over your second course. If you drank too much and stayed over, he put a tame bear in to share your bed (this resulted in a few deaths, but never mind that) or ordered that beads of amber be shaken through the peas or pearls be used to pepper fish (while delightful, this must have wreaked havoc with your teeth). Like his predecessor Caligula, he might serve a friend mock food: clay models of loaves of bread, wooden vitals, a dinner of glass, or an embroidered napkin depicting what you *would* have eaten, had you been allowed to do so (he might also send a jar of flies to your home). Varius would laugh and eat his own dinner while you sucked in your tummy. Varius invented a brilliant dinner game called "Chances": the guest chose a card and, on revealing his or her hand, was awarded (depending on the guest's luck or chance) with anything from the sublime to the ridiculous as a take-home present. You could leave with a hundred gold pieces or a dead dog (he also claimed he could give you a phoenix, too, if he felt like it).

Stylish and discerning, Varius's high standards meant he only liked to rest his head on cushions of rabbits' fur or made of the delicate feathers from the underside of a partridge's wings. He also insisted only on silk next to his skin and swam in pools perfumed with saffron. Clearly, he was having a very good time being an emperor. He gave colored banquets on different days; a yellow one on Monday, a blue one on Thursday (he also apparently liked his fish cooked in blue sauce—just like the water, get it?). Like Nero, he liked to wet his lips on a glass or seven of rose wine, made more piquant by powdered pinecones. Mastic and pennyroyal were added to flavor more ordinary wine. Everything was served on silver dishes, and guests lay on gold covers on couches. Humor of a sort was always just below the surface; Varius might seat you on a special deflating cushion so he could watch you sink slowly before the meal. Varius also added a great deal to the "themed party" genre; he liked to group people together as follows: sixteen diners with hernias, twelve guests with one eye, eight who were bald. He had great fun with geographically challenging meals where each course was at a different person's house, so guests had to charge between the different hills and districts of Rome. Meals of twenty-two enormous courses were held; between each gigantic course, guests had to have sex with women and bathe. Dressing up was always fun; Varius might dress as a confectioner or cook and set to work in the kitchen. Perhaps, though, Varius's whacky imagination could be off-putting, as when he prepared the beaky, doe-eyed heads of six hundred ostriches, the skull perhaps acting as a bowl for the succulent brain.

Rose Wine

Here's a rose wine recipe, left to us courtesy of Apicius—however, he warns that it causes rapid bowel movements! Don't use shop-bought roses; they've been sprayed with various nasties. Use ones picked from your own garden.

METHOD
"Make rose wine in this manner: rose petals, the lower white part removed, sewed into a linen bag and immersed in wine for seven days. Thereupon add a sack of new petals which allow to draw for another seven days. Again remove the old petals and replace then by fresh ones for another week. Then strain the wine through the colander. Before serving, add honey sweetening to taste. Take care that only the best petals free from dew be used for soaking."

The scandalmongers were out for Varius. He was too fond of magicians, they said, and studied the entrails of kidnapped young boys for omens. Though not to be recommended, something about this must have worked, and it was "seen" that Varius would die violently. With typical panache, Varius made some very pretty ropes (silk of course) in purple and gold should he have to hang himself. He had a handsome tower built for throwing himself from and also had lovely bespoke golden swords made in case stabbing himself was required. When the guards turned on him with their long knives, he hid in the latrine while lots of his friends died by being pierced up the anus. Dragged from the toilet, Varius was killed. His reviled and mocked body was yanked through the streets of Rome, dumped in a sewer, and then hurled into the greening Tiber. His mother was killed with him, a message to any upstart woman who dared to enter the senate.

THE MEAL THAT DEPOSED THE LAST SHAH

Shahs of Persia have not always been the kindest of rulers. When in 1873 the shah of Persia stayed under Queen Victoria's roof at Buckingham Palace in the Belgian Suite (heads of states are habitually housed there), he had one of his servants lie, prostrate and dog-like, at his bedroom doorway. The catch was that the servant was not supposed to fall asleep. When the shah woke, he heard gentle snores coming from near the door frame. Furious, he ordered the guards to beat our dozy friend, which they did, but so enthusiastically that he expired. Before a scandal should break, they disposed of the body, which, apparently, rests under the grass somewhere near Hyde Park Corner. This same shah was deeply impressed by the sight of an indoor lavatory at Buckingham Palace. Back home, the shah had taken to relieving himself wherever he fancied in his palace, leaving some dismal wretch in his retinue to clean up.

Our shah, Mohammed Reza Pahlavi, bore no relationship to this savage predecessor. He was the second and last king of the Pahlavi line. His father, Reza Shah, being a brutish military man, deposed the weak and venial Ahmad Shah in 1925. He chose Pahlavi as the name for his new dynasty. Mohammed and his twin sister, Ashraf, were born in 1919 in an alleyway in Tehran called Kucheh Roghani, which translates as "Greasy Lane." Auspicious or what? Their mother was the beautiful, literate, and convivial Tadj ol-Molouk. She could also afford to be feisty; as the mother of his firstborn son, Reza Shah could never divorce her. He had two subsequent wives and lived mostly with the third (Reza Shah and Tadj ol-Molouk were united, though, in their adoration of Persian cats). Reza was determined to modernize Persia, renaming it Iran. Reza forced European-style suits on the populace and ran an anti-veil campaign and turban-burning ceremonies. Women, he decreed, should "cast their veils, this symbol of injustice and shame, to the fires of oblivion." Ironically, the wearing of the chador (a cloak-like veil) became a symbol of anti-shah protest among women in the lead-up to Ayatollah Khomeini's revolution (while the Pahlavis increased the legal age of marriage for women to eighteen, the ayatollah reduced it to nine years old when he took power). Reza also abolished religious schools for their part in the Islamification of Persia and ordered that camels, as a symbol of Arabism, should vanish from his lands, with the result that hundreds were destroyed and many camels went into hiding (OK, their *owners* hid them). All this aside, the poor stayed poor, and the Pahlavis had very little understanding of the lives, passions, and needs of their subjects.

As the heir apparent, Mohammad was separated from his mother, Tadj ol-Molouk, and his sisters and brothers. His father wanted him to have a "manly education" at military school but also employed a French-born governess, Madame Arfa, who opened the mind of her twelve-year-old charge to European and Western culture—she taught him to eat French food.

When his father was forced to abdicate and went into exile in 1941, young Mohammed became the shah. Two years prior, Mohammed had married his beautiful, chilly first wife, Fawziah (the sister of Egypt's King Farouk), who had a miserable time in Iran. Fawziah caught malaria on her honeymoon by the Caspian Sea and then lay around in bed a lot when not playing cards. She moaned regularly about Iran; it was so primitive compared to the tinkling, diamanté, cosmopolitan glories of Egypt. Fawziah liked to bathe in milk, lowering her golden loveliness into a milky pool—until, that is, the shah's twin sister, Princess Ashraf, poured caustic detergent into Fawziah's bath. Eventually, as one does, Fawziah became involved with her tennis instructor, and then she found the shah in flagrante delicto with a well-known beauty, Pari Khanom. The marriage spluttered and died. Nightly, the shah would tap on Fawziah's door, seeking entry to the marital chamber, only to hear "Pour l'amour de Dieu partez!"—in other words, "For the love of God, go away!" Incidentally, when the shah's twin sister, Ashraf, visited Cairo to pay respect to her father's tomb, she went to her room to change for dinner. There she heard a strange rumbling in her wardrobe. Her frightened maid found King Farouk among the coat hangers!

Princess Ashraf was like a hard-done-by princess from the leaves of a children's story. The suitor for her hand in marriage was spurned because her sister preferred him. Ashraf instead had to marry some chinless wonder—the marriage was later annulled. Like her twin brother, she was very short—the shah wore elevator shoes—and, also like him, she survived an assassination attempt (he had five attempts made on his life; he loved having his photograph taken and one cunning assassin built a gun into a camera). Ashraf was a small, fierce feminist in a country where women weren't allowed to travel without their husband's consent. On tour in Iran, the Shiite clerics refused to shake the hand of the third wife of the shah, Queen Farah. Taking his sister's lead, Mohammed Reza was the first (and, ironically, the last) king of Iran to crown his wife, a radical act given that women didn't have the vote until the 1960s. Such top-down acts of emancipation, part of the shah's "White Revolution" in the early 1960s, was intended to illustrate the shah's beneficence but effectively began a war between the clergy, seeking an Islamic state, and the U.S.-backed shah.

When Fawziah raced to Egypt to seek a divorce, the shah fell—with some relief, no doubt—back into the ways of bachelorhood. In between wives, Mohammed was spartan in his personal habits. In private, he ran a shabby household at Echtessassi, complete with oddly assorted tablecloths and haphazard dishes. Bizarrely, though, this went alongside a dedication to punctuality like no other. Fereydun Javadi, a frequent guest at the court, recalled of the young shah's routine: "In Noshahr [a Caspian resort where the royal family stayed in summers] he came out of his room at 10 a.m. every single day—not one minute to ten, not one minute after 10. He was at the lunch table at one. Not one minute after or one minute before." Mohammed ate simple food in modest portions and booze held no allure. A rather special diet was also recommended for his delicate constitution. This seems to have involved a great deal of grilled meat—he was particularly partial to chelo kebab. "Cutlet and roasted chicken" were top on the list, claimed his servant Amir Pourshoja: "If you saw the remains of the chicken he ate you'd think the bones had been washed with Fab [a type of dishwashing soap]." After a thorough gargle in the morning, the shah was satisfied with a fresh orange juice, a little toast, coffee, a piece of feta, and last but not least, some delicious homemade Persian jam. He never managed to finish his plate, though he could count on his bulky, black German Shepherd, Beno, to have his eye on the buttery toast. The shah loved the Kalleh Pacheh breakfast soup made in his mother's house but again had to have a rather abstemious portion.

Kalleh Pacheh

Not a soup for the fainthearted, Kalleh Pacheh is based on a lamb's head and several of its hooves. You need to set aside a night and a day to make it and should drink it in the wee small hours for breakfast, with lavash bread crumbled into it and a cup of hot, black Persian chai.

INGREDIENTS

1 lamb's head, thoroughly cleaned
4 lamb's hooves, scoured
4 large onions, quartered
6 cloves of garlic, chopped

2 sticks of cinnamon
1 tbsp. turmeric
4 fresh bay leaves
Lemon

METHOD

Place the lamb's head and hooves into a large, commodious cooking pot. Cover with cold water and leave to soak overnight. The next day, drain and cover with fresh water. Now bring this to a boil and then drain off the water once more. Finally, top up with fresh water; add the onions, garlic, cinnamon, turmeric, and bay leaves. Simmer for 8 hours. When serving, squeeze a little lemon juice into each bowl.

Chelo Kebab

The best thing about chelo kebab is the wonderful encrusted rice that accompanies the kebab, but, as a damnable matter of courtesy, you have to offer the crust to your guest. You should try to fire up a charcoal grill for the meat kebab, if possible.

FOR THE KEBAB . . .

4 large onions, peeled and finely chopped

½ tsp. saffron threads, ground to a powder in a pestle and mortar

2 lb. boneless lamb, trimmed of fat and diced into 1 in. pieces

Sea salt

Black pepper

3 tbsp. melted butter

2 tsp. sumac

TO GARNISH . . .

2 tbsp. fresh cilantro, chopped

3 onions, quartered

FOR THE CHELO . . .

3 cups long-grain rice

9 cups cold water

1 tbsp. sea salt

1 cup melted butter or ghee

2 tbsp. plain yogurt

½ tsp. saffron threads, ground, and then dissolved in 4 tbsp. hot water

METHOD

Begin by marinating the kebab lamb. Puree the onion in a food processor. Pour into a bowl and add the saffron. Place the diced lamb in the bowl, cover, and marinate at room temperature for at least 2 hours or overnight.

An hour before you intend to eat, rinse the rice in lukewarm water and then drain it. Do this at least three times. In a deep saucepan, bring the water to a boil with the sea salt. Add the rice and cook it for 5–10 minutes. Stir it twice during this time to stop the grains from sticking together.

Drain the rice and then rinse it with lukewarm water. Clean your saucepan. In a bowl, whisk together the ½ cup of melted butter, 2 tablespoons of the rice, all the yogurt, and 1 tablespoon of the saffron-infused water. Pour this mixture over the base of the saucepan. This scrumptious concoction will eventually become the crust of the rice. A tablespoon at a time, add the rice to the pan; be gentle—don't disturb the crust layer. Mold the rice into a cone shape; it needs space to expand in the pot. Now cover the pot, place it on a medium heat, and cook, undisturbed, for 10 minutes.

Combine the remaining melted butter with 1 cup of cold water and the remaining 3 tablespoons of saffron-infused water. Uncover the rice and pour this over it. Now place a clean dishtowel over the rice; seal with the lid and cook on a low heat for another 45–50 minutes.

Remove the meat from the marinade and thread onto skewers. Season with sea salt and black pepper. Some 10 minutes before the chelo is ready, grill the lamb kebabs, brushing them with butter as they cook.

When the time is up for the chelo, fill a basin large enough to hold the rice saucepan with cold water. Plunge the base of the rice pan into the cold water; this will loosen the crust. Place a serving plate over the top of the rice pot and then upend it; the "cake" of chelo rice should pop out onto the serving plate.

Serve a portion of rice with the kebabs; sprinkle them with sumac and garnish with raw onions and chopped cilantro.

Eventually, the time came to find another wife. He couldn't drink Tadj ol-Molouk's soup forever, and so it was that he was shown a photograph of the lushly beautiful half-German, half-Persian sixteen-year-old Soraya Esfandiary Bakhtiary. Soraya was an innocent who loved Europe and Hollywood. When she went to language school in Britain, she reveled in the cinema, the paradise of lemonade supped in public, the liberty of wearing colorful turtlenecks. Persian schools were all rotten, mealy gray uniforms, homework, and the stink of the smoking stove that heated the rickety classroom. I'm not sure that she was the brightest, though. She was always petitioning to have caviar added to the palace's menu (the shah was allergic to it), raising its standard as a mouthful of Western luxury while seemingly unaware it was indeed an Iranian product. Mohammed's sister Shams traveled to London to catch up with Soraya, who was living in a bedsit and learning English at a private language school, in order to discuss the shah as a suitor: "'You know, Soraya, Mohammed Reza is a great deal older. He's not very tall . . . and he doesn't smile much. . . . On the other hand Mohammed Reza is a sincere man. He is loyal and simple. He is also very keen on sport. To appeal to him you should go in for sport. . . . He is afraid of his mother, Taj-al-Mulouk. You should show her respect . . . you should always be conciliating and give him children as well . . . a boy, naturally.'" Like her predecessor, Fawziah, Soraya had to decide after just one meeting whether she would accept Mohammed Reza's marriage offer. Unlike Fawziah, she thought he was magnificent looking. The answer was yes, and Soraya's London days were over. Merrily, Mohammed Reza's sisters teased him about the youthfulness of his bride. He cheerlessly replied, "In this country, empresses grow old very quickly. With the life which awaits her, she will very soon be obliged to forget her youth." It was determined that she meet with her husband-to-be twice a day, at lunch and dinner. Their marriage arrangements—or at least the measurement of her dress—were complicated by Soraya contracting salmonella a month before the wedding. Her recovery was very slimming but then further complicated by a relapse when, on a picnic with the shah, she gorged herself with caviar and chocolate truffles. The wedding was delayed. When the actual wedding came around on a snowy day on February 12, 1951, the train of Soraya's wedding dress was too heavy for her thinned form and had to be removed. The three hundred guests swallowed a wedding feast of "'pearls' from the Caspian Sea (caviar); consommé Imperial; cold salmon Ambassadeur; saddle of lamb; Shirin polov (rice with barberries, pistachios and strips of candied orange) with pheasant; asparagus with Hollandaise sauce; Glacé Madeleine; oranges; tangerines and apples." After the banquet, Soraya nearly fainted again.

Next it was time for the newlyweds to merge their pets. Not only did Soraya have two Skye terriers, called Tony and Plucky, plus a huge gangling wolfhound, Sita, but she also came with a seal, a gift from a Caspian fishery. The seal conversation went like this:

"Where are we going to keep the animal?" asked Mohammed Reza.

"Oh, very simple, we'll put it in the fountain in the conservatory."

"But that's fresh water. Seals need salt water."

"I'll fix that," Soraya said, and she poured the contents of a salt shaker into the fountain. Though she was clearly no marine biologist, Soraya proved to be a kind mistress to the seal, feeding it fish on a fork every midday and tolerating the seal's company as it slid alongside her through the palace, devoted and damp.

A desolate mood clung about the unkempt Echtessassi; the shah had had no housekeeper to keep things shipshape, and Soraya found the meals they shared unappetizing, unseasoned, bland, and dry. There was also a lamentable absence of condiments. When Soraya questioned the family doctor, Dr. Ayadi, he confided that the entire Pahlavi family were prey to hypochondria. In the clutches of an unhinged childhood doctor, when Mohammed, Ashraf, Shams, and the others were little, he diagnosed that they would all be prey to a terrible gastric blight if they did not stick to the dullest of diets. The boiled vegetable was to be their savior. After one too many a meal of brochettes and boiled carrot, Soraya decided to rebel— there was not even, she was shocked to discover, caviar on the table. She booted out the unpalatably dirty chefs Nassim and Suleiman, who were running a racket in the ancient kitchens there, masterminding their own market economy in kitchen scraps at the shah's expense. The very evening of their dismissal, her sister-in-law Shams said, "So, you have sacked Nassim and Suleiman?" Soraya was amazed that she knew; it was her first taste of low-level palace espionage. Nevertheless, dinners from now on, Soraya determined, would within her own house be controlled by her. She selected the menus and ensured that many European dishes were served, that good-quality fats were used for cooking, and that the milk did not carry bovine tuberculosis. There was no escape, however, from the interminable family meals with her in-laws that Soraya had to sit through, somber with boredom, always at half-past seven on the dot, followed by dull card games, bad films, endless cups of tea, and barbed comments hidden within the flitter of shallow conversations. Soraya had ridiculous rages and, frustrated, threw things out of palace windows. Mohammed and Soraya argued about her mother, the German Mrs. Esfandiary, who was in the habit of slinking after the sunset into her rooms with a bottle of whiskey, only to swan out under cover of night to sing German lieder to the moon. But none of this was enough to divide the couple; only the need for a son and heir did this. As it became increasingly clear that Soraya could not bear children, her days as the wife of the shah were marked.

Like Soraya, the shah's third wife, Farah Diba, was to realize that dinner with the Pahlavi clan was to be a daily ritual, in one or other of the palaces. Unlike Soraya, she gave Mohammed a son and heir, not that that would matter very much once the throne became defunct. Apart from the unpopular secularization of Persian society that his father had begun and Ayatollah Khomeini lurking in the background, Mohammed Reza's increasingly opulent lifestyle was easy to disapprove of if you were not a beneficiary.

No greater example of his excess can be found than in the shah's celebration of the twenty-five hundredth anniversary of the Persian Empire. It was October 1971. The shah had introduced modernist, Western reforms, but still in most villages there was no doctor, no safe drinking water, too little food, and no schools. The celebration was to mark the final, cataclysmic division between the shah and ordinary Iranians. Ayatollah Khomeini, exiled to Iraq, pronounced that those attending were "traitors to Islam and the Iranian people." Some peasants thought the shah was a distant, burnished god; 50 percent lived below the poverty line.

A colossal city of tents, in a star-shaped design, was erected on a plateau near the ruined pale-gold palace of Persepolis, symbolic home to the mighty, vanished kings of Persia, Cyrus, and Darius. Thirty kilometers of land around Persepolis had been sprayed to kill scorpions, and there had been a massive sweep of the area for snakes. Mr. Alam, the organizer, said he'd shoot anyone who didn't work to make the event a success and after that he'd shoot himself. The tents (actually prefabricated structures draped in plasticated tent materials) covered some 160 acres. The magnificence of ancient Persia, the feast implied, had been restored in the reign of the shah, known also as the "King of Kings," through modernity and secularization (the shah deliberately made a grand address to the mausoleum of Cyrus, just to hammer home the connections between them). The costs were so prohibitively high that the shah insisted they not be released; he was very good at bluffing over any mention of figures in interviews. The Parisian interior design firm of Maison Jansen fluttered into Persepolis. A couple of years previously, they had decorated the White House for Jacqueline Kennedy, and they wanted to bring the same magic to Persepolis. Over sixty heads of state were housed in the tents, each of which had a kitchen and a complete set of furniture. A maid slept in the kitchen so that when the guest felt hungry in the morning, breakfast was on hand. One African potentate brought ten personal guards, two of whom slept under his bed. Kings and queens sat taking tea outside their tents, with all the appearance of being on a royal campsite. The accommodation tents were surrounded by trees, all flown in from the forests of Versailles. Reportedly, fifty thousand songbirds were brought to Persepolis—many died within seventy-two hours for want of water; tiny Spanish sparrows fell from the branches.

The grand Persepolis anniversary was certainly not to the benefit of the ordinary Persians occupying the miserable villages nearby. Emancipation had not touched the women there, drawing water from wells in tins and wearing black face shields and black flowing garments, which made them appear like either the ancient, untouched feudal peasants they were or the precursors of Darth Vader. While the mighty dined on the breasts of peacocks laid on Limoges china, the poor had dry bread. Planes full of blocks of ice the size of garages blackened the skies; for the celebration itself, the shah closed Iran's borders. All the Baccarat crystal glasses twinkled in anticipation of the shah's guests. Elizabeth Arden makeup kits were handed out to female guests. The sleek kit was called "Farah" after the queen. Imelda Marcos cozied up in her tent with Christina Ford. Haile Selassie had taken his black Chihuahua with him, its neck in the embrace of a diamond collar. Nixon stood the shah up, so Vice President Spiro Agnew took his place. There were no less that sixteen presidents of various places there, nine kings and five queens, nine sheiks; all in all the assembled jet set represented sixty-nine countries. When food was served by the shah on less prestigious occasions, glorious, rich, buttery Persian dishes appeared at the table, crimsoned with smoky saffron, bitter sumac, or billowing with the aromas of rose and bitter orange. But not, ironically, on the anniversary of the Persian Empire. To satisfy high-powered, transatlantic stomachs, the owner of Maxim's in Paris, the famous Monsieur Louis Vaudable, supervised the feast, managing more than 160 chefs, drawn from Paris, Monte Carlo, and St. Moritz. He told his chef, Michel Menant, "You're about to make history." Waiters were flown in from as far afield as St. Moritz, themselves afraid since they had to fly to Iran by aircraft for the first time in their lives. On the evening that heralded the opening of festivities, the head waiter fainted with anxiety and had to be tranquilized so he could do his job. The kitchens were sizzling hot; chefs stood cooking, semi-naked, in bikini-style pants.

The menus, bound in blue silk and gold, offered guests a novel and delicious dish of tiny, delicate poached quails' eggs with golden imperial caviar—Farah complained that, shamefully, this was the only Persian dish on the entire menu—lobster mousse with Sauce Nantua, and roast saddle of lamb with truffles. Then platters bore down on the tables with fifty peacocks stuffed with foie gras, their tail feathers reattached; figs with raspberries; cream; and port wine. A sorbet of Moët et Chandon 1911 slipped down very well or melted uneaten among the napkins. Twenty-five thousand bottles of wine were provided. Reputedly, Persepolis cost the shah close to $100 million. He scoffed at implied or direct criticism by countering, "The twenty-five hundredth anniversary cost me less than the inauguration of the new president of the United States. . . . What do they think I should feed over fifty heads of state? Bread and radishes?" Not at all! After the fireworks, the army marched out dressed as ancient Persians while the modern great and good nodded with delight from among the rugs and hot-water bottles that had been supplied for them.

No doubt some of the guests at Persepolis had been recruited from Mohammed and Farah's many foreign trips. These visits were often full of comedy. Queen Farah remembered the grisly pleasure with which the Russians took her and the shah on a tour of the former imperial palaces of Nicholas II. Perhaps it was like having an executioner mulling over the private property of the deceased with his next victim? There were other brilliant moments in USSR, such as when they were watching *Swan Lake* performed by the Russian ballet. When the black swan sallied onto the stage, the Russian politician Alexei Kosygin leaned in to the shah and whispered, "It makes you think of NATO, doesn't it?" Then there was the visit of Britain's Princess Margaret in 1969. The shah wasn't impressed: "I had never met her before and she struck me as being rather coarse, indeed more than a little common. Her husband seemed likeable enough but it's said, how shall I put it, that he's not exactly a lady's man." Finally, there was the Sri Lankan ambassador, who had badly fitted false teeth that fell down the back of his throat while he was giving a speech. He had to fumble about with them.

Some visitors to Iran would have more sobering words for the shah, had they chosen to air their thoughts. Mrs. Sadat, the wife of the Egyptian president Anwar Sadat, had, of course, witnessed the overthrow of King Farouk in 1952. When they visited the shah in 1976, she saw opulent chocolate mousses caged within swans of spun sugar and served on plates of gold, a flight of stairs that seemed to be made of many-faceted crystal, trees into which exotic fruits had been woven, and piles of black caviar glistening on tables. Privately, she shook her head: "There will be a revolution here, I feel it," she predicted to her husband.

The remote, wooden shah could do nothing to stem the huge populist Islamic surge headed by the Muslim cleric Ayatollah Khomeini. The United States and the United Kingdom were rumored to be covertly backing the ayatollah. People whispered, "If you lift a mullah's beard you'll find 'Made in Britain' stamped on his chin." The BBC broadcast the ayatollah's speeches about the cinemas that would burn, and it was rumored that the shah had taken to opium. Revolution was on. The shah went into exile in 1978 but not before millions of dollars had been siphoned out of the country; suitcases were hurriedly packed with jewels and Dior dresses. The royal family were shaking out the royal palaces like so many moneyboxes; Princess Ashraf's furnishings were flown out to her homes in Manhattan or Paris or the Seychelles.

The shah left on a sumptuous, personal 707 plane. They first flew to Egypt, the shah in the cockpit, flying the plane with muffled sobs and tears in his eyes until it left Iranian airspace. Then they settled down to an in-flight lunch that had been prepared in the palace before they left and was now served by the shah's personal cook, Ali Kabiri. They had been offered exile in Egypt but were never to know a permanent home again. Iran became, for the last of the shahs, a longed-for nostalgic dreamworld; the Pahlavis even missed the smell of gasoline in the heat—the distinctive urban stink of Tehran. In her memoirs, written in exile, Farah remembered Iranian food with great nostalgia: "A slice of feta cheese on a slice of bread with a mint leaf on top or a few apricots that a friend brings me from home fill me with an incredible nostalgia. And the boiling hot tea accompanied with mulberries! When these mulberries are dried in the sun, they still have a little bit of sand that crunches when you chew. Recently, eating some of these grains of fruit that the king and I liked so much I found that one of them had a few grains of sand. I thought I had broken a tooth, but at the same time I felt a surge of happiness at having swallowed a little bit of Iranian soil."

FOOD AND DUTY: GEORGE VI AND HIS QUEEN, ELIZABETH

Elizabeth Bowes-Lyon, the redoubtable wife of George VI and Queen Mother to Elizabeth II, was proud of her Scottish roots. She grew up in Glamis Castle with her delightful mother and father, Lord and Lady Strathmore. "Life is for living and working at," Lady Cecilia Strathmore told Elizabeth. "If you find anything or anyone a bore, the fault is in yourself." Cecilia scorned the snobberies of her social class, complaining that "some hostesses feed royalty to their guests as zoo keepers feed fish to seals." Principled and true to her word, when their maid Mabel knocked over a family vase during some vigorous dusting and tearfully confessed to the crime, Cecilia held her hand, saying, "I hear you've been in the wars Mabel. . . . Accidents will happen. It was only a Ming." Lord Claude Strathmore was often taken for a farm laborer, as he belted his coat with old twine and offered a warming slug of whiskey to people who came across him. The family was not very well off. As soon as Claude's gun was heard blasting off in the grounds, the estate tenants knew a fine dinner was planned at the castle. Claude's catch of game was on its way to the kitchen and then the table.

Little Elizabeth's pet name was "the Merry Mischief," and whenever Claude and Cecilia's guests did turn up at Glamis, she and her brother David poured icy-cold water onto the guests' heads from high up in the turrets. Looking up, drenched guests would catch no more than a flash of small, round faces; the children were pretending they were defending Glamis Castle with boiling oil. When Elizabeth wasn't practicing draconian medieval warfare on gentlemen in frock coats, she was startlingly precocious, pulling her mother's friends aside with the invitation, "Shall us sit and talk?"

Autumns in Scotland were followed by several months in St. Paul's, Waldenbury, where various Bowes-Lyons had resided since the eighteenth century. There lived Elizabeth's little Shetland pony Bobs. She and David kept chickens in the "Flea House," where they also hid from their nurse. Up in the schoolroom, she and David laid aside their schoolbooks to toast bread on the fire, play Dumb Crambo among the pencil shavings, or chew silently on homemade toffee. Elizabeth's pet bullfinch—called Bobby—masterfully stalked over the nursery table, often eating off Elizabeth's plate. Whether he would have been allowed a beakful of her favorite chocolate cake is less likely; she loved it so much she'd materialize at the stillroom and request, "May I come in and eat more—*much* more of that chocolate cake than I liked to eat while it was upstairs." The cook, however, remembered her being far less formal: "That little imp! I was for ever chasing her out of my kitchen." Bobby, incidentally, having lived a happy and full life, was murdered by the cat, and had a pencil box as a coffin.

Homemade Toffee

INGREDIENTS

2 cups butter, plus 1 tbsp. for
  greasing
3 cups vanilla sugar

Generous pinch of sea salt
The seeds and pulp of one plump
  vanilla pod

METHOD

Preheat the oven to 180°C. Butter a baking tin. In a heavy-bottomed saucepan, melt the butter. Once the butter has melted into a slippery pool, add the vanilla sugar and sea salt and stir until the sugar has dissolved. Place a jam thermometer in the pot, turn the heat up, and wait for about 5 minutes, until the thermometer reaches a temperature of 120°C. Add the vanilla pulp, stir through, and then wait for about 15 minutes, until the temperature climbs to 150°C. The very moment the temperature peaks at 150°C, whip the pan off the heat and pour the toffee into the buttered tin. Leave to cool for at least an hour or two. Finally, it is time to attack the toffee with a hammer (quite seriously, you have to assault toffee in order to break it up into shards). Do not even attempt a conversation when eating.

Elizabeth's husband-to-be, the future King George VI, known then as Bertie, was growing up in a weaselly cottage on the Sandringham Estate in Norfolk. He and his brother David (Edward VIII, who abdicated his throne for Wallis Simpson) had an evil nanny who ended up in an asylum. Not that this deterred Bertie's boyhood vivacity—he tried to serve his French tutor tadpoles on toast. The evil nanny hit Bertie with a heavy rod when he stuttered. Nor did she feed the boys properly; Bertie developed rickets, normally a disease associated with the poor in the city slums, and he had to wear stiff, poky splints to straighten his knock-knees. He cried at night, as he had to wear the splints even for sleep. The cottage corridors smelled of boiled cabbage. It was tough. Even his father sniggered and mocked his stammer, encouraging his siblings to do likewise. Like his grandson Prince Charles, Bertie had sticky-out ears. When he was sent to the Royal Naval College, he was called "Bat Lugs," and his fellow cadets pricked him with pins to see if his blood was truly blue. These horrors and unkindnesses, while leaving him deeply ashamed of his stammer, also made him into a decent and generous person. The sort that Elizabeth Bowes-Lyon might just fall in love with.

But that was not for now. While Bertie was off serving in World War I, Elizabeth worked as a nurse in Glamis Castle, a chunk of which became a hospital.

In his autobiography, James Stuart recalled taking Bertie out in Brussels during demobilization (this may have been when Bertie lost his virginity). The small, quaint restaurants of Brussels offered delicious food and bottles of burgundy; they had particularly good fun in the Merry Grill restaurant. James became Bertie's equerry when he went to Cambridge and, as luck had it, was also a close friend of the Bowes-Lyons. Bertie and Elizabeth's meeting was destined. Finally, in May 1920 Elizabeth and Bertie danced together at a ball. He was in love almost instantaneously but had to fight off some stiff competition, including one suitor who tried to woo Elizabeth by dancing on the table while picking out a tune on the ukulele.

The couple's wedding was a jolly affair. The meal was designed by the Swiss chef to the royals, Gabriel "Chummy" Tschumi, with some dishes specially named to reflect the antecedents of the bride and groom: Consommé à la Windsor, Suprêmes de Saumon, Reine Mary, Côtelettes d'Agneau, Prince Albert, and Chapons à la Strathmore. Then there was ham and tongue in aspic, a "royal" salad, asparagus with creamy sauce, strawberries, and woven sugar baskets containing patisserie, which guests could take away. In his memoirs, *Royal Chef*, "Chummy" gave the recipe for the dish he invented for Lady Strathmore, Chapons à la Strathmore: "*Chapons à la Strathmore* is served cold with a vegetable salad in mayonnaise. To make it, you need a boiling chicken which is well cooked, cut in neat joints, and chaudfroided in a white chicken sauce. It is served on a flat dish covered with clear chicken jelly, and when this has set it is garnished with truffles and tips of tongue either cut into tiny squares or circles. The truffle and tongue garnishing takes a long time to prepare artistically, but it can give a very pleasant colour scheme if arranged well."

The newlyweds, finally in their own home at the large, beautiful, and well-appointed 145 Piccadilly, London, built a quiet and happy existence. When no public duties beckoned, Bertie and Elizabeth liked nothing better than to snuggle up in front of the fire, their supper on a tray. Occasionally, the quiet was shattered, as when Elizabeth had her father-in-law, George V, over for dinner. Queen Mary, she knew, liked simple and plain food (much to the chef's fury at Buckingham Palace, she scored though his menu suggestion of gateaux and penned in "stewed plums and semolina"). It all went very well, though. Fortunately, Elizabeth's staff was well versed in place setting: Brian Hoey records that George V was once served Dover sole, his place at the table set out with fish knives and forks. "What are these for?" he queried. The answer came back: This is how the middle class ate fish. "How extraordinary," marveled George.

Stewed Plums and Semolina

FOR THE PLUMS . . .

½ cup granulated sugar

1 cup water

1 lb. Victoria plums, stoned

FOR THE SEMOLINA . . .

½ cup semolina

1 pint full-fat milk

1 scant tbsp. granulated sugar

1 tsp. vanilla extract

METHOD

Put the sugar and water into a saucepan and bring to a gentle simmer until the sugar is dissolved. Now add the plums, cover, and cook for 10 minutes or until the plums are soft but not collapsed. Meanwhile, make the semolina. In a bowl, combine the semolina with 2 tablespoons of the milk to make a paste. Gradually add the rest of the milk, the sugar, and the vanilla extract. Pour this mixture into a saucepan and, stirring regularly, simmer over a medium heat for 10 minutes; the semolina will thicken. Serve with the warm stewed plums.

Elizabeth and George soon had two daughters, the little princesses Elizabeth, called "Lilibet," and Margaret. All seemed quiet in childhood for the princesses: a cozy nursery; their kindly nanny, Marion Crawford, whom they fondly called "Crawfie"; their lovely parents giving them baths and reading stories. When the family were trapped inside on rainy, wet days, Elizabeth might pop into the stillroom and make Scottish scones. Princess Margaret was rather like "Merry Mischief"; she kept her sister awake by singing "Old MacDonald Had a Farm" and making animal noises through the wall. Lilibet and Margaret competed to see who could eat the greatest number of brown bread slices lavishly spread with golden syrup. As the older princess (and future Queen Elizabeth II), Lilibet was eventually promoted from nursery eating to taking her lunch downstairs with her parents, where her nanny, Crawfie, recalled that Lilibet had to take spoonfuls of milk pudding, which her mother thought was very good for her. Finally, Lilibet looked sternly at Crawfie and said, "If it's good for me, I think Crawfie ought to have some too. It is good for her also." Lilibet liked to pretend Crawfie was a horse, particularly on very cold, frosty days when her nanny's breath steamed just like a horse. Lilibet had also inherited Queen Victoria's sense of diligence; when twelve-year-old Victoria heard that she was in line for the throne, she promised earnestly, "I will be good!" So all was quiet and merry with the little family at 145 Piccadilly. Quiet, that is, until the abdication of their Uncle David (Edward VIII) and their father's sudden, unwilling elevation to kingship.

Milk Pudding

INGREDIENTS

3 eggs

¾ cup sugar

1¼ oz. gelatin

2 tbsp. hot water

¾ pint milk

1 tsp. vanilla extract

METHOD

Beat the eggs with the sugar. Dissolve the gelatin in the hot water. Warm the milk, then gradually whisk it into the eggs. Place this eggy mixture in a saucepan and bring to a boil, stirring all the time. Add the gelatin and remove from the heat. Stir through the vanilla extract. Pour the milk pudding mixture into a bowl and allow to cool. Refrigerate for about 4 hours and serve.

Fortunately, George V was no longer around to witness the abdication. He would have found it considerably more shocking than the middle-class use of fish knives. Before his death, he had become increasingly infuriated by David's liaisons with married women, roaring at him, "You dress like a cad. You act like a cad. You are a cad. Get out!" Forced into kingship by David's passion for Wallis Simpson (David had lasted less than a year as Edward VIII), Bertie reluctantly laid aside his privacy and peace. On the day of the coronation, when Bertie was to metamorphose into George VI, the smell from frying pans of bacon and eggs and fried bread rose up to the Buckingham Palace windows as royal watchers, camping overnight in St. James's Park, prepared themselves a nice hot breakfast. The king-to-be, in contrast, couldn't stomach so much as a slice of toast because of the "sinking feeling inside." The deep Christian faith Bertie and Elizabeth shared helped them to face the future; such was Bertie's earnestness that once, over dinner, he demanded the opinion of a new lady-in-waiting on the Ten Commandments.

Even though Wallis called Elizabeth the "Dowdy Duchess," "that fat Scottish cook," and "Cookie" (she said she was shaped that way) and wouldn't hesitate to imitate her, Elizabeth continued to send the couple Christmas cards as the years rolled by. Many were found eventually in Edward's bath; he loved showers and found the bath a very useful vessel for storing correspondence. The attitude of Edward's former mistress, posh beauty Thelma Furness, toward Elizabeth was much warmer. When Thelma was imagining poverty, which she seemed to envisage as living in a bungalow, she said there was no one she'd find more cheering as her neighbor than Elizabeth. Slowly, and with humor, the family began to adjust to their role as the royal family. There were hilarious moments, as when the king, queen, and the two daughters dived under their tea table just in time to avoid General Eisenhower and a delegation of transatlantic guests who were touring Windsor Castle. Eisenhower and company breezed past, not noticing the giggling, rocking table.

Another transatlantic guest, Eleanor Roosevelt, visiting Buckingham Palace in 1942 and traveling under the code name "Rover," witnessed the family's determination to share the privations of war with the British people. Eleanor froze in her apartments, plastic sheeting was stretched across the capacious windows, and a spluttering little electric fire shed a thin heat. Although dinner was on gold-and-silver plates, Eleanor noted, "Our bread was the same kind of war bread every other family had to eat . . . nothing was ever served that was not served in any war canteen." Cunningly, war bread was brown—the British public was used to white—but the brown was thicker, more obstinate beneath the knife, and so the public ate less of it. When bombs hit Buckingham Palace, Elizabeth was relieved. It meant that the royal family could share the experience of the bomb-blitzed Londoners. By the time of Eleanor's visit, Bertie was exhausted and had tan makeup smeared on his face to mask his exhaustion. If a British Resistance movement was to be formed in the future, Bertie wanted to lead it. He kept a shotgun by his feverish pillow in case any cunning "Huns" parachuted onto the palace flower beds. When he wasn't sleeping, he patrolled the palace grounds, checking that it was properly blacked out. As Europe collapsed before Hitler, stray refugee royals began appearing at Buckingham Palace, down-at-the-heels and seeking shelter. A British destroyer delivered Queen Wilhemina of the Netherlands at Harwich port, luggage-less except for a tin hat (and some jewels she managed to remember)—she had escaped the Nazi Stormtroopers' clutches by only half an hour. Her large raincoat covered a voluminous nightdress beneath (being a large lady, the Windsors had a hard time finding clothes for her afterward at the palace). The Luxembourg royal family turned up at the train station, and King Haakon of Norway appeared, having dodged the Luftwaffe. All had evaded capture, foiling what they believed was Hitler's cunning scheme to "bag" as many monarchs as he could from invaded countries. Elizabeth, a good shot herself, practiced firing her shotgun at any rats that crossed her path. "I shall not go down like the others," she said firmly, referring to the other European royal houses.

When they could, the king and queen went to Windsor Castle (some twenty-five miles from London), where Lilibet and Margaret lived for five years. Whenever there was an air-raid warning, the girls donned their little siren suits (Winston Churchill loved wearing these) and solemnly trudged down to the Windsor Castle dungeons, their suitcases packed and looking for all the world, said Crawfie, as if they were off to catch a train. There they also stuck to wartime rations but, like Churchill or any members of the landed gentry, were able to enrich their table with game. Bertie dug up the lawns at Windsor and planted a victory garden. For pudding, however, the children were generally stuck with their grandmother Queen Mary's favorite: stewed plums, taken from Windsor's gnarled old plum trees. After that, they might spend an hour or so practicing (and giggling over) how to quash incendiary bombs. Determined to avoid excess, Bertie painted a black line around the bath in Windsor, marking out the three inches of water everyone was allowed.

Inevitably, the war threw Bertie and his prime minister, Winston Churchill, into frequent contact. In the basement of Buckingham Palace—which doubled as a bomb shelter—they had lunch on Tuesdays, often with Elizabeth. No other "ears" were allowed entry, and the three served themselves from a side table, though at times all food was forgotten. They learned to laugh together. When sandwiches appeared, Bertie joked, "I don't know what's in them. Sawdust, I suppose." The correspondence between the two men reveals an increasing warmth. The king would open his letters to Churchill with "My dear Winston," and by 1940 he vowed, "I could not have a better Prime Minister."

Then, marvelously, after all the horror and sacrifice, came Victory in Europe Day on Wednesday, May 8, 1945. Germany had surrendered; tears of relieved jubilation and gladness were shed. Ice cream returned with freedom. The king, queen, and Churchill, with Lilibet and Margaret in the background, stood waving from the balcony of Buckingham Palace before the cheering, dancing, singing, and weeping London crowds. After that, it was time for a jolly lunch of salmon kedgeree, lamb chops, salad, and crème caramel. The Buckingham Palace wine cellars were cracked open, and dark, cobwebby bottles of port materialized with champagne to pop and fizz. Not only that, but Churchill was invited back for dinner. Queen Elizabeth, her handgun packed away, with a light heart took an afternoon tea at 4 p.m. of cucumber sandwiches, dense sweet fruitcake, a puffy Swiss roll, and some joyous parcels of currant buns.

That night the venerable, silvery Queen Mary traveled to the palace, and Churchill arrived, face polished, medals pinned to his chest. That night they truly feasted. The cellars were raided again for Mouton Rothschild, Heidsieck champagne, and Riesling. First there was delicate poached turbot, then a melting partridge casserole, new potatoes (perhaps dug up from Windsor's victory garden?), and spring broccoli. Cherries and vanilla ice cream were for dessert. Then an airy richness of cheese soufflés. After toasting the Allied victory with port, Bertie and Winston smoked Winston's trademark long cigars together (even though Bertie secretly would have preferred one of his Senior Service cigarettes).

Partridge Casserole

INGREDIENTS

1 tbsp. butter
1 tbsp. olive oil
3 partridges, jointed
4 ribs of celery, cut into 1 in. pieces
6 rashers of streaky bacon, cut into
  1 in. pieces
Freshly ground black pepper

Sea salt
Saucepan-size piece of buttered
  greaseproof paper
1 tbsp. mushroom ketchup
3 glasses of port
3 tbsp. sour cream
A dash of dry sherry

METHOD

In a heavy-bottomed, deep saucepan, heat the butter and olive oil. Brown the partridge pieces in the oils and then remove from the heat. Next, add the celery and bacon to the buttery mess in the saucepan. Salt and pepper, turn down the heat to low, and then cover with the buttered greaseproof paper. Allow the celery and bacon to sweat for 10 minutes. After this time, return the partridges to the pan; pour over them the mushroom ketchup and port. Cover. Braise over a moderate heat until the partridge is cooked—this should take about 30 minutes. Now remove the partridges from the pan (cover them and keep them warm), turn up the heat beneath the pan, and reduce the partridge gravy by a third. Now add the sour cream and a dash of dry sherry. Cook for a further 3 minutes and then serve the partridges with the creamy port sauce poured over them.

Bertie's Senior Service habit proved to be the death of him. Having served his country generously and well, this unobtrusive monarch succumbed to lung cancer in 1952. Elizabeth believed he had sacrificed his health and thus life for his country. On the throne was a new queen, Lilibet, now Queen Elizabeth II, and our Elizabeth became the Queen Mother, a role she played for the next fifty-or-so years with great aplomb, bringing her own comic wisdom to the job. Margaret Rhodes recalled the Queen Mother having lunch with Queen Elizabeth. A very modest drinker, the queen surprised her mother by asking for a second glass of wine. "'Oh, my darling,' said her mother. 'Is that wise? After all you *are* the Queen and you have to reign all afternoon.'" When the British media reported that Prince Philip loved poetry, the Queen Mother responded, "How extraordinary. I have known Philip all these years yet I did not know he had a guilty secret. He likes poetry. Poor man. How dreadful." There was, perhaps, no love lost between the two; before he married Lilibet, the Queen Mother used to call him "the Hun." She loved ceremonial mishaps—someone riding in the wrong direction on a parade, another's braces snapping mid-bow. Or when socialite Elsa Maxwell curtsied to the queen (she compared herself to a buoy on a swell) but, as luck would have it, she landed on the queen's feet when she executed her second curtsey. The Queen Mother loved to go fishing in the afternoon or evening in Balmoral with her waders on and was very amused when a fellow fisherwoman once tried to curtsey to her in the water, only to have her waders fill up with sloshing Cairngorm water.

The Duchess of Grafton frequently traveled abroad with the Queen Mother and always found her very friendly to others at the dinner table. One host might warn her, "'So and so is a communist,' and she always said, 'But I love communists,' and would proceed to get on particularly well with them." Once, traveling in Africa on a long car journey with one of her ladies-in-waiting, she said, "Now I am going to have to close my eyes for ten minutes—you keep yours open, and if there's a crowd of people give me a nudge and I'll wave to them." After her rest, she woke up, bright eyed, and said, "Now you can go to sleep." She was also an excellent practical joker. When one dignitary turned up at Balmoral, she shook hands with him and said, "I'm so glad you have come to look at the boiler. It has been playing up for some time."

Elizabeth was a wonderful party girl. She loved dancing, especially doing the Congo around whichever palace she was in, singing songs like rowdy renditions of "Lloyd George Knew My Father," sometimes dressing up in a bowler hat and stick, inviting a series of toasts at Balmoral. Her pre-lunch line was "I do hope lunch is late, then we can have another drink or perhaps several." Over dinners in Balmoral, she would customarily propose a toast, "Hooray for . . . ," lift her glass, and everyone followed suit in a toast; then there would be cries of "Down with . . . ," and glasses would vanish beneath the table. Bobby the bullfinch was never forgotten. Her love of animals flourished; in Scotland she had Jock, a Highland pony, who was passionately keen on mince. Her beloved Scotland also offered an opportunity for picnics, a great royal preoccupation. The Queen Mum sent a note to her adoring and adored servant Bill Tallon, prioritizing the necessary preparations for a picnic: "I think I will take two small bottles of Dubonnet and gin with me this morning, in case it is needed." At Birkhall in Balmoral, according to her former equerry Ashe Windham, the Queen Mother liked to go down to her log cabin for a picnic almost every day. There they ate their way through a very tasty repast: "You start off with something fishy, like a mousse, and then usually a bit of cold ham or cold grouse, which might have been shot the day before. This is followed up by the traditional jam pies produced by the cook." She insisted that the best way to eat jam pies was to slice off the top and fill it with cream; then you had to try to actually eat it. "The old hands put a drop or two in the bottom, but the enthusiastic beginners fill it up to the top and suffer the consequences." One evening, again in Ashe's company, the Queen Mother had been the dinner guest in Prince Charles's log cabin. There he had made them an "interesting" meal of rather tough venison. Not being very partial to venison, as they were driving back in the Land Rover, the Queen Mother asked, "Ashe, are you feeling a little bit hungry?"

He said, "No, not really, Ma'am."

"Well," she said, "I am. I think we'll make some scrambled eggs when we get back to Birkhall." There they all marched into the kitchen. Ashe was in charge of making toast, while the "Queen Mother was cracking eggs into a basin and much whisking was going on, and shortly after midnight we had a great plateful of scrambled eggs on toast."

Food at Clarence House in London when the Queen Mother was the chief resident was reputedly pretty heavy going, like a slightly slipshod 1970s hotel, with deep-fried potato rissoles and liverish-looking stews. There was something beautifully ancient and perpetual about events there, from the Queen Mum's gin and Dubonnet tipple before lunch to the long memories and starchy habits of the ancient upper crust. A scattering of corgis would announce the Queen Mother's arrival. Cecil Beaton, the photographer and a friend of hers, was always fascinated by her "solid mountains" of hats. At her seventieth birthday party, he recalled that there was delicious caramel soufflé and, to suit the occasion, the Queen Mother was in a "sort of redingote of pale moth-coloured chiffon with pelisses covered with solid sequins, a big pearl and diamond necklace and tiara. She only needed a wand to fly to the top of the Christmas tree." He was very fond of her. At another lovely intimate lunch, he noted that she perched on the arm of the sofa and, when she spotted there was hardly any asparagus, took a small amount for herself. Her consumption of wine on top of the scant asparagus made her face very jolly and pink, and she confessed that her recurrent dreams were of being late and finding that no clothes had been put out for her to wear.

In Colin Burgess's book, *Behind Palace Doors*, he recalled sharing a hard-core lunch of chicken and mashed potatoes with the Queen Mum and her old guard of Sir Alistair Aird, her devoted lady-in-waiting Dame Frances Campbell-Preston, and the Queen Mum's silvery treasurer Sir Ralph Anstruther. The day was warm; the lunch was outside, the honeyed hum of bees was in the air. Several bottles of pugnacious, solid claret were consumed as the quartet struggled on, debating World War II. Burgess suddenly found that, one by one, midconversation, all four of the elderly diners fell fast asleep, and the burble of snores and sighs filled the air. Burgess sat silently, politely mute. Some thirty-five minutes passed. Burgess thought, *Well, I ought to ring the bell for the servants, I suppose.* No sooner had the bell tinkled than all four woke and immediately resumed their conversation. "And of course the Italians," blustered Sir Ralph, "simply gave in once the Germans had gone."

One Last Caramel Soufflé for the Road

INGREDIENTS

½ cup softened butter, plus an
   extra 1–2 oz. for buttering
   soufflé ramekins
1⅓ cups demerara sugar, plus
   an extra for ramekins
1 scant cup heavy cream

The seeds and pulp of 1 vanilla pod
A pinch of salt
2 egg yolks
1 tbsp. all-purpose flour
3 egg whites, at room temperature
2 tbsp. demerara sugar

METHOD

Preheat the oven to 200°C. Butter 5 small ramekins and pour some demerara sugar into each. Roll each ramekin from side to side, evenly distributing the sugar as it sticks to the butter. This gives each soufflé an outer shell of butter and brown sugar.

Now make the caramel sauce. Some will be incorporated into the soufflé mix, while the remainder will be reserved as a delicious caramel sauce to accompany the soufflés. In a deep saucepan, combine the cup and a third of demerara sugar with the cream, vanilla pulp, and pinch of salt. Stir until the sugar has dissolved. Let this bubble away gently for about 2 minutes and then drain off a scant cup of the sauce; reserve this for the accompanying caramel sauce.

Remove the remaining caramel sauce from the heat.

Whisk the egg yolks in a large bowl. Incorporate the flour thoroughly. Now, slowly whisk in the warm caramel sauce. Return the entire mix to the pan and, using a wooden spoon, keep stirring the mixture over a medium heat until it thickens, coating the back of the spoon. Remove from the heat and cool, continuing to stir until it is lukewarm. Allow to cool.

In a large, clean bowl, whisk the egg whites until they foam, then gradually add the 2 tablespoons of demerara sugar, whisking until you have a soft, shapely mass of egg whites. Using a large metal spoon, fold about a third of the egg whites gently into the cooled caramel sauce in the saucepan. Now fold the saucepan mixture gently through the egg white mass, using a figure-eight motion.

Fill each ramekin with the soufflé mixture and bake for 10–12 minutes in the oven. Gently warm the caramel sauce and serve with the soufflés.

Bibliography

Afkhami, Gholam. *The Life and Times of the Shah*. Berkeley, CA: University of California Press, 2009.

Aga Khan III. *The Memoirs of Aga Khan: World Enough and Time*. London: Cassell, 1954.

Aisin-Gioro, Pu Yi. *From Emperor to Citizen: The Autobiography of Aisin-Gioro Pu Yi*. Peking: Foreign Languages Press, 1964.

Alam, Asadollah. *The Shah and I: The Confidential Diary of Iran's Royal Court, 1969–1977*. New York: St. Martin's Press, 1992.

Alexander, Diana. *The Other Mitford: Pamela's Story*. Stroud, UK: History Press, 2012.

Almedingen, E. M. *The Romanovs: Three Centuries of an Ill-Fated Dynasty*. London: Bodley Head, 1966.

Anand, Sushila. *Daisy: The Life and Loves of the Countess of Warwick*. London: Piatkus, 2008.

Aronson, Theo. *Heart of a Queen: Queen Victoria's Romantic Attachments*. London: Murray, 1991.

Asquith, Lady Cynthia. *Queen Elizabeth: Her Intimate and Authentic Life*. London: Hutchinson, 1937.

Astor, Michael. *Tribal Feelings*. London: Murray, 1963.

Azar, Helen. *The Diary of Olga Romanov: Royal Witness to the Russian Revolution*. Yardley, PA: Westholme Publishing, 2014.

Balsan, Consuelo Vanderbilt. *The Glitter and the Gold*. London: Hodder, 2011.

Barlett, Donald, and James Steele. *Howard Hughes: His Life and Madness*. London: Deutsch, 2003.

Basu, Shrabani. *Curry: The Story of the Nation's Favourite Dish*. Stroud, UK: Sutton Publishing, 2003.

———. *Victoria and Abdul*. Stroud, UK: History Press, 2010.

Battye, Evelyn. "Imperial Tutor: Sir Reginald Fleming Johnston (1874–1938)." *Country Life*, September 25, 1986.

Beaton, Cecil. *The Unexpurgated Beaton: The Cecil Beaton Diaries as They Were Written*. London: Weidenfeld and Nicolson, 2002.

Behr, Edward. *Hirohito: Behind the Myth*. London: Hamilton, 1989.

———. *The Last Emperor*. London: Macdonald, 1987.

Berry, Wendy. *The Housekeeper's Diary: Charles and Diana before the Break-Up*. New York: Barricade Books, 1995.

Birmingham, Stephen. *Duchess: The Story of Wallis Warfield Windsor*. London: Macmillan, 1969.

Blanch, Lesley. *Farah, Shahbanou of Iran: Queen of Persia*. London: Collins, 1978.

Blunt, Wilfrid. *The Dream King: Ludwig II of Bavaria*. London: Hamilton, 1970.

Bower, Tom. *Fayed: The Unauthorised Biography*. London: Macmillan, 1998.

Brady, Frank. *Onassis: An Extravagant Life*. London: Futura Publications, 1978.

Brown, Peter Harry. *Such Devoted Sisters: Those Fabulous Gabors*. London: Robson Books, 1986.

Brown, Peter Harry, and Pat H. Broeske. *Howard Hughes: The Untold Story*. New York: Penguin, 1996.

Burg, Katerina von. *Ludwig II of Bavaria: The Man and the Mystery*. London: Windsor Publications, 1989.

Burgess, Colin. *Behind Palace Doors*. London: John Blake, 2007.

Burrell, Paul. *A Royal Duty*. London: Penguin, 2003.

Callas, Evangelia. *My Daughter—Maria Callas*. London: Frewin, 1967.

Callas, Jackie. *Sisters*. London: Macmillan, 1989.

Campbell, Lady Colin. *Diana in Private*. London: Warner, 1992.

Collins, Joan. *Passion for Life*. London: Constable, 2013.

Collis, Maurice. *Nancy Astor*. London: Faber and Faber, 1960.

Cooper, Duff. *The Duff Cooper Diaries*. Edited by John Julius Norwich. London: Weidenfeld and Nicolson, 2005.

Cowles, Virginia. *The Astors: The Story of a Transatlantic Family*. London: Weidenfeld and Nicolson, 1979.

———. *The Rothschilds: A Family of Fortune*. London: Weidenfeld and Nicolson, 1973.

Crawford, Marion. *Happy and Glorious!* London: George Newnes, 1953.

———. *The Little Princesses*. London: Orion, 2002.

———. *Queen Elizabeth*. London: Purnell and Sons, 1952.

Cullen, Tom. *The Empress Brown: The Story of a Royal Friendship*. London: Bodley Head, 1969.

Dalley, Jan. *Diana Mosley: A Life*. London: Faber and Faber, 1999.

Dampier, Phil, and Ashley Walton. *What's in the Queen's Handbag: And Other Royal Secrets*. Sussex, UK: Book Guild, 2007.

Daniel, Sarah. *Lord Rothschild's Favourite Recipes*. London: Stourton Press, 1989.

De Courcy, Anne. *Diana Mosley*. London: Vintage, 2004.

Deghy, Guy, and Keith Waterhouse. *Café Royal: 90 Years of Bohemia*. London: Hutchinson, 1955.

De-la-Noy, Michael. *Queen Victoria at Home*. London: Constable, 2003.

Devee, Sunity. *The Autobiography of an Indian Princess*. London: Murray, 1921.

Devonshire, Deborah. *Wait for Me! Memoirs of the Youngest Mitford Sister*. London: Murray, 2011.

Doren, Mamie van. *Playing the Field: My Story*. New York: Putnam, 1987.

Duff, David. *Elizabeth of Glamis*. London: Magnum Books, 1977.

———. *George and Elizabeth: A Royal Marriage*. London: Collins, 1963.

———, ed. *Victoria in the Highlands: The Personal Journal of Her Majesty Queen Victoria*. London: Muller, 1968.

Edgren, Gretchen. *Inside the Playboy Mansion: If You Don't Swing, Don't Ring*. London: Aurum Press, 1998.

Edwards, Anne. *The Grimaldis of Monaco*. London: HarperCollins, 1992.

———. *Throne of Gold: The Lives of the Aga Khans*. London: HarperCollins, 1996.

Edwards, John. *The Roman Cookery of Apicius*. London: Rider, 1985.

Englund, Steven. *Princess Grace*. London: Orbis, 1984.

Erickson, Carolly. *Her Little Majesty: The Life of Queen Victoria*. London: Robson Books, 1997.

Ernst, Jimmy. *A Not-So-Still Life*. New York: Pushcart Press, 1984.

Escoffier, Auguste. *Auguste Escoffier: Memories of My Life*. New York: Van Nostrand Reinhold, 1996.

Esfandiary Bakhtiary, Soraya. *Palace of Solitude*. London: Quartet Books, 1991.

Fielding, Daphne. *The Face on the Sphinx: A Portrait of Gladys Deacon, Duchess of Marlborough*. London: Hamilton, 1978.

Fletcher, Joanne. *Cleopatra the Great*. London: Hodder, 2009.

Fort, Adrian. *Nancy: The Story of Lady Astor*. London: Cape, 2012.

Francatelli, Charles Elme. *Chef to Queen Victoria*. Edited by Ann Currah. London: Kimber, 1973.

Fuhrman, Joseph. *Rasputin: The Untold Story*. Hoboken, NJ: Wiley, 2013.

Furness, Thelma, and Gloria Vanderbilt. *Double Exposure*. London: Muller, 1959.

Gabor, Zsa Zsa. *One Lifetime Is Not Enough*. London: Headline, 1992.

Gabor, Zsa Zsa, and Gerold Frank. *Zsa Zsa Gabor: My Story*. London: Arthur Barker, 1961.

Gage, Nicholas. *Greek Fire: The Story of Maria Callas and Aristotle Onassis*. London: Pan Books, 2001.

Gardner, Ava. *Ava: My Story*. London: Bantam Press, 1990.

Gaury, Gerald de. *Faisal: King of Saudi Arabia*. London: Arthur Barker, 1966.

Gerard, Francis. *The Romance of Ludwig II of Bavaria*. London: Hutchinson, 1899.

Getty, John Paul. *As I See It*. London: W. H. Allen, 1976.

Gladstone, William. *Gladstone to His Wife*. Edited by A. Tilney Bassett. London: Methuen, 1936.

Goodall, Sarah, and Nicholas Monson. *The Palace Diaries: Twelve Years with HRH Prince Charles*. London: Mainstream Publishing, 2006.

Graham, Sheilah. *Beloved Infidel: The Education of a Woman*. London: Cassell, 1959.

Granger, Stewart. *Sparks Fly Upward*. New York: G. P. Putman's Sons, 1981.

Graves, Charles. *Royal Riviera*. London: Heinemann, 1957.

Gregory, Martin. *Diana: The Last Days*. London: Virgin, 1999.

Grenfell, Joyce. *Darling Ma: Letters to Her Mother, 1932–1944*. London: Hodder and Stoughton, 1988.

———. *In Pleasant Places*. London: Macmillan, 1979.

Guggenheim, Peggy. *Out of This Century: Confessions of an Art Addict*. London: Deutsch, 1979.

Guinness, Jonathan. *The House of Mitford*. London: Hutchinson, 1984.

Hack, Richard. *Hughes: The Private Diaries, Memos and Letters: The Definitive Biography of the First American Billionaire*. Beverly Hills, CA: New Millennium Press, 2002.

Hane, Mikiso, trans. *Emperor Hirohito and His Chief Aide-de-Camp: The Honjō Diary, 1933–36*. Tokyo: University of Tokyo Press, 1967.

Harrison, Rosina. *Gentlemen's Gentlemen: My Friends in Service*. London: Sphere Books, 1978.

———. *Rose: My Life in Service*. London: Cassell, 1975.

Hepburn, Katharine. *Me: Stories of My Life*. New York: Knopf, 1991.

Higham, Charles. *Howard Hughes: The Secret Life*. London: Sidgwick and Jackson, 1993.

———. *Wallis: Secret Lives of the Duchess of Windsor*. London: Sidgwick and Jackson, 1988.

Hill, James. *Rita Hayworth: A Memoir*. London: Robson, 1983.

Hilton, Conrad. *Be My Guest*. Englewood Cliffs, NJ: Prentice-Hall, 1957.

Hilton, Lisa. *The Horror of Love*. London: Weidenfeld and Nicolson, 2011.

Hitler, Adolf. *Hitler's Table Talk, 1941–1944: His Private Conversations*. 3rd ed. Edited and translated by Norman Cameron and R. H. Stephens. New York City: Enigma Books, 2000.

Hoey, Brian. *At Home with the Queen: Life through the Keyhole of the Royal Household*. London: HarperCollins, 2003.

———. *Invitation to the Palace: How Royalty Entertains*. London: Grafton Books, 1989.

———. *The Royal Train: The Inside Story*. Yeovil, UK: Haynes, 2008.

———. *The Royal Yacht* Britannia. Newbury Park, CA: Haynes, 2012.

Hogg, James, and Michael Mortimer, eds. *The Queen Mother Remembered: The Intimate Recollections of Her Friends*. London: BBC Books, 2002.

Holden, David, and Richard Johns. *The House of Saud*. London: Sidgwick and Jackson, 1981.

Hoyt, Edwin P. *The Vanderbilts and Their Fortunes*. London: Muller, 1963.

Hubbard, Kate. *Serving Victoria: Life in the Royal Household*. London: Chatto and Windus, 2012.

Hussein, King of Jordan. *Uneasy Lies the Head: The Autobiography of His Majesty King Hussein of the Hashemite Kingdom of Jordan*. London: Heinemann, 1962.

Ingram, Kevin. *Rebel: The Short Life of Esmond Romilly*. London: Weidenfeld and Nicolson, 1985.

Jenkins, Graham. *Richard Burton, My Brother*. London: Joseph, 1988.

Jerrold, Clare. *The Married Life of Queen Victoria*. London: Nash, 1913.

Johnston, Reginald. *Twilight in the Forbidden City*. Oxford: Oxford University Press, 1993.

Kanroji, Osanaga. *Hirohito: An Intimate Portrait of the Japanese Emperor*. Los Angeles: Gateweay Publishers, 1975.

Kanter, Judith. *Bridesmaids: Grace Kelly and Six Intimate Friends*. New York: Pocket Books, 1990.

Kapuściński, Ryszard. *Shah of Shahs*. London: Penguin, 2006.

Kavaler, Lucy. *The Astors: A Family Chronicle*. London: Harrap, 1966.

Kay, Richard. *Diana: Untold Story*. London: Boxtree, 1998.

King, Greg. *The Duchess of Windsor: The Uncommon Life of Wallis Simpson*. London: Aurum Press, 1999.

———. *The Mad King: The Life and Times of Ludwig II of Bavaria*. London: Aurum Press, 1996.

Kobal, John. *Rita Hayworth: The Time, the Place and the Woman*. London: W. H. Allen, 1977.

Korda, Michael. *Charmed Lives*. London: Penguin, 1979.

Lamont-Brown, Raymond. *Edward VII's Last Loves*. Stroud, UK: Sutton, 1998.

———. *John Brown: Queen Victoria's Highland Servant*. Stroud, UK: Sutton, 2000.

Lang, Theo. *My Darling Daisy*. London: Joseph, 1966.

Langtry, Lillie. *The Days I Knew*. London: Hutchinson, 1925.

Leigh, Wendy. *True Grace: The Life and Times of an American Princess*. London: J. R. Books, 2007.

Lincoln, W. Bruce. *The Romanovs: Autocrats of All the Russias*. London: Weidenfeld and Nicolson, 1981.

Lippman, Thomas. "The Day FDR Met Saudi Arabia's Ibn Saud." *The Link* 38, no. 2 (April–May 2005): 1–16.

Lovell, Mary S. *The Mitford Girls: The Biography of an Extraordinary Family*. London: Little, Brown, 2001.

Maddison, Holly. *Down the Rabbit Hole*. New York: HarperCollins, 2015.

Magnus, Philip. *King Edward VII*. London: Penguin, 1967.

Martin, Ralph. *The Woman He Loved*. London: W. H. Allen, 1974.

Massey, Christian de. *Palace: My Life in the Royal Family of Monaco*. London: Bodley Head, 1986.

Maxwell, Elsa. *I Married the World*. London: Heinemann, 1955.

Mayer, Catherine. *Charles: The Heart of a King*. London: W. H. Allen, 2015.

McBride, Barrie St. Clair. *Farouk of Egypt*. London: Hale, 1967.

McDougald, Charles. *The Marcos File*. San Francisco: San Francisco Publishers, 1987.

McGrady, Darren. *Eating Royally: Recipes and Remembrances from a Palace Kitchen*. Nashville, TN: Thomas Nelson, 2007.

McIntosh, Christopher. *Ludwig II of Bavaria: The Swan King*. London: I. B. Taurus, 1997.

Meneghini, Battista. *My Wife Maria Callas*. London: Bodley Head, 1991.

Milani, Abbas. *The Shah*. New York: Palgrave Macmillan, 2011.

Mitford, Diana. *A Life of Contrasts*. London: Gibson Square, 2009.

Mitford, Jessica. *Hons and Rebels*. London: Gollancz, 1989.

Moore, Terry. *The Beauty and the Billionaire*. New York: Pocket Books, 1984.

Morton, Frederic. *The Rothschilds*. London: Secker and Warburg, 1962.

Mosely, Charlotte. *The Mitfords: Letters between Six Sisters*. London: Fourth Estate, 2007.

Mosely, Nicholas. *Rules of the Game: Sir Oswald and Lady Cynthia Mosley*. London: Secker and Warburg, 1982.

Mosley, Leonard. *Hirohito: Emperor of Japan*. London: Weidenfeld and Nicolson, 1966.

Mossolov, A. A. *At the Court of the Last Tsar*. London: Methuen, 1935.

Navarro Pedrosa, Carmen. *The Untold Story of Imelda Marcos.* Worthing, UK: Littlehampton Book Services, 1987.

Noor, Queen Consort of Hussein, King of Jordan. *Leap of Faith: Memoirs of an Unexpected Life.* London: Weidenfeld and Nicolson, 2003.

Obolensky, Serge. *One Man in His Time.* London: Hutchinson, 1960.

Pahlavi, Farah. *An Enduring Love: My Life with the Shah, a Memoir.* New York: Miramax Books, 2004.

Pahlavi, Mohammed Reza. *The Shah's Story.* London: Joseph, 1980.

Palmer, Lilli. *Change Lobsters—and Dance.* London: W. H. Allen, 1976.

Parker, Matthew. *Goldeneye: Where Bond Was Born: Ian Fleming's Jamaica.* London: Random House, 2014.

Pasternak, Anna. *Princess in Love.* London: Bloomsbury, 1994.

Patterson, Jerry. *The First Four Hundred: Mrs. Astor's New York in the Gilded Age.* New York: Rizzoli, 2000.

Piggott, F. S. G. *Broken Thread: An Autobiography.* Aldershot, UK: Gale and Poulden, 1950.

Plimpton, George. *Truman Capote: In Which Various Friends, Enemies, Acquaintances, and Detractors Recall His Turbulent Career.* London: Picador, 1998.

Plowright, Joan. *And That's Not All.* London: Orion, 2002.

Plutarch. *Plutarch's Lives of Caesar, Brutus and Antony.* Edited by Martha Brier. London: Macmillan, 1909.

Portalès, Guy de. *Ludwig II of Bavaria: The Man of Illusion.* London: Thornton Butterworth, 1929.

Price, Willard. *The Son of Heaven: The Problem of the Mikado.* London: Heinemann, 1945.

Pryce-Jones, David. *Unity Mitford: A Quest.* London: Weidenfeld and Nicolson, 1976.

Quinn, Tom. *Backstairs Billy: The Life of William Tallon, the Queen Mother's Most Devoted Servant.* London: Robson Press, 2015.

Rappaport, Helen. *Ekaterinburg: The Last Days of the Romanovs.* London: Hutchinson, 2008.

Ravensdale, Mary, and Irene Curzon. *In Many Rhythms: An Autobiography.* London: Weidenfeld and Nicolson, 1953.

Regan, Simon. *Charles: The Clown Prince.* London: Everest Books, 1977.

Reich, Cary. *The Life of Nelson A. Rockefeller: Worlds to Conquer.* New York: Doubleday, 1996.

Rhodes, Margaret. *The Final Curtsey: A Royal Memoir by the Queen's Cousin.* London: Umbria Press, 2011.

Robinson, Jeffrey. *Rainier and Grace.* London: Simon and Schuster, 1989.

Rose, Norman. *The Cliveden Set: Portrait of an Exclusive Fraternity.* London: Pimlico, 2001.

Roth, Cecil. *The Magnificent Rothschilds*. London: Robert Hale, 1939.

Rothschild, Edmund de. *A Gilt-Edged Life: Memoir*. London: Murray, 1998.

Rothschild, Mrs. James de. *The Rothschilds at Waddesdon Manor*. London: Collins, 1979.

Russell, Jane. *An Autobiography: My Path and Detours*. New York: Watts, 1985.

Russell, Polly. "The History Cook: The Playboy Gourmet." *Financial Times*, June 21, 2013.

Sabit, Adel. *A King Betrayed: The Ill-Fated Reign of Farouk of Egypt*. London: Quartet, 1989.

Sanders, George. *Memoirs of a Professional Cad*. London: Scarecrow Press, 1992.

Sassoon, Jean P. *Princess*. London: Doubleday, 1992.

Seagrave, Sterling. *The Marcos Dynasty*. London: Macmillan, 1988.

Shawcross, William. *The Shah's Last Ride: The Story of the Exile, Misadventures and Death of the Emperor*. London: Chatto and Windus, 1989.

Shlaim, Avi. *Lion of Jordan: The Life of King Hussein in War and Peace*. London: Allen Lane, 2007.

Simmons, Simone, and Susan Hill. *Diana: The Secret Years*. London: Michael O'Mara Books, 1998.

Sinclair, David. *Dynasty: The Astors and Their Times*. London: J. M. Dent, 1983.

Slater, Leonard. *Aly: A Biography*. London: W. H. Allen, 1966.

Smith, Sally Bedell. *Diana: The Life of a Troubled Princess*. London: Aurum Press, 1999.

Spada, James. *The Secret Lives of a Princess*. London: Sidgwick and Jackson, 1987.

Sparks, Fred. *The $20,000,000 Honeymoon: Jackie and Arnie's First Year*. New York: Bernard Geis, 1970.

Speer, Albert. *Inside the Third Reich*. New York and Toronto: Macmillan, 1970.

Stadiem, William. *Too Rich: The High Life and Tragic Death of King Farouk*. London: Parkway Publishing, 1991.

Stancioff, Nadia. *Maria Callas Remembered*. London: Sidgwick and Jackson, 1988.

Stanford, Peter. *Bronwen Astor, Her Life and Times*. London: HarperCollins, 2000.

St. James, Isabella. *Bunny Tales: Behind Closed Doors at the Playboy Mansion*. Philadelphia: Running Press, 2009.

Stoney, Barbara, and Heinrich Weltzien, eds. *My Mistress the Queen: The Letters of Frieda Arnold, Dresser to Queen Victoria, 1854–9*. London: Weidenfeld and Nicolson, 1994.

Stuart, Amanda Mackenzie. *Consuelo and Alva Vanderbilt: The Story of a Mother and Daughter in the Gilded Age*. London: Harper Perennial, 2005.

Suetonius. *The Lives of the Caesars*. Translated by J. C. Rolfe. London: William Heinemann, 1970.

Sykes, Christopher. *Nancy: The Life of Lady Astor*. London: Granada Publishing, 1979.

Taheri, Amir. *The Unknown Life of the Shah*. London: Hutchinson, 1991.

Taraborrelli, J. Randy. *The Hiltons: The True Story of an American Dynasty*. New York: Grand Central Publishing, 2014.

Tschumi, Gabriel, and Joan Powe. *Royal Chef*. London: Kimber, 1974.

Vickers, Hugo. *Gladys, the Duchess of Marlborough*. London: Weidenfeld and Nicolson, 1979.

Villiers, Gerard de. *The Imperial Shah: An Informal Biography*. London: Weidenfeld and Nicolson, 1975.

Vining, Elizabeth Gray. *Windows for the Crown Prince*. London: Joseph, 1952.

Wallace, Carol, and Clare MacColl. *To Marry an English Lord*. London: Sidgwick and Jackson, 1989.

Watson, Vera. *The Queen at Home*. London: W. H. Allen, 1952.

Watts, Steven. *Mr. Playboy: Hugh Hefner and the American Dream*. Hoboken, NJ: Wiley, 2008.

Wayne, Jane Ellen. *The Life and Loves of Grace Kelly*. London: Robson Books, 1991.

Weigall, Arthur E. P. Brome. *The Life and Times of Cleopatra*. London: Kegal Paul, 2004.

Welch, Frances. *The Russian Court at Sea*. Exeter, UK: Short Books, 2011.

Weld, Jacqueline. *Peggy, the Wayward Guggenheim*. London: Bodley Head, 1986.

Wharfe, Ken, and Robert Jobson. *Diana: Closely Guarded Secret*. London: Michael O'Mara Books, 2002.

Williams, Emrys. *Bodyguard: My Twenty Years as Aly Khan's Shadow*. London: Golden Pegasus Books, 1960.

Wilson, Bee. "Musical Chairs with Ribbentrop." *London Review of Books* 34, no. 24 (December 20, 2012): 20–22.

Wilson, Christopher. *A Greater Love: Charles and Camilla*. London: Headline, 1994.

Wilson, Derek. *The Astors, 1763–1992: Landscape with Millionaires*. London: Weidenfeld and Nicolson, 1993.

Windsor, Edward. *A King's Story: The Memoirs of H.R.H. the Duke of Windsor*. London: Cassell, 1951.

Windsor, Wallis Warfield. *The Heart Has Its Reasons: The Memoirs of the Duchess of Windsor*. London: Sphere, 1980.

Winstone, H. V. F. *Captain Shakespear*. London: Quartet Books, 1978.

Wray, Fay. *On the Other Hand*. New York: St. Martin's Press, 1988.

Young, Gordon. *The Golden Prince: The Remarkable Life of Prince Aly Khan*. London: Hale, 1955.

Zeffirelli, Franco. *The Autobiography of Franco Zeffirelli*. London: Weidenfeld and Nicolson, 1986.

Index